T0298365

THE LAWS AND ECONOMICS OF CONFUCIANISM

Tying together cultural history, legal history, and institutional economics, *The Laws and Economics of Confucianism: Kinship and Property in Pre-industrial China and England* offers a novel argument as to why Chinese and English pre-industrial economic development went down different paths. The dominance of Neo-Confucian social hierarchies in Late Imperial and Republican China, under which advanced age and generational seniority were the primary determinants of sociopolitical status, allowed many poor but senior individuals to possess status and political authority highly disproportionate to their wealth. In comparison, landed wealth was a fairly strict prerequisite for high status and authority in the far more "individualist" society of early modern England, essentially excluding low-income individuals from secular positions of prestige and leadership. Zhang argues that this social difference had major consequences for property institutions and agricultural production.

Taisu Zhang is an associate professor of law at Yale Law School and works on comparative legal history – specifically, economic institutions in modern China and early modern Western Europe – comparative law, property law, and contemporary Chinese law. *The Laws and Economics of Confucianism: Kinship and Property in Pre-industrial China and England* is his first book. In dissertation form, it was the recipient of Yale University's Arthur and Mary Wright Dissertation Prize and the American Society for Legal History's Kathryn T. Preyer Award. Dr. Zhang is a founding board member of the International Society for Chinese Law and History.

CAMBRIDGE STUDIES IN ECONOMICS, CHOICE, AND SOCIETY

Founding Editors

Timur Kuran, Duke University
Peter J. Boettke, George Mason University

This interdisciplinary series promotes original theoretical and empirical research as well as integrative syntheses involving links between individual choice, institutions, and social outcomes. Contributions are welcome from across the social sciences, particularly in the areas where economic analysis is joined with other disciplines such as comparative political economy, new institutional economics, and behavioral economics.

Books in the Series:

Terry L. Anderson and Gary D. Libecap *Environmental Markets: A Property Rights Approach*, 2014

Morris B. Hoffman *The Punisher's Brain: The Evolution of Judge and Jury*, 2014

Peter T. Leeson *Anarchy Unbound: Why Self- Governance Works Better Than You Think*, 2014

Benjamin Powell *Out of Poverty: Sweatshops in the Global Economy*, 2014

Cass R. Sunstein *The Ethics of Influence: Government in the Age of Behavioral Science*, 2016

Jared Rubin *Rulers, Religion, and Riches: Why the West Got Rich and the Middle East Did Not*, 2017

Jean-Philippe Platteau *Islam Instrumentalized: Religion and Politics in Historical Perspective*, 2017

The Laws and Economics of Confucianism

Kinship and Property in Pre-industrial China and England

TAISU ZHANG

Yale University

CAMBRIDGE
UNIVERSITY PRESS

University Printing House, Cambridge CB2 8BS, United Kingdom

One Liberty Plaza, 20th Floor, New York, NY 10006, USA

477 Williamstown Road, Port Melbourne, VIC 3207, Australia

314-321, 3rd Floor, Plot 3, Splendor Forum, Jasola District Centre, New Delhi-110025, India

79 Anson Road, #06-04/06, Singapore 079906

Cambridge University Press is part of the University of Cambridge.

It furthers the University's mission by disseminating knowledge in the pursuit of education, learning and research at the highest international levels of excellence.

www.cambridge.org
Information on this title: www.cambridge.org/9781107141117
DOI: 10.1017/9781316493328

First published 2017

A catalogue record for this publication is available from the British Library

Library of Congress Cataloging in Publication data
Names: Zhang, Taisu, author.
Title: The laws and economics of Confucianism : kinship and property in pre-industrial China and England / Taisu Zhang.
Description: Cambridge [UK] ; New York : Cambridge University Press, 2017. |
Series: Cambridge studies in economics, choice, and society | Includes bibliographical references and index.
Identifiers: LCCN 2017011389 | ISBN 9781107141117 (Hardback)
Subjects: LCSH: Kinship (Law)–China–History. | Kinship (Law)–England–History. |
Property–China–History. | Property–England–History. | Confucianism–Philosophy. |
Confucianism and law | Confucianism–Economic aspects. |
BISAC: BUSINESS & ECONOMICS / Development / Economic Development.
Classification: LCC K705 .Z43 2017 | DDC 330.1/70951–dc23 LC record available at https://lccn.loc.gov/2017011389

ISBN 978-1-107-14111-7 Hardback
ISBN 978-1-316-50628-8 Paperback

To my family.

Contents

Acknowledgments

I owe my deepest gratitude to Peter Perdue and James Whitman, for generously sharing their extraordinary wisdom and knowledge, for engaging my often underdeveloped ideas with patience and good cheer, and for giving me wonderful academic examples to which to aspire. Valerie Hansen and Steven Pincus also provided exceptionally penetrating and insightful feedback over the course of many years. I will forever be in their debt.

I have benefited enormously from the comments and suggestions provided by many colleagues and mentors: Kenneth Pomeranz, Madeleine Zelin, the late Jonathan Ocko, Wang Zhiqiang, Robert Ellickson, Bruce Ackerman, William Alford, Melissa Macauley, John Langbein, Ralf Michaels, Jedediah Purdy, Paul Haagen, Barak Richman, James Boyle, Stuart Benjamin, Mathias Reimann, Nicholas Howson, Chiu Pengsheng, James Oldham, Harold Tanner, Chen Li, Jamie Horsley, Jeffery Prescott, Susan Jakes, Sulmaan Khan, C.J. Huang, Wang Yingyao, and Qiao Shitong. Three anonymous referees provided thorough and helpful reviews to Cambridge University Press during the submission process, for which I am deeply grateful.

I have had the good fortune to work with a truly excellent collection of editors at Cambridge University Press: Timur Kuran, Karen Maloney, Joshua Penney, and Kristina Deutsch. They have been a model of good judgment, professionalism, and efficiency throughout this long process.

I thank the following institutions for granting me access to their collections and archives: the First National Historical Archives in Beijing, the Zhejiang University History Department, the Shanghai Jiaotong University History Department, and the Fudan University History Department. Part of the project was generously funded by a Prize Fellowship from the Yale Council for East Asian Studies.

While working on this book, I taught first at Duke University and then at Yale Law School, where I was once a student. I cannot imagine better places to be a professional academic. They have provided the kind of robust and endlessly inspiring intellectual life that elevates the teaching and scholarship of all who take part in it.

My love of history – as a systematic academic subject – began, back in my undergraduate days, under the tutelage of Jonathan Spence and Donald Kagan. They showed me both the nuance and the grandeur that accompanies serious historical research and inspired me to follow, however meekly and tentatively, in their footsteps.

Finally, like most other things in life, I could not have written this book without the unconditional love and support of my family. Their companionship – intellectual and otherwise – has sustained me, and continues to do so, through the numerous ups and downs that are part of any attempt to begin an academic career. To them the book is dedicated.

Introduction

OVERVIEW

The aim of this book is, in one sentence, to demonstrate a chain of causation between cultural norms, legal institutions, and macro-level economic outcomes in early modern pre-industrial China and England. It argues that the dominance of kinship networks in later Qing and Republican society (1860–1949), operating under broadly "Confucian" norms of social ranking, allowed many relatively poor individuals to possess status and political authority highly disproportionate to their wealth. Under these norms, advanced age and generational seniority were much stronger determinants of sociopolitical status than wealth. In comparison, landed wealth was a fairly strict prerequisite for high status and authority in the far more "individualist" society of early modern England (specifically 1500–1700), essentially excluding low-income individuals from secular positions of prestige and leadership. Directly reflecting the much higher sociopolitical clout of lower-income households in rural China, Chinese customary laws governing the selling and collateralizing of land protected their economic interests far more vigorously than comparable English institutions.

Over time, this institutional divergence had significant economic consequences. By the early eighteenth century, a sizable majority of English land was concentrated under capitalist management, with the yeomanry and smallholders in steady decline. In comparison, even by the mid-twentieth century, Chinese agriculture remained predominantly household-based, indeed at the cost of comparatively low labor productivity and, more importantly, low levels of capital accumulation by potential entrepreneurs. Landownership, while not precisely "equally" distributed, was nonetheless far less concentrated and disparate than in England. The best explanation for these deep structural differences is precisely that Chinese property

1

institutions were much more "poor friendly," in that they allowed cash-needy landowners – who were usually poor – to collateralize land without risking permanent loss of title. This severely discouraged the permanent selling of land and, correspondingly, the accumulation of land into larger, capitalist farms. Property institutions were therefore an essential nexus that linked cultural differences concerning kinship and social organization to macro-level economic divergence.

"RECULTURALIZING" CHINA'S RELATIVE ECONOMIC DECLINE

The study of early modern China's "relative decline," an eternal topic in global history, has experienced a fairly thorough "deculturalization" in recent years. The field has come a long way since the early and mid-twentieth century, when the equating of "Confucian" culture or religion with economic irrationality – both individual and institutional – and stagnation, or the equating of "Western" values with rationality and growth, was almost *de rigueur*.[1] Since then, scholars across the social sciences have become well acquainted with the numerous empirical problems in that equation: the precise content of "Chinese culture," however one defines that term, is tremendously diverse, whether between different schools of thought, different eras, or different geographic regions. Even if done with the utmost care, broad generalizations are inherently risky. More importantly, cultural differences, if they existed, did not necessarily have economic significance. The individual economic behavior of Chinese peasants, farmers, merchants, or even officials was not obviously different from that of their peers in, say, England or France. China had no "Protestant work ethic," but her people attempted to maximize personal economic gain no less persistently or rationally. With few exceptions, scholars now hasten to distance themselves from Max Weber, Karl Polanyi, and the sweeping "Eurocentric" cultural paradigms with which they are associated.

The result of all this, however, is that "cultural factors" – commonly defined as social norms and beliefs that are embraced and internalized without empirical discovery or analytical justification[2] – are now virtually invisible

---

[1] MAX WEBER ON LAW IN ECONOMY AND SOCIETY (Max Rheinstein ed., 1954); MAX WEBER, THE RELIGION OF CHINA: CONFUCIANISM AND TAOISM (1920); KARL POLANYI, THE GREAT TRANSFORMATION: THE POLITICAL AND ECONOMIC ORIGINS OF OUR TIME (New York: Rinehart, 1944).

[2] Avner Greif, *Cultural Beliefs and the Organization of Society: A Historical and Theoretical Reflection on Collectivist and Individualist Societies*, 102 J. POL. ECON. 912 (1994); Robert C. Ellickson, *Law and Economics Discovers Social Norms*, 27 J. LEGAL STUD. 537 (1998).

in most recent studies of Sino-European divergence. This is especially apparent in the work of the "California School" scholars – Kenneth Pomeranz, R. Bin Wong, the late Andre Gunder Frank, and others.[3] Often spoken of in collective terms because they share a strongly revisionist perspective on global economic history and because many of them taught in California at some point, these scholars have engineered a thoroughly new interpretation of how, and why, the Chinese economy "fell behind." As late as 1750, perhaps 1800, the Chinese and Western European economies were remarkably similar. Structurally, both were significantly commercialized and on the cusp of industrialization; both were predominantly agricultural and self-contained, although the importance of international trade was ever-increasing; finally, both recognized and protected private property rights through law and custom. In terms of living standards, the core regions of China – the Lower Yangtze in particular – compared quite favorably to England and Holland, two of Europe's most advanced economies.

That much is consensual. When it comes to explaining the relative decline that followed, "California School" scholars diverge widely. Pomeranz famously argued that England pulled ahead largely because it had easier access to coal and its North American colonies, allowing it to escape the natural resource constraints that limited the Chinese economy. More recently, he has suggested that property institutions, specifically those governing land leasing, may have deepened the divergence in the later nineteenth century. Wong and Jean Rosenthal, in contrast, highlight the role of frequent wars in stimulating the urbanization of Europe and its investment in capital-intensive technologies – whereas the relative unity of China boosted its agrarian economy but also damaged the likelihood of industrialization.[4] In earlier work, Wong and others also questioned the effectiveness of the Qing state's economy management.[5] Frank agrees with Pomeranz that natural resources were part of the explanation, but also suggests that the low price of labor in China discouraged investment in capital-intensive technology.[6]

---

[3] KENNETH POMERANZ, THE GREAT DIVERGENCE: CHINA, EUROPE, AND THE MAKING OF THE MODERN WORLD ECONOMY (2000); R. BIN WONG, CHINA TRANSFORMED: HISTORICAL CHANGE AND THE LIMITS OF EUROPEAN EXPERIENCE (1997); ANDRE GUNDER FRANK, REORIENT (1998).

[4] R. BIN WONG & JEAN-LAURENT ROSENTHAL, BEFORE AND BEYOND DIVERGENCE: THE POLITICS OF ECONOMIC CHANGE IN CHINA AND EUROPE (2011).

[5] WONG (1997). *See also* PETER C. PERDUE, CHINA MARCHES WEST: THE QING CONQUEST OF CENTRAL EURASIA 537–65 (2005), which makes a similar argument.

[6] FRANK (1998).

What these theories share in common, however, is a largely exclusive focus on easily measurable noncultural factors: the supply of natural resources, labor costs, and wars. There is little discussion of values, social discourse, or religious beliefs. Much of this is on purpose. Frank explicitly states that exceptionalist portrayals of European culture are racist.[7] The others employ less incendiary language but are no less eager to avoid any analysis that might be considered Eurocentric – cultural analysis has, as discussed earlier, been particularly vulnerable to such accusations. Wong, for example, expressly argues against the notion that Sino-English differences in political culture had significant macroeconomic consequences.[8]

These scholars are hardly alone in their avoidance of cultural analysis. Within the field of Chinese history, recent studies by Christopher Isett, David Faure, and Debin Ma argue that legal institutions played a central role in China's relative decline,[9] whereas older works by Philip C. C. Huang and Ramon Myers place somewhat greater emphasis on "purely economic"[10] factors such as population pressures and land scarcity.[11] Despite their differences, neither group seriously incorporates cultural factors into their analysis. Faure, who addresses this more explicitly than the others, suggests that cultural factors were often the product of institutions and political policy.[12] The underlying argument seems to be that they were not, therefore, independent variables in economic growth, even if one can intelligibly speak of "cultural differences" between East and West.

Most scholars working from the European side of the comparison but with some express interest in China – Robert Brenner, Robert Allen, Daron Acemoglu, James Robinson, Patrick O'Brien, and others – have likewise placed primary, often exclusive emphasis on labor and capital costs, access to maritime trade and colonies, and legal and political institutions.[13] Acemoglu

---

[7] *Id.* at 4.   [8] WONG (1997), at 151.

[9] CHRISTOPHER ISETT, STATE, PEASANT AND MERCHANT IN QING MANCHURIA: 1644–1862 (2007); DAVID FAURE, CHINA AND CAPITALISM: A HISTORY OF BUSINESS ENTERPRISE IN MODERN CHINA (2006); Debin Ma, *Economic Growth in the Lower Yangzi Region of China in 1911–1937: A Quantitative and Historical Analysis*, 68 J. ECON. HIS. 355–92 (2008).

[10] Lillian Li, *Review of* State, Peasant and Merchant in Qing Manchuria: 1644–1862, 38 J. OF INTERDISCIPLINARY HIST. 644–46 (2008).

[11] PHILIP C.C. HUANG, THE PEASANT ECONOMY AND SOCIAL CHANGE IN NORTH CHINA (1985); RAMON H. MYERS, THE CHINESE ECONOMY, PAST AND PRESENT (1980).

[12] FAURE (2006), at 95–97.

[13] *E.g.,* THE BRENNER DEBATE 10–63 (T.H. Aston & C.H.E. Philpin eds., 1987); Robert Brenner & Christopher Isett, *England's Divergence from China's Yangtze Delta: Property*

and Robinson, in particular, draw from a deep tradition of new institutional economics[14] in arguing that Europe's economic rise benefited tremendously from its legal and political institutions: checks and balances between government entities that limited the arbitrary use of state power, and – as a result – secure property and contract rights that stimulated the private economy. In comparison, cultural factors are generally "just not important" in understanding global economic divergence.

The one subarea of global economic history where culture still makes a somewhat frequent appearance is the history of science and technology, and even there its appearance is controversial. Joel Mokyr and Margaret Jacob, for example, argue that England's economic development benefited tremendously from its "scientific culture" that spurred technological advancement and, eventually, large-scale industrialization.[15] This argument is echoed from the Chinese side by Jack Goldstone, who is perhaps the only "California School" scholar to expressly emphasize cultural and intellectual factors. Although China and the Islamic world did possess highly advanced scientific traditions, these traditions were also fundamentally subordinate to "classical and religious orthodoxy" and therefore slower to make the technological breakthroughs necessary for mechanical industrialization.[16]

Relations, Microeconomics, and Patterns of Development, 61 J. OF ASIAN STUD. 609 (2002); ROBERT ALLEN, THE BRITISH INDUSTRIAL REVOLUTION IN GLOBAL PERSPECTIVE (2009); Daron Acemoglu, Simon Johnson, & James Robinson, *The Rise of Europe: Atlantic Trade, Institutional Change, and Economic Growth*, 95 AM. ECON. REV. 546 (2005); DARON ACEMOGLU & JAMES A. ROBINSON, WHY NATIONS FAIL: THE ORIGINS OF POWER, PROSPERITY AND POVERTY (2010); Patrick O'Brien, *State Formation and the Construction of Institutions for the First Industrial Nation, in* INSTITUTIONAL CHANGE AND ECONOMIC DEVELOPMENT (Ha Joon Chang ed., 2007).

[14] *E.g.*, DOUGLASS C. NORTH & ROBERT PAUL THOMAS, THE RISE OF THE WESTERN WORLD: A NEW ECONOMIC HISTORY (1976); DOUGLASS C. NORTH, INSTITUTIONS, INSTITUTIONAL CHANGE AND ECONOMIC PERFORMANCE (1990). Of course, the notion that secure property rights were exclusive to Western Europe has long since been discredited. *See, e.g.*, Joseph P. McDermott, *Charting Blank Spaces and Disputed Regions: The Problem of Sung Land Tenure*, 44 J. OF ASIAN STUD. 13 (1984); Peter C. Perdue, *Property Rights on Imperial China's Frontiers, in* LAND, PROPERTY, AND THE ENVIRONMENT (John Richards ed., 2001); Madeleine Zelin, *A Critique of Rights of Property in Prewar China, in* CONTRACT AND PROPERTY IN EARLY MODERN CHINA 17 (Madeleine Zelin, Jonathan K. Ocko, & Robert Gardella eds., 2004a).

[15] JOEL MOKYR, THE ENLIGHTENED ECONOMY: AN ECONOMIC HISTORY OF BRITAIN 1700–1850 (2010); MARGARET JACOB, SCIENTIFIC CULTURE AND THE MAKING OF THE MECHANICAL WEST (1997).

[16] JACK GOLDSTONE, WHY EUROPE? THE RISE OF THE WEST IN GLOBAL HISTORY (2008).

Such arguments encounter deep opposition on several fronts. Benjamin Elman and others have pointed out, for example, that traditional accounts of Chinese science – which Goldstone largely follows – seriously underestimate the intellectual independence, creativity, and rigor of Qing scientific research under *kaozheng* scholars.[17] Alternatively, many economic historians have argued that the impact of scientific research on pre-nineteenth century English development was questionable: Traditional historiography has arguably exaggerated both the impact of the natural sciences on mechanical technology and the impact of mechanical technology on economic growth.[18] In any case, "scientific culture" proponents are but a small minority in the overall divergence literature and, moreover, focus on a very narrow and specific kind of culture. Serious discussion of broader sociopolitical culture – of norms that governed group organization, personal interaction, and social hierarchies – has distinctly fallen out of favor.

Much of this is obviously for the better. Given the empirical missteps of earlier scholarship, "culture" is clearly something that should be employed with care and precision, something that complements, rather than obscures, serious economic analysis. More substantively, there is little downside to recognizing, for example, that individual Chinese were as economically rational and aggressive as their Western European peers and that Chinese social culture was diverse and fluid. That said, the precipitous decline of cultural analysis leaves a number of fundamental questions unanswered. Many, perhaps most, of the noncultural divergence theories discussed earlier are simply logically incomplete: the explanatory factors on which they rely – population trends, wars, institutions – beg for explanation themselves.

Nowhere is this more evident than in the role of institutions. Institutions are, as any legal historian or social scientist will attest, inherently human constructs that undergo constant scrutiny and are often susceptible to change. It is therefore imperative to carefully consider why – and how – institutions exist in the first place, before employing them as analytical starting points in a study of economic divergence. One would otherwise find it difficult, if not impossible, to understand how these institutions

---

[17] BENJAMIN ELMAN, ON THEIR OWN TERMS: SCIENCE IN CHINA (2005).

[18] *E.g.*, ALLEN (2009); POMERANZ (2000), at 47–49; A. MUSSON, ALBERT EDWARD & ERIC ROBINSON, SCIENCE AND TECHNOLOGY IN THE INDUSTRIAL REVOLUTION (1969); DAVID S. LANDES, THE UNBOUND PROMETHEUS: TECHNOLOGICAL CHANGE AND INDUSTRIAL DEVELOPMENT IN WESTERN EUROPE FROM 1750 TO THE PRESENT (1969).

functioned in real socioeconomic contexts – and, in turn, to accurately analyze their broader economic significance. What prompted England and other Western European countries to create economically efficient institutions? More interestingly, why do economically inefficient institutions survive in China long enough to become seriously detrimental? Especially in the latter case, the durability of these institutions was clearly supplied by something other than macro-level economic welfare. But what was that "something," and how did it coexist with the individual pursuit of material wealth?

If we take these questions seriously, then social culture must be reintroduced into the comparative study of Sino-English economic history or indeed almost any comparative study of economic history – not as sweeping generalizations that created fundamental differences in individual economic behavior, but as specifically defined background conditions for institutional change and divergence.[19] To this end, I argue in the following pages that economically significant institutional differences between the two countries derived, in the end, from cultural norms of kinship and social hierarchy. In doing so, I break down the elusive connection between cultural norms and economic outcomes into more empirically manageable "subconnections": kinship and social hierarchy norms shaped distributions of social authority; distributions of social authority regulated the negotiation of property institutions; property institutions affected macroeconomic outcomes.

Traditional "cultural explanations" of global divergence tend to suffer from two deficiencies. First, they often misunderstand, or at least seriously oversimplify, the very cultural factors they discuss. This is, for example, the most common accusation lodged against Max Weber's "Protestant work ethic" thesis[20] or against its many contemporary variations – David Landes' *The Wealth and Poverty of Nations* is a famous example[21]: that they simply mischaracterize the nature of Protestantism in England and,

---

[19] For an economic theory of cultural influence in institutional choice, *see* Greif (1994) at 912. NORTH (1990) also discusses the theoretical possibility that cultural norms can influence political and legal institutions but does not formally model it or provide empirical verification. There have been very few attempts to verify these theoretical insights on a larger empirical scale or to rigorously apply them to broader historical trends.

[20] MAX WEBER, THE PROTESTANT WORK ETHIC AND THE SPIRIT OF CAPITALISM (Peter Baehr & Gordon C. Wells trans., Penguin 2002); WEBER (1920).

[21] DAVID LANDES, THE WEALTH AND POVERTY OF NATIONS: WHY SOME ARE SO RICH AND SOME SO POOR (1999).

far more seriously, the nature of traditional Confucianism, Islam, and other non-Western belief systems.[22] Second, and perhaps more fundamentally, they often overestimate the impact of cultural factors on everyday economic life, even in premodern times. Perhaps swayed by the expansive coverage of everyday life in religious texts – both the Bible and the *Analects*, for example, contain extremely detailed guidelines for individual behavior – they seem to assume that religious beliefs actually micromanaged how individuals sell and buy property, use resources, make social connections, and create economic institutions. Ample historical research has shown that such micromanagement was, in fact, very limited, and that individual economic behavior was similarly self-interested across different societies.[23]

In light of these deficiencies, a major advantage of this book's approach is that it recognizes significantly larger doses of economic rationality in both Chinese and English individuals than these "Weberian" "cultural explanations." Of the three "subconnections" just identified, the latter two are completely consistent with "rational actor" models of individual economic behavior, delineating how basically rational, self-interested individuals react to established norms of kinship and social hierarchy and then to the property institutions that consequently emerge. Cultural factors such as kinship and social hierarchy norms feature prominently only in the first subconnection, and only to the extent that they can be clearly defined and empirically demonstrated.

In fact, even the first subconnection is not necessarily inconsistent with the assumption of individual rationality. One could argue that cultural factors simply influence individual utility functions – by making certain activities more psychologically desirable and others less so – but do not cause any irrational decision making per se. After all, rational-actor models only assume that people attempt to maximize their personal utility but do not specify what the content of that utility is.

Nonetheless, the kinship and social hierarchy norms that I study are distinctly "cultural" in the sense that, by at least the seventeenth century,

---

[22] *E.g.*, H.M. Robertson, Aspects of the Rise of Economic Individualism: A Criticism of Max Weber and His School (1950); Robert M. Marsh, *Weber's Misunderstanding of Chinese Law*, 106 Am. J. Sociology 281 (2000); Gale Stokes, *The Fates of Human Societies: A Review of Recent Macrohistories*, 106 Am. Hist. Rev. 508–25 (2001).

[23] Acemoglu & Robinson (2010), at 56–63; Stokes (2001); Timur Kuran, The Long Divergence: How Islamic Law Held Back the Middle East (2010); Pomeranz (2000), at 91–105; Li Bozhong, Agricultural Development in Jiangnan, 1620–1850, at 107–08 (1998).

there is much evidence that they had been morally internalized by large segments – probably the overwhelming majority – of their respective populations. Such evidence is particularly strong for the Ming and Qing, by which time Confucian doctrines of kinship bonding and patrilineal hierarchy had routinely been spoken of in highly moralized and philosophical language for centuries, with legions of scholars and officials proclaiming them to be "inviolable and eternal" principles of human society. Of course, by the late nineteenth and early twentieth century, some intellectuals had begun to question their validity, but broader social acceptance of such skepticism, or even widespread support among elites, did not emerge until the later 1940s at the earliest.

One could further examine how, and why, kinship norms became broadly internalized in the first place, but there is room in this book only for a general sketch. In short, private kinship networks began to emerge *en masse* during the tenth and eleventh centuries, as the Song government loosened up legal prohibitions against extended ancestor worship by non-aristocrats. The Ming government further eased such prohibitions and eventually granted full ancestral worship rights to all commoners. But well before these institutional clogs had been removed, pent-up private demand for extended worship rights was already driving the rapid proliferation of large kinship networks in most macroregions, across highly diverse ecological, economic, and political conditions. By the sixteenth century, they had become the dominant mode of social organization and had evidently become a central part of China's sociocultural fabric.

Because this study focuses on the nineteenth and twentieth centuries, I take these internalized kinship norms more as an analytical starting point, an independent variable, than as something to be thoroughly explained. The primary objective, as stated earlier, is to demonstrate sequential historical causation between morally internalized kinship norms, legal institutions, and patterns of landholding and use in early modern China and England. In doing so, I argue for the "reculturalization" of China's relative economic decline, albeit with – hopefully – sufficient economic and social sophistication and some healthy skepticism of traditional cultural "paradigms."

INSTITUTIONAL COMPARISONS

The institutional comparison that I focus on is, at heart, a functionalist one. It stems from a question that might have been drawn from the Personal Finance Section of the *Wall Street Journal*: how did landowners cope with large emergency cash needs in early modern China and England? For small sums, they could often get by through borrowing money on their good name, without the use of collateral, but for large sums – to cover a funeral or wedding, for example – creditors in both countries generally demanded collateral. In these early modern economies, despite prevalent commercialization and perhaps some nascent industrialization, land was by far the most valuable source of capital and hence the most important source of collateral for large-sum loans. The legal and quasi-legal instruments facilitating such collateralization fundamentally affected the market for both temporary and permanent conveyances of land and, therefore, were some of the most crucial institutional cogs in the economy. In sixteenth- and seventeenth-century England, this role was filled by the mortgage, whereas in Qing and Republican China it was filled by the *dian*, or conditional sale.

Compared with modern Anglo-American mortgages, the "classic mortgage" of sixteenth- and seventeenth-century England was a much duller instrument. Modern mortgages allow, of course, repayment schedules of up to several decades, generally permit the mortgagor to maintain possession of the property, and in cases of default arrange foreclosure auctions to raise the collateral's full market value.[24] The classic mortgage was not nearly as lenient to mortgagors. They conveyed full title or a long term-of-years to mortgagees, including the right of possession.[25] Crucially, most local customs dictated that they must repay their debts within a very short time frame – generally six months to a year after the initial conveyance – or the mortgagees would automatically obtained fee simple ownership.

Until the early eighteenth century, common-law courts enforced these customary deadlines quite ruthlessly, so much so that Chancery felt compelled to aid beleaguered mortgagors by establishing the "equity of redemption," allowing judges to extend redemption deadlines and demand foreclosure auctions on final default.[26] These reforms did not, however, harden into established doctrine until the mid-eighteenth century, and even then their preeminence over common-law rules was questionable.

---

[24] DAVID A. SCHMUDDE, A PRACTICAL GUIDE TO MORTGAGES AND LIENS 7 (2004).

[25] *See* WILLIAM BLACKSTONE, 2 COMMENTARIES ON THE LAWS OF ENGLAND 157–58 (Univ. of Chicago Press, 1979); A.W.B. SIMPSON, A HISTORY OF THE LAND LAW 242–43 (1986).

[26] David Sugarman & Ronnie Warrington, *Land Law, Citizenship, and the Invention of "Englishness": The Strange World of the Equity of Redemption, in* EARLY MODERN CONCEPTIONS OF PROPERTY 111, 113 (John Brewer & Susan Staves eds., 1996).

The cash-needy landowner in early modern China faced far more favorable institutional conditions. Most Qing and Republican land transactions were not permanent sales, but rather *dian* ("conditional") sales, where the conditional "seller" conveyed land to the "buyer" for 60 to 80 percent of the property's full market value, but retained the right to redeem *at zero interest*. The *dian* buyer's interest in lending money under such an arrangement was not monetary interest but whatever profit the land could yield before the seller redeemed. He was therefore often protected by contractually established "guaranteed-usage periods" (*xian*) of one or more years, during which the seller could not redeem. In addition, he could obtain full ownership of the land if the *dian* seller agreed to convert the transaction into a permanent sale (*mai*), upon which the seller would receive "additional payments" (*zhaotie*) that made up the difference between the original transaction price and the land's present market value.

Most significantly, *dian* customs generally allowed *dian* sellers to retain redemption rights *ad infinitum*. As one local custom stated, *dian* sales "could be redeemed after several hundred years, and the price of redemption would always remain the same."[27] Similar customs were commonplace throughout China's core regions, particularly North China and the Lower Yangtze. Many explicitly forbid the original contract from setting any redemption deadline. Others allowed redemption rights to be exercised "any time after the guaranteed-usage period's expiration." These rules were not for show. Under their influence, very few *dian* contracts attempted to establish redemption deadlines, and most *dian* sales were apparently redeemed at some point. In more than a few cases, a *dian* seller or his descendants would attempt to redeem after astonishingly long periods – sometimes a century.

This was an institutional arrangement rife with social tension. During the decades that often passed between *dian* sale and redemption request, families might move, original contractors might die, usage rights might be transferred to a third party, or economic conditions might change dramatically. The swelling volume of related disputes brought before local courts eventually pushed the Qing government into action. It made several attempts to limit the redemption window of *dian* sales, ordering first in the *Qing Code* that all contracts must explicitly indicate whether they were permanent sales or *dian* sales[28]

---

[27] Minshangshi Xiguan Diaocha Baogaolu [Research Report on Civil and Commercial Customs] [*hereinafter* XGDC] 505 (Sifa Xingzheng Bu ed., 1930).

[28] Da Qing Lü Li [The Great Qing Code] [*hereinafter* DQLL] § 95–107 (1905).

and then, in the 1758 *Board of Finance Regulations*, that regular *dian* sales must be redeemed within ten years or be converted to a permanent sale, with at most a one-year extension.[29]

Enforcement of these legal rules was weak at best. Due to their lack of coercive authority, Qing local magistrates were hesitant, even afraid, to formally adjudicate cases where central laws and regulations conflicted with local custom. By the Republican era, the government had basically admitted that Qing rules against excessive redemption were unenforceable: early Republican-era governments extended the national deadline for land redemption to sixty years, a clear concession to local custom.[30] After 1929, the newly victorious Nationalist government attempted to impose a thirty-year deadline nationwide,[31] but surveys of Northern Chinese peasants conducted a decade later suggest that their efforts were ineffectual. Most peasants had no knowledge of the deadline, and most who did believed that no one followed it.

For *dian* sellers, these customary norms offered tremendous advantages with limited downside. Land was, to most rural residents in these early modern times, the single most valuable kind of property, not only because of its high market value, but also because it was the foundation for most economic production. As various Qing- and Republican-era sources repeatedly claim, landowners generally sold land *only* when financial conditions made it absolutely necessary, and therefore, they usually preferred redeemable *dian* sales to permanent ones.[32] Under these conditions, an institutional framework that effectively eliminated the danger of default and seizure was highly attractive to cash-strapped landowners.

By contrast, this framework did *dian* buyers few favors. The constant danger of redemption after the guaranteed-usage period's expiration seriously decreased the land's value to buyers by discouraging both long-term investments to improve the land and use of the land as a reliable source of

---

[29] 1 QINGDAI GE BUYUAN ZELI: QINDING HUBU ZELI (QIANLONG CHAO) [REGULATIONS OF QING BOARDS AND MINISTRIES: IMPERIAL BOARD OF FINANCE REGULATIONS (QIANLONG ERA)] 83, 148–49 (Fuchi Shuyuan ed., 2004).

[30] 6 FALING JILAN [EDITED COLLECTION OF LAWS AND REGULATIONS] 179–80 (Sifa Bu ed., 1917).

[31] ZHONGHUA MINGUO MINFA DIAN [CIVIL CODE OF THE REPUBLIC OF CHINA], arts. 912, 924 (1929).

[32] *See* PHILIP C.C. HUANG, CODE, CUSTOM, AND LEGAL PRACTICE IN CHINA: THE QING AND THE REPUBLIC COMPARED 73 (2001); Madeleine Zelin, *The Rights of Tenants in Mid-Qing Sichuan: A Study of Land-Related Lawsuits in the Baxian Archives*, 45 J. ASIAN STUD. 499, 515 (1986).

capital or collateral.[33] The tremendous attractiveness of *dian* customs to potential land sellers also drained the supply of permanent land sales, further exacerbating the difficulty of secure land accumulation. Despite all this, the demand for *dian* sales remained high during times of relative peace, driven by some combination of population growth, commercialization, and nascent industrialization.[34] All in all, "land pawning" was a strikingly low-risk affair in early modern China, especially when compared with the perils of English mortgaging.

Not surprisingly, the economic identities of creditors and debtors were broadly similar across the two countries: both mortgagors and *dian* sellers were generally much poorer than mortgagees and *dian* buyers. The academic literature is remarkably consistent on these points. The institutional protection of *dian* sellers was therefore also the protection of poor against rich. Likewise, the harsh treatment of mortgagors in English custom usually meant harsh treatment of smallholders and tenants in favor of aggressively expanding gentry and capitalist farmers. Poorer households in both societies would therefore have preferred "*dian* rules" over "mortgage rules," but only the Chinese got them.

ECONOMIC CONSEQUENCES

To almost any social scientist, the institutional contrast between *dian* and mortgage triggers two immediate questions. First, what were its broader socioeconomic consequences? Second, how did this contrast emerge in the first place? The same two questions can be asked of almost any cross-society legal or institutional comparison, but are very rarely tackled by the same study, or even the same scholar. Such tunnel vision allows, perhaps, for a cleaner argument, but is ultimately unsatisfactory. As argued earlier,

---

[33] *See* Robert C. Ellickson, *The Cost of Complex Land Titles: Two Examples from China* (Yale Law & Econ. Research Paper no. 441, 2011), *available at* http://papers.ssrn.com/sol3/papers.cfm?abstract_id=1953207.

[34] This is discussed in greater detail in Chapter 3, Section B. *See generally*, Ho Ping-ti, Studies on the Population of China, 1369–1953 (1959). For population growth and its impact on land and produce prices in the Lower Yangtze, *see* Huang Jingbin, Minsheng yu Jiaji: Qingchu zhi Minguo Shiqi Jiangnan Jumin de Xiaofei [Civilian Welfare and Household Economics: Resident Consumption in the Lower Yangtze from the Early Qing to the Republic] 70–71 (2009). Population growth in urban areas was much faster than elsewhere. *Id.* at 17. For national figures, *see* Robert B. Marks, *China's Population Size during the Ming and Qing* 3 (on file with author).

no answer to the first question is complete without serious consideration of the second. Likewise, it is probably impossible to understand the historical rationales for an institution without also understanding its broader socio-economic consequences. The two questions should be answered in tandem.

I start here with the first question, if only because it offers a more obvious explanation for the historical significance of *dian* redemption norms. Did the *dian*-mortgage contrast have major economic conse-quences? It should be pointed out immediately that this is *not* equivalent to asking, "Does this explain the Great Divergence?" I argue that the institutional contrast did indeed facilitate deep structural differences between the two economies, but do not systematically measure how sig-nificant those structural differences ultimately were to either China's relative decline or "the rise of the West" – that panorama of economic developments that led to European dominance in industrialization, living standards, technological advancement, and military prowess. Attempting such a measurement would balloon this study to unreadable lengths and is better reserved for future research. Instead, the Introduction and Conclu-sion offer some abbreviated thoughts on why – as many scholars continue to believe – the structural differences were potentially important to broader Sino-English economic differences, and how one should go about proving that.

But let me begin by outlining these structural differences. Within the wide-ranging debates on China's relative decline, one of the few points of general agreement is that, relative to England, China lacked "managerial" or "capitalist" farming – defined as agricultural production that relied more on employed labor than on household labor.[35] Most scholars would agree that household-level production dominated Chinese agriculture until the Communist era. In comparison, by the early eighteenth century, English agriculture – including a large portion of open-fields agriculture – was predominantly capitalist, whereas it had been largely household-based in the sixteenth century.[36] Relatedly, "landlords" probably owned less than

---

[35] *See, e.g.*, MARK ELVIN, THE PATTERN OF THE CHINESE PAST (1973); LI WENZHI ET AL., MING QING SHIDAI DE NONGYE ZIBEN ZHUYI MENGYA WENTI [THE QUESTION OF "SHOOTS OF AGRICULTURAL CAPITALISTM" IN THE MING AND QING] (1983); PHILIP C.C. HUANG, THE PEASANT FAMILY AND RURAL DEVELOPMENT IN THE LOWER YANGTZE REGION, 1350–1988, at 58–76 (1990); HUANG (1985); SUCHETA MAZUMDAR, SUGAR AND SOCIETY IN CHINA: PEASANTS, TECHNOLOGY AND THE WORLD MARKET 192–250 (1998); LI (1998), at 85–87.

[36] *See* Leigh Shaw-Taylor, *Working Paper on Agrarian Capitalism* 4, 17–18 (2008), *available at* www.geog.cam.ac.uk/research/projects/occupations/abstracts/paper7.pdf; ROBERT

40 percent of arable land in China throughout the later Qing and Republic eras, with no clear upward trend, whereas conventional estimates of landownership by large landowners went from 65 to 75 percent of total land in 1690, to 85 percent in 1790, and to 90 percent by 1873.[37]

Historians traditionally believed that the higher labor productivity on managerial farms created enormous agricultural surpluses that directly stimulated English industrial growth.[38] Likewise, they often saw China's relative lack of agricultural capitalism as a crippling liability that prevented robust economic development. Although more recent scholarship continues to agree that capitalist agriculture substantially boosted productivity, some, particularly Robert Allen, have questioned whether the increase was large enough to explain England's overall economic preeminence.[39] Pomeranz has also suggested that whatever labor productivity boost China would have gained by transitioning to capitalist agriculture was significantly smaller than previously imagined – too small, in fact, to explain much about the Great Divergence.[40] The debate remains somewhat inconclusive. Peer Vries, for example, has recently argued that scholars have been too hasty in dismissing the economic significance of capitalist agriculture, even if Allen and Pomeranz's reduced estimates are correct.[41]

More importantly, one could argue that the transition to capitalist farming was important for reasons other than simply increasing agricultural labor productivity. Most notably, it also aided industrial development by concentrating landed capital into the hands of wealthy entrepreneurs. Indeed, the idea that "primitive accumulation" of capital, specifically land, was crucial to Western industrialization has been central to Western

---

C. ALLEN, ENCLOSURE AND THE YEOMAN: THE AGRICULTURAL DEVELOPMENT OF THE SOUTH MIDLANDS 1450–1850, at 73, tbl. 4–4, 78–104 (1992); THE BRENNER DEBATE (1987).

[37] Some of the literature on Chinese landownership is summarized and critiqued in Joseph W. Esherick, *Number Games: A Note on Land Distribution in Prerevolutionary China,* 7 MODERN CHINA 387, 397, 405 (1981). On England, *see* J.V. Beckett, *The Pattern of Landownership in England and Wales, 1660–1880,* 37 ECON. HIST. REV. 1 (1984).

[38] ALLEN (1992), at 2–5, 18–19 (summarizing the field prior to 1992).

[39] ALLEN (1992), at 17–19, 218–27; Peter C. Perdue, *China in the World Economy: Exports, Regions, and Theories,* 60 HARV. J. OF ASIATIC STUD. 259, 272–75 (2000).

[40] POMERANZ (2000), at 73.

[41] Peer Vries, *The California School and Beyond: How to Study the Great Divergence?,* 8 HISTORY COMPASS 730–51, 742–43 (2010). Moreover, Allen has been criticized, based on his own data, for heavily understating the importance of capitalist farming to pre-1700 English agriculture. Shaw-Taylor (2008), at 6–7. His admission that capitalist farms were ultimately more efficient than household farms has allowed some to use his own observations against him. *See* Brenner & Isett (2002), at 626.

economic thought since Adam Smith and Karl Marx and remains highly influential among political economists today.[42] Correspondingly, recent histories of Chinese business development have argued that the lack of capital concentration among late Qing entrepreneurs forced companies to either operate at inefficiently small scales or become joint ventures, which was difficult and costly under contemporary legal conditions.[43] The concept of limited liability, for example, did not exist in Qing business transactions, making investors far more reluctant to join entrepreneurial projects. Although eighteenth-century English legal institutions were not necessarily any friendlier to capital pooling – limited liability did not become commonly available to companies until the nineteenth century[44] – the concentration of wealth represented and facilitated by agricultural capitalism may have allowed English proto-industrialists to bypass this institutional difficulty. In other words, because individual English landowners possessed far larger estates than their Chinese counterparts, they had much less need to form potentially burdensome joint ventures.

None of this is to say that pre-industrial capital accumulation has been *impossible* historically without agricultural capitalism.: Both the Dutch and the Japanese economies – economies that may have benefited from the existence of a strong state apparatus controlling large amounts of capital – arguably cleared the "capital accumulation barrier," if you will, without the emergence of large-scale managerial agriculture.[45] Even so, based on the information currently available to scholars, one cannot dismiss the notion that agricultural capitalism played a major role in facilitating English

---

[42] ADAM SMITH, AN INQUIRY INTO THE NATURE AND CAUSES OF THE WEALTH OF NATIONS 111 (Joseph Nicholson ed., 1895); KARL MARX, 1 CAPITAL ch. 31, *available at* www.marxists.org/archive/marx/works/1867-c1/ch31.htm (1867, last accessed December 7, 2010). These ideas continue to be influential in modern political economics. *See, e.g.*, MICHAEL PERELMAN, THE INVENTION OF CAPITALISM: CLASSICAL POLITICAL ECONOMY AND THE SECRET HISTORY OF PRIMITIVE ACCUMULATION (2000); DAVID HARVEY, THE NEW IMPERIALISM, 145–46, 149 (2005); ELLEN MEIKSINS WOOD, THE ORIGIN OF CAPITALISM 57–59 (1999).

[43] MADELEINE ZELIN, THE MERCHANTS OF ZIGONG: INDUSTRIAL ENTREPRENEURSHIP IN EARLY MODERN CHINA 223–68 (2005); William C. Kirby, *China, Unincorporated: Company Law and Business Enterprise in Twentieth Century China*, 54 J. ASIAN STUD. 43 (1995).

[44] Ron Harris, *The Private Origins of the Private Company: Britain 1862–1907* (2009), *available at* http://papers.ssrn.com/sol3/papers.cfm?abstract_id=1613206.

[45] THOMAS C. SMITH, THE AGRARIAN ORIGINS OF MODERN JAPAN (1959); HE WENKAI, PATHS TOWARDS THE MODERN FISCAL STATE: ENGLAND, JAPAN, AND CHINA (2014); JAN DE VRIES, THE FIRST MODERN ECONOMY: SUCCESS, FAILURE, AND PERSEVERANCE OF THE DUTCH ECONOMY, 1500–1815 (1997).

industrialization or, for that matter, the notion that the Chinese economy could have benefited from more concentrated landholding. Agricultural capitalism may only have been one path among several that could have led to sufficient capital accumulation, but one can still ask why the Chinese economy chose not to take it. The claim here is simply that the relative lack of land concentration in the Chinese economy was one of its most distinctive and potentially significant characteristics. At the very least, it is something that is worth explaining in detail.

Explaining this structural difference has, in fact, proven fairly difficult. England was not always a land of managerial farms, nor was the transition easy. English agriculture was, as noted earlier, predominately household-based even in the sixteenth century, whereas the size of England's agricultural population actually increased by *at least* 30 percent – quite possibly by as much as 75 percent – between 1500 and 1700.[46] Even in 1700, 60 to 80 percent of England's population was agricultural.[47] Meanwhile, England's vaunted textile industry remained very modest in size until the late eighteenth century, as did the overseas trade.[48] The creation of managerial farms during the sixteenth and seventeenth centuries was therefore the fundamental reorganization of a predominantly agricultural society and not the transition between an agricultural society and a manufacturing-based one. Rather than driving people from farming into industrial shops, it more often involved the contentious process of purchasing land from smallholders, creating large farms, and then reemploying the land-deprived poor as wageworkers. Given that Qing China's core economic regions also possessed secure property rights, active markets for commodities and land, technological development, and significant urbanization,[49] what saved Qing and Republican smallholders from a similar fate?

---

[46] The 30 percent figure is obtained by combining data in Robert C. Allen, *Economic Structure and Agricultural Productivity in Europe, 1300–1800*, 3 EURO. R. OF ECON. HIST. 1, 11 (2000), and Theofanis C. Tsoulouhas, *A New Look at Demographic and Technological Changes: England, 1550 to 1839*, 29 EXPLORATIONS IN ECON. HIST. 169, 176–77 (1992) (using data from Wrigley and Lindert).

[47] S. Todd Lowry, *The Agricultural Foundation of the Seventeenth-Century English Economy*, 35 HIST. OF POL. ECON. 74, 75 (2003); Allen (2000).

[48] RALPH DAVIS, THE INDUSTRIAL REVOLUTION AND BRITISH OVERSEAS TRADE 63 (1979); Acemoglu, Johnson, & Robinson (2005).

[49] On market integration for agricultural produce, textiles, and other personal goods in the Chinese economic core, *see, e.g.*, LILLIAN M. LI, FIGHTING FAMINE IN NORTH CHINA 196–220 (2007); LI (1998) at 107–08; HUANG (1985), at 118–20; CHINESE HISTORY IN ECONOMIC PERSPECTIVE 35–99 (Thomas G. Rawski & Lillian M. Li eds., 1992). As POMERANZ (2000), at 86–87, points out, market development in pre-1800 Western Europe does not seem more advanced. On the protection of private property, *see*

Over two decades of academic discussion has produced no consensus.[50] Some have argued that labor was simply too expensive for managerial farming in China. More commonly, scholars have emphasized one or more institutional or legal factors theoretically related to one's ability to amass large, consolidated farms: Chinese family division customs, which divided family estates equally among male heirs and therefore deconcentrated landownership; the weaker power of eviction Chinese landlords had against tenants; and lineage rights of first refusal, which, by forcing land sellers to seek buyers among relatives before offering it to outsiders, purportedly limited a Chinese landowner's ability to sell his land. Anglo-American property law scholars will find this latter explanation particularly intuitive. American legal historians generally believe that "[m]odernity ... fosters alienability ... As groups modernize, they ... relax traditional restrictions on transfer."[51] Arguing that Chinese agricultural inefficiencies stemmed from the inalienability of land certainly applies these ideas in a straightforward fashion. Empirically, however, the argument is untenable. Existing evidence suggests that lineage rights of first refusal did very little to obstruct the efficient transaction of land in China's core socioeconomic regions. Similarly, the evidence fails to show that either family division customs or the lack of eviction rights significantly impeded the spread of managerial farming.[52]

The noninstitutional explanations have their own difficulties. Data from rural labor markets indicate that most North China and Lower Yangtze peasants who possessed surplus land found it more productive and profitable to employ wage labor than to rent out the surplus. This distinguishes much of Chinese agriculture from, for example, seventeenth-century Dutch agriculture, where there were few economies of scale to be gained and where

McDermott (1984); Zelin (2004a); Perdue (2001). On the marketability of land, *see* THOMAS BUOYE, MANSLAUGHTER, MARKETS AND MORAL ECONOMY: VIOLENT DISPUTES OVER PROPERTY RIGHTS IN EIGHTEENTH CENTURY CHINA (2000). For the underestimated pace of Chinese technological development, *see* LI (1998); and MAZUMDAR (1998), at 120–91. On urbanization in China, a recent literature survey is Yu Tongyuan, *Ming Qing Jiangnan Zaoqi Gongyehua Shehui de Xingcheng yu Fazhan* [*The Creation and Development of Jiangnan Industrial Society in the Ming and Qing*], 2007(11) SHIXUE YUEKAN [J. OF HIST. SCI.] 41, which argues that 20 percent of the *Jiangnan* population around 1700 was urban, while 30 percent was nonagricultural. This is comparable with even the most optimistic estimates on English urbanization in 1700.

[50] These debates are discussed in Chapter 3.
[51] Robert C. Ellickson, *Property in Land*, 102 YALE L.J. 1315, 1376–77 (1993). *See also* JESSE DUKEMINIER & JAMES E. KRIER, PROPERTY 197–220 (5th ed. 2002).
[52] See discussion at Chapter 6, Section B.

managerial farming therefore made little economic sense.[53] The existence of economic incentives in large parts of China that favored managerial farming suggests, therefore, that its relative scarcity might be attributed to institutional forces. But if not straightforward inalienability, family division rules, intralineage first-refusal rights, or tenant security, then what?

It turns out that the *dian*-mortgage contrast goes a very long way toward supplying an explanation. The extraordinary harshness of English mortgage default rules benefited large-scale land accumulation in two ways. First, it made default and seizure a fairly common affair. More importantly, however, it drove large numbers of cash-strapped smallholders into selling their land permanently. Better to sell land for its full value than to mortgage it at a lower value and run the significant risk of default and uncompensated loss of title. Large landowners looking to expand their holdings therefore could tap into a fairly robust supply of permanent sale offers.

In Qing and Republican China, however, the unlimited right of redemption in *dian* sales meant that smallholders had little incentive to permanently alienate their land. If they needed a lump sum to cover immediate needs, a conditional sale was usually satisfactory, while also preserving the option of zero-interest redemption. If, however, they simply wished to maximize the sale price of their land (an uncommon motive because the value of land in an agrarian society lay not only in its monetary price but also in the livelihood it secured), then the practice of *zhaotie* in conditional sales would allow them to take advantage of future increases in land value. Permanent alienation was therefore unattractive and rarely used – this, in turn, drove up the price of permanent sales, benefiting smallholders even more. Farmers who acquired land under a *dian* sale, however, found it highly difficult to obtain secure and permanent ownership. Not only did this impede the concentration of farmland and the development of capitalist agriculture, but it also militated against long-term capital investments that could potentially have boosted both land and labor productivity. All in all, the institutional contrast between *dian* and mortgage contributed substantially to both the capitalization of the English agrarian economy and the lack thereof in China.

SOCIAL AND CULTURAL ORIGINS

This brings us to the second, arguably more important, question in this study: How did this institutional contrast emerge in the first place? In

---

[53] de Vries (1997).

particular, how did the economically inefficient *dian* redemption norms survive centuries of fairly rapid economic change – from well before the Qing to the mid-twentieth century – without being revoked or simply ignored? If the goal is to "reculturalize" the study of economic divergence, it may seem tempting to simply say that "Chinese culture dictated unlimited *dian* redemption." We must, however, resist that temptation. In fact, one would be hard-pressed to find a widely articulated moral or religious norm in Imperial China that said anything about whether collateralized land should be subject to default. This is precisely where the few previous attempts to address these questions have misstepped and perhaps why recent studies of economic divergence have felt free to largely ignore them. There are additional steps to take before we can bring cultural factors into the analysis.

Several legal historians have argued that *dian* redemption norms derived directly from a moral and ideological embrace of "permanence in land-holding" ideals in "precommercial" societies. Philip Huang, for example, believed that interminable redemption rights were a natural normative component of subsistence economies: the prevalence of subsistence agriculture was mutually reinforcing with mores that shamed the loss of ancestral property and glorified the stable descent of land from generation to generation.[54] Others have suggested that Chinese peasants simply possessed a strong sentimental attachment to land and, consequently, were highly loathe to lose it[55] – this may simply have reflected, of course, the higher economic and social value of land in pre-industrial societies.

The evidence presented in support of these arguments, however, is thin – generally no more than vague moralizing by scholar-officials on the importance of land. Moreover, the higher economic value of land in pre-industrial societies pushed in two opposite directions. Apart from encouraging landowners to retain their properties, it also encouraged them to aggressively acquire new property. The stubbornly high demand for land sales, both permanent and *dian*, from around 1870 to the 1930s certainly suggests that the latter dynamic was consistently at work in times of relative peace despite the prevalence of highly burdensome *dian* customs. The attractiveness of landownership alone is therefore an inadequate explanation for the existence of those customs. Consider also the comparison with England. Early modern English landowners, too, had a strong sentimental attachment to

---

[54] HUANG (2001), at 74.
[55] MELISSA MACAULEY, SOCIAL POWER AND LEGAL CULTURE: LITIGATION MASTERS IN LATE IMPERIAL CHINA 234 (1998).

land, made all the more powerful by the dependency of sociopolitical status on landed wealth,[56] but this clearly did not prevent their customs from limiting redemption windows and tenancy security. If anything, the strong psychological premium placed on landownership actually encouraged larger landowners to champion such limitations.

More importantly, the characterization of early modern Chinese society as "precommercial" has been severely challenged in recent scholarship. Studies of grain price fluctuations within and across macroregions indicate considerable market integration, suggesting that large portions of the rural economy had become market integrated. This directly contradicts older assumptions about the dominance of subsistence agriculture. Evidence of market integration is robust not only in core macroregions such as the Lower Yangtze and North China but also in frontier regions such as Gansu.[57]

Unsurprisingly, market penetration went hand-in-hand with individual economic rationality: most households were both calculating and resourceful. They invested in land when profitable, employed excess labor in nonagricultural production, reacted swiftly to fluctuations in land or commodity prices,[58] and, as demonstrated below, tirelessly promoted economic institutions and norms that favored their own interests. Certainly the existence of strong lineages promoted communal solidarity, but even within lineages, households often clashed over property, debt, and the rules that governed them. It seems highly unlikely that such a commercialized and economically aggressive society sustained moral ideals of "permanence in landholding," especially when there is almost no positive evidence of their existence.

Quite the opposite, such "ideals" were largely embraced only by those who could economically benefit from them. Almost no high-income households expressed support. *Dian* and permanent tenancy customs were therefore the result of intense and prolonged negotiation between highly self-interested parties rather than simple moral derivatives of "precommercial" ideals. Bargained equilibriums could emerge where moral uniformity did not. The assumption of basic self-interested rationality also applies easily to the formation and maintenance of English property

---

[56] Sugarman & Warrington (1996), at 121–35.

[57] *See* discussion at *supra* note 49. On market integration in Gansu, *see* Peter C. Perdue, *The Qing State and the Gansu Grain Market, 1739–1864, in* CHINESE HISTORY IN ECONOMIC PERSPECTIVE (1992), at 100.

[58] Lynda S. Bell, *Farming, Sericulture, and Peasant Rationality in Wuxi County in the Early Twentieth Century, in* CHINESE HISTORY IN ECONOMIC PERSPECTIVE (1992), at 207, 226–29, 232–39.

customs. While traditional Marxist accounts of early modern English history exaggerate the importance of *class*-based conflict,[59] it was, as many have argued, still a place of considerable ruthlessness when it came to property acquisitions, evictions, and enclosures. As a general theoretical matter, individuals may rationally choose to tolerate and abide by undesirable property norms for many reasons: to signal willingness for future cooperation, for example, or to avoid the material and reputational costs of noncompliance. The problem, however, is why similarly self-interested bargaining over property norms in both China and England led to dramatically different institutional outcomes.

The answer, I argue, lies in the different ways Chinese and English society allocated status and political authority. Specifically, sociopolitical status correlated tightly with wealth in early modern England but far less closely in China. Throughout the Qing and Republic, a Chinese individual's social position and status depended, according to broadly "Confucian" norms of social hierarchy, on his age and generational seniority within his patrilineal descent group, which commonly included several dozen households in North China and considerably more in southern regions. In contrast, the importance of kinship ties in rural English society precipitously declined in late medieval and early modern times, leading to, by the sixteenth century, a substantially "individualist" sociolegal order.[60] The tighter social fabric of rural China was indisputably "hierarchical" – elder kinsmen wielded extensive legal and customary authority over younger relatives – but also conferred, in aggregate, large status benefits on lower-income households: Because status was so closely tied to age and generational seniority, the system guaranteed significant status mobility within most individual lifetimes. People automatically gained status as they aged, theoretically independent of personal wealth.

A major theme of Chinese history during the Second Millenium was the gradual erosion of the central government's control over local communities. Geographic expansion and population growth tended to outstrip increases in state capacity throughout the Song, Yuan, Ming, and Qing dynasties, which meant that local communities increasingly had to

---

[59] R.S. NEALE, CLASS IN ENGLISH HISTORY 96 (1981) (noting that early modern English society was "neither order based nor class based").

[60] ALAN MACFARLANE, THE ORIGINS OF ENGLISH INDIVIDUALISM: FAMILY, PROPERTY, AND SOCIAL TRANSITION (1978); David Cressy, *Kinship and Kin Interaction in Early Modern England*, 113 PAST & PRESENT 38, 41 (1986); H.R. French & Richard Hoyle, *English Individualism Refuted and Reasserted: The Case of Earls Colne (Essex), 1550–1750*, 56 ECON. HIST. REV. 595 (2003).

self-govern.[61] This required closer forms of sociopolitical organization and therefore drove the proliferation of extended kinship networks across rural China, generally organized according to Neo-Confucian principles of age-based and generational seniority. Kinship networks varied from region to region in terms of size, the extent of their corporate landholdings, and the specific codes of conducts they imposed on their members, but a basic adherence to "gerontocratic" – if you will – principles of sociopolitical organization characterized the great majority of these networks in virtually all macroregions.[62]

By at least the fifteenth century, these "Confucian" norms of kinship-based hierarchy had become deeply embedded within the moral and ideological mainstream of Chinese society, and there were very few dissenting voices at any level of society. State sponsorship of these values was often substantial, especially in the tenth and eleventh centuries, but came and went rather unpredictably, as did any macroeconomic rationales that initially may have supported them. In other words, purely functionalist explanations for their longevity and reach are extremely problematic. By the Ming and Qing, scholars, officials, merchants, and farmers alike spoke of them in such intensely reverential, almost religious language – as inviolable "heavenly principles" of human behavior – that it seems highly implausible that no widespread and deep moral internalization had taken place.

In practice, of course, wealth remained a valuable social asset, but even so, lower-income seniors did frequently obtain status and authority quite disproportionate to their wealth. The evidence that follows indicates, for example, that slightly less than half of political leadership positions in a common village could be occupied by below-average landowners of advanced age and generation. Even this mildly weaker claim is comparatively striking. By most accounts, large landowners virtually monopolized positions of sociopolitical authority in rural English society.[63] This was

---

[61] Robert M. Hartwell, *Demographic, Political, and Social Transformations of China*, 42 HARV. J. ASIATIC STUD. 365 (1982). On the limited size and reach of the Qing bureaucracy, *see* CH'U TUNG-TSU, LOCAL GOVERNMENT IN CHINA UNDER THE CH'ING (1962); BRADLEY W. REED, TALONS AND TEETH: COUNTY CLERKS AND RUNNERS IN THE QING DYNASTY (2000); JOHN R. WATT, THE DISTRICT MAGISTRATE IN LATE IMPERIAL CHINA (1972); WILLIAM T. ROWE, CHINA'S LAST EMPIRE: THE GREAT QING 31–62 (2009). On examination degree quotas, *see* Benjamin A. Elman, *Political, Social, and Cultural Reproduction via Civil Service Examinations in Late Imperial China*, 50 J. ASIAN STUD. 1 (1991).

[62] See Chapter 5 for a detailed discussion.

[63] KEITH WRIGHTSON, ENGLISH SOCIETY, 1580–1680, at 43 (2003); H.R. French, *Social Status, Localism and the "Middle Sort of People" in England, 1620–1750*, 166 PAST & PRESENT 66 (2000).

not necessarily because, as some older studies have suggested, that political status depended *entirely* on wealth. We now know, for example, that active participation in public affairs and extended residency in the locality were similarly important factors. Rather, significant landholding was probably only a *prerequisite* for high status, if an explicitly acknowledged and widely moralized one. Nonetheless, small landowners and tenants were generally excluded from the ranks of the local political elite. Their cumulative social status and authority were therefore significantly weaker than those of Chinese farmers of similar economic rank.

Higher sociopolitical status naturally led to stronger bargaining positions in the negotiation of property norms, and vice versa. There is considerable evidence that high-status but low-income political elites played a central role in advocating and protecting *dian* redemption norms that favored the generally poor *dian* seller.[64] In comparison, the political dominance of large landowners in England allowed them to shape both legal and customary institutions very much to their liking. There was, in fact, a distinct long-term trend in the history of English property institutions toward favoring the interests of the "landed class," and away from the equitable treatment of smallholders. Differences between Chinese and English property norms reflected, therefore, the different power balances at play in such negotiations, which, as discussed earlier, were deeply self-interested and aggressive affairs.

The redemption of pawned land was hardly the only area where Chinese property norms were more egalitarian than English ones. For example, Qing and Republican local customs also favored poorer households over richer ones in crucial aspects of tenancy regulation. Most notably, Lower Yangtze customs regularly allowed and protected the right of "permanent tenancy" (*yong dian*), in which landlords lost the right to raise rents or evict tenants.[65] Early modern English landlords suffered no comparable handicaps and were notoriously ruthless in the eviction of tenants and consolidation of estates.[66] The model of custom formation presented here

---

[64] See discussion at Chapter 4, Section C.

[65] *E.g.*, HUANG (2001), at 99–118; KATHRYN BERNHARDT, RENTS, TAXES, AND PEASANT RESISTANCE: THE LOWER YANGTZE REGION, 1840–1950, at 21–27 (1992).

[66] *See* THE BRENNER DEBATE (1987); R.W. Hoyle, *Tenure and the Land Market in Early Modern England: Or a Late Contribution to the Brenner Debate*, 43 ECON. HIST. REV. 1 (1990). Although scholars involved in the "Brenner debate" vehemently disagreed over whether landlord aggression could explain the seventeenth-century Anglo-French economic divergence, all agreed that such aggression was indeed prevalent in England.

may explain, therefore, several key differences between Chinese and English property institutions, although length limitations allow detailed examination of only one.

All in all, cultural factors appear quite sparsely in my thesis, directly affecting only the initial distribution of social status. They made no explicit mandate – none of actual behavioral significance at least – regarding either the personal pursuit of wealth or the specific content of property institutions. However, because the distribution of status essentially laid the "ground rules" and basic political conditions for more self-interested socioeconomic activities, these narrowly defined cultural factors had tremendous institutional and macroeconomic impact nonetheless. We need not revert back to big, Weberian "cultural paradigms" that purportedly impeded individual economic ambition and rationality to bring culture, at least in the narrow sense of status distribution norms, back into global economic history.

BASIC SETTINGS AND TERMINOLOGY

Geographically, this book focuses on the Lower Yangtze and North China. It makes little sense to compare England with *all* of China due to the enormous size difference. It is far more manageable to highlight the more developed areas with relatively stable sociopolitical conditions. Both the Lower Yangtze and North China are "core" regions that fit this description. Moreover, the Lower Yangtze was the richest region in the country, whereas North China was the relative "hotbed" of Chinese managerial farming.[67]

Why compare China with England and not with, say, France? There have been major recent works that have pursued the latter comparison,[68] but for the most part, "divergence studies" still tend to focus on England and China. While there are unavoidable path-dependency issues at work here, there are nonetheless some clear substantive advantages to sticking with the traditional China–England comparison. First, the fact that England was the "first industrial economy" is still enormously significant. It remains the best example – perhaps the only example – of an economy that "industrialized organically," that industrialized without aspiring to an external example, without attempting to

---

[67] HUANG (1985), at 69–84; LI WENZHI ET AL. (1983), at 215–17.
[68] WONG & ROSENTHAL (2011).

copy industrial technologies and methods of production that were developed elsewhere. If we are to explain why China economically declined relative to "the West," then at some point the question of why China economically declined relative to "the first industrial economy in the West" becomes unavoidable. Better to tackle it head on, especially when, as noted below, the pre-1700 English economy *was* reasonably comparable to the nineteenth- and early twentieth-century economy of the Lower Yangtze and North China.

Second, the Sino-English divergence has a layer of genuine historical significance that other Sino-European comparisons cannot compare with: England, not any other European country, defeated and humiliated China in the Opium War, starting the so-called century of humiliation that defined, and continues to define, so much of modern Chinese history.[69] Shocked and embarrassed by its own industrial and military ineptitude, China eventually sunk into a century-long period of self-doubt and cultural chaos, starting with the slow demise of the dynastic system and the erosion of intellectual faith in "Confucianism" and ending with the Communist revolution.[70] England was not merely the "first industrial economy" but also the Western power that arguably did the most – or, at the very least, struck the first and most symbolic blow – to make China aware of its own material weaknesses.

Temporally, I cover roughly two centuries of English history, from 1500 to 1700, but focus more on the better-studied seventeenth century. Whereas English agriculture was largely household-based – supplemented, of course, by some communal pooling of labor and capital – prior to the sixteenth century, by 1700, agricultural capitalism had achieved

---

[69] JOHN DELURY & ORVILLE SCHELL, WEALTH AND POWER: CHINA'S LONG MARCH TO THE TWENTY-FIRST CENTURY (2013).

[70] The psychological and ideological damage done by the perception of material weakness is a prevalent theme in numerous books on late Qing and early Republican intellectual history. *See, e.g.*, MARY C. WRIGHT, THE LAST STAND OF CHINESE CONSERVATISM: THE T'UNG-CHIH RESTORATION, 1862–1874 (1988); BENJAMIN I. SCHWARTZ, IN SEARCH OF WEALTH AND POWER: YEN FU AND THE WEST (1964); JOHN KING FAIRBANK, TRADE AND DIPLOMACY ON THE CHINA COAST; THE OPENING OF THE TREATY PORTS, 1842–1854 (1953); JOSEPH RICHMOND LEVENSON, CONFUCIAN CHINA AND ITS MODERN FATE: A TRILOGY (1968). One must be careful, however, in evaluating the stronger claim that China's modern intellectual and cultural history was *only* a reaction against the Western impact. Benjamin Elman's scholarship has, for example, emphasized that the groundwork for this reaction was laid by internal developments in Confucian thought going back to the sixteenth century. BENJAMIN A. ELMAN, FROM PHILOSOPHY TO PHILOLOGY: INTELLECTUAL AND SOCIAL ASPECTS OF CHANGE IN LATE IMPERIAL CHINA (1984).

basic predominance. The sixteenth and seventeenth centuries also represented the heyday of classic common-law mortgages: by the late seventeenth century, "equity courts" began to challenge some of their institutional conventions. Although my coverage of English history relies heavily on the well-developed secondary literature, I also draw on an array of primary legal sources to illustrate the major mortgage institutions of this period.

On the Chinese side, I focus on the later nineteenth and early twentieth centuries. While this may seem odd, the analytical goal here is to match societies that were economically comparable – which, in the end, tends to mean "reasonably similar." Both late Qing and Republican China and seventeenth-century England boasted significantly commercialized economies on the cusp of industrialization; both were predominantly agricultural and self-contained, although the importance of international trade was ever increasing; and finally, both recognized and protected private property rights through law and custom. Rigorous analysis and comparison would be impossible without these broad similarities.

In fact, compared with earlier periods in Chinese history, the later nineteenth and early twentieth centuries may actually offer a more poignant set of economic circumstances. Fresh off a series of humiliating defeats at the hands of foreign powers and trying to recover from the Taiping Rebellion, China's political and economic elites badly wanted to industrialize the economy as fast as possible. Why this proved to be an elusive goal – why the Chinese economy "stayed down" – despite their newfound sense of urgency, is perhaps an even more compelling question than why, still largely unaware of Western progress, the Chinese economy fell behind in the first place.

This does mean, of course, that this book will only have indirect, if thematically significant, connections to the "Great Divergence" debate proper, which focuses on why China "fell behind." That said, "Confucian" kinship networks, infinite "dian" redeemability, and a relative lack of managerial farming were all very much characteristic of eighteenth century China as well as the nineteenth and twentieth, which certainly suggests that the analysis performed here could conceivably be replicated in an earlier era. However intuitively appealing that may be, that is a different project.

My analysis of Chinese sociolegal and economic history relies on a large variety of primary sources – legal codes and cases, compilations of customary law, land contracts, rural sociological surveys, lineage registries, and local gazetteers. The bulk of these sources falls within 1865–1940, a period of relative stability for most rural communities – despite, of course, serious turmoil at the level of national and international politics – and therefore a more suitable arena for the sort of structural analysis done here. I do attempt, when there is corroborating evidence, to make reasonable projections back as far as the mid-eighteenth century, thereby also covering most of the Qing. For example, *dian* customs in the 1930s were broadly similar to what they were around 1755; kinship networks were prevalent and sociopolitically powerful in rural China throughout the Qing and Republic; and capitalist agriculture was always insignificant.

The English side of the analysis makes use of the usual legal historian's repertoire–cases, records of customs, treatises, and commentaries–but also relies somewhat heavily on surveys of the secondary academic literature. This is a strategic choice driven partially by space limitations and partially by the fact that the preexisting literature on early modern English law and economic change is substantially more developed and exhaustive than that on late imperial and Republican China. The book does, of course, make every effort to utilize this literature comprehensively and accurately.

A few comments on terminology: First, almost any use of the term "Confucian" among historians will usually encounter several basic objections. For starters, many will point out, following in the tradition of Joseph Levenson, that the term "Confucianism" can be applied, at any given time, to multiple schools of thought that disagree on fundamental philosophical and moral issues.[71] During the Qing, for example, scholars separated into several major factions, most notably the "Song Learning" and "Han Learning" schools, each of which advocated a different moral philosophy and indeed a different set of canonical texts. There was no one set of values and doctrines that uniquely deserved the label "Confucian." Second, even the major schools of thought underwent dramatic change from era to era. Third, historians tend to be highly sensitive to the fact that "Confucianism," however defined, did not monopolize religious faith or moral discourse during any late Imperial dynasty, but rather shared the stage with other religions and philosophies – Buddhism and Daoism were perhaps the most visible ones, but there were also many local popular religions, cults, and variations of the major religions.

Fortunately, these now-standard forms of skepticism have fairly little effect on this particular study. Most importantly, I do not attempt to deal with any unified concept of "Confucianism," but only with a relatively

---

[71] LEVENSON (1968); THOMAS A. WILSON, GENEALOGY OF THE WAY: THE CONSTRUCTION AND USES OF THE CONFUCIAN TRADITION IN LATE IMPERIAL CHINA (1995).

narrow set of social norms – the ranking of related individuals by age and generational seniority – that most scholars would label, at least in the Chinese context, as basically "Confucian." Of the three major systemized religions in late Imperial China, only "Confucianism," however defined, consistently endorsed this norm as a foundational moral principle. Moreover, virtually no school of thought that could be plausibly labeled "Confucian" during the Second Millennium – none to my knowledge, at least – expressly disagreed with this principle. It is a major unifying theme amid the sometimes chaotic philosophical disagreements that Chinese scholars and officials regularly indulged in, which also meant that its basic normative shape and content remained largely stable during the latter dynasties.

Finally, although kinship hierarchies did indeed "share the stage" with other religions and value systems in actual social life, the format of these hierarchies was similar enough across different geographic regions that it seems rather unlikely that other value systems substantially interfered with their basic operation. Economic conditions did, as discussed below, lead a minority of Qing South China lineages to adopt different organizational principles, but even then, there was not enough institutional variation to indicate that other religions had played a significant normative role. For these reasons, it is possible, at least in this study, to speak coherently of "Confucian" values influencing the spread of kinship hierarchies, standard objections to the conceptual use of "Confucianism" notwithstanding.

The use of "egalitarian" in this book also deserves some explanation. Although the term "egalitarian" may be used to describe any kind of equality-promoting behavior or policy,[72] within the confines of this study, it specifically describes institutions and actions that promote the political and economic interests of lower-income households. It is also used in a purely descriptive sense, without ideological connotations attached. Finally, "customary law" and "custom" are also terms that often mean different things to different people.[73] Here they refer to social "rule[s]

---

[72] Egalitarianism (Stanford Encyclopedia of Philosophy), *available at* http://plato.stanford .edu/entries/egalitarianism/ (last visited March 7, 2013) ("An egalitarian favors equality of some sort: People should get the same, or be treated the same, or be treated as equals, in some respect").

[73] *See, e.g.,* the discussion at Gerald G. Postema, *Custom, Normative Practice and the Law,* 62 Duke L.J. 707 (2012) (summarizing preexisting definitions of custom and customary law and arguing that they are wrong); C.M.N. White, *African Customary Law: The Problem of Concept and Definition,* 9(2) J. African L. 86 (1965) (describing several different definitions of "customary law").

acknowledged by the population of a particular locality as having a *binding force*."[74] In some fields, such rules are more commonly referred to as "social norms."[75]

Finally, there is the title of the book, *Laws and Economics of Confucianism: Kinship and Property in Pre-industrial China and England*: *Laws and Economics of Confucianism* is, quite obviously, a play on the numerous articles titled "the law and economics of X" that have emerged in the legal academy over the past two or three decades.[76] This book shares a number of thematic concerns with these articles, including both its concern with the socioeconomic origins and economic consequences of legal institutions, and also its attempts to grapple with the utility and limitations of individual economic rationality – so the word play seemed appropriate enough. That said, I make no claim to provide anything remotely resembling a comprehensive economic analysis of "Confucianism," however defined, and therefore chose the softer phrasing "the laws and economics" rather than "the law and economics."

I employ the word "laws" somewhat loosely, using it to cover both formal state law and local customary law – the latter, not the former, is the focus of the book. *Customary Laws* might have been slightly more accurate, but *Customary Laws and Economics of Confucianism* would likely fail to alert many readers of this book's thematic connection to the law and economics literature. Moreover, there are many scholars who consider customary law a necessary part of any functional legal apparatus and would therefore agree that "customary law" is indeed "law."[77] "Confucianism" is employed, as noted earlier, in a very narrow sense. I do not attempt to comprehensively define the parameters of "Confucianism," but would insist that seniority-based kinship hierarchies – the core explanatory element of this book – were

---

[74] Jerome Bourgon, *Uncivil Dialouge: Law and Custom Did Not Merge into Civil Law under the Qing*, 23 LATE IMPERIAL CHINA 50, 53 (2002). Many scholars use "customary law" and "custom" interchangeably. *E.g.*, POSTEMA (2012). This book does as well. To some, however, "custom," especially in the context of Chinese legal history, may also refer to habitual practices that do not necessarily have any normative force. *See* Shiga Shuzo, *Qingdai Susong Zhidu zhi Minshi Fayuan de Kaocha* [*Research on the Legal Origins of Civil Law and Adjudication in the Qing*], *in* MING QING SHIQI DE MINSHI SHENPAN YU MINJIAN QIYUE [CIVIL ADJUDICATION AND CIVIL CONTRACTS IN THE MING AND QING] 54 (Wang Yaxin & Liang Zhiping eds., Wang Yaxin et al. trans., 1998).

[75] *See* Richard H. McAdams, *The Origin, Development, and Regulation of Norms*, 96 MICH. L. REV. 338, 340 (1997b) (defining "social norms").

[76] *E.g.*, Richard A. Posner, *The Law and Economics of Contract Interpretation*, 83 TEXAS L. REV. 1581 (2005); Devon W. Carbado & Mitu Gulati, *The Law and Economics of Critical Race Theory*, 112 YALE L.J. 1757 (2003).

[77] *See, e.g.*, LAWRENCE LESSIG, CODE AND OTHER LAWS OF CYBERSPACE (1999).

distinctively "Confucian" within the historical context of pre-industrial China and England.

The conceptual ambiguities and intellectual disagreements that any general intellectual or religious category inevitably generates are no reason to stop using these categories altogether. I certainly do not claim that there was any "essential version" or "orthodox version" of Confucianism or even of "late Qing/Republican Confucianism," but do believe that seniority-based kinship hierarchies were a core feature of almost all major versions of "Confucian ethics" in the Second Millenium. This argument is, in fact, developed in some detail over the course of an entire chapter. The title *Laws and Economics of Confucianism* does justice, therefore, to this book's main themes. It does not touch on the English side of the comparison, but this is less problematic when, as noted earlier, the book's primary historical contributions are concentrated on the Chinese side. In any case, its comparative nature is made clear by the subtitle, *Kinship and Property in Pre-industrial China and England*. "Confucianism" refers to the primary explanatory factor of this comparative exercise, not its core subject – which, ultimately, is the social origins and economic consequences of pre-industrial property institutions.

STRUCTURE AND METHODOLOGY

Chapter 1 introduces the basic institutional framework and socioeconomic settings of *dian* transactions. Existing studies on Qing and Republican *dian* institutions disagree over a number of key issues, including the precise content of central regulations and the extent to which they were enforced. The first two chapters focus, therefore, on carefully presenting the institutional comparison between Chinese conditional sales and English mortgages, drawing particular attention to the complex relation between customs and formal law. In general, although the central government made several legislative and regulatory attempts to impose deadlines on *dian* redemption, enforcement at the county level or below was nearly nonexistent. In practice, customary law took precedence over state-made rules.

Chapter 2 discusses the evolution of the English mortgage from late medieval times to the early eighteenth century. While medieval lending institutions were relatively benign toward borrowers – resembling, in many aspects, *dian* norms – over the centuries they became increasingly harsh and ruthless, until, by the late fifteenth century, the "classic mortgage" had become the predominant financial instrument through which land was collateralized. Not coincidentally, other English property institutions, especially those governing tenancy relations, also became dramatically less poor friendly during this period.

Chapters 3 to 5 provide a "cultural" explanation for this institutional divergence. Chapters 3 and 4 demonstrate how "Confucian" kinship norms sustained economically inefficient but egalitarian *dian* institutions throughout the socioeconomic turbulence of the nineteenth and twentieth centuries, while social individualism and ranking by landed wealth helped large landowners in early modern England to seize control of property institutions. The idea that *dian* norms derived directly from "precommercial" ideals of "permanence in landholding" is examined and rejected in favor of a more structuralist thesis that incorporates larger doses of individual economic rationality and aggressiveness. Here again, the English side relies on a reasonably well-developed secondary literature, whereas the Chinese side is unpacked into several subarguments, each backed by primary historical evidence. A wide array of sources, including county-level case archives, village-level contract collections, Japanese surveys of Republican rural society, lineage registries, and local gazetteers, are used.

Chapter 5 then considers how "Confucian" kinship norms became entrenched in the Chinese ideological and religious mainstream. Moving in much broader strokes than the previous chapters and relying primarily on secondary literature, it outlines the rise of localized lineage groups during the Song and their gradual social and moral entrenchment during the Yuan, Ming, and Qing. The state plays a visible but complicated role in this process. Although government support for lineage building, particularly its consistent moral advocacy of Confucian social hierarchies, was sometimes quite substantial, it was not always reliable and usually doled out with much reluctance. For considerable parts of the Ming and, Qing, state policy actually turned very hostile to lineage self-governance, but with limited effect. Throughout the Second Millennium, private demand for extended ancestor worship rights and kinship self-governance was clearly the primary driving force behind the proliferation of "Confucian" kinship networks and hierarchies.

As should be quite obvious by this point, the main objective of this book is explanatory, not descriptive. The first two chapters do trace the evolution of *dian* and mortgage institutions in early modern China and England, but the core of the book is devoted to explaining them. This also explains the ordering of Chapters 3 through 5. Although the causal arrows I argue for run from cultural norms to kinship hierarchies to property institutions, in an analytical exercise in explanation, it is logically easier to work backwards, from the phenomenon being explained to the "level one explanation" and then to the deeper "level two explanation" that underlies the "level one explanation." Consequently, Chapter 5 should follow Chapters 3 and 4, which, in turn, should follow Chapters 1 and 2.

Chapter 6 examines the economic significance of the *dian*-mortgage comparison. It begins by discussing the socioeconomic backgrounds of *dian* sellers, *dian* buyers, mortgagors, and mortgagees. In both China and England, during the periods on which I focus, smallholders were far more likely to collateralize their land than larger landowners. The stronger redemption rights in *dian* sales therefore were tremendously beneficial to smallholders but aggravating and inconvenient to their wealthier neighbors – whereas the tables were turned in English mortgages. The chapter further argues that this contrast can substantially explain both the rise of capitalist agriculture in England and the lack thereof in China. Existing explanations, both institutional and "purely economic," are considered and rejected. I then lay out the specific mechanisms through which *dian* redemption norms obstructed land accumulation, whereas mortgage institutions accelerated it. Although the English side of this story is fairly well studied, the Chinese side requires the verification of several testable hypotheses via primary economic and legal sources.

The Conclusion returns to broader theoretical and historical themes, some already introduced: To what extent do the narratives here shed light on the broader "Great Divergence"? Given the balance they attempt to strike between value internalization and self-interested rationality, how do they relate to the growing literature on behavioral economics and cognitive psychology? In particular, how much do they contribute to the theoretical study of social norms and property?

It also introduces – briefly – a separate issue that may possess significant contemporary relevance: by demonstrating that "Confucian" kinship norms promoted economic egalitarianism – despite doing so at considerable cost to productivity and capital accumulation – this study urges a more nuanced reconsideration of Confucianism's role in Chinese history. Conventional wisdom, particularly in mainland China, tends to portray Confucianism as both economically oppressive *and* inefficient. The arguments here suggest, however, that some core Confucian institutions were inefficient precisely *because* they promoted economic equality. This book has no intent of taking sides in the well-publicized debates on whether China needs a "Confucian revival," but given how extensively both sides in that debate have used "historical arguments," it does encourage them to at least get their history right.

Finally, a word on methodology: Given that there are, essentially, two primary data points – the analysis focuses more on the commonalities between the Lower Yangtze and North China or between different parts of England than the differences, which means that each country is treated, in the final analysis, as one big data point – in this comparison, the core analytical moves employed here are necessarily qualitative and case study-based rather than quantitative. The primary methodology I employ at each level of analysis is more or less the following: What are the preexisting explanations for a certain phenomenon? Are they supported by available data? If not, what would a logically coherent alternative hypothesis look like – one in which the temporal and geographic scopes of the explanatory factors match the scope of the phenomenon being explained? What are the empirically demonstrable features of this hypothesis? Are the existing data consistent with these features – more so than with preexisting theories?

This is not to say that there are no statistical elements in this analysis. Quite the opposite, particularly on the Chinese side, there are quite a few, some central to the argument. When answering, "Did a certain phenomenon exist?", I have also tried to answer the natural follow-up: "To what extent?". Nevertheless, these attempts at estimation do not amount to *quantitative analysis*. Providing estimations of, for example, "what percentage of the contracts in a certain archive were *dian* sales" is not the same thing as running a statistical regression of the correlation between kinship hierarchies and customs of infinite *dian* redeemability. Not only is the existing evidence too piecemeal – the localities for which we have good evidence of the former are rarely the same localities for which we have good evidence of the latter – but there likely was, as argued later, insufficient variation within the two Chinese macroregions I focus on to support a meaningful regression. Quantitative social scientists may find this unsatisfactory, but then again, the primary challenge of history, even relatively recent history, is to make sense of often limited data. An empirical economist may choose to avoid a certain historical topic if the data are not good enough to support the field's conventional methods, but historians rarely have that luxury: their task is simply to make the best of sense of history we can. If this demands qualitative, rather than quantitative, analysis, as it usually does, then so be it.

1

Dian Sales in Qing and Republican China

Like most comparative studies of economic institutions, I begin with a functional question: how do landowners cope with large emergency cash needs? One could ask this of any human society, but it carries particular socioeconomic significance in pre-industrial but commercialized societies – where agriculture remained the most important source of livelihood and capital, but where land had become a marketable commodity, with both ample supply and demand and sophisticated legal instruments of conveyance. In such economies, landowning households typically held much more of their net worth in real property than in currency or personal property and often faced the issue of converting real property into currency. The legal instruments through which such conversion occurred were therefore of foundational importance to the functioning of land markets and the flow of capital.

In both societies that I study – later Qing and Republican China and sixteenth- and seventeenth-century England – landowners had two primary means of converting real property into currency: either they could sell the property outright, or they could collateralize it for a large loan. As discussed in later chapters, the basic economic circumstances under which landowners in both societies sold or collateralized land were broadly similar: land transactions were generally last resorts in times of emergency, used only when the monetary need, generally triggered by a wedding, funeral, or imminent loan repayment, exceeded what unsecured personal borrowing and the pawning of personal property could bring in. The institutional rules of collateralizing land, however, were dramatically

Portions of this chapter were previously published in Taisu Zhang, *Property Rights in Land, Agricultural Capitalism, and the Relative Decline of Pre-Industrial China*, 13 SAN DIEGO INT. L.J. 129 (2011).

different between the two societies. This chapter explores the Chinese side
of the story, whereas Chapter 2 explores the English side.

The great majority of Qing and Republican land transactions were *dian*
sales, sometimes translated as "conditional sales," in which a landowner
"sold" property but reserved the right to redeem it at a later time – it was,
in effect, a mortgage in which the mortgagee obtained temporary title and
use over the collateral until the mortgagor repaid. In almost all Lower
Yangtze or South China contract archives that scholars have discovered,
dian sales dramatically outnumbered permanent sales, in many cases by
more than eleven to one.[1] In North China, where well-preserved contract
archives have been much harder to come by, village surveys nonetheless
suggest that a large majority of local land sales were conditional rather than
permanent.[2]

Dian sales were hardly the only means of borrowing money in the Qing
and Republican economies – the pawning of personal items was a widespread practice, as was unsecured borrowing in small amounts – but if
landed collateral was involved in a loan, then generally a *dian* sale would
have to take place.[3] One often sees, for example, the following chain of
events in court disputes and rural surveys from these periods: a landholder
takes out an unsecured loan from a wealthier neighbor, agrees to pay
interest of a certain percentage, and pledges to pay the loan back within
a certain time frame. With the deadline looming, the landowner finds that
he (it was usually a he) cannot afford to redeem the land, but asks for a
grace period during which interest continues to accumulate and promises
to *dian* sale some of his land to the creditor if he defaults yet again. The
terminology for this stage of the transaction varies widely from village to
village, from *dang* to *ya* or even *dian*, but it was clearly designed as a
transitory step into a formal collateralized loan.[4] Once the final *dian* sale
was triggered, the original landowner's total debt would be repaid out of its

---

[1] See Qingdai Ningbo Qiyue Wenshu Jijiao [Qing Contracts from Ningbo] [*here-
inafter* Ningbo Contracts] (Wang Wanying ed., Tianjian Guji Press 2008); Shicang
Qiyue [Shicang Contracts] (Cao Shuji ed., Zhejiang Univ. Press 2010); Yang
Guozhen, Ming Qing Tudi Qiyue Wenshu Yanjiu [Research on Land
Contracts in the Ming and Qing] (1988).

[2] *E.g.*, 3 Chugoku Noson Kanko Chosa [Investigation of Rural Chinese Customs]
[*hereinafter* Mantetsu Surveys] 243–74 (Committee for the Publication of the Rural
Customs and Practices of China ed., Iwanami Shoten Press 1958).

[3] Liu Qiugen, Zhongguo Dian Dang Zhidu Shi [A History of Pawning and *Dian*
in China] 272–303 (1995).

[4] 3 Mantetsu Surveys, at 243 (using the term *dian*); 4 Mantetsu Surveys, at 511 (using
dang); 5 Mantetsu Surveys, at 547 (using *ya*).

proceeds, effectively terminating the loan and starting a new kind of financial relationship between the two sides.

In theory, *dian* sales were simple affairs: the original owner "sold" land, generally at some 60 to 80 percent of its full market value,[5] under the condition that he could later redeem it at the *original price* – no interest was charged, unlike in most forms of unsecured borrowing.[6] Tenants, who generally enjoyed decent security of tenure in China's economic core, could also transfer their rights of possession through these instruments.[7] In either situation, usage rights to the land changed hands with the *dian* sale, allowing the buyer to use the land as he wished until the seller redeemed.

The *dian* buyer's interest in lending money under such an arrangement was therefore not monetary interest, but rather whatever profits the land could yield before redemption. He was often protected, therefore, by contractually established "guaranteed-usage periods," usually called *xian*, of one or more years.[8] The seller could potentially reimburse the initial payment before these periods expired, but could only regain usage rights after expiration. However, he was under no obligation to redeem immediately on the expiration: as long as the contract did not expressly set a deadline for redemption, he could redeem at "any time after the guaranteed-usage period had expired."[9]

In any kind of *dian* sale, the seller might decide to part with this right of redemption, either because he could not afford to redeem or because he had simply lost interest in the land – perhaps because he planned to leave the region. When this happened, the *dian* buyer would obtain full ownership rights, but would have to pay the seller an "additional payment" (*zhaotie*) equal to the difference between the original sales price and the

---

[5] HUANG (1985), at 176; Henry McAleavy, *Dien in China and Vietnam*, 17 J. ASIAN ST. 406 (1958); MACAULEY (1998), at 231.

[6] Both the *Qing Code* and earlier Ming laws simply define *dian* as a sale that could be redeemed. DQLL, at 95.03; MINGDAI LÜLI HUIBIAN [COLLECTED LAWS AND PRECEDENTS OF THE MING], chap. 5–2, III–21 (Huang Zhangjian ed., 1979). On redemption at the original price, *see* LIANG ZHIPING, QINGDAI XIGUAN FA: SHEHUI YU GUOJIA [QING CUSTOMARY LAW: SOCIETY AND STATE] 93 (1996); WU XIANGHONG, DIAN ZHI FENGSU YU DIAN ZHI FALÜ [THE CUSTOMS AND LAWS REGULATING *DIAN* SALES] 35 (2009). In fact, in the several hundred *dian* contracts examined over the course of this project – discussed in detail in Section A of this chapter and then again in Chapter 4, none attempt to set an interest rate.

[7] *See* discussion by Brenner & Isett (2002). Tenants were free to transfer or sublease their tenancy rights. *See* Kenneth Pomeranz, *Land Markets in Late Imperial and Republican China*, 23 CONTINUITY & CHANGE 101, 131 (2008).

[8] LIANG (1996); McAleavy (1958), at 403, 406–07.   [9] WU (2009), at 100–03.

present market value of the land.[10] Similar to foreclosure sales for modern Anglo-American mortgages, this procedure protected the *dian* seller from losing land at less than full market value.

It should be immediately clarified that the concept of *dian* employed here is a functional one. It refers to a general category of land transactions that followed the basic institutional contours outlined earlier: land conveyances used as collateral for large loans. The specific legal labeling varied from place to place and often from contract to contract. *Dian* was by far the most common label, not to mention the formal label employed by the *Qing Code* and other government documents, but such terms as *dang* ("pawning") and even *mai* ("sale") or *yongmai* ("perpetual sale") were often employed in local life. In the latter cases, local custom tended to distinguish a *mai* ("sale") from a *juemai* ("irredeemable sale"): the former could be redeemed and also gave the "seller" a right to demand additional payments, whereas the latter was a truly permanent conveyance.[11] The mere label reveals no reliable information about the specific institutional framework of the transaction. Instead, one must look at the terms and governing rules. For conceptual simplicity, in this book, the term "*dian* sale" refers to all redeemable exchanges of land for money in which the creditor/buyer gained some usage rights – which he may or may not choose to rent back to the debtor – and some form of partial title over the transacted land. From this basic functional perspective, a redeemable sale and a loan secured by landed collateral in which the creditor could use the land until redemption were essentially identical.

To further illustrate these points, consider the following sample contracts, the former drawn from Republican North China, and the latter from late Qing Zhejiang:

Liu Yongxiang, the *dang* seller, due to inconveniences, now *dian* sells land in the Xiyuan region of his village, totaling six *mu*, to Zhao Luojian for three years. He will remain on the land as a tenant, paying two *jiao* of rent for each *mu*.
                    Middleman Zhao Yufeng; Village Head Hao Duodong; Vice Village Head Zhao Qini.[12]

Dianxin, because of a lack of money, now willingly sells (*mai*) a piece of his land, passed on from his grandfather. The land is a seed plot, covering one hill, and has

---

[10] These practices are summarized in HUANG (2001), at 74–75. Market value appraisals were generally conducted by local community members with accounting expertise but sometimes also involved finding other potential buyers and then asking the *dian* buyer to match their offer.

[11] See discussion below and also in Chapter 4 for specific examples of such contracts.

[12] 3 Mantetsu 247.

an area of 0.2 *mu*. Its specific parameters are: to the east, it borders Rongyang's land; to the south, it borders Runzhu's land; to the west, it borders a ditch; to the north, it borders Anfa's land. This land is willingly sold to Kunshan. The contract has been agreed upon by all three sides, and carries a sum of 8,400 wen. The money has been paid in full upon the signing of the contract. After the sale, the buyer shall have full freedom to plant and harvest. The land is free from any dispute by relatives. This is voluntary on both sides, and there is no complaint by anyone. To provide written proof for the future, they establish this *yongmai* contract as reference.

Also: the land taxes for this land are transferred with the sale.

– Eleventh Year of Daoguang (1831), Eleventh Month, signed by Dianxin
– Witnessed by his brother Changfa, middleman Wenrui, and drafter Qisen[13]

The terminology varies wildly in these two contracts: the first one uses both *dang* and *dian* but is clearly referring to a kind of transaction that would fall neatly under the functional parameters discussed earlier. Liu *dian* sells land to Zhao, remains as tenant, and guarantees Zhao the right to collect rent for at least three years – that is, Liu will not fully redeem the land for at least three years. At the time the contract was documented by researchers in 1942, the three-year period had yet to pass.

In the latter contract, the terms *mai* and *yongmai* are used, which might suggest a permanent sale, but it is clear from other contracts in this archive that only contracts designated as *juemai* ("final sale") were unredeemable, whereas *yongmai* contracts were fully redeemable and would only become *juemai* after a series of "additional payments" (*zhaojia*), in the local terminology. In fact, across the Lower Yangtze, the customary distinction between a *mai* – which carried a possibility of redemption and of additional payments – and a final, nonredeemable *juemai* was very commonplace, with the former greatly outnumbering the latter. We see this not only in the Ningbo contract archives but also in the other major contract archive, Shicang, which was discovered in recent years.[14]

Returning, however, to the Ningbo sample contract under discussion: *zhaojia* and *juemai* arrangements were commonly documented as addenda to the original contract. These arrangements, too, fall within the functional concept of *dian* employed in this book. No guaranteed-usage period is specified here, which suggests that the "seller" could redeem as soon as he found the funds to do so. The fact that no *juemai* or *zhaojia* addendum is attached suggests that Dianxin or his descendants likely redeemed at some point.

---

[13] Ningbo Contracts 2.
[14] Shicang Contracts, Contents & Introduction (2010). For more specific statistics on the kinds of contracts in each archive, *see* Chapter 4, Section C, for a detailed discussion.

In both contracts, middlemen and witnesses are employed, often chosen from the contractors' relatives: Zhao Yufeng and Zhao Qini were both related to Zhao Luojian, whereas both contractors and all witnesses in the second contract belonged to the same clan – hence the omission of their surnames. In the first contract, the village chief and his second-in-command were present to lend credibility to the proceedings. In the second, gravitas was provided by the middleman Wenrui and the drafter Qisen, both clan seniors who knew how to read and write and were therefore present at many contract signings.

A number of practical questions arose from this basic institutional framework. Chief among these was the issue of redemption: could the parties set a deadline for redemption? The two examples just given do not provide for any deadlines, but could the parties have fixed one if they so desired? Were they free to set any deadline they pleased, or were there regulatory upper or lower boundaries? Taking a step back, if the original contract failed to expressly provide a deadline, would a default deadline apply, either by law or by custom?

Historians have struggled with these issues for some time but have yet to generate substantial consensus. Some have argued that norms on all levels, from the *Qing Code* down to local custom, approached *dian* sales from a basic presumption of permanent landownership: the universal assumption was that farmers were reluctant to sell land and that this reluctance deserved legal and customary protection.[15] Laws and customs alike, therefore, expressly allowed *dian* sellers to redeem after extended periods or might simply refuse to recognize any contractually set deadline for redemption. In effect, they often granted *dian* sellers an interminable right of redemption, good for decades or even centuries after the original transaction. More recent writings on the subject seem to reach the opposite conclusion: Qing laws and customs operated under the assumption that real property was a fully alienable commodity and should not be subject to extended periods of conditional ownership. Correspondingly, they prohibited redemption of *dian* sales after a certain period, commonly a decade or so, and recognized contractually established deadlines.[16]

---

[15] HUANG (2001), at 71–98. *See also* MACAULEY (1998), at 230–45; YANG (1998), at 279; Yang Guozhen, *Shilun Qingdai Minbei Minjian de Tudi Maimai* [*Discussing Land Transactions in Qing Northern Fujian*], 1 ZHONGGUOSHI YANJIU [STUDIES ON CHINESE HISTORY] 29 (1981).

[16] BUOYE (2000), at 94; POMERANZ (2000), at 70–73.

Part of the problem is that these studies generally relied on incomplete analyses of the existing evidence: they have yet to seriously explore local customs on redemption deadlines and, perhaps more problematically, have often relied on inaccurate or partial interpretations of the formal law. A more comprehensive survey of relevant law and custom suggests that the actual situation fell somewhere in the middle. Local customs in the regions I studied do indeed display a prevalent social sympathy for attempts to maintain permanent landownership. They generally did not recognize redemption deadlines, permitting *dian* sellers to retain redemption rights indefinitely. Central-level authorities, however, displayed strong hostility to such practices and nominally banned redemption after ten years. Faced with this conflict between law and custom, local magistrates generally left conditional land sale disputes to mediation and, when compelled to issue a statement, tended to express support for local customs. While probably just a prudent act of self-preservation, this nonetheless shielded local customs from hostile legal regulations. Qing and Republican property institutions did, therefore, favor strong redemption rights in practice, even though they may have opposed them as a matter of formal legal theory.

The remainder of this chapter is organized as follows: Section A examines how county-level customs throughout China regulated conditional sales contracts. Section B then describes how various pieces of Qing and Republican legislation handled such transactions. Section C argues that local courts very rarely enforced these laws and regulations that contradicted local customs.

A Local Custom

The term "custom," as legal historians generally use it, refers to "rule[s] acknowledged by the population of a particular locality as having a *binding force*."[17] As medieval Canonists saw it, "custom resonate[d] within law, while ordinary practice pertain[ed] to the domain of fact."[18] In essence, a custom was a habitual practice that had acquired normative status. It may be, as so many legal or social-science concepts are, a Weberian "ideal type,"[19] but this does not necessarily detract from its usefulness in describing, however approximately, rules that *govern* social behavior, either due to

---

[17] Bourgon (2002), at 53.   [18] *Id.* at 54.
[19] 1 Max Weber, Economy and Society: An Outline of Interpretative Sociology 20–21 & note 5, at 57–58 (Guenther Roth & Claus Wittich eds., Ephraim Fischoff et al. trans., Bedminster Press 1968).

fear of sanction or internalization,[20] rather than merely describe it. Modern property rights scholars often call these rules "social norms,"[21] but legal historians probably remain more familiar with the term "custom."

Attempts to apply this concept, usually translated as *xiguan*, to Qing legal practice have sometimes stirred considerable controversy. Historically, the concept did not come into widespread use in China until the early twentieth century, when Republican jurists began searching for local "customs" in their attempt to draft a formal civil law code.[22] Perhaps confused by this importation of legal terminology, academic attempts to search for references to "custom" in Qing adjudication have sometimes imposed a normative dimension to terms that, in their original context, had none. As Shiga Shuzo has famously pointed out, early attempts to frame references to *renqing* ("human sentiment") in some Qing court decisions as examinations of "local custom" overlooked the fact that those references were merely observations of habitual social fact.[23] That is, they merely noted that local people tended to behave in a certain way and did not infer that those tendencies could constitute a binding *norm*, either on local people or on judicial decision making. Thus, when Qing court decisions spoke of *renqing*, they often treated it as factual information and not as a source of *law*. This conceptual ambiguity is only made worse by the tendency of preexisting studies to employ the word "custom" without defining it at all.[24]

Regardless of the state of previous scholarship, this book applies the term "custom" strictly in its normative sense. Although it might be difficult to find precise equivalents to custom in Qing legal terminology, it would nonetheless be ridiculous to assume that Qing localities had no normative property customs of their own. For example, *dian* sales had been one of the most important forms of land transaction for longer than the dynasty itself,[25] but heavy central regulation did not come into existence until the latter part of the eighteenth century. The myriad of disputes triggered by *dian* sales were somehow resolved in the absence of formal law, allowing ample opportunity for the development of local custom. In fact, a number of sources do indicate the existence of well-established customs by the mid-Qing. These include a few mediation records in the county archive

---

[20] McAdams (1997b), at 340.   [21] *Id.*

[22] Sui Hongming, Qingmo Minchu Minshangshi Xiguan Diaocha zhi Yanjiu 18–76 (2005).

[23] Shiga (1998).   [24] Bourgon (2002).

[25] Ming attempts to regulate *dian* sales are clear evidence of this.

cases discussed earlier and, more importantly, early-twentieth-century surveys that sought to emulate the French *enquéte par turbe*.

The surveys were initiated in 1903 by the Qing court, but were repeatedly interrupted due to insufficient funding and personnel, and not completed until 1923 under Cao Kun's Beiyang government.[26] The original intent, shared by both Qing and Republican authorities, was to gather information for the drafting of a new civil code.[27] The researchers in charge explicitly sought to identify "local customs" (*xiguan*) that possessed binding force and indeed produced a vast collection of local practices that, at least as presented in the final report, were clearly normative in nature: numerous researchers commented on the "strong binding force" of certain customs, or how they could be used to "combat" nonconforming actions.[28] Republican-era jurists took the normative nature of these customs seriously enough to designate them a *formal source of law* in the new Civil Code of 1929: "where the Code is silent, the courts shall apply custom."[29] At the time, the survey reports were the only extensive compilation of Chinese custom in existence.

There are, of course, other potential sources of information on local economic customs: as early as the Ming Dynasty – perhaps even before – and throughout the Qing, scholars and officials encouraged local communities to establish "county pacts" (*xiangyue*) as a source of order and regulation.[30] Some of these survive in writing. A large number of local lineages enacted lengthy codes of conduct for lineage members, which often included detailed regulations on contract making and the selling of property. Finally, Qing merchant guilds generally enjoyed considerable rule-making authority over local commercial activity and would often publish these economic customs via steel engravings. The later chapters

---

[26] Sui (2005).   [27] *Id.* at 18–19, 58–59.   [28] XGDC, at 153, 175, 194, 364.

[29] Zhonghua Minguo Minfa Dian [The Civil Code of the Republic of China] art. 1 (1929).

[30] Terada Hiroaki, *Ming Qing Shiqi Fazhixu zhong de "Yue" de Xingzhi* [The Nature of *Yue* in Ming and Qing Legal Order], *in* Ming Qing Shiqi de Minshi Shenpan yu Minjian Qiyue (1998), at 178. *See also* William Rowe, Saving the World: Chen Hongmou and Elite Consciousness in Eighteenth-Century China 102–03 (2003) (discussing the positive assessment of *xiangyue* by prominent officials); Conrad Schirokauer & Robert P. Hymes, *Introduction, in* Ordering the World: Approaches to State and Society in Sung Dynasty China 1 (Robert P. Hymes & Conrad Schirokauer eds., 1993) (discussing social organizational principles in Song China). The local creation of written custom was prevalent in the Qing. *See* Terada (1998); Sun Lijuan, Qingdai Shangye Shehui de Guize yu Zhixu: Cong Beike Ziliao Jiedu Qingdai Zhongguo Shangshi Xiguan Fa [The Rules and Order of Qing Commercial Society: Interpreting Qing China's Commercial Customary Law from Stele Inscriptions] (2005).

of this study use a number of these sources, but in general, they are of varying quality and relevance and cannot approach the systematic coverage that the government custom surveys attempted to provide. They do, at least, reinforce the surveys' basic assumption that local communities engaged in extensive economic self-regulation and, therefore, should have little difficulty in identifying normative "customs."

Despite the geographic diversity of the survey, its reports on *dian* sales reveal considerable uniformity among local customs on the issue of *dian* redemption: nearly all surveyed counties, for example, had customary prohibitions against redeeming conditionally sold land between the initial sowing of seeds and the final harvest.[31] Most prohibited early redemption if the contract had set a guaranteed-usage period.[32] More importantly for the purposes of this book, almost none of the several hundred surveyed counties – and, indeed, only one county in North China or the Lower Yangtze – imposed any customary deadline on redemption.[33] Instead, the general assumption seemed to be that redemption rights would exist indefinitely and could be exercised in any year after the guaranteed-usage period, if one existed.

As one particularly explicit Fujian custom stated, *dian* sales of land "could be redeemed even after several dozen or even several hundred years, and the price of redemption would always remain the same regardless of changes in land value."[34] While such colorful language was rare, customs that expressly made redemption possible "at any time" existed in *all* reporting provinces and were particularly abundant in North China, the Middle and Lower Yangtze, and South China.[35] Many explicitly forbid the original contract from setting any redemption deadline.[36] In comparison, a *very* small number of customs – only three in the entire survey – expressly

---

[31] *See, e.g.,* XGDC, at 28, 30, 40, 67, 79, 84, 132, 141, 153, 157, 175, 194, 257, 291, 349, 418.

[32] These were common. *See, e.g.,* XGDC, at 141, 153, 157, 175, 194, 257, 278, 279, 291. Exceptions include XGDC, at 225, 488, 234, 262, and 547, which allowed redemption at *any* time, regardless of any contractually established guaranteed-usage period.

[33] Deqing County, Zhejiang Province, guaranteed redeemability for only thirty years, which would still be unimaginably long by the English standards discussed in Chapter 2. XGDC, at 480–81. I can only find two other counties that imposed a mandatory deadline, both in Gansu Province. Xunhua imposed a three- or five-year redemption deadline for all *dian* sales. Jingyuan capped redeemability at sixty years. XGDC, at 684, 695. Numerous other counties in Gansu supported unlimited redeemability. *See, e.g.,* XGDC, at 690, 691, 696.

[34] XGDC, at 505.

[35] A partial list: XGDC, at 28, 29, 67, 81, 225, 234, 262, 319, 356, 364, 370, 488, 505, 524, 547, 570, 586, 600, 631 (dealing explicitly with burial grounds) and 645, 646, 690, 691, 696, 722, 822, 1160.

[36] Examples include XGDC, at 234, 262, 524, 547.

limited indefinite redeemability to contracts that imposed no clear dead-line.[37] Far more often, customs simply stated that redemption rights could be exercised "at any time after the guaranteed-usage period's expiration."[38]

A number of customs prohibited redemption during guaranteed-usage periods and between sowing and harvest, but made no express statement on redemption deadlines.[39] Many of these do note, however, that if the seller failed to redeem before sowing time, "he would have to wait until the following year," implying that redemption rights were viable for some extended period of time.[40]

The question, of course, is for how long? A simple answer would be "until whatever deadline the contract sets," but as scholars have known for some time, the vast majority of *dian* contracts did not set any deadline. For example, in a sample of some 500 *dian* contracts from Qing and Republican Zhejiang, covering two villages and several dozen households, *none* imposed a redemption deadline.[41] Quite the opposite, it was common practice in both North China and the Lower Yangtze to incorporate some version of the following language into *dian* contracts: "If there is not enough cash to redeem [after the guaranteed usage period had passed], the buyer will continue to till the land with no deadline. Once the original amount has been paid, the land will revert to the original owner."[42] All this is completely consistent with what we saw in the preceding paragraph and suggests that even when the early-twentieth-century custom surveys were silent on the issue of redemption deadlines, the general normative pre-sumption was simply that no deadlines should be imposed. Moreover, as discussed in considerable detail in Chapter 6, there is much evidence to suggest that *dian* sellers regularly exercised their right of redemption. For example, in the Zhejiang contract archives discussed earlier, probably no more than a small fraction of *dian* sales were eventually converted to permanent conveyances.[43]

All things considered, there is very good reason to believe that most local communities in the Chinese core supported unlimited redeemability. A few localities, in fact, went a step further and prohibited permanent

---

[37] I can find only three examples of this: XGDC, at 586, 688, 818.

[38] Examples include every custom cited in note 113 below, except those also cited in note 114.

[39] *See, e.g.,* XGDC, at 141, 153, 157, 175, 194, 257, 278, 279, 291.

[40] *See, e.g.,* XGDC, at 55, 378, 548, 291, 940.   [41] NINGBO (2008); SHICANG (2010).

[42] TIANCANG QIYUE WENSHU CUIBIAN nos. 17, 71, 91, 130, 198, 279 (Hugh T. Scogin & Zheng Qin eds., 2001); XGDC, at 312.

[43] *See* Chapter 6, Section C.

land selling of *any* kind: even irrevocable sales could be redeemed as long the original owner still possessed a copy of his original deed.[44] Such statements were highly unusual – we can only imagine the tremendous economic inefficiencies that would have arisen had they been remotely widespread – but nonetheless seemed to share in whatever socioeconomic rationale that provided for unlimited redeemability in *dian* contracts.

The uniformity of such customs across geographic regions indicates that the practice had deep social and historical roots – these are the focus of Chapters 4 and 5 – and had therefore existed long before the late-Qing- and Republican-era custom surveys "discovered" them. Indeed, as discussed later, Qing officials made concerted efforts to combat unlimited *dian* redemption as early as the mid-Qianlong era – a campaign that Republican governments carried on well into the twentieth century. This suggests that such norms were widespread by at least the mid-eighteenth century and, considering how long it could take for the central government to address perceived "problems" in local commercial self-regulation, possibly much earlier.

The idea that Qing and Republican society favored permanent land-ownership ideals, including the specific claim that *dian* sales were unlimitedly redeemable, has recently come under criticism by Thomas Buoye. Based on surveys of provincial homicide cases, Buoye claims that Qing landowners often made *dian* sales "to raise cash to invest in trade or business" and in increasingly "innovative" ways that "indicated a good deal of commercial savvy."[45] This suggests, Buoye believes, that the "ideal of permanent landownership" was in decline and that local communities would not have tolerated long-term conditional ownership of land.

The problem is that Buoye's factual observations are not at all inconsistent with the presumption that *dian* sales were permanently redeemable. If anything, they might actually support it. Even if landowners were increasingly willing to engage in complex *dian* sales, they could nonetheless have assumed that redemption rights were unlimitedly viable. In fact, strong customary protection of redemption rights made "innovative" *dian* sales significantly less risky for landowners and, therefore, should theoretically have boosted their willingness to experiment with complex title arrangements.

---

[44] *See, e.g.*, XGDC, at 28, 319, 225.
[45] Thomas Buoye, *Litigation, Legitimacy, and Lethal Violence, in* CONTRACT AND PROPERTY (2004), at 94, 106, 113; BUOYE (2000), at 94.

A more material challenge to the aforementioned observations comes from Zhou Yuanlian and Xie Zhaohua, who argue that most *dian* sale contracts in the Lower Yangtze *did* contain a contractual deadline, usually three or five years, for redemption.[46] This argument seems to stem, however, from a straightforward misinterpretation of contractual language. Zhou and Xie note, for example, that certain Anhui contracts contained the clause "can be redeemed after three years" and interpret this to mean that the seller must redeem *within* three years.[47] The various sources examined earlier, however, make it abundantly clear that such language almost always meant "*cannot* redeem within three years" – in other words, it guaranteed that the *dian* buyer would enjoy usage rights for at least three years – but says nothing about redemption deadlines.

B The *Qing Code* and Other Central Regulations

Compared to the seller-friendly tendencies of most local customs, formal Qing civil law came to exhibit considerable hostility toward the unlimited redemption of *dian* sales, although this was a slow and extended process. Earlier editions of the *Qing Code* make little mention of *dian* sales. The central statute on this subject was Statute 95, "*Dian* Sales of Land or Real Estate" (*Dian Mai Tianzhai*), which sets three rules[48]: (1) the *dian* buyer must register the contract with local officials and pay the accompanying tax,[49] (2) the *dian* buyer must not impede redemption after the guaranteed-usage period has passed, and (3) the *dian* seller must not sell the contracted land to any other party before he fully redeems it. These are, of course, very narrow rules that fail to address most *dian* sales-related complications. They do not tell us, for example, whether contracts could set any redemption deadline the parties desired or how to handle a contract that did not expressly indicate either a *dian* sale or an irrevocable one.

Realizing these inadequacies, the Qing Court issued several addenda during the eighteenth century. The first, promulgated in 1730, banned the redemption of sales expressly labeled as "irrevocable sales." If no such phrase existed, *or* if the contract "set a guaranteed-usage period,"

---

[46] Pomeranz (2008), at 130–31; Zhou Yuanlian & Xie Zhaohua, Qingdai Zudianzhi Yanjiu [Research on Qing Tenancy and *Dian* Institutions] 312–13 (1986); Huang (1985), at 176.

[47] Zhou & Xie (1986), at 124.   [48] DQLL, at 95.00.

[49] Later edicts effectively voided this rule by granting tax exemptions to *dian* contracts. *Id.* at 95.09.

"then the property shall be redeemable."[50] In addition, should the *dian* seller eventually decide to irrevocably sell his land to the *dian* buyer, he could henceforth demand only one additional payment.[51] Finally, any attempt by the seller to prematurely redeem before the guaranteed-usage period had expired would carry criminal liability.[52]

A 1744 addition by Emperor Qianlong attempted to further crack down on ambiguously worded contracts that failed to specify whether the sale was redeemable or not, banning redemption of such contracts if "a long time has already passed."[53] This vague edict paved the path for a more detailed 1753 substatute that stipulated that any ambiguous contract made after 1723, but before 1753, could be "redeemed in accordance with this sub-statute."[54] Ambiguous contracts made before 1723 would, however, be considered irrevocable sales that carried no possibility of either redemption or additional payment. From 1753 onward, all new contracts were required to expressly indicate their legal status, either as a *dian* or a *juemai*, through the phrases "to be redeemed" or "sold irrevocably, never to be redeemed."[55]

All things considered, the *Qing Code* left a substantial amount of contractual freedom to private parties. Most importantly, it did not impose any upper boundaries on *dian* redemption deadlines or, indeed, even require that contracts specify a deadline. Philip Huang, for one, considers this lack of regulation a commitment to "a precommercial ideal of permanence in landholding."[56] Whether a laissez-faire approach can really be

---

[50] *Id*. at 95.03.   [51] *Id*.   [52] *Id*.

[53] 14 QING SHILU [RECORD OF THE QING] chap. 436 (Zhonghua Shuju ed., 1985).

[54] DQLL, at 95.07.

[55] Some scholars have proposed a more ambitious but somewhat less literal interpretation: the substatute meant that *any* ambiguous contract, whether drawn before or after 1753, would be presumed redeemable for thirty years. HUANG (2001), at 74; MACAULEY (1998), at 240–41. The evidence is drawn from a paper by Kishimoto Mio that records three murder cases from the *Xing'an Huilan* that purportedly adjudicated "according to the 30-year rule." HUANG (2001), at 74, note. None of the three cases expressly applied any such rule. Instead, they simply ruled that since the original contracts were ambiguous and too much time had passed, the land in question was no long redeemable. Kishimoto Mio, *Ming Qing Shidai de "Zhaojia Huishu" Wenti* [*The Issue of "Zhaojia" and "Dian" Redemption in the Ming and Qing*], in III-4 ZHONGGUO FAZHISHI KAOZHENG [EMPIRICAL STUDIES ON CHINESE LEGAL HISTORY] 423, 457–58 (Terada Hiroaki ed., Zheng Minqin trans., 2003). They do not tell us whether those contracts were made before or after 1753. There is therefore no way to identify the precise statutory rationale of the judgments. *See also* Terada Hiroaki, *Shindai Chuuki no Ten Kisei ni Mieru Kigen no Imi ni*, in TOUYOU HOSHI NO TANKYUU 339, 347–51 (1987) (refuting any attempt to apply DQLL 95.07 to post-1753 contracts).

[56] HUANG (2001), at 74.

interpreted as supporting any specific "ideal" of landholding is debatable,[57] but the substatutes did at least tolerate that ideal.

While this is certainly a reasonable reading of the *Qing Code,* the code itself hardly presents a comprehensive and accurate view of Qing *dian* sales regulation. Most scholarship in English, with the notable exception of an early article by Henry McAleavy,[58] seems to assume, either implicitly or explicitly, that the code constituted the *only* Qing legal authority on *dian* sales.[59] Chinese and Japanese scholars have done better only very recently and have begun to give the *Board of Finance Regulations (Hubu Zeli)* some well-deserved attention.[60]

This was a set of fairly fluid regulations issued by the Board of Finance at five-year intervals beginning in 1776. Since the board's official duties centered on the administration of land and tax, the regulations naturally focused on similar issues and in much greater detail than the *Qing Code.* The authority to draft such regulations came directly from the emperor, who would occasionally delegate certain areas of regulation to the board for discussion and drafting. Some Chinese historians suggest that these regulations eventually came to function as a "civil code" of sorts, thus directly challenging the traditional assumption that the Qing only had a "criminal code."[61]

The central government invested considerable energy in publicizing and enforcing the *Board of Finance Regulations.* In 1793, for example, a conditional sale between a Jiangsu Board of Punishments official and some private landowners came to the attention of Qianlong himself, who then

---

[57] Chapter 4 discusses this in greater detail.

[58] Henry McAleavy does not explicitly discuss any other legal authority but does, based on the *Taiwan Shiho,* notice the existence of the crucial "eleven year rule" in the *Hubu Zeli,* discussed below. McAleavy (1958), at 411. Macauley does recognize the existence of the *Hubu Zeli* as an alternative source of legal regulation but does not mention the "eleven year rule." MACAULEY (1998), at 241.

[59] *See, e.g.,* HUANG (2001); Buoye (2004). Neither of the two main essay collections in the Chinese legal history field, CIVIL LAW IN QING AND REPUBLICAN CHINA (Kathryn Bernhardt & Philip C. C. Huang eds., 1994) or CONTRACT AND PROPERTY (2004), mention any statutory source other than the *Qing Code* and some scattered edict collections in their bibliographies.

[60] *See, e.g.,* Lin Qian & Zhang Jinfan, *Zailun* Chongde Huidian, Hubu Zeli *de Falü Shiyong* [*Restudying the Legal Application of the Chongde Huidian and Hubu Zeli*], 5 FAXUE QIANYAN [FRONTIERS OF LEGAL SCHOLARSHIP] 197 (2003); 8; ZHONGGUO FAZHI TONGSHI [HISTORY OF CHINESE LAW] 436 (Zhang Jinfan ed., 1999); ZHONGGUO MINFA SHI [THE HISTORY OF CHINESE CIVIL LAW] 602–03 (Kong Qingming, Hu Liuyuan & Sun Jiping eds., 1996); Terada (1987), at 352–60.

[61] Lin & Zhang (2003).

directed the *Bureau of Laws and Regulations* (*Luli Guan*) to outline the relevant legal authorities. The bureau's response memo stated that "in both this case and future disputes that concern residency [*hukou*] and land [*tiandi*], the *Board of Finance Regulations* should be applied."[62] By at least the early Jiaqing era, court memoirs were referring to the *Board of Finance Regulations* as a commonly accepted source of legal authority, noting that exceptions to it could not be granted without express approval of the emperor.[63]

This was not lost on private legal commentators. The mid-Qing writer Bao Shichen, for example, noted that "each Board issues its own regulations [*zeli*], and these too are eternally binding."[64] By the Xianfeng era, private land contracts expressly listed both the *Qing Code* and the *Board of Finance Regulations* as binding legal authorities, suggesting that the *Board of Finance Regulations* had penetrated very deeply into local economic life.[65] At the very least, officials at both provincial and county levels kept copies of the *Board of Finance Regulations* in their archives, well aware that they would have to apply them in their daily administration. As the famous legal scholar Wang Youhuai observed, "[A]ll *yamen* officials, whether high or low, were instructed to place in their archives distinct copies of all laws and regulations they had to obey. If any were missing, they were punished as if they had lost an official document."[66] Wang then provides a list of legal authorities that these local bureaucrats had to possess: the *Qing Code*, the *Board of Civil Appointments Regulations* (*Libu Zeli*), the *Board of Finance Regulations*, and several dozen others. The legal landscape of the Qing was clearly far more complicated than just the *Qing Code*.

The Qianlong series of *Board of Finance Regulations* made two crucial changes to *dian* sales law: first, the *Board of Finance Regulations* now allowed the buyer of a *dian* to sell his conditional ownership,[67] at which point the third-party purchaser would assume all the rights and obligations of the original buyer. Second, and more drastically, if the *dian* seller

---

[62] *Id.*   [63] *Id.*

[64] Zhongguo Jindai Sixiang Jia Wenku: Bao Shichen Juan [Collected Works of Early Modern Chinese Thinkers: Bao Shichen] 415 (Liu Ping & Zheng Dahua eds., 2013).

[65] Lin & Zhang (2003).

[66] Wang Youhuai, 3 Qiangu Beiyao [Essentials of Finance and Grain] 57 (1893).

[67] 1 Qingdai Ge Buyuan Zeli: Qinding Hubu Zeli (Qianlong Chao) [The Regulations of Qing Boards: The Imperially Decreed Board of Finance Regulations (Qianlong Era)] [*hereinafter*, HBZL] 148 (Fuchi Shuyuan ed., 2004).

failed to redeem within eleven years of the original sale, the *dian* buyer could claim full ownership by assuming tax responsibilities for the property (*tou shui guo hu*).[68] After ten years, the seller could ask for, at most, a one-year extension, after which redemption would be at the discretion of the buyer.[69] There was only one exception: when bannermen sold land to Han Chinese, they were guaranteed redemption rights for twenty years.[70]

Court documents claim that the official legislative intent behind these rules was to "eliminate social conflict" and "prevent litigation."[71] These somewhat cryptic phrases seem to suggest that the central government was indeed aware of the widespread protection of unlimited *dian* redemption by local customs – there were, in fact, several memoirs by local magistrates on this very issue[72] – and, moreover, felt burdened by the social disputes they frequently generated. Quite plausibly, then, the regulations amounted to a direct and conscious assault on customary rights of *dian* redemption.

As with almost any Imperial court document, one might question whether "eliminating social conflict" and "preventing litigation" were merely rhetorical flourishes that shielded some other rationale, but there is no good reason to assume so. Qing local governments famously suffered from an often-crippling lack of both financial and human resources.[73] This was at least partially a conscious decision by the central government: citing a more streamlined bureaucracy as one its primary policy objectives, the Qing Court systematically withdrew from direct management of local economic and social affairs, leaving tax-collection, dispute-settlement,

---

[68] HBZL, at 83, 148–49; ZHONGGUO FAZHI TONGSHI (1999), at 435; Terada (1987), at 357–58. There has been some debate over whether this ten-year limit was a deadline for redemption or merely an upper limit for guaranteed-usage periods – the language is somewhat ambiguous and could support either interpretation. *See* GUO JIAN, DIANQUAN ZHIDU YUANLIU KAO [VERIFYING THE ORIGINS OF *DIAN* INSTITUTIONS] 196 (2009) (supporting the latter interpretation); Terada (1987), at 357–58 (supporting a version of the former interpretation, in which the buyer *could* terminate the seller's right of redemption after eleven years if he chose to). However, discussions of the rule in Imperial memorials, in which officials pleaded with the Jiaqing emperor to allow impoverished bannermen to retain redemption rights after the eleven-year deadline, make it fairly clear that Qing officials, at least, tended to follow the former interpretation. Lin & Zhang (2003). I see no solid reason to challenge them.

[69] ZHONGGUO FAZHI TONGSHI (1999), at 435. The buyer did not have to exercise this claim immediately. Terada (1987), at 357–58.

[70] ZHONGGUO FAZHI TONGSHI (1999), at 435.   [71] Lin & Zhang (2003), at part 3.

[72] *Id.*   [73] CH'U (1962); REED (2000).

and regulatory powers to local guilds, lineages, and other social groups.[74] Compared with earlier dynasties, the Qing employed roughly the same number of local officials, despite dealing with a population that was several times larger.[75] "Preventing litigation" was therefore a very real and pressing issue.

In any case, the *Board of Finance Regulations* were clearly unwilling to tolerate unlimited *dian* redemption rights and extended uncertainly in land titles: no matter the circumstance or contractual language, *dian* sellers had at most ten or twenty years to redeem and could receive only one additional payment if they made the sale irrevocable. The drafters of these rules were quite ready to sacrifice the *dian* seller's interest in redemption for legal clarity and perhaps administrative simplicity. This is a very different picture from what the *Qing Code* offers on its own.

Republican-era statesmen and jurists followed their mid-Qing predecessors in treating the concept of unlimited *dian* redemption with considerable skepticism and hostility. The government researchers who conducted the commercial customs survey, for example, would often label customs that protected unlimited redemption as "evil" or "backwards." In the higher echelons of law and policymaking, politicians agreed that unlimited *dian* redemption created economically inefficient amounts of legal uncertainty and therefore should be eliminated.

Despite this rhetorical hostility, Republican-era lawmakers actually chose to extend the ten-year redemption deadline in the *Board of Finance Regulations*, first to sixty years in a 1915 piece of legislation titled *Rules for Clearing Dian Relations in Real Property* (*Budongchan Diandang Qingli Banfa*) and then to thirty years in the 1929 *Republican Civil Code*. The former came, of course, at a time when the country was descending into warlordism and civil war and was therefore frequently subject to somewhat arbitrary revision and reinterpretation by different warlord factions within their respective spheres of influence. In Zhejiang, for example, a 1917 provincial "interpretation" of the *Rules for Clearing Dian Relations in Real Property* stated that *dian* sales could not be redeemed after thirty years

---

[74] *See* ROWE (2009) at 32–33. For an overview on guilds, *see* Christine Moll-Murata, *Chinese Guilds from the Seventeenth to Twentieth Centuries*, 53 INT'L REV. OF SOC. HIST. 213 (2008).

[75] HO PING-TI, THE LADDER OF SUCCESS IN IMPERIAL CHINA; ASPECTS OF SOCIAL MOBILITY, 1368–1911 (1962). The book's definition of *social mobility* has been controversial. *See* the literature review in F. W. MOTE, IMPERIAL CHINA 900–1600, at 126–34 (2003) and in BENJAMIN ELMAN, A CULTURAL HISTORY OF CIVIL EXAMINATIONS IN LATE IMPERIAL CHINA 647–50, 656, 659 (2000).

rather than sixty. Leaving aside the politically meaningless problem of whether such an interpretation was constitutionally allowable, there did seem to be some general consensus that a ten-year legal deadline was too short. As the next section will argue, this consensus probably had much to do with the enormous difficulty of enforcing such a deadline in local adjudication.

C Local-Level Adjudication

The true socioeconomic significance of central legislation and rule making depends, of course, on whether they were actually enforced in the official resolution of relevant disputes. This was largely the domain of local magistrates and clerks, far removed from the high politics of Beijing. The *Qing Code*, in particular, expressly discouraged the appeal of commonplace "residency, marriage, or land" (*huhun tiantu*) disputes from their court of original jurisdiction, a preference that Republican courts were apparently eager to embrace.[76] Whether central regulations on *dian* redemption could indeed supplant contradictory local customs largely depended, therefore, on the adjudicatory behavior of entry-level officials and their staff.

Local adjudication is naturally best studied through case records, which generally fall into one of three categories: (1) serious criminal cases compiled by Qing provincial governments or the Imperial court – Republican case archives at the provincial level or above remain largely inaccessible to researchers[77]; (2) privately written casebooks, usually compiled by retired officials based on their personal adjudication experience[78]; and (3) local county-level archives, such as the famous Baxian, Baodi, and Danxin archives or, more recently, the Republican-era Longquan archives.[79]

---

[76] DQLL, at 334.05.

[77] Mainly the XINGKE TIBEN (TUDI ZHAIWU LEI), archived at the First National Archives in Beijing, and the XING'AN HUILAN, which has been edited and published by multiple presses. Books using these sources include BUOYE (2000) and DERK BODDE & CLARENCE MORRIS, LAW IN IMPERIAL CHINA (1967).

[78] *E.g.*, QIU HUANG, FUPAN LUCUN [RECORDINGS OF MAGISTRATE DECISIONS], *in* 1 MING QING FAZHI SHILIAO JIKAN [COLLECTION OF LEGAL MATERIAL FROM THE MING AND QING] 371 (National Library of China ed., 2008); FAN ZENGXIANG, FANSHAN PIPAN [DECISIONS AND ORDERS FROM FANSHAN] (Shanghai Guangyi Bookstore ed., 1915).

[79] Historians have recently discovered a fourth in Nanbu County. Yasuhiko Karasawa, Bradly W. Reed, & Matthew H. Sommer, *Qing County Archives in Sichuan: An Update from the Field*, 26 LATE IMPERIAL CHINA 114 (2005). It remains relatively unknown in Western academia. Mainland Chinese scholars have better access. *See, e.g.*, LI ZAN, WAN QING ZHOUXIAN SUSONG ZHONG DE SHENDUAN WENTI [THE ISSUE OF ADJUDICATION IN LATE QING COUNTY-LEVEL LITIGATION] (2010).

Among these, both the first and second categories are largely unhelpful for our present purposes. The great majority of private collections, particularly those that provide complete and well-edited case records, only incorporate cases that, in the editor's judgment, possess significant explanatory force or set good examples for future adjudication.[80] As such, they have a strong tendency to incorporate only the highest-quality decisions, which, needless to say, present a severely skewed image of local adjudication – in other words, they present it in far too positive a light. Because there is no way to effectively neutralize this overwhelming selection bias, private case collections appear here only in peripheral, complimentary roles. In later chapters, where the goal is to study fact patterns and not judicial behavior, they become much more useful.

Qing central and provincial case archives suffer from a different kind of selection bias. Because Imperial law strongly discouraged the appeal of "household, marriage, and land" (*huhun tiantu*) cases to the provincial level unless a strong criminal element was present,[81] adjudication at the provincial level or beyond focused almost exclusively on serious crimes. The largest category actually seemed to be homicide.[82] In addition, Qing law explicitly separated *huhun tiantu* disputes from more serious cases not only in the availability of appeal but also in the level of discretion that local magistrates enjoyed. For example, a magistrate could diverge from the prescribed punishments in the *Qing Code* for *huhun tiantu* cases. Thus, instead of receiving a physical beating, the losing side would generally pay damages or obey a court injunction.[83] More importantly, the magistrate could allow *huhun tiantu* cases, but not serious criminal charges, to end informal mediation.[84] It is therefore impossible to project patterns of judicial behavior found in provincial homicide cases onto the processing of ordinary civil cases.

---

[80] *See, e.g.,* QIU (2008), at 375–77.

[81] *See* Jonathan Ocko, *I'll Take It All the Way to Beijing: Capital Appeals in the Qing*, 47 J. ASIAN STUD. 291, 295 (1988) ("[N]o appeals of minor civil cases could be accepted"); Qiang Fang, *Hot Potatoes: Chinese Complaint Systems from Early Times to the Late Qing*, 68 J. ASIAN STUD. 1105, 1121 (2009) (noting that *huhun tiantu* cases could not be appealed beyond the prefecture level).

[82] BUOYE (2000), at 1–16.

[83] LIBU CHUFEN ZELI [CONDUCT REGULATIONS OF THE BOARD OF PERSONNEL], *cited in* ZHONGGUO FAZHI TONGSHI (1999), at 676–77; Mark Allee, *Code Culture, and Custom: Foundations of Civil Case Verdicts in a Nineteenth-Century County Court, in* CIVIL LAW IN QING AND REPUBLICAN CHINA 122, 126–27 (Kathryn Bernhardt & Philip C. C. Huang eds., 1994).

[84] PHILIP C. C. HUANG, CIVIL JUSTICE IN CHINA: REPRESENTATION AND PRACTICE IN THE QING 119 (1996).

This leaves us with the third category: county-level case archives. There are, as noted earlier, three major archives that have been employed in historical research since the 1980s: Baxian, in Sichuan; Baodi, in Hebei; and Danxin, in Taiwan. Combined, these archives offer detailed case records of several thousand civil disputes ranging from the late Qianlong era to the early 1910s. A couple hundred are now housed at Stanford University, courtesy of Philip Huang and his research teams from the 1990s. For our present purposes, these cases are especially valuable because they generally occurred after the issuance of the *Board of Finance Regulations*, and therefore shed some light on how the regulations were enforced by late eighteenth- and nineteenth-century magistrates. I focus here on a sample of twenty-six *dian*-related disputes, ranging from 1770 to 1890, but pre-dominantly concentrated within two thirty-year periods: 1770–1800 and 1860–1890.[85]

Much more recently, scholars have unearthed a Republican-era case archive from Longquan County in southern Zhejiang. This new discovery holds 18,434 cases from 1910 to 1949, including 10,614 civil suits and 7,820 criminal cases – smaller than Baxian, but larger than Baodi and Danxin. Moreover, rapid progress has been made in digitizing the entire collection, allowing scholars to run comprehensive searches for certain categories of cases. For example, within the 10,614 civil suits, 430 stemmed from a dispute concerning *dian* sales, of which 386 focused on whether the *dian* seller should be allowed to redeem.[86] Assuming that the preservation of cases contained no inherent selection bias – there is no reason to assume otherwise – this suggests that perhaps 4 to 5 percent of civil disputes were

---

[85] Baodi County Archives [*hereinafter* Baodi] 194, 1839.2.23; Baodi 96, 1846.95.8; Baodi 96, 1846.100.6; Baodi 103, 1863.117.27; Baodi 104, 1865.5.22; Baodi 109, 1870.22.8; Baxian County Archives [*hereinafter* Baxian] 6:1:722, 1770.7; Baxian 6:1:739, 1774.8; Baxian 6.1:746, 1775.3; Baxian 6.1:749, 1775.10; Baxian 6:1:761, 1777.3; Baxian 6:2:1413, 1796.11; Baxian 6:2:1415, 1797.1; Baxian 6.2.1418, 1797.3; Baxian, 6:2:1416, 1797.6; Baxian 6:2:1427, 1797.6; Baxian 6.2:1428, 1797.8; Baxian 6.2:1430, 1797.8; Baxian 6:2:1421, 1807.4; Baxian 6.4:1707, 1851.8; Danxin County Archives [*hereinafter* Danxin] 23201, 1868.10.23; Danxin 23202, 1873.10.18; Danxin 23205, 1879.2.18; Danxin 23206, 1879.11.6; Danxin 23208, 1881.11.21; Danxin 23209, 1882.3.8. See also Shen Yanqing, *Huaiqing Yigao* 525–27, *in* 1 JINDAI ZHONGGUO SHILIAO CONGKAN no. 0378 (Shen Yunlong ed., Taibei, 1966), for a private collection case from the same time period, which touches upon similar issues, and displays a similar mindset.

[86] Longquan Dang'an Hebian Mulu [Index of Collected Archives from Longquan] [*hereinafter* Longquan Index] (December 5, 2011) (unpublished index, on file with the Zhejiang University History Department). Search with keywords "典," "当," "押," and "赎."

dian related, with over 85 percent of those related directly to redemption disputes. My sample here consists of eighty randomly selected *dian*-related cases, of which sixty-five specifically focused on the redemption issue.

The Baxian, Baodi, and Danxin sample suggests, first and foremost, that county magistrates were generally reluctant to issue formal decisions on *dian*-related cases. Within the twenty-six-case sample, only nine reached a formal court decision, whereas the other seventeen ended through some out-of-court process, usually community mediation.[87] A cursory glance at this ratio suggests a clear willingness to allow mediation. More importantly, the nine formally adjudicated cases were mostly "easy cases" that did not involve the more provocative rules in either the *Qing Code* or the *Board of Finance Regulations*. In particular, *none* involved the issue of redemption deadlines. Two examples will suffice to illustrate this. In the first, the Baxian county government had sold land confiscated from a temple that was engaged in illegal activities.[88] That land, however, had previously been conditionally sold to several parties, who now petitioned for repayment. The magistrates determined that they had no relation to the temple's crimes and arranged compensation. This case does not, in fact, involve *any* legal rule discussed earlier but was morally straightforward. The second case involved a peasant who had conditionally sold land to another,[89] but had later made the sale irrevocable and had received the additional payment. A few years afterwards, he attempted to reclaim the land by cutting down its trees for sale. The magistrate found for the new owner, and no other result was possible unless he assumed that *irrevocable* sales could be redeemed.[90]

More interesting, one case actually saw the magistrate explicitly disobey a *Qing Code* statute: in a 1796 case from Baxian, one Yang Panlong had conditionally purchased a piece of land from his neighbor, Liu Hongzhi.[91] A few years later, he asked Liu to redeem it. Liu agreed but also wanted to sell it outright to a third party. He therefore proposed to pay his debt to Yang through the revenue from that third-party sale. Yang disagreed and brought the case to court, where the magistrate ordered Liu to proceed with his sale and pay Yang afterwards. This clearly contradicted Statute

---

[87] The nine formally adjudicated ones are Baodi 103, 1863.117.27; Baodi 96, 1846.95.8; Baodi 194, 1839.2.23; Baxian 6:1:722, 1770.7; Baxian 6:2:1413, 1796.11; Baxian 6:2:1415, 1797.1; Baxian, 6:2:1416, 1797.6; Danxin 23206, 1879.11.6; Danxin 23209, 1882.3.8.
[88] Baxian 6:1:722.   [89] Baxian 6:2:1415, 1797.1.
[90] Similar cases are Danxin 23209, 1882.3.8 and Baodi 194, 1839.2.23.
[91] Baxian 6:2:1413, 1796.11.

95 of the *Qing Code*, which, as noted earlier, stated that no land under a *dian* sale contract could be sold unless the seller first redeemed it in full.

On the other hand, *no* case that potentially involved the mandatory ten-year redemption deadline ever reached a formal court decision. Such cases were instead mediated out of court, and they account for eight of the seventeen unadjudicated cases, most involving an outright attempt to redeem and others involving a *dian* seller claiming "sharecropping rights" over the transacted land, but all seeing at least eleven years pass between the original transaction and the suit.[92] Several of these cases involved attempts to redeem contracts made many decades ago: in an 1865 Baodi case, for example, Zhao Yong sought to redeem land that his great-grandfather conditionally sold in 1788.[93] When the *dian* buyer's descendant refused, Zhao cut down his wheat. While this would have been a clear-cut decision for the current owner if the magistrate enforced the *Board of Finance Regulations*, he allowed it to end in mediation, where, as discussed later, the mediator apparently recognized Zhao's claim to the land. A Danxin magistrate in charge of a similar 1881 case involving a *dian* sale from 1835 actually went beyond this.[94] While he did not formally issue a decision, he told the grand nephew of the original seller: "[T]he land was conditionally sold by your granduncle to Su Gong ... How can his grandson Su Li refuse to allow redemption?"[95] This magistrate clearly ignored the eleven-year limit on redemption.

Some cases also involved additional payment claims on top of the redemption attempts. In another 1797 Baxian case, two brothers attempted to squeeze further additional payments out of their grandfather's *dian* sale contract, even though it had become legally irrevocable over thirty years ago due to the grandfather's acceptance of an additional payment.[96] They

---

[92] Baodi 104, 1865.5.22; Danxin 23208, 1881.11.21; Baxian 6:2:1418, 1797.3; Baxian 6:1:761, 1777.3; Baxian 6:2:1430, 1797.8; Danxin 23201, 1868.10.23; Danxin 23202, 1873.10.18; Danxin 23205, 1879.2.18. All of these involve *dian* sellers claiming an ownership stake in the transacted land at least eleven years after the original transaction. Apart from these eight redemption-related cases, the other nine unadjudicated cases are Baodi 109, 1870.22.8 (involving a price dispute over the added value to a piece of conditionally sold land); Baodi 96, 1846.100.6 (involving a sharecropping agreement over a piece of conditionally sold land); Baxian 6.4:1707, 1851.8 (involving ownership of an ancestral gravesite on a transacted property); Baxian 6:1:739, 1774.8 (likewise); Baxian 6:2:1421, 1807.4 (likewise); Baxian 6:2:1427, 1797.6 (likewise); Baxian 6.1:749, 1775.10 (conditionally selling the same piece of land multiple times); Baxian 6.2:1428, 1797.8 (likewise); Baxian 6.1:746, 1775.3 (likewise).
[93] Baodi 104, 1865.5.22.   [94] Danxin 23208, 1881.11.21.   [95] *Id.*
[96] Baxian 6:2:1418, 1797.3.

returned to the land and, using what must seem like an unimaginative tactic by now, cut down its bamboo, stating that their ownership interests had yet to terminate and that they were reclaiming their rights. This case also went to mediation, but the case record does not document the mediation result. The other five cases involving contested redemption offer basically similar fact patterns to the three described above.[97]

Despite its quantitative limitations, this case sample offers a coherent picture of judicial passiveness: local magistrates strongly preferred to leave *dian* sales disputes, especially ones that involved prolonged redemption claims, to mediation and usually declined to enforce potentially controversial regulations. While most cases that did reach a formal decision adhered to the published law – a conclusion reached by several previous studies[98] – a few did not. In some mediated cases, moreover, the magistrate expressly indicated his disagreement with central regulations. All in all, coercive enforcement of central-level laws and regulations was weak at best.

These observations agree exceedingly well with the conventional historiographic opinion that Qing local governance was weak. As scholars have explored in considerable detail, Qing county magistrates were commonly hampered by an acute shortage of funds, personnel, and social connections.[99] State policy not only prohibited magistrates from serving within 500 *li* of their hometown but also expected them to pay staff salaries out of their own pockets. Apart from the handful of personal clerks and secretaries the average county magistrate could afford, nearly all *yamen* staff members were local residents who received most of their income not from their meager official stipend but in the form of processing and filing fees from private parties.[100] County magistrates routinely dealt, therefore, both with sociogeographic unfamiliarity and also with a staff that was deeply embedded within local society yet financially independent of the magistrates themselves. To make matters even worse, the Qing state kept the size of its bureaucracy largely stable throughout the entire dynasty despite rapid demographic growth that led to a doubling of the population by the early nineteenth century and a tripling by the dynasty's end.

---

[97] Baxian 6:1:761, 1777.3; Baxian 6:2:1430, 1797.8; Danxin 23201, 1868.10.23; Danxin 23202, 1873.10.18; Danxin 23205, 1879.2.18. See also Shen, *Huaiqing Yigao* 525–27.

[98] HUANG (1996), at 17; Buoye (2004), at 99–100. These conclusions do not contradict my conclusions here, which simply argue that difficult cases involving a law-custom split were usually left to mediation – the magistrate was not violating any legal rule by allowing this.

[99] CH'U (1962); REED (2000).   [100] REED (2000).

Given these circumstances, it is completely unsurprising that county governments – underfunded, understaffed, and facing an increasingly daunting bureaucracy-to-population ratio – generally refrained from challenging local interest groups or customs. Nor, in fact, did they have much positive incentive to. As noted earlier, real property disputes that lacked a criminal element were typically handled only at the county level, without possibility of appeal. This meant that deference to local custom, even when formal Qing law demanded otherwise, was unlikely to attract any negative attention from higher authorities.

Of course, the mere fact that magistrates tended to leave *dian* sales disputes to informal mediation does not necessarily mean that mediation outcomes relied substantively on local custom. To be sure, it would be very counterintuitive if they somehow did not – there is a strong logical expectation that local communities will attempt to enforce rules they set for themselves, especially when state authorities are both unwilling and unable to challenge their judgment – but some positive evidence is nonetheless desirable. Fortunately, of the eight mediated disputes that potentially involved the ten-year deadline, two do indicate how the mediation proceedings eventually concluded. Although this is obviously too small a sample to generate concrete conclusions on its own, these cases nonetheless offer compelling insights when read jointly with the custom surveys examined in Section A.

Both of these cases were mentioned earlier. The first is the 1881 Danxin case involving a *dian* sale from 1835.[101] As noted earlier, the magistrate issued no verdict but did observe to the grand nephew that "the land was conditionally sold by your granduncle to Su Gong ... How can his grandson Su Li refuse to allow redemption?"[102] The case record then indicates that the dispute was eventually resolved through mediation. This strongly suggests that the final mediation result allowed redemption, although potentially with some financial concessions to the buyer's grandson. Since the magistrate's comment was a clear violation of the *Board of Finance Regulations*, the motivation for his comments lay elsewhere, either in his personal sense of equity or in prudent deference to local custom. The latter motivation agrees, of course, with my argument that *dian* redemption customs were socially influential. If, however, unlimited *dian* redemption was somehow an issue of moral equity to the magistrate,

---

[101] Danxin 23208, 1881.11.21.　　[102] *Id.*

then perhaps I have actually *underestimated* the social importance of permanent landownership ideals.

The other case, the Zhao Yong incident from Baodi, had a very similar fact pattern. The record shows that communal mediators took control and reached a settlement: the original seller's great-grandson, who had cut down wheat from the contracted land, could keep the crops but would also allow the original buyer's family to keep using the land for the time being.[103] The original contract would *not*, however, be replaced by an irrevocable deed. While this may seem to be a mutual compromise, the fact remains that the original contract was over eighty years old by this point, so *any* acknowledgment of the great-grandson's claim suggests that the mediators were somewhat sympathetic to his redemption claim. As with all individual mediation results, it is uncertain whether the mediators were consciously following local custom or simply trying to appease both sides. As argued in Section A, however, local customs in North China, where Baodi is located, did support indefinite redeemability vigorously. The concurrence between these customs and the specific outcome in this case is at least suggestive.

It seems likely, therefore, that local customs played a material role in communal mediation of *dian* disputes. In any case, the very fact that most local *dian* redemption customs continued to contradict official law well into the early twentieth century itself constitutes fairly convincing proof that local enforcement of the ten-year regulatory deadline was weak. As noted earlier, despite much rhetorical condemnation of *dian* redemption customs, Republican lawmakers actually extended the mandatory redemption deadline for *dian* sales from ten to sixty years – later cut down to thirty years – even though commercialization of land had increased substantially since the mid-Qing.[104] They seemed to realize that the ten-year deadline was simply unenforceable and chose to concede some ground to local customs.[105]

Despite these concessions, Republican local courts were only marginally more effective at enforcing legal *dian* redemption deadlines than their Qing predecessors.[106] Within the eighty-case sample of *dian*-related cases from Republican-era Longquan, sixty-five cases, as noted earlier, focused specifically on *dian* redemption. Twenty-five of the sixty-five cases

---

[103] Baodi 104, 1865.5.22.   [104] ZHONGHUA MINGUO MINFA DIAN (1930), at arts. 912, 924.
[105] Philip Huang has, somewhat oddly, interpreted this as a partial rethinking of the "precommercial" logic of rural society. HUANG (2001), at 88–99.
[106] *See* Appendix A, Part I.

featured express claims that the *dian* buyer's redemption rights had expired after a certain period of time, a ratio of 38 percent. Of these twenty-five cases, sixteen involved *dian* contracts that had been made more than thirty years prior to the redemption attempt, the oldest of which was made seventy-two years prior. In at least five of the twenty-five cases, the *dian* buyer expressly petitioned the magistrate to disregard local customs and enforce government regulations, citing in particular 1917 provincial interpretations of the *Regulations on Clearing Land Tenure*, which, contrary to the sixty-year *dian* redemption limit in the regulation's original text, banned redemption of *dian* contracts after thirty years.[107] After 1929, of course, the governing legal text should simply have been the newly enacted *Civil Code*, which banned *dian* redemption after thirty years.

Whether before or after 1929, the local court's enforcement efforts were both tepid and rather incoherent. In only one of the sixteen cases involving contracts of thirty years or longer did it enforce the relevant legal authority and ban redemption.[108] One other redemption attempt was rejected due to procedural missteps: the *dian* seller failed to show up in court.[109] In three other cases, the court actually allowed redemption despite the passage of thirty-eight, fifty, and fifty-nine years, and made no mention whatsoever of the legal deadlines.[110] The remaining eleven cases were settled via communal mediation. It seems highly unlikely that such erratic adjudicatory behavior could have significantly dented the reach and authority of local custom, especially when the great majority of *dian* redemption cases were still settled via external mediation.

There is evidence to suggest that local customs continued to exert profound influence over communal mediation: five of the eleven settled cases also record the basic terms of settlement, all of which gave basic recognition to the *dian* seller's right to redeem.[111] In three cases he was allowed to redeem outright, and in two he was paid an extra sum to temporarily withdraw his redemption request. In no case was he compelled to permanently surrender the property to the *dian* buyer.

---

[107] *Id.* [108] Longquan County Archives [*hereinafter* Longquan] M003-01-02147 (1920).
[109] Longquan M003-01-01119 (1919).
[110] Longquan M003-01-00038 (1919) (fifty-nine years); Longquan M003-01-00586 (1921) (thirty-eight years); Longquan M003-01-15483 (1932) (fifty years).
[111] *See* Longquan M003-01-00642 (1919); Longquan M003-01-00787 (1947); Longquan M003-01-01166 (1920); Longquan M003-01-11063 (1922); Longquan M003-01-15821 (1943).

Despite its inconsistent behavior, in terms of adhering to and enforcing the written law, the Longquan court's behavior nonetheless may have represented a actual improvement, however minor, over the general state of Qing county-level adjudication. At the very least, Longquan judges were occasionally willing to pass formal judgment on *dian* redemption cases, whereas the magistrates from the Qing sample punted the issue back to mediation in every instance. Actual enforcement of the thirty-year redemption deadlines also occurred from time to time, if very unreliably.

This apparent "improvement" may or may not have been real, but if it was, how should we understand it? Perhaps more importantly, does it pose any problems for the general argument that local courts did little to curb "dian" redemption customs? A thirty-year deadline was, of course, less at odds with local custom than the ten-year Qing rule and therefore less risky to enforce, but this does not fully explain why Longquan judges may have been more eager to adjudicate. Even under a thirty-year deadline, the path of least resistance was still to send potentially controversial cases back to mediation.

These marginal improvements, if they existed, were probably not the result of any stronger state control over local communities – quite the opposite, central-level state authority only weakened after the Qing collapse because the new Republican governments were rife with in-fighting, warlordism, and local factionalism. Even after the Nationalist Party unified much of the country in 1928–1929, the new central government in Nanjing made relatively little progress in expanding its control over rural localities despite an initially spirited reform program. As several studies have documented, attempts to revamp local governance structures rarely generated substantive administrative efficiency.[112] Certainly the new Republican state ushered in new local discourses about political rights, religion, and even law, but it exercised comparatively minimal coercive authority over most local interest groups, such as lineages, guilds, and religious groups. In other words, while post-1929 local officials and judges were arguably more eager to engage local communities than passive Qing magistrates, who were primarily interested in maintaining stability, such engagement required, as it did during the Qing, the consent and cooperation of local society. It could not simply be forced on it.

---

[112] *E.g.*, KENNETH POMERANZ, THE MAKING OF A HINTERLAND: STATE, SOCIETY, AND ECONOMY IN INLAND NORTH CHINA, 1853–1937 (1993); PRASENJIT DUARA, CULTURE, POWER AND THE STATE: RURAL NORTH CHINA, 1900–1942, at 169–73 (1988); HUANG (1985).

More plausibly, the well-documented legal "modernization" efforts of the late Qing and early Republican eras may indeed have had some effect on judicial behavior, although it is near-impossible to measure how much. Judges were encouraged, both by their peers in their profession and by higher-level government authorities, to actively enforce "rational" laws and policies against "backwards" local customs and to follow the standards of professionalism that "civilized" nations – Western countries, in other words – expected of their judges.[113] The somewhat lower mediation rate in Longquan *dian* redemption cases may suggest that some judges were tentatively embracing this new professional identity.

It seems unlikely, however, that this made much difference in the larger scheme of things. The fact remains that the *dian* seller was barred from redeeming in only two of sixteen cases involving a thirty-year or older *dian* contract. The vast majority of *dian* sellers – including those who never brought a case to court – could apparently ignore the thirty-year legal deadline with no consequence. After all, even if Republican judges adopted a somewhat more active adjudicatory mentality than their Qing predecessors, their coercive authority was just as limited, if not more so. Ultimately, my evidence suggests that from the eighteenth century to the 1940s, customary law was the predominant authority governing *dian* redemption. Consequently, *dian* contracts generally operated under the normative presumption that sellers could enjoy an unlimited right to redeem.

---

[113] Xu Xiaoqun, Trial of Modernity: Judicial Reform in Early Twentieth-Century China, 1901–1937 (2008).

2

Mortgages in Early Modern England

At the start of the seventeenth century, England, despite the leading role it would later play in global trade and commerce, was home to a commercializing but largely agrarian economy not unlike the late Imperial Chinese economy. Foreign trade had yet to emerge as a major economic force, industrialization was yet a century away, and some 80 percent of the workforce was agricultural. Crucially, however, the English agrarian economy was in the midst of a fundamental structural change from household-level production by small tenants and yeoman to concentrated, "capitalist" farms run by large landowners or tenants. While later stages of this transition relied heavily on en masse expulsion of tenants and enclosure of estates by large landlords, through the sixteenth and early seventeenth centuries, the major driving force was the commercial transaction of land or tenancy rights from smallholders to larger farms. To facilitate such transactions, active land markets emerged throughout rural and urban England involving unprecedentedly large shares of the English population. Unlike eighteenth- and nineteenth-century land markets, which were largely the domain of the very wealthy, small tenants and yeomen were highly active in these earlier markets, although usually in the less fortunate position of conveyor.

Similar to their Chinese counterparts, early modern English smallholders were usually reluctant to sell or collateralize land. They lived, after all, in a predominantly agrarian society that offered limited off-farm employment opportunities, where land was not merely a guarantee of livelihood but also the most important indicator of social status. Nonetheless, when small-sum loans and pawning were insufficient to meet pressing financial

Portions of this chapter were previously published in Taisu Zhang, *Property Rights in Land, Agricultural Capitalism, and the Relative Decline of Pre-Industrial China*, 13 SAN DIEGO INT. L.J. 129 (2011).

needs, tapping into one's landed wealth was generally the only way out. But how did they do this, and how did their options compare with those that were available in pre-industrial China?

The two primary options, in both England and China, were to sell land outright or to use it as collateral. Echoing Chapter 1, this chapter searches for the functional English equivalent to the *dian* sale: did English real property norms allow landholders to exchange their land for most of its full value while retaining rights of redemption – in other words, to collateralize it? For how long were those redemption rights valid? Did English laws or customs impose mandatory deadlines?

The short answers are, in sequence, "Of course," "Not for long," and "Usually yes." English law and custom did recognize a right of redemption for certain transactions, but such rights were, in general, only secure for short periods of time. No English law or custom ever *guaranteed* an indefinitely viable right of redemption for any kind of transaction or even acknowledged the possibility of creating one. Quite the contrary, many local customs mandated a *one-year* redemption period for mortgages. Thus redemption windows were generally quite limited and, moreover, were enforced with extraordinary rigor until the late seventeenth century. This created a transaction system that was perhaps cleaner and less dispute prone than Qing conditional sales but also much harsher on the conveyor. All in all, landholders who wished to collateralize their property enjoyed an overwhelmingly stronger right of redemption in Qing and Republican China than in early modern England.

One preliminary issue that haunts any study of English property rights is the status of copyhold land – that is, land technically owned by the lord of the manor but then rented out to tenants. More precisely, were the rules for copyhold transactions substantively different from those governing the transactions of freehold land? By at least the fourteenth century, copyholders were transacting and conveying their land in roughly the same ways as a freehold tenant, and by the later sixteenth century, any major normative difference on this issue had effectively vanished.[1] The main differences were that copyholds could only change hands through a "surrender and

---

[1] *See generally*, ERIC KERRIDGE, AGRARIAN PROBLEMS IN THE SIXTEENTH CENTURY AND AFTER 32–93 (1969) (arguing that by the sixteenth century, copyhold and freehold were effectively equivalent for most legal questions); J.H. BAKER, AN INTRODUCTION TO ENGLISH LEGAL HISTORY 348–50 (3d ed. 1990); S.F.C. MILSOM, HISTORICAL FOUNDATIONS OF THE COMMON LAW 165 (2d ed., 1981) ("Although the copyhold [by the early seventeenth century] had equal protection, it retained its separate identity for three useless centuries).

admittance" in the lord's court, but this was more a formality than anything else.[2] Otherwise, copyhold conveyances employed conditions, limitations, remainders, trusts, and mortgages just like freeholds.[3] These were governed mainly by local customs, but the substantive distinction between custom and law on these issues had begun to blur by as early as the fourteenth century, when royal courts began to enforce "reasonable" customs,[4] and had certainly become rather insignificant in our era of interest (*ca.* 1500–1700). Courts of equity had recognized copyhold claims well before the reign of Henry VIII, and by at least the sixteenth century, even the sluggish common-law courts had caught up, applying common-law rules to copyholds via writs of trespass.[5]

More importantly, common-law rules on real property had possessed deep customary roots ever since their creation in the twelfth century. Instead of imposing some abstract or foreign system, they generally attempted to reinforce manorial custom, which was actually quite uniform across different geographic regions.[6] The normative difference between common law and custom, at least with regard to land, was simply not that large to begin with. While custom frequently differed from the common law in issues such as fines and services to the lord, it seemed to recognize the same modes of transaction and, moreover, applied largely similar rules to them. As Alan Harding has observed, manor courts "often imitated . . . the legal processes which protected the freeman at Common Law."[7]

[2] *See, e.g.*, BLACKSTONE 2 (1979), at 371 ("And, as in admittances upon surrenders, so in admittances upon descents . . . the lord is used as a mere instrument"); SIMPSON (1986), at 170 ("The practice of actually holding courts [for surrender and admittance] passed out of use in many manors").

[3] *See, e.g.*, BAKER (1990), at 350 (discussing conditional and limited remainders in copyhold); SIMPSON (1986) at 243 ("[Mortgages by demise] could be used for both freehold and leasehold property"); University of Nottingham, Copyhold Land, www .nottingham.ac.uk/mss/learning/skills/deeds-depth/copyhold.phtml (last visited May 6, 2009) (noting that copyholds could be "bought and sold, inherited by descendents, left in a will, mortgaged, and settled, just like freehold estates").

[4] Albert Kiralfy, *Custom in Mediaeval English Law*, 9 J. LEGAL HIST. 26, 28–30, 32–33 (1988).

[5] WILLIAM HOLDSWORTH, 7 A HISTORY OF ENGLISH LAW 306 (2d ed., 1937) ("[T]he grants made by the copyholder were subject to the ordinary rules of law"); CHARLES MONTGOMERY GRAY, COPYHOLD, EQUITY, AND THE COMMON LAW 23–34, 54–66 (1963).

[6] This is the thesis of S.F.C. MILSOM, THE LEGAL FRAMEWORK OF ENGLISH FEUDALISM (1976); Kiralfy (1998), at 28–29 ("In principle the custom of each manor was separate, but obviously the basic principles would be similar though adapted to local geography and conditions").

[7] ALAN HARDING, A SOCIAL HISTORY OF ENGLISH LAW 95 (1966).

Indeed, when legal treatises, including Bracton and Blackstone, attempted to analyze the rules of land conveyance, they sometimes drew as much from customary sources as they did from legal cases.[8] All in all, although the distinction between copyhold and freehold was undoubtedly important in many circumstances – most obviously in security of tenure but also when the copyholder wished to sue his lord[9] or when the Statute of Uses was concerned – it did not seem to substantively affect the basic rules and categories of conveyance by the sixteenth century. Because this chapter examines both legal and customary norms, it does not need to maintain a rigid separation of copyhold and freehold throughout.

Section A surveys the main categories of revertible land transactions – fees "upon condition" and "upon limitation" – and considers their comparability with Chinese conditional sales. Following this discussion, Section B hones in on the most comparable subcategory, mortgages, and carefully examines the legal and customary regimes that regulated mortgage redemption. It argues that English mortgagors could only retain an unchallengeable right of redemption for very short periods, at least when compared with Qing practices. Section C then examines a few other transactional instruments that bear some resemblance to conditional sales. While theoretically intriguing, none of these instruments were accessible enough to the common landholder to possess much economic significance. Section D looks back at the evolution of mortgages up to the seventeenth century and identifies similar trends in other aspects of English property law.

A Narrowing the Range of Inquiry

To most students of modern Anglo-American law, the default example of real property transactions that allowed eventual redemption is, of course, the mortgage. In the "classic" English mortgage, which was predominant from the fifteenth century to the early twentieth century,[10] the mortgagor conveyed ownership rights to the mortgagee but retained rights of

---

[8] *See, e.g.,* BLACKSTONE (1979), at 156 note q; HENRY DE BRACTON, 2 DE LEGIBUS ET CONSUETUDINIBUS ANGLIAE 69 (Samuel E. Thorne trans., 1970), *available at* Bracton Online, http://hlsl5.law.harvard.edu/bracton/ (discussing the law of lay assizes).

[9] The difference really was more procedural than substantive: *see* KERRIDGE (1969).

[10] As discussed below, the "classic" mortgage was quite prevalent by at least Littleton's time; *see* THOMAS DE LITTLETON, LITTLETON'S TENURES IN ENGLISH § 332 (Eugene Wambaugh ed., 1903). It remained largely predominant until the Law of Property Act of 1925, 15 & 16 GEORGE V. c.20.

redemption until a fixed date. Other forms of "mortgages" or "gages" had been in use since Anglo-Saxon times but followed the same general principles. Much of the following discussion will therefore focus on comparing English mortgages with Chinese conditional sales.

Before we plunge in, however, we must also consider whether to focus *exclusively* on mortgages. In English legal history, the idea that a real property conveyance could "revert" back to the conveyor was certainly *not* exclusive to mortgages. There are, of course, revertible terms-of-years and life-estates, where reversion would automatically occur on termination of either a fixed period of years or the receiver's life, but these are hardly comparable with Chinese conditional sales. More relevantly, there are also cases where the reversion could *cut short* what otherwise would be a more extended estate. As early as Bracton's time, a conveyance could be either "conditional" or "unconditional." In the former, the conveyor would have a reversion if some specified event – generally if the receiver failed to have heirs of his body – occurred.[11] By Blackstone's time, jurists had broken down such transactions into further subcategories: they could either be "upon condition" or "upon limitation."[12] Thus, when Blackstone speaks of a "conditional deed" or conveyance, he only refers to the former subcategory, instead of Bracton's broader concept. Simply put, a conditional conveyance gives the conveyor an *option* of retrieving the property, whereas a limitation simply returns ownership without any action on his behalf. We should note here that this book employs Blackstone's terminology, not Bracton's.

The "classic" English mortgage outlined earlier was, as post-Blackstone jurists were fond of pointing out, "subject to a condition": the mortgagor could choose to terminate the mortgagee's ownership on timely payment of all debt and interest.[13] The condition for reversion here was, of course, timely repayment, but a somewhat trickier question is whether *all* conditional conveyances that could return ownership on repayment – in other words, allowed *redemption* – were necessarily mortgages. If not, then we need to identify these nonmortgage conditions and survey the relevant normative apparatus. The same considerations also apply to limitations: if mortgages did not fall within the limitations category, then we must conduct a separate search for conditional sale-equivalents among conveyances "upon limitation." Ultimately, is it worthwhile to search extensively

---

[11] Bracton (1970), at 71–83.   [12] Blackstone (1979), at 154–55.
[13] Frederick Pollock & Frederic William Maitland, 2 The History of English Law before the Time of Edward I 123 (1968); Holdsworth (1937), at 375.

for nonmortgage transaction instruments that allowed redemption? A deeper look into the medieval roots of mortgages and conditional transactions suggests that the answer is "No."

Although mortgages might appear to be a subset of conveyances subject to condition by Blackstone's time, in earlier centuries they were very much unrelated. In Bracton's time, for example, "conditional" grants of real property usually referred to a very specific kind of transaction: the conveyor would convey land to "R and the heirs of his body" or perhaps to "H and W and to the heirs of H begotten on W."[14] Whereas such language would seem to create an entail, that is, "to R and then *only to* the heirs of his body," legal convention in the mid-thirteenth century interpreted it as "to R if he has heirs of his body" or "to H and W if they have children."[15] Thus, once R had a heir, he would immediately obtain full ownership over the transacted land and would be free to alienate it in whatever way he chose. By the time of the statute *De Donis Conditionalibus*, issued in 1285,[16] this was apparently the most prominent kind of conditional conveyance. As legal historians are well aware, the statute altered the formal legal interpretation of these contractual forms and created what later would be known as the "entail,"[17] but the point here is that the early origins of conditional conveyances had nothing to do with *powers of redemption*. There were, of course, other forms of conditional conveyance even in Bracton's time. The conveyor might demand that the land not be alienated to men of religion, that he should have preemption rights should alienation occur, or even that the land not be alienated at all.[18] Should these conditions fail, the conveyor would have a power of reversion. A central theme in all these conditional conveyances, including the classic "heirs of his body" format, was, however, that they limited the *grantee's* behavior but did not give the *conveyor* any way to actively initiate a reversion. That is, whether the reversion would occur depended on the grantee's actions, and not the conveyor's. Indeed, when Bracton discusses various kinds of conditions, he notes that there are three kinds: those that depend "on the donee," those that depend on some third party, and those that are "fortuitous."[19] Conditions that depend on the conveyor

---

[14] POLLOCK & MAITLAND (1968), at 18; MILSOM (1976), at 173–75.

[15] BRACTON (1970), at 81–82, 267–68.

[16] 13 EDWARD I., STATUTE OF WESTMINISTER II c.1 (1285).

[17] POLLOCK & MAITLAND (1968), at 19.

[18] GLOUCESTER CATHEDRAL, 1 HISTORIA ET CARTULARIUM: MONASTERII SANCTI PETRI GLOUCESTRIAE 179, 181, 188, 194, 222, 302, 337 (William Henry Hart ed., 1863).

[19] BRACTON (1970), at 71–72.

are noticeably missing. This seemed to be generally true of all recorded conditional conveyances until mortgages began adopting a "conditional conveyance" format in the fifteenth century.

In their earliest form, mortgages were not conditional conveyances at all. The term "conveyance" implies that some transfer of formal title, whether in fee simple, for a term of years, or for life, has occurred, but in Glanvill's time (*ca.* 1180), no such transfer accompanied the establishment of a "gage" – broadly defined as a landed security for debt.[20] Instead, the "gagor" simply put the "gagee" in possession of the transacted land, but without giving him any formal right to the land.[21] Glanvill separated gages into "living gages" (*vivum vadium*) and "dead gages" (*mortuum vadium*). In the former, the transacted land's annual yield counted toward the gagor's debt as long as the gagee was in possession, whereas in the latter, it did not.[22] The latter, which is the namesake of modern mortgages, also triggered the issue of usury: depending on one's viewpoint, the annual yield could count as a form of interest.[23] This was sinful but legal,[24] and most creditors apparently had few qualms about it, as evidenced by their gradual abandonment of living gages in favor of mortgages over the following two centuries.[25]

Mortgages could be either "for a term" or "without a term." In the former case, the mortgagor had a fixed term for repayment but would be obliged to formally transfer ownership rights to the mortgagee on default.[26] When, however, it was "without a term," then the mortgagee could bring a motion in court at any time to compel repayment within some "reasonable" period, after which he could "do what he pleases with the gaged thing."[27]

The problem with these antique gages is, naturally, the gagee's lack of either legal or customary title. Judges in both royal and local courts found it difficult to determine what, exactly, the gagee was entitled to.[28] Theoretically speaking, he had no legal claim to the gaged land and was only

---

[20] Ranulf de Glanvill, Tractatus de Legibus et Consuetudinibus Regni Angliae x. 6–12 (G.D.G. Hall ed., 1965).

[21] *Id.* at x. 8.

[22] *Id.* These concepts apparently had Roman roots. *See* H.W. Chaplin, *The Story of Mortgage Law*, 4 Harv. L. Rev. 1, 5–8 (1890).

[23] Pollock & Maitland (1968), at 119.

[24] *Id.* For a fuller discussion of usury, *see* James M. Ackerman, *Interest Rates and the Law: A History of Usury*, Ariz. St. L.J. 61 1981.

[25] Littleton no longer mentions the "living gage" – for him a "dead gage" is simply one that is not paid to date. Littleton (1903). *See also,* Baker (1990), at 353.

[26] Glanvill (1965), at x. 8.   [27] Pollock & Maitland (1968), at 120.   [28] *Id.* at 121.

entitled to recover his debt.[29] In practice, however, the judges were often unable to compel monetary repayment and thus could *only* offer relief through compelling formal and permanent conveyance.[30] How they justified such conveyance remains somewhat ambiguous, but later jurists correctly point out that they must have attempted to invent some kind of new and imaginary estate category to accommodate gages[31] – perhaps an "estate of gage" that would stand beside "estate of years," "estate in fee simple," and so on. In effect, such a construction would not be so different from the "lien theory" mortgages that predominate in many modern American states and, by virtue of the Law of Property Act of 1925, in England and Wales as well.[32]

By the later thirteenth century, a legally "cleaner" kind of mortgage had become predominant: the mortgagor would convey land to the mortgagee for a fixed term of years, at the end of which he could either redeem or convey full ownership.[33] The main difference between this form and the fifteenth-century "classic" mortgage was that it guaranteed the mortgagee a fixed-term ownership regardless of redemption: the mortgagor could not compel reversion during the fixed term, even if he paid off all his debt. Despite its relative inflexibility, this format at least saved jurists the trouble of creating a new legal estate fitting more or less reasonably into the traditional term-of-years category.

Not until the fifteenth century did the "classic" mortgage finally replace these archaic forms. Because mortgages and conditional conveyances had been quite unrelated until this point, their legal merger required alterations on both sides. Mortgages were now conveyances of either full ownership or a very long term-of-years – generally over 100 years[34] – and could be redeemed at any time prior to the deadline, which, as discussed below, was usually six months to a year after the initial transaction. If a long term-of-years was used, the right of redemption did not terminate on the end of the term-of-years but on default of the contractual debt, which, of course, was not nearly as distant into the future. On default, either the full ownership would become absolutely free from future reversion or the long

---

[29] GLANVILL (1965), at x. 11.   [30] POLLOCK & MAITLAND (1968), at 121.

[31] *Id.* (noting that there was an "attempt to treat the rights of the gagee in the land as rights of a peculiar character").

[32] Law of Property Act of 1925, 15 & 16 GEORGE V. c.20.

[33] POLLOCK & MAITLAND (1968), at 122; Chaplin (1890), at 8.

[34] *E.g.*, Bamfield v. Bamford (1675), 73 PUBLICATIONS OF THE SELDEN SOCIETY 183. *See also*, BLACKSTONE (1979), at 157–58; SIMPSON (1986), at 242–43.

term-of-years would "swell" into full ownership.[35] In addition, the legal concept of conditional conveyance evolved to accommodate a new kind of condition: that reversion would become possible on repayment of debt or, in other words, redemption. As noted earlier, this condition was qualitatively different from traditional conditions – be it "failing to have heirs of one's body" or "attempting certain kinds of alienation" – in that it allowed the *conveyor* to initiate reversion. By Blackstone's time, jurists had firmly embedded such conditions within the legal framework of conditional conveyances, placing them alongside these more traditional conditions.[36] We must remember, however, that the emergence of active redemption as a recognized legal condition directly reflected the need to formalize mortgages. It would be odd, therefore, if we could find a redeemable conditional conveyance that was somehow *not* a mortgage.

The definition of "mortgage" after the fifteenth century further confirms this impression. According to case decisions, statutory language, and legal treatises, a "mortgage," whether at law or at custom, was simply "any arrangement whereby a loan was secured by a conveyance of real property."[37] Because *any* redeemable conveyance of land was, theoretically, a secured debt – and vice versa – the concept of "mortgage" was most probably broad enough to incorporate all conveyances that involved active redemption. The diverse legal forms that a mortgage could assume only emphasized the broad scope of its basic concept. A mortgage might well be a conditional conveyance or a rigid term-of-years (which was still in use, albeit very rarely, in the sixteenth century), but it did not necessarily attach itself to any particular form of legal estate. Instead, it embodied a fundamental "intent" – to secure debt through conveyance of land – that could take any one of several legal shapes.[38] Indeed, we find this broad definition of "mortgage" in legal authorities from the fifteenth century onward, and it remained predominant until at least the late nineteenth century, even though mortgages had been firmly and almost exclusively bound to conditional conveyances for centuries by then. Finally, a basic survey of the main legal sources for the sixteenth and seventeenth centuries, including the *English Law Reports* and the *Publications of the Selden Society*, does not

---

[35] The possibility of such "swelling" made some jurists very uncomfortable. *See* the discussion at LITTLETON (1903), at §§ 216–18.

[36] BLACKSTONE (1979), at 155.

[37] BAKER (1990), at 353. For similar statements from earlier jurists, *see* Seton v. Slade (1802), 7 Ves. 265, 32 Eng. R.; Mortgagees Legal Cost Act, 58 & 59 Victoria c.25 (1895); and W.F. BEDDOES, A CONCISE TREATISE OF THE LAW OF MORTGAGE 2–5 (2d ed., 1908).

[38] SIMPSON (1986), at 242.

reveal any case or custom where a redeemable conditional conveyance of land was classified as anything *but* a "gage" or mortgage.[39]

The same can be said about conveyances "subject to limitation," which were known as "determinable fees" when the conveyance was of fee simple.[40] Because, however, such conveyances never formally overlapped with mortgages, the relevant legal history is considerably simpler than that of conditional conveyances. As noted earlier, the main difference between these conveyances and conditional conveyances was that they would automatically revert as soon as the condition occurred, without any action by the conveyor, whereas conditional conveyances gave the conveyor a *power* of reversion. Bracton, however, does not seem to draw any such distinction,[41] suggesting that its emergence was a somewhat later development. Indeed, the first mention of determinable fees in the law reports was apparently in a 1467 statement by Judge Choke:

As if I give lands to a man to have to him and his heirs in fee *so long as* John A'Down has issue of his body, in that case the feofee will hold of his Lord etc.; yet if John A'Down dies without heir of his body, etc., in that case I may well enter, etc. But not by escheat, etc., but because the feoffment is determined.[42]

In this early case, the determinable fee in question clearly shared much in common with the early conditional conveyances that we discussed earlier. In both cases, the condition was that the receiver must have heirs of his body. The primary indication that this was a determinable fee – and not a conditional one – was the phrase "so long as," which was interpreted as providing for immediate reversion on the condition's occurrence.[43] The determinable fee that made ownership contingent on possessing heirs of one's body seemed to be fairly prevalent in the fifteenth century. It is also the subject of an in-court debate between Judges Vavasour and Townshend, with the former arguing that all determinable fees were void under the statute *Quia Emptores* – issued in 1290 to ban subinfeudation[44] – whereas

---

[39] *E.g.*, Manning v. Burgess (1663), 1 Ch. Cas. 29; Roscarrick v. Barton (1672), 1 Ch. Cas. 216; Bamfield v. Bamford (1675), 73 PUBLICATIONS OF THE SELDEN SOCIETY 183. The customs are mainly found in 18 PUBLICATIONS OF THE SELDEN SOCIETY (1904) and 21 PUBLICATIONS OF THE SELDEN SOCIETY (1906).

[40] For a discussion of limitations in general, *see* BLACKSTONE (1979), at 154. For a discussion of determinable fees, *see* Richard R.B. Powell, *Determinable Fees*, 23 COLUM. L. REV. 207 (1923).

[41] BRACTON (1970), at 69 (speaking of "limitations" and "conditions" as if they were the same).

[42] Statement of Choke, J. (1466), YEAR BOOK 7 Edward IV 12a, pl. 2.

[43] BLACKSTONE (1979), at 155.   [44] 18 Edward I 1 (1290).

the latter considered them valid.[45] Regardless of Vavasour's position, determinable fees clearly did exist throughout the early modern era and, as modern legal historians have argued in some detail, probably were legally valid.

By the sixteenth century, court decisions began to discuss additional kinds of limitations. Some, such as the various conditional conveyances discussed earlier, prohibited alienation,[46] whereas others stipulated that the receiver would have ownership so long as a certain tree within the estate or a local church should stand.[47] In later times, limitations might also limit how the receiver could use the conveyed land. For example, he could only use the land to benefit a certain charity school. As with traditional conditional conveyances, all these limitations depended either on the receiver's conduct or on some outside force that neither receiver nor conveyor could directly control. Prior to *Collier v. Walters* in 1873,[48] I have been unable to find a single instance where a determinable fee might revert on an action by the *conveyor*. These limitations were, as noted earlier, fundamentally different from the act of redeeming, which could only be initiated by the conveyor.

Collier v. Walters offers, in fact, the best proof that early modern limitations did not incorporate the possibility of redemption. In that case, Judge Jessel examined a determinable fee that very much resembled a mortgage: reversion would occur on repayment of debt. After searching through an "enormous" number of cases, Jessel determined that "there is not any authority to be found" for any such limitation and promptly ruled it void.[49] Of course, the very existence of this case indicates that such conveyances did occasionally emerge in practice, but Jessel's frustration suggests that this was rare. In any case, the main comparison I attempt to draw in this study is a legal one, between Chinese and English land transaction *norms*. Thus the fact that English norms, apparently both legal and customary, did not recognize a redeemable determinable fee means that conveyances subject to limitation were not very comparable with Chinese conditional sales. All in all, the various developments and legal authorities examined earlier strongly suggest that mortgages were the *only*

---

[45] Statements of Vavasour J. & Townshend J. (1497), YEAR BOOK 13 Henry VII (Easter Term) fol. 24.

[46] Christopher Corbet's Case (1579), 2 ANDERSON 134, 1 Co. REP. *83b.

[47] Statement of Counsel (1535), YEAR BOOK 27 Henry VIII. 29 pl. 20; Stamp v. Clinton (1615), 6 Co. REP. Pt. XI *46b, 1 ROLL 95, 101; Walsingham's Case (1573), 2 PLOWDEN 547, 75 ENGLISH REP. 805.

[48] Collier v. Walters (1873), LAW REPORTS 17 Equity 252.   [49] *Id.* at 261.

recognized instruments of transaction in common law, equity, or custom that contained a right of *redemption*.

B Mortgages

The central issue, therefore, is whether English mortgages and Chinese conditional sales were different enough to have affected the extent of managerial farming. As should be apparent by now, the two had much in common: they both involved the conveyance of land in exchange for a lump sum, and both imbue the conveyor with certain rights of redemption. Of course, these are what make the two instruments comparable in the first place. Moving on to the details, however, we begin to find more differences than similarities, although of varying importance.

One possible difference lies in the amount of money that such transactions involved. *Dian* sales usually commanded about 70 to 80 percent of the land's full market value, but we do not seem to have much pricing information on English mortgages. As discussed below, sixteenth- and seventeenth-century mortgagors frequently complained to courts of equity that they were in danger of losing their land for insufficient value, suggesting that most mortgages secured somewhat less than 100 percent of the land's full value. This, however, is as far as legal sources will take us. However, even if there was a price discrepancy between conditional sales and English mortgages, it probably had few economic consequences. Neither country seemed to possess laws or customs that dictated pricing behavior, so any discrepancy in transactional value was the result of private negotiation rather than *institutional* or *normative* determination. Therefore, if we wish to study how land transaction norms affected – rather than merely reflected – economic growth or agricultural development, then negotiated price discrepancies do not seem meaningful.

Those familiar with modern mortgages will probably notice rather obvious differences in the distribution of possession rights. In modern English and American mortgages, the mortgagee generally does not possess the transacted land until default,[50] whereas Chinese conditional sales

---

[50] Lien theory mortgages, established in England by the Law of Property Act of 1925, 15 & 16 GEORGE V. c.20, do not give the mortgagee a right of immediate possession because he or she has no title to the land until foreclosure. Under "title theory" mortgages, still in use in about ten states, the mortgagee does have, as he would under the classical English mortgage, a right of possession, but this is almost never exercised. This is something that American law students learn before taking the bar, but for a quick summary, *see* SCHMUDDE (2004), at 7.

allowed the buyer to maintain possession until redemption. This distinction, if true, would be economically significant. A conditional sales buyer who exercised his right of possession would, until redemption or conversion into an irrevocable sale, have little incentive to either improve the land or use it as a source of long-term capital. A mortgagor who retained possession, however, could more or less control his own destiny and would therefore have greater incentive to keep the land in good condition.

Unfortunately, this institutional difference is much more pronounced in modern times than it was in the sixteenth and seventeenth centuries. As mentioned earlier, the basic theory of English mortgages underwent significant revisions in the Law of Property Act of 1925. This law attempted to fit all English mortgages into a uniform "lien theory," which gave the mortgagee only a power of foreclosure on default and therefore did not entitle him to preforeclosure possession.[51] In contrast, the classic English mortgage discussed earlier conveyed ownership rights to the mortgagee, whether for a long term-of-years or for full ownership, and, at least in theory, allowed the mortgagee to take immediate possession unless the contract expressly covenanted otherwise.[52] Mortgagees would often decline possession in actual practice,[53] but at least the normative possibility was no different from Chinese conditional sales. It makes somewhat more sense to draw a distinction in the late seventeenth century, when courts began to actively discourage preforeclosure mortgagee possession. They did this by holding the mortgagee to a higher standard of maintenance and management: "calling the mortgagee very strictly to account, not only for all rents and profits actually received, but for all rents and profits which *ought with due diligence* to have been received."[54] It does seem possible to draw an institutional distinction between active discouragement of mortgagee possession and the relative neutrality of Chinese conditional sales, but this would be a rather mild difference whose actual effect is difficult to measure. Mortgagee possession remained somewhat common even in Blackstone's time and, as far as we can tell, may not have declined very much since the mid-seventeenth century.[55] In any case, a late-seventeenth-century institutional divergence cannot really explain why English peasants created

---

[51] SCHMUDDE (2004). [52] BLACKSTONE (1979), at 158–59. [53] *Id.* at 159.

[54] Backs v. Gayer (1684), 1 VERN 258; Blacklock v. Barnes (1725), SEL. CASES OF THE KING 53. See also, R.W. Turner, *The English Mortgage of Land as a Security*, 20 VA. L. REV. 729, 730 (1934).

[55] Blackstone seems to be fairly familiar with contemporary instances of mortgagee possession. BLACKSTONE (1979), at 158–59. However, since at least the early seventeenth century, courts of equity had declared that the mortgagor was the true owner of the land and, barring

more managerial farms than their Chinese counterparts – this agricultural divergence probably started much earlier.

In the end, the primary institutional difference between Chinese conditional sales and English mortgages lies in the regulation of redemption deadlines and default. Whereas conditional sales customs, as emphasized earlier, usually *guaranteed* the seller an indefinitely viable right of redemption, the notions of limited redeemability and default had been central to English mortgages since at least Bracton's time. The Bractonian "gage for years" was, as the term implies, only redeemable for a fixed term-of-years – if the mortgagor redeemed, then the mortgaged land would revert at the end of that term. By the time Littleton wrote his treatise on tenures, he described mortgages as a conveyance "upon such condition, that if the [mortgagor] pay to the [mortgagee] *at a certain day* [for example], 40 *l.* of money, that then the [mortgagor] may reenter."[56] This basic format remained virtually unchanged for at least three centuries. Thus Blackstone could claim that a mortgage is where "a man borrows of another a specific sum (*e.g.* 200 *l.*) and grants him an estate in fee, on condition that if [he] shall repay the mortgagee the said sum of 200 *l.* on *a certain day mentioned in the deed*, that then the mortgagor may [reclaim the land]."[57] Indeed, of the various mortgage forms discussed earlier, the only two that appeared to have no fixed deadline for redemption were the "living gage" and the "mortgage without a term," both of which were extremely archaic forms that only Glanville mentions. The latter could, in fact, be harsher to the mortgagor than the mortgages "with a term" because it entitled the mortgagee to seek court-directed foreclosure *at any time.* The court may well give the mortgagor a short window of redemption, but this was discretionary and uncertain. However, "living gages" did not necessarily involve redemption at all: the mortgagee might simply take possession of the land and enjoy its profits until they offset the loan. Unless the mortgagor attempted to redeem at some point, this could take as long as necessary but still had to end at some point. In any case, use of living gages died out before the fifteenth century.

We can assume, then, that early modern English mortgages generally – perhaps universally – carried deadlines for redemption. Theoretically speaking, there was no law that prevented a mortgage contract from stating that "this deed shall be forever redeemable," but no normative authority

---

unusual circumstances, should not lose possession before default. Emmanuel College, Cambridge v. Evans (1625), 1 CHANCERY REPORTS 10; BAKER (1990), at 355–56.

[56] LITTLETON (1903).   [57] BLACKSTONE (1979), at 158.

ever acknowledges this possibility. More likely than not, they would have found it inconceivable. But what about contracts that, whether purposely or not, failed to state an express deadline? It is hard to imagine that they simply created Glanvillian mortgages that were "without a term." By the nineteenth century, courts would regularly apply default redemption deadlines in such cases: any use of the term "as mortgagor" would automatically imply a half-year redemption period unless expressly made otherwise.[58] While the law books give little information on the precise origins of this rule,[59] we do know that sixteenth- and seventeenth-century mortgages generally gave one-year redemption periods, with few exceptions. Collections of mortgage contracts at, for example, the University of Nottingham demonstrate remarkable homogeneity in this regard.[60] It is unclear, however, if courts applied this one-year period by default in cases of contractual silence. As far as we know, the legal treatises and law reports of the time mention no such default rule for either common law or equity.

If, however, we backtrack a little to the fourteenth and fifteenth centuries and search the existing customs records, customs *mandating* one-year redemption periods begin to show up. For example, in the customs compilations of the Selden Society, many localities that have preserved their medieval mortgage customs report a mandatory one-year redemption period.[61] There is, in fact, good reason to suspect that such customs were quite prevalent in England throughout the late medieval and early modern periods. The striking uniformity of sixteenth- and seventeenth-century mortgage contracts in this regard strongly suggests the existence of some underlying normative force. It would otherwise be very difficult to understand why most contracts converged onto a one-year time frame, which, by this time, would be just as random as any other schedule. Since no such rule existed in either common law or equity, the most likely normative source clearly would be local custom. All in all, the existing evidence strongly suggests that one-year redemption periods had deep roots in

---

[58] Turner (1934), at 736. See also, BEDDOES (1908), at 1.

[59] Turner suggests that it may have originated in the later seventeenth or early eighteenth century but provides no concrete evidence. Turner (1934), at 731.

[60] University of Nottingham, Mortgage by Demise, www.nottingham.ac.uk/manuscriptsand specialcollections/researchguidance/deedsindepth/mortgaged/demise.aspx (last visited July 5, 2013) ("The date for repayment is usually given as one year from the date of the mortgage"); University of Nottingham, Mortgage by Conveyance, www.nottingham.ac.uk/ manuscriptsandspecialcollections/research guidance/deedsindepth/mortgaged/conveyance .aspx (last visited July 5, 2013) ("The date for repayment is usually given as one year from the date of the mortgage").

[61] See the customs at 18 PUBLICATIONS OF THE SELDEN SOCIETY 143, 145, 147, 193 (1904).

historical practice and that they were a common customary norm in the early modern period.

Redemption deadlines mean very little, of course, if courts of either law or custom refuse to enforce them, but lack of enforcement was almost certainly not an issue in pre-eighteenth-century England. Common-law courts, at least, were notoriously harsh in enforcing default provisions. As legal historians have been fond of pointing out since at least Blackstone's time, the date for repayment was strictly adhered to at common law.[62] Once the date had passed, if only for a day or two, the mortgagee would theoretically have an absolute right of exclusion against the mortgagor, even if the amount of the loan were *less* than the land's full market value.[63] The harshness of this rule is remarkable, especially in a comparative perspective. In the event of permanent alienation, Chinese conditional sales customs would compel the buyer to provide the seller with "additional payments" and thereby pay him the transacted property's full market value.

How frequently mortgagees actually used this rule is less clear. Many mortgagees were probably willing to grant repayment extensions, if for no other reason than to accumulate more interest.[64] However, given the high level of concern in later-seventeenth-century equity courts, we can safely assume that a substantial number of mortgagees *did* successfully exercise these exclusion rights. Because I focus here on *institutional* comparisons, I necessarily focus more on whether creditors *could* exercise these rights than on how many of them actually did. As far as the evidence can show, common-law courts were perfectly willing to enforce deadlines.

The only question is whether other legal or customary authorities would have applied softer rules. Between customary authorities and courts of equity, the two other major sources of property-related adjudication, the former had a far longer history of regulating mortgages, dating back to at least the twelfth century. Its rules were indeed softer than common-law norms, but not by much. In the medieval customs of one Lancashire borough, for example, default did not give the mortgagee an immediate right of possession, but rather a right of sale.[65] He must sell the land for its

---

[62] Wade's Case (1602), 5 Co. Rep. 114; BLACKSTONE (1979), at 158; BAKER (1990), at 355; Sugarman & Warrington (1996), at 113.

[63] BLACKSTONE (1979), at 158; BAKER (1990), at 355; Sugarman & Warrington (1996), at 113.

[64] For a survey of foreclosure and debt practices among high-income groups, *see* Christopher Clay, *Property Settlements, Financial Provision for the Family, and Sale of Land by the Greater Landowners, 1660–1790*, 21 J. BRIT. STUD. 18 (1981).

[65] 18 PUBLICATIONS OF THE SELDEN SOCIETY 143.

full value, take what is owed to him, and return the rest to the mortgagor. The rule did not, however, seem to prohibit the mortgagee himself from being the purchaser, so he could potentially pay the difference to the mortgagor and then assume full ownership. For our purposes, however, whether the mortgagee purchases the land is of little consequence. The central point is that default would lead swiftly to permanent alienation from the mortgagor, whether to the mortgagee or to some other buyer. If the default did not lead to an immediate transfer to the mortgagee – which would make it effectively a permanent sale – then at least it would irrevocably throw the land into the open market. In the larger scheme of things, this might actually have been more economically efficient.

The customs of Romney, in Kent, were somewhat more complicated.[66] The Selden Society records preserve two different sets of customs for this locality, one in the mid-fourteenth century and one in the late-fifteenth. Despite the shifting of mortgage forms between these two dates, mortgage redemption customs remained largely stable. Once default occurred, the mortgagee would come to the local court and demand repayment. The court would then publish this request for eight days and, should the mortgagor still fail to redeem, convey full ownership to the mortgagee. If, however, the full value of the land exceeded the mortgagor's debt, the mortgagee would have to pay the difference. No public sale was necessary.

All other mortgage redemption customs in the Selden Society records resemble one or both of the preceding. They generally guaranteed mortgagors the full value of their land while also providing for permanent alienation – if the mortgagee demanded immediate satisfaction – within a few weeks of default.[67] By any measure, these customs were much more accommodating to the mortgagor than the common-law rule, but nonetheless gave the redemption deadline significant normative weight. Because, as mentioned earlier, most customs also mandated "year-and-a-day" redemption periods, it was virtually impossible for English mortgages to mutate into the century-long affairs that Chinese *dian* sales frequently became, unless, for some reason, it made sense for the mortgagee.

Probably not until the later seventeenth century did any English court substantially interfere with contractual redemption deadlines. In 1654, the Court of Chancery decided *Duchess of Hamilton v. Countess of Dirlton* and,

---

[66] *Id.* at 144–46.

[67] Apart from the customs discussed earlier, see also 18 PUBLICATIONS OF THE SELDEN SOCIETY 143–44, 147, 192–93, 289. The longest extension is found on page 289, which gave roughly one month – between Michaelmas and All Saints Day.

for the first time, outlined "the equity of redemption."[68] By the mid-eighteenth century, there was a fixed format for this. As a matter of equity, default of payment gave the mortgagee not an absolute right of ownership but only a right to foreclosure. This meant an action of foreclosure in court, where the judge would discretionarily decide whether to compel immediate satisfaction or, if the mortgagor could show cause, to extend the redemption period for a "reasonable time."[69] In time, this came to mean six months but in some unusual cases could reach two years.[70] Once the extension expired, the mortgagor could then obtain a decree of absolute foreclosure, which generally severed any tie between the mortgagee and the transacted land. In extreme cases of injustice, the court might choose to reopen redemption even after many years or could perhaps compel a sale, but such cases were very rare.[71] Alternatively, the mortgagee could exercise a *power of sale* immediately after the first default but could not attempt to purchase the land himself.[72]

Despite the equity of redemption's eventual legal importance, it has little significance for our present inquiry. As noted earlier, English agriculture had become largely managerial as early as 1700, which meant that tenant-driven land accumulation took off during the sixteenth and seventeenth centuries. The equity of redemption, however, did not become firmly established until the eighteenth century[73] and therefore had very little impact on the process of accumulation. Although the *Duchess of Hamilton* decision appeared in 1654, the Chancery was of two minds for the rest of the seventeenth century, with Lord Nottingham in favor of equitable redemption and Lord North against. In, for example, the 1681 case of *Newcombe v. Bonham*, North refused to allow equitable redemption, reversing Nottingham's earlier decision and ordering immediate alienation.[74] Meanwhile, common-law courts adhered to their strict default rules until at least *Roscarrick v. Barton*, which was decided in 1672.[75] All in all, courts of equity played no significant role in regulating mortgage redemption until well after the takeoff of managerial farming. Within our period of interest,

---

[68] (1654), 1 Сн. Rep. 165.

[69] Sugarman & Warrington (1996), at 113; Sheldon Tefft, *The Myth of Strict Foreclosure*, 4 U. Сні. L. Rev. 575, 576–78 (1937).

[70] Tefft (1937). [71] *Id.* at 579–80.

[72] *Id.* at 580–81; Blackstone (1979), at 159 ("[T]he mortgagee may ... compel the sale of the estate, in order get the whole of his money immediately ...").

[73] *E.g.*, Burgess v. Wheate (1750), 1 Eden 177, 96 English Reports 67.

[74] Newcombe v. Bonham (1681), 1 Vern 7 (Ch.), 1 Vern 214, 1 Vern 232, 2 Vern 264.

[75] Roscarrick v. Barton (1672), 1 Сн. Cas. 216.

common-law and customary norms probably predominated and, as demonstrated earlier, usually provided for strictly enforced one-year redemption periods that were indeed drastically different from Chinese norms.

C Other Transactional Instruments

Apart from these more "organic" forms of land transaction, English law also recognized a number of statutory transaction forms. These generally did not stem from popular usage, but were instead created by royal decree to meet certain economic needs. Two of these forms, the "statute merchant" and the "statute staple,"[76] were somewhat similar to mortgages. "They are both," according to Blackstone, "securities for debts ... whereby the lands of the debtor are conveyed to the creditor, till out of the rents and profits of them his debt may be satisfied: and during such time ... he is tenant by statute merchant or statute staple."[77] These were, in essence, Glanvillian "living gages" preserved until the early modern period and, unlike mortgages, did not carry a fixed deadline for redemption. They were not, however, freely available for everyday use. Because they were created by statutory decree, one during Edward I's reign and the other during his grandson's,[78] the state maintained rather tight control over their procedural application. To create such a security, the transacting parties needed to appear before the mayor of an authorized "staple," of which there were only a handful in England, and register their agreement.[79] Moreover, prior to 1532, they were only available to registered traders.[80] Although Henry VIII loosened this particular restriction, the registration requirement remained untouched, effectively preventing most rural people from using these instruments.

Another theoretically possible transaction that bears some resemblance to Qing conditional sales would be a term-of-years conveyance that was then rented back to the conveyor.[81] For example, the conveyance would be for thirty years at perhaps £300, whereas the yearly rent paid by the

---

[76] Blackstone (1979), at 160. *See also,* A.W.B. Simpson, A History of the Common Law of Contract: The Rise of Assumpsit 87–88, 126–35 (1975). Also, in the statute of *elegit,* land could be held as security for debt under an action by a sheriff, but only after initial default. Blackstone (1979), at 160–61. Thus the land was not conveyed as part of the original credit transaction but instead as a postdefault *seizure.* This is not very comparable with either mortgages or conditional sales.

[77] Blackstone (1979), at 160.

[78] 13 Edward I. *De mercatoribus* (1285); 27 Edward III st. ii., c.9 (1353).

[79] Blackstone (1979), at 160.   [80] 23 Henry VIII 8 c.6 (Eng.) (1531).

[81] My thanks to Bruce Ackerman for pointing out this possibility.

conveyor would be £12. The term-of-years deed in this situation effectively constituted security for a £300 loan, repayable in thirty years with £60 of interest. However, unlike the fifteenth-century mortgage that employed a long (generally over 100 years) term-of-years as security, this kind of transaction would not expressly constitute a loan security because the contract would not mention any "debt" or formal obligation of repayment. The "rent" would be set through a separate deed of tenancy. Using such a legal fiction, the conveyor could theoretically avoid the generally short repayment time frames of mortgages while still "transacting" his land for an immediate lump sum. Although the potentially extended repayment schedule does indeed resemble Qing conditional sales, most other aspects of this transactional instrument are fundamentally different and, in general, far less advantageous to the conveyor. Most importantly, it would be an extremely inflexible way of securing a loan: without the purchaser's consent, the conveyor had no way of regaining ownership either sooner or later than the fixed term. In addition, the conveyor would also have a yearly repayment obligation, which could easily become a significant burden if some unforeseeable financial misfortune fell on him. The longer the term-of-years, the more likely this would be. These inflexibilities most probably made such transactions fairly unattractive to landholders. In any case, existing legal treatises and case archives contain very few, if any, instances of such transactions, and one may reasonably suspect that they had relatively little socioeconomic importance. When legal sources discuss terms-of-years as loan security, they generally refer to the long term-of-years format that fifteenth-century mortgages frequently employed. As noted earlier, these were considered a form of mortgage and were therefore subject to the relevant customs and laws.

Ultimately, English law and custom do not seem to recognize any mode of land transaction that was both redeemable for indefinite periods and easily available to the general population. Inaccessible statutory instruments aside, the mortgage was probably the only transaction mode that contained *any* right of redemption – but nonetheless of a fundamentally different quality than what we find in Chinese customs. The difference between an indefinitely viable right of redemption and a strictly enforced deadline, usually for a year, is simply enormous.

D Trends

One of the striking things about the brief history of English mortgages presented here is that English institutions of land collateralization became, over time, steadily less accommodating to the original landholder. During the twelfth and thirteenth centuries, it was still possible to establish "living gages" in which the debtor did not face any fixed deadline to redeem. By the fifteenth century, however, this comparatively debtor-friendly instrument had fallen into disuse, replaced almost completely by mortgages that required repayment within a fixed term and would strip away his right of redemption on default. On the bright side, many local customs still guaranteed the defaulting debtor a foreclosure sale, so he might at least recoup the full market value of the collateral. The deterioration of the debtor's institutional position accelerated, however, during the sixteenth and seventeenth centuries. An increasing number of local customs cut down on repayment windows to the point where mortgage contracts generally demanded redemption within a year of the original transaction. In addition, the foreclosure sale was gradually replaced, both normatively and in practice, by automatic full conveyance to the creditor on default, even if the initial mortgage sum fell far short of the land's full value. Clearly, borrowers faced harsher institutional conditions as England moved into its early modern era.

Many historians have portrayed the sixteenth to eighteenth centuries as an era in which the balance of sociopolitical power shifted dramatically in favor of larger, richer landowners at tremendous cost to small tenants and yeomen.[82] Traditionally, they have cited the weakening of tenant rights as a primary example. A large portion of English tenants during medieval times were copyholders who enjoyed fairly generous terms of tenancy. Pursuant to most manorial customs, most copyholds had no fixed term, paid only a nominal rent, could be inherited, sold, mortgaged, or subleased just as freehold land, and were not subject to direct evictions. Creation of copyholds, however, had slowed to a trickle during the fifteenth and sixteenth centuries and had largely vanished by the later seventeenth century. In fact, landlords encumbered by copyholds devoted tremendous effort toward rolling back the security of copyhold tenancies throughout the sixteenth and early seventeenth centuries, often by unilaterally raising inheritance and conveyance fees or by raising rents. Copyholders who converted their holdings into leasehold land under such pressure became tenants in the

---

[82] The Brenner Debate (1987); Kerridge (1969), at 36–37; Hoyle (1990), at 7–12, 17–18 (placing the start of conscious landlord encroachment at around 1550); R.W. Hoyle, *An Ancient and Laudable Custom: The Definition and Development of Tenant Right in North-Western England in the Sixteenth Century*, 116 Past & Present 24, 29–36 (1987).

modern sense: they held only for a fixed term of years and could not pass the tenancy to their heirs without the landlord's express approval.

Similar sociopolitical dynamics also seem to underlie the institutional trend toward harsher legal and customary treatment of mortgagors. Small-holders faced large cash shortages much more often than wealthier land-holders. Consequently, they had a significantly greater economic need to sell or mortgage land[83] and were damaged particularly severely by the increasing harshness of mortgage redemption rules. However, these rules were highly beneficial to mortgagees and potential land buyers and, as discussed in Chapter 3, were deeply involved in the emergence of large capitalist farms across England.

---

[83] ALLEN (1992); Leigh Shaw-Taylor, *The Rise of Agrarian Capitalism and the Decline of Family Farming in England*, 65 ECON. HIST. REV. 26 (2012).

3

Kinship, Social Hierarchy, and Institutional
Divergence (Theories)

The preceding chapters have laid out a rather stark institutional contrast between Qing and Republican land collateralization instruments and their early modern English counterparts. Whereas Qing and Republican *dian* sellers were customarily allowed to retain redemption rights indefinitely at no interest, early modern English mortgagors would generally lose their land if they did not redeem within one year. Because *dian* sales and mortgages served largely identical functions within their respective economies – both were, as discussed earlier, the primary instrument of land collateralization available to rural landholders – this institutional divergence meant that cash-needy Chinese landholders faced a profoundly different set of economic incentives and options than English landholders under similar circumstances. The same could be said, of course, for potential land buyers and lenders on the other end of the bargain. This immediately begs two questions: First, how did these differences emerge? Second, what were their consequences?

This chapter and the next two examine the socioeconomic rationales underlying the institutional divergence – the issue of consequences is then picked up in Chapter 6. In particular, they provide a detailed explanation for why the norm of infinite *dian* redeemability maintained such a strong grip over the Chinese rural land market throughout the nineteenth and early twentieth centuries. Adding to the intrigue is that the wealthiest segments of Chinese society were also those that were most vocally hostile to such norms, which were indeed, as argued in some detail below, probably detrimental to their general economic interests. One has to wonder why these economic elites tolerated – or, perhaps, were forced to tolerate – such an inconvenient institutional arrangement.

Because this is a study in comparative history, this book attempts to formulate an explanation that also addresses the Sino-English comparison, one that can help us understand why English property institutions moved in a different direction. It argues that the answer lies in the ways Chinese – and English – society allocated sociopolitical status and rank. Crudely summarized, Chinese social hierarchies were substantially gerontocratic, whereas English ones were wealth-based. The former produced a class of relatively impoverished but high-status seniors who were instrumental in promoting and, in the case of *dian* redemption norms, establishing poor-friendly property institutions. Early modern English society, in comparison, was dominated by larger, wealthier households that tended to pursue their own institutional interests, often at serious socioeconomic cost to smallholders.

This argument rests on three fundamental pillars. First, this book must demonstrate that social tension and bargaining over *dian* and mortgage redemption norms were, as alluded to in previous chapters, split largely across smallholder–large landowner – poor versus rich, in other words – lines. The crucial point is to provide evidence that smallholders did indeed prefer longer redemption deadlines, infinite if possible, whereas larger landowners preferred to shorten them. Additionally, there ideally should be at least a theoretically coherent account of *why* they had these preferences – and, if they did, why customs that favored one side's preferences over the other's nonetheless were generally obeyed by both. In other words, there should be a theoretical account of both preference formation *and* norm creation.

Second, this book must demonstrate that social status in pre-industrial rural China correlated more strongly with seniority than wealth – that, specifically, there existed a substantial class of high-status but relatively poor seniors – whereas wealth was the predominant status determinant in early modern England.

Third, the book must demonstrate that there is good reason to believe that these different patterns of status distribution can actually explain the institutional divergences outlined in Chapters 1 and 2. Is there, for example, any compelling evidence that low-income but high-status seniors effectively championed infinite *dian* redeemability in the Chinese countryside?

For the sake of structural clarity, this chapter provides a concentrated delineation of the basic theoretical model – if it can be called that – whereas Chapter 4 supplies empirical support, focusing on the three points outlined earlier. The presentation of the model will proceed as follows: Section A discusses preexisting theories on the origins of *dian* redemption norms. I argue that they rely on cultural assumptions that are both empirically unfounded and analytically unhelpful. Section B combines rational-choice economic analysis and narrowly defined elements of social culture to present a new model of how *dian* and mortgage institutions were created and sustained. The model does three basic things. First, it explains why smallholders in both societies probably would have preferred longer redemption windows and why larger households were likely opposed. Second, and perhaps most importantly, it explains how the predominance of different status hierarchies in rural China and England could have led to very different property institutions. Finally, it explains why larger Chinese landowners, having "lost" the negotiation over *dian* redemption norms, nonetheless would have obeyed them and, indeed, would have continued to lend money to smallholders through *dian* contracts. Section C briefly explores some of the broader theoretical ramifications of the model. Chapter 4 provides empirical support.

A Preexisting Theories

Among Chinese legal historians, the traditional explanation for the customary protection of *dian* and permanent tenancy rights has been an exceedingly straightforward, almost simplistic, one. They derived directly from a cultural dislike of permanent land alienation – a moral and ideological embrace of "permanence in landholding" in "precommercial" societies. Philip Huang, for example, believed that interminable redemption rights were a natural normative component of subsistence economies that lacked strong market integration: the prevalence of subsistence agriculture was mutually reinforcing with norms that shamed the loss of ancestral property and glorified the stable descent of land from generation to generation.[1] Similarly, Melissa Macauley and others have suggested that Chinese peasants generally possessed a strong sentimental attachment to land and, consequently, were highly loathe to lose it.[2] Such attachment was purportedly reflected in the terms often used to describe property rights: title ownership, for example, was "the bone of the land," whereas usage rights were the "skin."[3] These terms suggest, to some, that peasants considered land an intimate extension of their own bodies. Such psychological intimacy reflected once again the closer connection between peasant and land in subsistence agriculture. Less abstractly, it may simply have reflected the higher economic and social value of land in pre-industrial societies.

---

[1]   HUANG (2001), at 74.   [2]   MACAULEY (1998), at 234.   [3]   *Id.*

The evidence presented in support of these arguments, however, is thin – generally no more than some relatively vague comments by literati officials on the importance of land. The mere existence of terms such as "bone of the land," however, lends itself to multiple interpretations, not necessarily this one. For example, it might simply have existed in opposition to "skin of the land," signaling that title ownership was a more fundamental and significant right than usage. There is no good reason to favor one interpretation over the other. Similarly, the higher economic value of land in pre-industrial societies pushed in two opposite directions. Apart from encouraging landowners to hold onto their properties, it also encouraged them to aggressively acquire property from other landowners. The stubbornly high demand for land sales, both permanent and *dian*, from around 1870 to the mid-1930s certainly suggests that the latter dynamic was consistently at work in times of relative peace despite, one might add, the prevalence of highly hostile *dian* customs. The attractiveness of landownership alone is therefore an inadequate explanation for the existence of those customs.

Consider also the comparison with England. Early modern English landowners, too, had a strong sentimental attachment to land, which was made all the more powerful by the strong correlation of sociopolitical status with landed wealth,[4] but this clearly did not prevent their customs from limiting redemption windows and tenancy security. If anything, the strong psychological premium placed on landownership actually encouraged larger landowners to champion such limitations. Cultural perceptions of land in China and England had surprisingly much in common despite common characterization of one as "precommercial" and the other as "commercialized."

Moreover, these cultural characterizations run deeply contrary to much recent scholarship arguing that Qing and Republican society was, in fact, highly commercialized and economically aggressive: Studies of grain price fluctuations across several geographic regions indicate considerable market integration, suggesting that considerable portions of even the rural population relied on market activity for both income and food.[5] This directly contradicts older assumptions about the dominance of subsistence agriculture and, correspondingly, the dire lack of specialization and commercialization. Evidence of market integration is robust not only in core macroregions such as the Lower Yangtze, the Middle

---

[4] Sugarman & Warrington (1996), at 121–35; WRIGHTSON (2003), at 43; French (2000).
[5] *See* sources cited in Introduction, notes 43, 49.

Yangtze, and North China, but also in more peripheral provinces such as Gansu and Fujian. The Lower Yangtze was, of course, the epitome of early modern Chinese commercialization, boasting bustling commodity markets for food, textiles, tools, and even small machinery that affected a significant majority of households. Perhaps 15 percent of the *rural* workforce was completely nonagricultural, and most agricultural households also engaged in some textile or craft production.[6] Few households lived independently of local markets, which connected to a larger network of trade and commerce covering the entire region and affecting commodity prices nationwide.

Unsurprisingly, market penetration went hand-in-hand with relatively high levels of individual economic rationality: households regularly displayed highly rational decision making and considerable resourcefulness. They invested in land when profitable, employed excess labor in nonagricultural production, carefully negotiated property and credit transactions, reacted swiftly to fluctuations in land or commodity prices,[7] and, as demonstrated below, tirelessly promoted economic institutions and norms that favored their own interests. Certainly the existence of strong lineages promoted considerable communal solidarity, but even within lineages, households had few qualms about clashing – verbally and often physically – over property, debt, and the rules that governed them. Qing and Republican society was not "precommercial," which calls into question how it could have sustained moral ideals of "permanence in landholding."

In fact, it probably did not. The evidence presented next strongly suggests that such "ideals," insofar as they could be called "ideals" at all, were widely advocated only by those who could economically benefit from them. Almost no high-income households expressed support for them. Quite the opposite, many openly complained about the inconveniences of *dian* customs and permanent tenancy to their neighbors and kinsmen, but also through official venues. This could occasionally fuel widespread communal debate, which, in all likelihood, was precisely the desired effect.

There is, however, a crucial difference of degree between unhappiness over customs, however serious, and outright rejection of them. The evidence here points predominantly to the former, not the latter. For example, many grumbling *dian* buyers nonetheless acknowledged that customary law, however unreasonably, did allow *dian* sellers to redeem land decades after the original transaction. Few seemed prepared to openly deny its

---

[6] Yu (2007).   [7] Bell (1992).

regulatory legitimacy, even as they passively resisted this "evil custom" through a bewildering array of delay tactics and subterfuge. Certainly they would welcome a change in the rules – the complaining and even the delay tactics nudged in this direction – but until that happened, rules remained rules: to be worked around, tested for potential loopholes and weaknesses, and sometimes campaigned against, but not ignored outright. The parallels to contemporary legal practice, especially in common-law countries, are deeply intriguing.

B Toward a New Model

All this strongly suggests that *dian* and permanent tenancy customs were the result of intense and prolonged negotiation between highly self-interested parties rather than simple moral derivatives of "permanency in landholding" ideals. There was not nearly enough internalized consensus to sustain such ideals, but bargained equilibriums nonetheless could emerge where ethical uniformity did not. As a general theoretical matter, individuals may choose to tolerate undesirable property norms for many rationalistic reasons: a desire to maintain good relationships with those who favor the norms or, similarly, to signal a willingness to cooperate in the future; fear of material or reputational retribution; or even a straight-forward calculation that fighting over the norm is not worth the physical or psychological effort.

The assumption of basic self-interested rationality also applies to the formation and maintenance of English property customs. While traditional Marxist accounts of early modern English history exaggerate the amount of *class*-based conflict present in the early modern English countryside,[8] it was nonetheless, as noted earlier, a place of considerable ruthlessness when it came to property acquisitions, evictions, and enclosures. As numerous scholars have noted, the fourteenth-century English Black Death wiped out such a large portion of the population that traditional communal ties became severely weakened in its aftermath. Market integration had also made tremendous headways by the seventeenth century, as had urbanization and nonagricultural production. With them came a rise in both productivity and "industriousness," measured by both hours worked

---

[8] WRIGHTSON (2003). *But see* E.P. Thompson, *Eighteenth-Century English Society: Class Struggle without Class?*, 3 SOC. HIST. 133–65 (1978), which summarizes and criticizes "anticlass" interpretations of English social history.

and the amount of attention to personal finances.[9] All this suggests a population that had become fairly rational – economically rational, that is – and strongly self-interested a few centuries before Adam Smith.

Of course, it is much better to demonstrate economic rationality than to merely assume it. There have been, as noted earlier, major studies that tend to support a basic assumption of rationality, but some independent analysis would nonetheless be useful. This section therefore argues that smallholders – in both societies – theoretically had strong, economically rational reasons to prefer longer redemption windows, whereas large landowners likely preferred the opposite. Chapter 4 demonstrates that these theoretical preferences do indeed match the sociolegal behavior documented in the available historical evidence, including cases, contracts, and social surveys.

Perhaps the easiest way to understand the institutional incentives of individual households is to consider how they were affected by the institutional arrangements discussed in Chapters 1 and 2. The early modern English landholder who needed a large cash inflow is probably as good a place to start as any. He faced, to put it lightly, an extremely unpalatable set of choices. In most cases, he had to either mortgage some of his property or sell it outright, but there were obvious downsides to either option. Not only did mortgaging usually bring in less than the property's full market value, but it also carried a substantial risk that the landholder would lose the land permanently at that discounted price. Generally, his redemption right was only good for a very short period of time. Moreover, until the "equity of redemption" became firmly established in the eighteenth century, the mortgagee could simply seize the property on default, with no foreclosure process to make up whatever difference existed between the loan and the property's full value. This obviously placed the mortgagor under tremendous pressure to redeem on time, but given the small redemption window and limited financial means he usually faced – households in good financial shape rarely had to sell or mortgage land in the first place – very often the only way out was to mortgage or sell more of his property, creating a vicious cycle that potentially led to financial ruin.

Mortgaging was therefore a highly unattractive option, but the alternative was not much better. To be sure, selling land outright guaranteed a higher transaction price and created fewer longer-term complications, but

---

[9]   *See* JAN DE VRIES, THE INDUSTRIOUS REVOLUTION: CONSUMER DEMAND AND THE HOUSEHOLD ECONOMY, 1650 TO THE PRESENT (2008); JOHN BROAD, TRANSFORMING ENGLISH RURAL SOCIETY: THE VERNEYS AND THE CLAYDONS, 1600–1820 (2004) (examining the rural entrepreneurship of gentry families).

it also guaranteed permanent loss of the property. In a society were land was *the* primary source of economic production and sociopolitical status, people were willing go to great lengths to keep it. From a purely economic point of view, because the availability of well compensated off-farm, nonagricultural employment was very limited prior to mid-eighteenth century, it rarely made economic sense for a landholder to voluntarily sell his land in the absence of pressing financial need. In other words, when people sold or mortgaged land, it was usually because external circumstances forced them to. Throw in the substantial sociopolitical status benefits of landholding,[10] and one can easily understand why the choice between mortgaging and selling outright was both highly difficult and deeply unpleasant.[11] For the great majority of landholders with large cash needs, English law and custom provided them with only bad options.

While the relationship between landholding and high sociopolitical status was much more ambiguous in China – a subject that is explored in detail below – the basic economic incentives that the Chinese rural population faced were not so different from those of their early modern English counterparts. They, too, operated in an economy where agricultural was the predominant source of production and income, where other sectors of the economy had yet to really take off, and where rural-urban migration was fairly minimal. Consequently, they, too, were usually very reluctant to sell land and, when faced with substantial cash needs that could not be met via small-sum, unsecured borrowing, preferred to first explore options other than the permanent selling of land.

When they did so, however, they could count on an institutional framework that was highly protective of their economic interests. Not only did *dian* sellers generally pay no interest, but they also had decades or more to scrape together funds for redemption. Local customs did deprive them of some contractual freedoms, but the loss was minimal: they could not contractually establish a deadline for redemption even if they wanted to. However, they had little reason to want that. Removing the possibility of default hardly meant removing the possibility of permanent alienation altogether. If, after the original contract, the *dian* seller ever wished to permanently convey his land, he could simply request an additional payment (*zhaotie*) and convert the *dian* sale into a permanent one. Until then, it certainly did not hurt to leave other options open, especially

---

[10] Chapters 4 and 5 discuss these status benefits in greater detail.

[11] This also explains why social demand for the equity of redemption was so high in late-seventeenth-century England. *See* Sugarman & Warrington (1996).

because the right to *zhaotie* guaranteed that he would receive the full market value of his land should he ever choose to fully alienate. Land prices were either stable or rising throughout most of the later Qing and Republic[12] – the major exceptions being the Taiping rebellion years and the Japanese invasion – thus further decreasing the economic risk of extended *dian* relations.

A more serious concern might be that the inability to impose redemption deadlines could prevent the landowner from negotiating higher *dian* prices, which amounted to only 60 to 80 percent of what a permanent sale would command. There *were*, however, ways to negotiate a higher price: rather than agreeing to a redemption deadline, the two sides could establish a longer guaranteed-usage period (*xian*), which gave *dian* buyers greater economic security and larger returns to their loan. In practice, Qing and Republican *dian* contractors commonly used guaranteed-usage periods of one, three, five, or ten years, with longer periods associated with higher *dian* prices.[13] Guaranteed-usage periods did create inconveniencies for *dian* sellers who were eager to redeem at the earliest convenience, but in the overall balance of things, this seems to have been a relatively small price to pay for absolute institutional protection against default.[14] Moreover, as discussed in later chapters, guaranteed-usage periods were often less than guaranteed: *dian* sellers frequently attempted and, in many cases,

---

[12] On rising land prices prior to 1840, *see* Li Wenzhi, *Lun Yapian Zhanzheng qian Dijia he Goumai Nian* [*On Land Prices and Purchase Years before the Opium War*], 1988(2) ZHONGGUO SHEHUI JINGJI SHI YANJIU [STUD. OF SOC. & ECON. HIST.] 1. On rising Lower Yangtze land values before and after the Taiping, *see* BERNHARDT (1992), at 248–49. After the mid-nineteenth century, exposure to foreign trade actually *increased* market integration and the profitability of most forms of agricultural production. *See, e.g.*, THOMAS G. RAWSKI, ECONOMIC GROWTH IN PREWAR CHINA (1989) (attributing early-twentieth-century growth to market integration driven by the foreign presence); LILLIAN M. LI, CHINA'S SILK TRADE: TRADITIONAL INDUSTRY IN THE MODERN WORLD, 1842–1937 (1981) (positively assessing the impact of foreign trade on silk production); ROBERT PAUL GARDELLA, HARVESTING MOUNTAINS: FUJIAN AND THE CHINA TEA TRADE, 1757– 1937 (1994) (discussing the growth of the tea trade after the mid-Qing). On growing land productivity, *see* Philip C.C. Huang, *Development or Involution in Eighteenth-Century Britain and China?*, 61 J. ASIAN STUD. 501, 512 (2002) (arguing that land productivity increased despite declining labor productivity).
[13] *See, e.g.*, ZHOU & XIE (1986), at 124, 312–13.
[14] Implicit in this statement is, of course, an assumption that the utility value of land to a farmer was so high that a measurable increase in the likelihood of redemption generated an expected utility gain that outweighed the corresponding dip in *dian* prices (or whatever guaranteed-usage period the seller would have to accept to negate the dip). Considering that even with infinite redeemability, *dian* prices remained at 60 to 80 percent of full market value, this seems to be an acceptable assumption.

did redeem land before the period had passed, much to the buyers' discontent. Some even claimed that by customary law, guaranteed-usage periods held no binding force. Needless to say, buyers often disagreed, but even the existence of such a debate reinforces the extent to which *dian* customs favored sellers.

All things considered, *dian* redemption norms were so favorable to *dian* sellers that landholders theoretically should have had little incentive to permanently sell land at all. For those who needed to meet an immediate financial need, the problems created by the somewhat lesser monetary value of a *dian* sale were almost always outweighed by the unlimited redemption rights that it conveyed. Indeed, even if the goal was simply to wrench as much sale value as possible from the property, a *dian* sale nonetheless would be preferable in most cases because the *dian* seller could then use a *zhaotie* transaction to take advantage of future increases in property value. Only in those relatively rare cases where the landholder needed to sell the entire piece of land immediately at the highest possible price – perhaps if he was planning to move away permanently – was a permanent sale the optimal choice. Unsurprisingly, then, the vast majority of land contracts scholars have found from the nineteenth and early twentieth centuries have been *dian* contracts rather than permanent sales. In some archives, the ratio could be as high as eleven *dian* contracts to every permanent sale.[15] Moreover, there is fairly good evidence to suggest that the considerable majority of *dian* contracts were, in fact, eventually redeemed by the debtor rather than permanently sold off to the creditor via "additional payment" procedures.[16]

But why would *dian* sellers prefer establishing a blanket rule on redemption deadlines, rather than simply granting both sides in the transaction full contractual freedom? A customary norm that mandated an infinite right of redemption did theoretically damage their contractual freedom – with, as noted earlier, at least *some* economic consequences, however minor. The answer probably lies in the different bargaining positions they faced in one-on-one contract negotiations and in general norm negotiation. Because most *dian* sales were made under considerable financial stress, which severely cut into the seller's bargaining power, it probably was not in his interest to personally negotiate redemption terms under a normative assumption of complete contractual freedom and flexibility. Rather, he probably would have preferred to establish, under more

---

[15] Ningbo Contracts (2008); Shicang Qiyue (2010); Yang (1988).
[16] *See* Chapter 6, Section C.

economically neutral conditions, an a priori redemption deadline that covered all future *dian* sales. In other words, if *dian* sellers truly wished to maximize their bargaining position – and thereby obtain, in the great majority of cases, superior outcomes – they would have pursued a blanket redemption deadline instead of a rule of free contract. Theoretically, the a priori deadline could range from immediately after the sale to, essentially, infinity. Among the possibilities, having a blanket rule of infinite redeemability, as explained earlier, clearly offered *dian* sellers the highest expected economic utility.

The only hypothetical *dian* sellers who really lost out under the Chinese customary regime, and indeed would have fared better under the English system, were those who were completely certain that they could repay within a very short period of time – a year or less – but also urgently needed to obtain a loan worth significantly more than the percentage of full market value commonly issued by *dian* buyers. Such people were, in all likelihood, extremely rare in real life. In fact, they never emerge at all in the several thousand pages of primary sources used for this study. Presumably, if a potential *dian* seller were completely and predictably able to repay within such a short period of time, he very rarely would have needed to make the sale in the first place.

To summarize, due to the economic primacy of land and the paucity of alternative employment opportunities, rural households likely had extremely strong incentives, in either society, to retain or, in the case of collateralized borrowing, redeem their land whenever possible. Potential migration, particularly rural-urban migration, might have tempered this incentive, but it was usually a fairly distant prospect in these early modern economies and, given the extremely low wages in proto-industrial production, often a deeply undesirably one. The conversion of smallholders to wage labor was rarely voluntary and frequently coercive. Moreover, the looming power imbalances in one-on-one term negotiations over collateralized borrowing contracts – which themselves would have stemmed from the high reluctance to lose land – meant that potential *dian* sellers or mortgagors likely would have preferred to collectively negotiate fixed redemption windows *a priori* rather than accept a general norm of free contract. Combined, these incentives meant that most potential borrowers would have preferred a custom resembling the infinite-redeemability norm that governed *dian* sales – whereas English mortgage redemption customs would have run contrary to their core economic interests.

Before we proceed further, it is useful to have a clearer sense of what, exactly, were the common socioeconomic identities of *dian* sellers and buyers. The high economic value of arable land in these pre-industrial societies meant that, as alluded to earlier, the primary impetus for land-holders, whether Chinese or English, to sell or mortgage land was serious financial stress: upcoming weddings, funerals, or large debts coming due.[17] Median- or lower-income rural households in particular usually could only meet these financial demands through the selling or mortgaging of land. Outside these circumstances – in which a failure to raise cash could trigger severe social penalties – they rarely put their land up for sale or mortgage.

This created some fairly strong income-based divisions between sellers/debtors and buyers/creditors. Larger landholders rarely needed to sell land to make ends meet, whereas smallholders frequently did. Chapter 6 provides a detailed empirical illustration of these claims, but some of the more compelling empirical nuggets are worth previewing here. In some North China villages, for example, nearly 90 percent of documented land mortgagors and sellers during the later 1930s came from the bottom half of landholders, whereas only 3 percent belonged to the top 25 percent.[18] Moreover, nearly all existing contract archives from Qing and Republican China suggest that land mortgages and sales gener-ally involved a few large landholders accumulating land from dozens of poorer neighbors.[19] The same was true of England, where existing his-torical sources document a steady flow of land from smallholders to wealthier households in the early modern era but very little in the other direction. In other words, the great majority of debtors – mortgagors or *dian* sellers – were smallholders, whereas the great majority of creditors – mortgagees or *dian* buyers – were larger landowners holding greater amounts of monetary capital. The debtor versus creditor division was therefore usually also a clash between poor and rich, in which most

---

[17] On China and England, *see* THE BRENNER DEBATE (1987), at 10–63, 236; Phillipp R. Schofield, *Dearth, Debt and the Local Land Market in a Late Thirteenth-Century Village Community*, 45 AGRICULTURAL HIST. REV. 1 (1997); Govind Sreenivasan, *The Land-Family Bond at Earls Colne (Essex) 1550–1650*, 131 PAST AND PRESENT 3 (1991) (docu-menting the unwillingness of English peasants to sell land); Zvi Razi, *Family, Land and the Village Community in Later Medieval England*, 93 PAST & PRESENT 3 (1981). A similar situation existed in Tokugawa Japan; *see* SMITH (1959), at 159 ("[Mortgaging documents] show that borrowing by peasants usually originated in poverty"); WILLIAM CHAMBLISS, CHIARAIJIMA VILLAGE: LAND TENURE, TAXATION, AND LOCAL TRADE, 1811–1884, at 36–37 (1964) (noting that selling or mortgaging land tended to indicate declining economic fortunes); Tsutomu Ouchi, *Chiso kaisei zengo no nominsho no bunkai to jinushisei*, in 1 CHISO KAISEI NO KENKYU 37 (Uno Kozo ed., 1957).

[18] 3 MANTETSU SURVEYS, at 5; 4 MANTETSU SURVEYS, at 218.

[19] See discussion in Chapter 6.

smallholders in a community likely sympathized with the interests of debtors, whereas larger landowners more readily imagined themselves in the shoes of creditors.

How, then, should we understand the economic interests of these relatively well-off creditors? Here again, it is probably best to begin by considering how they were affected by the specific institutional arrangements discussed in previous chapters. Compared with its highly favorable treatment of *dian* sellers, customary law placed *dian* buyers in a very awkward economic position. Certainly they could enjoy, at basically no cost,[20] the land's produce and other economic values for some period of time, which explains their willingness to contract in the first place, but otherwise *dian* redemption norms did them no favors. The constant danger of redemption – after the guaranteed-usage period had passed, but sometimes even before that – seriously decreased the land's value to them both by discouraging long-term investments to improve the land and by discouraging long-term use of the land itself as a source of capital or collateral. There is indeed evidence suggesting that, particularly in North China, land held as *dian* collateral – or, for that matter, under a fixed-term tenancy arrangement, where the tenant likewise lacked strong incentives to invest in long-term improvements – was only 70 to 80 percent as productive as land farmed by its permanent owner.[21] If the goal was to maximize the production capacity of land, then obtaining land via a *dian* contract was not nearly as good as getting it via permanent sale.

If, however, the goal was to permanently acquire land – either via the default of collateralized debt or a straightforward permanent sale – then allowing a norm of unlimited *dian* redeemability was probably one of the worst possible institutional outcomes. First, it effectively eliminated the possibility of involuntary debt default and subsequent forfeiture of collateral. Moreover, the overwhelming attractiveness of *dian* sales to potential debtors dramatically decreased the supply of permanent sales, thereby making it much more difficult to accumulate land. If we assume, as urged earlier, that pre-industrial landowners (mainly smallholders) rarely sold or collateralized their land unless forced to by exogenous financial duress – and therefore that the total supply of land on the market, via both permanent and *dian* sales, was largely unaffected by transactional institutions – then increasing the institutional attractiveness of *dian* sales to

---

[20] That is, assuming that the land was eventually redeemed – which, as discussed in Chapter 6, Section C, probably happened more often than not.

[21] Akira Nagano, Zhongguo Tudi Zhidu de Yanjiu [Research on China's Land Institutions] (Qiang Wo trans., 2004), at 116–28.

potential debtors/sellers was effectively equivalent to decreasing the attractiveness of permanent sales. In other words, the more they could rely on infinitely redeemable *dian* sales to meet financial needs, the less they needed to permanently sell land. As noted earlier, well over 90 percent of surviving land transactions in local archives, and in some cases over 95 percent, were *dian* sales, the considerable majority of which seemed to be redeemed at some point.[22] Permanent alienation, in comparison, was a rare event, which meant that wealthier households had a very difficult time prying full title away from less affluent smallholders – and therefore, as discussed in greater detail in Chapter 6, were not nearly as economically dominant as large landowners were in early modern England. Naturally, this led to considerable grumbling among village-level economic elites, not to mention the occasional petition to local governmental authorities to intervene against "evil" and "backward" customs, which, as noted earlier, was rarely effective.[23]

One has to wonder, then, why, given these detrimental consequences, Chinese rural economic elites tolerated infinite *dian* redeemability at all. There are two different levels to this question. First, why didn't they fight harder to prevent or undermine its establishment? Second, assuming that the norm had already been established, why didn't they simply refuse to engage in *dian* sales? In other words, why were they both institutionally and economically complicit, apart from the occasional complaint or petition, in sustaining a norm that damaged their economic interests? The remainder of this section focuses largely on the first question, but before it does that, it should probably spend a few paragraphs addressing the second question. Even with the unwanted burden of infinite redeemability, "dian" sales nonetheless provided substantial economic value to creditors, which helps to explain why they did tolerate its existence over long periods of time, if grudgingly.

In fact, not only did large landowners continue to make *dian* purchases – existing contract archives suggest that many Lower Yangtze landlords made more than ten per year – but they routinely paid *dian* prices that, as noted earlier, hovered at around 70 to 80 percent of the land's full market value.[24] This begs the additional question of why the prices of *dian* sales were not discounted more severely given the significant inconveniences they imposed on *dian* buyers. The answer probably lies in the opportunity costs involved with bidding up the price of permanent

---

[22] *See* Chapter 6, Section C.   [23] *See* Chapter 1, Section C.
[24] HUANG (1985), at 176; McAleavy (1958), at 406; MACAULEY (1998), at 231.

transactions: For all the inconveniences they caused, *dian* sales nonetheless offered a fair amount of economic value to buyers. If the seller eventually redeemed, the buyer would at least have enjoyed – given the usually low rates of inflation in this era[25] – essentially free use of the land for several years. To be sure, such use was usually suboptimal, given the disincentives to making permanent improvements to the land, but even so, land productivity on *dian*-sold land could, as noted earlier, nonetheless reach some 70 to 80 percent of optimal productivity.[26] In other words, in terms of raw agricultural produce, a series of *dian* purchases was worth, to most buyers, 70 to 80 percent of the value of a comparably sized permanent purchase minus transaction costs. It therefore made little sense for them to bid up the price of permanent sales to several times the price of *dian* sales. The relatively limited discounting of *dian* sales simply may have reflected these economic rationales.

Moreover, for a relatively wealthy landholder sitting on a small pile of excess cash, attractive investment opportunities rarely existed outside the land market. China did experience moderate proto-industrial growth throughout the middle and late Qing, but at a macro level, such growth was actually outpaced by agricultural expansion. Recent quantitative estimates suggest that for most of the pre–Opium War era, nonagricultural production steadily accounted for some 25 percent of gross domestic product (GDP).[27] Between 1850 and 1910, however, it actually shrank to less than 20 percent of GDP despite the Qing state's professed interest in stimulating industrialization.[28] The causes for this relative contraction are obviously highly complex, but one contributing factor was likely the differential tax rates applied to agricultural and nonagricultural activity. Facing a serious fiscal crisis during and immediately after the Taiping Rebellion, the Qing state doubled its tax revenues between 1850 and 1900 and doubled them yet again after 1900. Nearly all this revenue growth came from nonagricultural sources, elevating the "real tax rate" on non-agricultural production from barely more than 1 percent in 1850 to well

---

[25] The major exception was the final decade of the nineteenth Century.

[26] NAGANO (2004), at 116–28.

[27] Stephen Broadberry, Guan Hanhui, & Li Daokui, *China, Europe and the Great Divergence: A Study in National Accounting*, Working Paper, London School of Economics (2014); Ye Ma & Tianshu Chu, *Living Standards in China between 1840 and 1912: A New Estimation of Gross Domestic Product per capita*, Paper presented at the European Historical Economics Society Conference (2013).

[28] Broadberry, Guan, & Li (2014); Ma & Chu (2013).

above 6 percent in 1900.[29] In comparison, the total volume of agricultural taxes remained stagnant at some 70 to 80 million taels per year throughout this period despite fairly rapid rural recovery and expansion following the Taiping crisis.[30] By 1900, the real tax rate on agriculture had actually fallen well below 1 percent, compared with 1 to 1.5 percent in 1850.[31] In other words, whereas agricultural production and nonagricultural production were taxed at comparable rates prior to the Opium War, the latter was taxed at least seven to eight times more heavily than the former by the end of the century. The causes of this exceedingly strange fiscal strategy extend, of course, far beyond the scope of this book, but suffice to say, it likely had a substantial dampening effect on private investment in nonagricultural economic activity.

Adding to these woes was the fact that investing in nonagricultural sectors generally meant assuming greater financial risk than simply investing in land. As a number of scholars have argued, Qing law and custom did not allow investors to purchase limited-liability shares in commercial businesses, which meant that most nonagricultural investments – textiles, salt production, and so on – carried some risk of financial loss beyond the initial volume of investment.[32] As the economy became more volatile in the nineteenth century, both before and after the midcentury crisis, investors across the country, but particularly in the Yangtze regions, became increasingly wary of assuming such risk and correspondingly reduced their exposure to nonlanded assets.[33] Land, in comparison, was a "limited-liability asset." Even if the value of land went to zero, the landowner would still only lose the value of his investment

---

[29] Revene estimates come from Luo Yudong, Zhongguo Lijin Shi (2010); Yang Duanliu, Liushiwu Nian lai Zhongguo Guoji Maoyi Tongji 122–23 (1931); Zeng Yangfeng, Zhongguo Yanzheng Shi 27–30 (1936); Wu Zhaoxin, Zhongguo Shuizhi Shi 116–20 (1937). Production estimates come from Ma & Chu (2013).

[30] Guan Jiyu, Tianfu Huiyao 426–27 (1944); Feng Huade, *Hebei Sheng Ding Xian Yuan Tianfu*, 4 Zhengzhi Jingji Xuebao 487 (1936); Li & Jiang (2005); Wang Yeh-chien, Land Taxation in Late Imperial China (1973); Zhou Tang, Zhongguo Caizheng Lungang 23, 297 (1911); Liu Jinzao, Qingchao Xu Wenxian Tongkao chap. 68 (1936); Zhou Yumin, Wanqing Caizheng yu Shehui Bianqian (2000); 2 Zhongguo Jindai Jingji Shi 987 (Wang Jingyu ed., 2000).

[31] Ma & Chu (2013).

[32] Zelin (2005); William C. Kirby, *China Unincorporated: Company Law and Business Enterprise in Twentieth-Century China*, 54 J. Asian. Stud. 43 (1996).

[33] Madeleine Zelin, *Managing Multiple Ownership at the Zigong Salt Yard*, in Contract and Property in Early Modern China 230 (Madeleine Zelin, Jonathan K. Ocko, & Robert Gardella eds., 2004b); Tomoko Shiroyama, China during the Great Depression: Market, State, and the World Economy, 1929–1937 (2008).

and no more. Even if we disregard agriculture's relative macroeconomic strength vis-à-vis other sectors, simple risk aversion likely would have driven many, perhaps most, investors into the land market.[34]

In fact, due to a potent combination of slow but steady population growth and growing land productivity, land prices rose steadily for most of the nineteenth and early twentieth centuries.[35] Population growth is, of course, a somewhat combustible issue in late Qing history. Historians have argued about the pace and distribution of Qing demographic expansion for decades, with no clear consensus in sight.[36] Nonetheless, there is at least a basic consensus that the populations of North China and the Lower Yangtze trended upward for most of the eighteenth, nineteenth, and early twentieth centuries but also grew at a somewhat slower rate than the national average, largely due to outward migration.[37] The most commonly cited statistics suggest that the population of the Lower Yangtze grew by perhaps 35 percent from 1750 to 1850, much of it in urban areas, whereas the national average might have been around 80 percent.[38] It then plunged by 40 to 50 percent during the early years of the Taiping Rebellion. After 1865, it grew quite rapidly until the Second Sino-Japanese War came to the region in the early 1940s, recovering to around 80 percent of 1850 levels – an increase of some 50 to 60 percent.

A similar situation existed in North China, where the population grew by around 20 percent between 1750 and 1850 and then by another 3 to 5 percent between 1850 and 1875. A massive famine that lasted from 1875 to 1878 then caused a roughly 10 percent population decline. Between 1880 and 1950, the population regained its upward momentum, growing by around 50 percent despite significant losses during the Sino-Japanese War and the 1945–1949 Civil War.[39]

---

[34] A number of scholars have also argued that population growth drove investment in agriculture because it decreased the price of agricultural labor. *See* ZHAO GANG, ZHONGGUO TUDI ZHIDU SHI, chap. 5 (2006); *see also* Martin Heijdra, *The Socio-Economic Development of Rural China During the Ming, in* 8 THE CAMBRIDGE HISTORY OF CHINA 417, 525–26 (Denis Twitchett and Frederick Mote eds., 1998).

[35] See discussion surrounding *infra*, notes 40–41.

[36] Summarized in Robert B. Marks, *China's Population Size during the Ming and Qing: A Comment on the Mote Revision* 3, Comments delivered at the 2002 Meeting of the Association of Asian Studies (on file with author).

[37] Ho PING-TI (1959), at 136–68.   [38] See discussion at note 34, Introduction.

[39] Xing Long, *Jindai Huabei Nongcun Renkou Liudong ji qi Xiaozhang* [*Demographic Mobility and Change in Early Modern Rural North China*], 2000(4) LISHI YANJIU, *available at* http://economy.guoxue.com/article.php/1480.

The point of this brief sketch is simply to make the case that population growth likely exerted significant upward pressure on land prices during the period on which I focus (1865–1940). Demographic growth did *not*, however, lead to significant decreases in per capita income. Instead, total output kept pace with the expanding population in large part because more intensive farming techniques and market-driven specialization drove up land productivity.[40] This, in turn, drove up both the economic value of land and rental rates for newly created tenancies.[41] Correspondingly, land prices likely fell during periods of severe population decline – the early Taiping years in the Lower Yangtze and the 1875–1878 famine in North China – but otherwise tended to grow steadily and often quite rapidly.[42]

Combined, these factors – the strength of the agricultural sector and investor risk aversion – were likely powerful enough to explain why neither creditor demand for *dian* sales nor *dian* prices collapsed in the face of strongly debtor-friendly redemption norms. Land was still a highly attractive investment, arguably more attractive, in fact, than investment in other sectors, and even a somewhat oppressive set of *dian* customs still offered quite substantial economic value to creditors. That said, infinite redeemability was clearly something that seriously damaged their general interests in both efficient land use and permanent land accumulation.

To appreciate how much better wealthy landowners could have had it – had they been able to establish customary or legal norms in full accordance with their socioeconomic interests – one need only look to the early modern English comparison. There they only had to endure a single of year of uncertainty. More importantly, given the long odds of successfully redeeming within one year, most potential debtors probably preferred to simply sell the land outright, making permanent transactions the dominant mode of conveyance on the land market, far outnumbering mortgages. In fact, to the extent that some households still chose to mortgage, their creditors likely appreciated it because it gave them a fairly

---

[40] Broadberry, Guan, & Li (2014); Ma & Chu (2013).

[41] After the mid-nineteenth century, exposure to foreign trade further boosted market integration levels. *See, e.g.,* RAWSKI (1989) (attributing early-twentieth-century growth to market integration driven by the foreign presence); LI (1981) (positively assessing the impact of foreign trade on silk production); GARDELLA (1994) (discussing the growth of the tea trade after the mid-Qing). On growing land productivity, *see* Huang (2002), at 501, 512 (arguing that land productivity increased despite declining labor productivity). On increasing pressure from landlords to increase rent levels throughout the nineteenth and early twentieth centuries, *see* BERNHARDT (1992).

[42] Huang (2002); Li (1998).

strong likelihood of obtaining full title at less than full market value on default.[43] Consequently – Chapter 6 addresses this causal relationship in more detail – the English rural economy evolved from smallholder domination in the fifteenth and sixteenth centuries to a managerial farm-driven mode by 1700, whereas in China smallholders retained their dominant position throughout the Qing and Republic.

How, then, should we summarize the institutional incentives of potential creditors – who were, as discussed earlier, predominantly large and wealthy landowners – in either economy? They would not have minded a "free contract" arrangement in which all redemption deadlines were negotiated on an individual basis. The likely financial desperation of the borrower in such circumstances would have worked to their advantage. If there was a predetermined deadline, they would have preferred a shorter one to a longer one. In fact, the shorter the deadline, the more their economic interests would have been enhanced. That said, given the extremely high value of land, they had reasonably strong incentives to continue lending even if the normative deadlines were extremely long and inconvenient. They would have, in other words, preferred the English arrangement to the Chinese one but likely would have continued to participate in the collateral market even under the Chinese arrangements.

What, then, explains the Sino-English institutional divergence? It cannot be the basic economic incentives of richer and poorer landholders, which were, as argued earlier, likely similar across both economies. A far more plausible candidate is the distribution of sociopolitical capital between rich and poor, which shaped, for both sides, the cost of negotiating for a norm, including, most importantly, the reputational and material risks of contradicting other community members.

"Social status" is, following sociological convention, the relative rank that an individual holds in a social hierarchy based on honor or prestige.[44] It is conceptually distinct from, if practically connected to, both the legal or institutional ranking of individuals discussed in Chapter 1 and one's relative material wealth. Honor and prestige hierarchies inevitably exist in human society so long as people need any kind of leadership, although, as demonstrated below, they can be based on dramatically different

---

[43] This was precisely what the "Equity of Redemption" sought to curb.

[44] *See, e.g.,* Yoram Weiss & Chaim Fershtman, *Social Status and Economic Performance: A Survey,* 43 EURO. ECON. REV. 801, 802 (1998); Britannica Online Encyclopedia (Academic Version), Social Status, www.britannica.com/EBchecked/topic/551450/social-status (last visited July 1, 2012) ("Social status [is] the relative rank that an individual holds ... in a social hierarchy based upon honour or prestige").

factors – physical prowess, wealth, religious or moral piety, age, and lineage, to name a few.[45] Generally, the reputational costs of contradicting a higher-status person outweigh those of contradicting a lower-status one.

This suggests a fairly straightforward model of norm negotiation: individual property owners, predominantly male household heads in early modern societies, negotiated for property norms based on their perceived self-interest. When considering whether to back a particular norm, they considered both material and reputational consequences – which, of course, are mutually affecting entities, if conceptually distinct. Both kinds of consequences, but particularly the latter, are influenced by the social status of allies and adversaries: all other things being equal, higher-status adversaries can inflict stronger reputational damage, which often leads to material costs as well, whereas higher-status allies can convey stronger reputational rewards. All other things being equal, there is greater incentive to compromise with, or even yield to, accumulatively higher-status adversaries than to lower-status ones. Consequently, higher-status people are more capable of negotiating favorable outcomes. In other words, because they hold higher bargaining power, property norms are more likely to reflect their preferences.

Correspondingly, I argue below that differences in status distribution explain differences in property institutions between China and England. Smallholders cumulatively possessed much higher social status in China than in England and were therefore able to negotiate favorable property norms in the former but not in the latter. This allows us to incorporate large doses of self-interested rationality into the analysis: if and when richer households conceded certain property norms to poorer ones, it was not because they shared in a vaguely defined "precommercial" ideal but because the cost of prolonged tension was too high.

The claim that lower-income Chinese households cumulatively possessed (relatively) formidable social status coexists rather uncomfortably, of course, with some fairly deep-rooted popular perceptions on Chinese law and society. Indeed, one of the oldest and most persistent assumptions that scholars have made about Chinese law and custom is that it was "hierarchical" and oppressive. Insofar as scholars even acknowledged that China had "law" – and such acknowledgment is not universal to this day – they rarely failed to describe that "law" as, more or less, "a moral code

---

[45] *See* Xiaotian Zhang, *Status Inconsistency Revisited: An Improved Empirical Model*, 24 Euro. Sociol. Rev. 155, 156 (2008) (noting the complex factors that affect the calculation of social status).

calling for inequality and hierarchy"[46] and therefore more a tool for political control than something that could give rise to genuine "rule of law." For many, the study of Chinese law and custom was, and remains, no more than the "scholarly study of obsequious submission to authority and hierarchy."[47]

The many logical problems with this reasoning aside, the more fundamental question is: "Hierarchical" in what sense? "Hierarchy" is a profoundly ambiguous and analytically useless term unless it is further specified and explained: Hierarchy of whom over whom? Under what conditions? With what kinds of privileges? Although many scholars have made the "Imperial Chinese law and society were hierarchical" argument, few have addressed these questions with detail or nuance. For a very long time, the dominant image of Chinese legal hierarchies in both Communist China and Western academic circles was simply one of "Oriental despotism" and systematic class oppression. Law and local custom alike were created by a narrow class of elites who used institutions at all levels – including, but not limited to, unfair advantages in government recruiting, uneven tax duties, and favorable property norms – to protect their core self-interests, largely to the political *and* economic detriment of other classes.[48] As one legal article put it, "[f]or centuries, Chinese concepts of property rights were rooted in strongly autocratic Confucian doctrine that enshrined and vindicated hierarchy,

---

[46] Ugo Mattei, *Three Patterns of Law: Taxonomy and Change in the World's Legal Systems*, 45 AM. J. COMP. L. 5, 39 (1997). For similar sentiments, *see, e.g.,* ZHANG JINFAN, ZHONGGUO FALÜ DE CHUANTONG YU JINDAI ZHUANXING [THE TRADITIONS AND EARLY MODERN TRANSFORMATION OF CHINESE LAW] 72 (1997); GEOFFREY MACCORMACK, THE SPIRIT OF TRADITIONAL CHINESE LAW 52–144 (1996); ROBERTO UNGER, LAW IN MODERN SOCIETY: TOWARDS A CRITICISM OF SOCIAL THEORY 93 (1976); BODDE & MORRIS (1967), at 29–38; Amir N. Licht et al., *Culture Rules: The Foundations of the Rule of Law and Other Norms of Governance*, 35 J. COMP. ECON. 659, 660, 684 (2007); John O. Haley, *Law and Culture in China and Japan: A Framework for Analysis*, 27 MICH. J. INT'L L. 895, 906 (2006); James Q. Whitman, *Enforcing Civility and Respect: Three Societies*, 109 YALE L.J. 1279, 1320 (2000); Albert H.Y. Chen, *Towards a Legal Enlightenment: Discussions in Contemporary China on the Rule of Law*, 17 UCLA PAC. BASIN L.J. 125, 130 (2000) (summarizing the academic consensus in mainland China that traditional Chinese legal culture was "hierarchical and oppressive"); Teemu Ruskola, *Law, Sexual Morality, and Gender Equality in Qing and Communist China*, 103 YALE L.J. 2531, 2531–37 (1994).

[47] THOMAS B. STEPHENS, ORDER AND DISCIPLINE IN CHINA: THE SHANGHAI MIXED COURT 1911–27, at 115 (1992).

[48] G.W.F. HEGEL, THE PHILOSOPHY OF HISTORY 112 (J. Sibree trans., 1956); STEPHENS (1992); KARL A. WITTFOGEL, ORIENTAL DESPOTISM: A COMPARATIVE STUDY OF TOTAL POWER (1957); Chen (2000); ZHANG (1997).

authority and inequality."[49] For the most part, this remains the academic dogma in mainland China, with major legal history narratives decrying almost universally the "feudal" and "oppressive" nature of Imperial institutions.[50]

Such oppression purportedly contributed to late Imperial China's severe economic disparity, lack of social mobility, and, ultimately, relative material decline[51]: elite domination stifled free entrepreneurialism and technological innovation, created tremendous social unrest, and left the rural economy vulnerable to natural disasters. Insofar as Chinese immigrants have been economically successful in other parts of the world, such as Southeast Asia, their success supposedly stems from the disintegration of traditional sociopolitical hierarchies and greater mobility in immigrant communities.[52]

The image of a dominant Chinese elite ruling the country is not entirely unsubstantiated. Chinese legal culture, even in the Ming and Qing, certainly privileged certain social groups over others. The emperor was largely beyond formal legal sanction, and the law afforded special economic and legal statuses, including exemption from most taxes and legal prosecution, to his extended family.[53] More generally, Manchu bannermen possessed economic privileges not available to Han Chinese throughout the Qing, whereas high-level national examination degree holders enjoyed significant political and social advantages over lower-level scholars or non-degree-holders.[54]

To portray these privileges as the main symptoms of class-based institutional oppression is, however, to exaggerate both the number and clout of these elites. They occupied, first of all, only a *tiny* portion of the population.

---

[49] Paul Cantor & James Kraus, *Changing Patterns of Ownership Rights in the People's Republic of China: A Legal and Economic Analysis in the Context of Economic Reforms and Social Conditions*, 23 VAND. J. TRANSNAT'L L. 479, 483 (1991).

[50] Chen (2000).

[51] Some of the best-known examples include ACEMOGLU & ROBINSON (2010), at 117 (attributing Chinese underdevelopment to the unchecked power of its ruling elite); JÜRGEN HABERMAS, THE POSTNATIONAL CONSTELLATION: POLITICAL ESSAYS 124 (M. Pensky trans., 2001) (arguing that Asian societies must discard their hierarchical legal institutions to achieve capitalist modernity); ERIC L. JONES, GROWTH RECURRING: ECONOMIC CHANGE IN WORLD HISTORY 130–46 (1988); WITTFOGEL (1957).

[52] LAWRENCE E. HARRISON, WHO PROSPERS: HOW CULTURAL VALUES SHAPE ECONOMIC AND POLITICAL SUCCESS 15 (1992); Amy L. Chua, *Markets, Democracy, and Ethnicity: Toward a New Paradigm for Law and Development*, 108 YALE L.J. 1, 30–31 (1998).

[53] ZHANG (1997), at 84–112; Chen Peipei, *Qingdai Falü Tequan Yanjiu [A Study of Legal Privileges in the Qing]* (2007) (unpublished M.A. thesis, Anhui University), *available at* http://cdmd.cnki.com.cn/Article/CDMD-10357-2007193110.htm.

[54] *See* CH'U (1962), at 168–92.

Due to stubborn government refusal to expand examination degree quotas in proportion to population growth, degree-holders of *any* level became extremely rare by the nineteenth century – far lower than 1 percent of the total population.[55] Imperial clan members were, of course, even rarer. Even bannermen did not exceed a few percentage points of the total and, in any case, had lost much of their privileged status by the nineteenth century.[56] To put this in a comparative perspective, titled nobility comprised perhaps 2 percent of England's population during the early modern era,[57] to say nothing of the far more numerous landed gentry. More importantly, as discussed earlier in some detail, the Qing state was extraordinarily limited by both contemporary and modern standards: its relatively small size severely dampened tax collection and law enforcement powers and forced it to leave most local administration and rulemaking duties to communal, guild, or kinship-based self-governance.

Correspondingly, some scholars – optimistically, perhaps most historians – now recognize that the inequalities between official and commoner were not nearly the most important source of hierarchy in Chinese law and custom.[58] That position rightly belonged to what this book calls "Confucian kinship hierarchies": the institutionally enshrined inequalities between different family members that affected virtually every branch of Chinese society. Parents naturally occupied a higher legal and social position than their offspring, older relatives over younger ones, and, on some economic issues, men over women. Examples are legion in all Imperial legal codes from the Tang to the Qing[59]: physically assaulting a parent was punishable by death, whereas beating one's child was perfectly acceptable. Likewise, it was a far more serious offense for a junior relative to injure or defraud a senior one than vice versa. Even disobedience or rudeness to a senior relative could constitute a crime or at least a punishable offense in one's lineage or local community. It

---

[55] Elman (1991) at 1, 14–15; MATTHEW H. SOMMER, SEX, LAW AND SOCIETY IN LATE IMPERIAL CHINA 8 (2000) ("By the eighteenth century, all but a tiny percentage of the population could be considered free commoners").

[56] MARK C. ELLIOTT, THE MANCHU WAY: THE EIGHT BANNERS AND ETHNIC IDENTITY IN LATE IMPERIAL CHINA (2001).

[57] M.L. BUSH, THE ENGLISH ARISTOCRACY: A COMPARATIVE SYNTHESIS 35 (1984).

[58] *See, e.g.,* William P. Alford, *The Inscrutable Occidental: Roberto Unger's Uses and Abuses of the Chinese Past,* 64 TEXAS L. REV. 915, 931 (1986); Avner Greif & Guido Tabellini, *Cultural and Institutional Bifurcation: China and Europe Compared,* 100(2) AM. ECON. REV.: PAPERS & PROCEEDINGS 1 (2010); Teemu Ruskola, *The East Asian Legal Tradition, in* THE CAMBRIDGE COMPANION TO COMPARATIVE LAW 257, 263–64 (Mauro Bussani & Ugo Mattei eds., Cambridge Univ. Press 2012).

[59] ZHANG (1997), at 113–35; 8 ZHONGGUO FAZHI TONGSHI (1999), at 208, 256–57, 508.

was only natural in such a society, then, that legal *and* customary authority over major socioeconomic decisions, particularly those regarding land or marriage, almost always resided with the household patriarch. To the average individual, his or her relatives also enjoyed certain economic privileges over nonrelatives: Many local customs dictated, for example, that landowners offer their land to relatives first when exploring sale options and only sell to nonrelatives if those offers were unsuccessful. While scholars have debated the economic significance and enforceability of these customs, their wide-spread existence is undeniable.[60]

Kinship hierarchies retained much of their vitality even after the Qing's collapse. Republican legal codes, ranging from the patchwork codes drafted during the Beiyang era to the far more systematic criminal and civil codes drafted by the Nanjing government, narrowed the range of privileges afforded to senior relatives but did not eliminate them altogether.[61] For example, killing or assaulting a senior relative continued to be punished more severely than usual homicide or assault.[62] More importantly, the great majority of local communities continued to recognize and enforce traditional kinship hierarchies throughout the Republican era, and many do so even today.[63]

Despite their immense importance, how Confucian kinship hierarchies actually affected the distribution of sociopolitical status and economic wealth is, however, poorly understood, if at all. By and large, historians and social scientists have yet to seriously consider that question. Certain scholars of considerable reputation but questionable exposure to Chinese history, most infamously Jurgen Habermas, have attempted to dismiss their compatibility with economic and social "modernity" in broad but clearly misguided strokes. Because familial hierarchies are fundamentally incompatible with normative certainty and predictability – a notion that the remaining portions of this book ardently dispute – "Asiatic societies cannot participate in capitalistic modernization without taking advantage of the achievements of an

---

[60] 8 Zhongguo Fazhi Tongshi (1999), at 267–68. *See also* the discussion on lineage first-purchase rights at Chapter 3, Section B.

[61] Liu Guoqiang, *Qingmo Minguo shiqi xingfadian jianshe zhong qinshu lunli guanxi de chuancheng yu biange* [*Continuity and Change in the Treatment of Kinship Ties in Late Qing and Republican Criminal Codes*], 2012(4) Daode yu Wenming [Morality and Civilization] 67.

[62] *Id.*

[63] Feng Erkang, 18 Shiji yilai Zhongguo jiazu de xiandai zhuanxiang [The Modern Turn of Chinese Lineages Since the 18th Century] 214–313 (2005).

individualistic legal order."[64] Still others, particularly mainland Chinese scholars, attempt to conflate kinship hierarchies with the class-oppression thesis discussed earlier, arguing that the former encouraged habitual submission to authority that supported the latter.[65]

There may be some truth to this, but if we think systematically about their mechanisms, kinship hierarchies really should have *weakened* class- and wealth-based oppression. In the very limited sense that related laws and customs recognized status differences between different individuals, kinship institutions were indeed "hierarchical." From a broader perspective, however, the term "hierarchical" masks some fairly unique but extremely important characteristics. Unlike in other social hierarchies that tied status strictly to heritage, including most feudal or caste-based societies, the category of privileged persons was an extremely fluid one under Confucian norms. As one aged and had children, one automatically gained legal and customary authority over younger generations. Normatively, neither wealth nor education (unless it led to an examination degree) affected status within kinship groups. A wealthy nephew owed the same social obligations to a penniless uncle as a penniless nephew to a wealthy one.

This all leads to a rather counterintuitive deduction about "Confucian" kinship hierarchies: at least in theory, their institutional inequalities between senior and junior relatives should have promoted, rather than damaged, status mobility simply because everyone ages and most reproduce. Moreover, because kinship hierarchies were disconnected from wealth, they should have empowered significant numbers of low-income but high-status individuals against their wealthier kin and, therefore, should have helped to level the cumulative sociopolitical balance between rich and poor. It was, hypothetically, a system where individual hierarchy led to macro-level equality.

No one should doubt that social reality was far more complicated, but as these two chapters will demonstrate, even in practice, Confucian social hierarchies generated enough status mobility to inject much socioeconomic egalitarianism into China's property and contract institutions – in fact, significantly more than what one finds in early modern English norms. Late Imperial and Republican property customs often offered far more protection to the economically disadvantaged than comparable institutions in early modern England. More importantly, they did so precisely

---

[64] HABERMAS (2001), at 124. *See also* Greif & Tabellini (2010), at 5 (questioning whether kinship institutions might affect China's "capacit[y] in bringing about the modern economy and adjusting to it").

[65] Chen (2000); 8 ZHONGGUO FAZHI TONGSHI (1999), at 257–60, 264–66.

because kinship norms remained strong in Chinese legal culture, whereas English society had become, to quote Alan Macfarlane, "individualistic."[66] This hardly meant that affluent Chinese households harbored greater sympathy toward poorer kinsmen than their English peers – the opposite was often true – but rather that Chinese kinship hierarchies encouraged status egalitarianism among even the most self-interested of people.

The higher cumulative social status of poorer Chinese households derived, therefore, from the "Confucian" emphasis on generational hierarchies: the ranking of lineage members by generational seniority, theoretically independently of wealth, created large numbers of high-status seniors from low-income households. In comparison, historians generally agree that beyond a narrow class of nobility, kinship ties were no longer of primary socioeconomic importance for most rural Englishmen by the sixteenth century.[67] More importantly, in the resulting "individualist" social order, substantial personal wealth was almost always a prerequisite for status and authority.[68] Consequently, large landholders possessed a virtual monopoly over positions of political leadership and social prestige, whereas low-income households had very little representation among these ranks. Short of outright rejection of the existing social order, an extremely costly and therefore usually noncredible threat, they had minimal bargaining power in social norm negotiation. They might appeal, perhaps, to social ideals of distributive justice, sympathy, or charity, but the strength of such ideals was highly questionable in either country, easily eroded by more pragmatic concerns of self-interest, and certainly incapable of preventing widespread social tension and conflict over property norms. The end result, naturally, was that English property customs gave relatively weak protection to the economic interests of small landowners and tenants. Their Chinese counterparts did far better due to the presence of many high-status seniors among them.

One potential complication to consider is whether ranking by generational seniority in China *excluded* ranking by wealth. Within a kinship group, seniority could, in theory, generate a "complete" ranking of all family members: older generations ranked, first of all, higher than younger ones. Within the same generation, men ranked higher than women, and with certain stated exceptions, elder men ranked higher than younger men. There was neither need nor room for further ranking based on wealth. In practice, the exclusion of ranking by wealth was certainly far from absolute.

---

[66] MACFARLANE (1978).   [67] *Id.*; Cressy (1986); French & Hoyle (2003).
[68] WRIGHTSON (2003), at 46; French (2000).

A notable minority of lineages in South China – which is not within the geographic scope of this book – made relatively high personal wealth a precondition for obtaining leadership positions. High-income households in North China rarely enjoyed such privileges, but some did openly propose that landed wealth should be a prerequisite for political authority., Lower Yangtze lineages, however, often expressly frowned on ranking members by wealth, insisting that higher status corresponded only to "generational seniority, high morality, and intelligence" and, occasionally, that "lineage members should never be differentiated by wealth." The highest political positions in both Lower Yangtze and North China villages were, indeed, often occupied by senior individuals from well-connected kinship groups who owned little or no land. That they were further able to substantively influence customary property law should come as no surprise.[69] In any case, what matters most is the comparison with England, where, in a large majority of localities, landed wealth was an express prerequisite for sociopolitical authority.

Scholars have, on occasion, presented alternative theories on why lower-income peasants could possess relatively high social status in Qing and Republican China, but these are, by and large, unpersuasive. At least one recent book on Lower Yangtze land rights has attempted to attribute the relatively high status of smallholders there to physical and economic conditions. It argues that the very nature of rice agriculture made it impossible for richer peasants to seriously discriminate against their poorer neighbors: Farms, even larger ones, were generally so small that peasants had to cooperate heavily with each other to achieve efficient irrigation, seeding, and harvesting, which precluded the possibility of dominance by higher-income households.[70] While the empirics of this book have been much maligned, the argument would be highly questionable even if it were sound. It presents, first of all, a chicken-and-egg problem: the social status of poorer households depended on the dominance of small-scale agriculture, but that dominance itself, as argued both earlier and later, depended on higher status for poorer households and corresponding property institutions. Which came first?

More importantly, Qing and Republican labor utilization statistics tend to disprove this argument. The vast majority of farms, excluding the 5 to 10

---

[69] The statements made here are argued in detail at Chapter 4, Section B.
[70] Zhang Peiguo, Jindai Jiangnan Xiangcun Diquan de Lishi Renleixue Yanjiu [A Historical Anthropological Study of Early Modern Land Rights in the Lower Yangtze] 279–89 (2002).

percent of land under managerial farming, employed far more labor than economically optimal: the average male laborer could handle around 1.6 acres of rice paddy, but the great majority worked less than a quarter of that. Even on relatively larger farms, most laborers worked at less than half their capacity.[71] Given this enormous labor surplus, higher-income households might not suffer much during seeding and harvest even if cooperative production relations became somewhat strained. Irrigation was a more complicated issue, but strong mutual reliance there, where one uncooperative link could sabotage the entire system, made lower-income households at least as eager as higher-income ones to avoid communal tension, canceling any potential effect on status distribution. In comparison, the social dominance of kinship norms, which did not depend on the social status of low-income households, offers an explanation that is logically cleaner, empirically sound, and also applicable to wheat-producing regions such as North China.

A major difference between this model and many other game theory–based theories of norm creation is that it does not assume self-interested rationality on *all* levels of human decision making,[72] but instead recognizes that normative internalization potentially plays an important role in distributing social status. As the considerable sociological literature on "status inconsistency" observes, norms that determine status distribution are frequently "inconsistent" with any meritocratic consideration, whether wealth, preexisting sociopolitical authority, physical prowess, intelligence, or education.[73] This suggests the influence of internalized norms, perhaps of religious or moral beliefs, but also potentially of racial, ethnic, or gender bias. Unlike tenancy or land transaction norms, people are commonly exposed to status-distribution norms – something as simple as "respect the elderly" – from a very young age, often in the form of ethical exhortations, thus increasing the likelihood of widespread internalization.

There is considerable reason to suspect that the social dominance of Confucian generational hierarchies in early modern China was largely the result of normative internalization. Chapter 5 addresses this issue in much greater detail, but it is nonetheless helpful to preview its basic arguments here. Most importantly, Confucian kinship hierarchies had simply existed for so long and on such a massive scale that it would be shocking if no significant internalization had taken place. Kinship hierarchies were a staple of Chinese social life since at least the wave of local lineage building around AD 900. By the seventeenth century, they were an indisputable

---

[71] *See* discussion at Chapter 6.   [72] *See* discussion below at Section C.
[73] Zhang (2008).

cornerstone of local social organization in "core" macroregions. Not coincidentally, local lineage building correlated with the rise of Song and Ming Neo-Confucianism, which systematized the legal and social enforcement of kinship hierarchies with unprecedented metaphysical rigor. Correspondingly, one finds, in every era, an overwhelming amount of writing that proclaimed embeddedness within kinship hierarchies as "the natural way of heaven," including political documents, moral and philosophical treatises, lineage registries, or local gazetteers.

Moral internalization coexisted, of course, with a variety of functionalist factors. With a few exceptions, the Song, Ming, and Qing governments promoted lineage building as a cost-effective way to establish local order and decentralize the political elite. Government sponsorship contributed, therefore, to the popularity of Confusion kinship hierarchies, as did the many socioeconomic functions that kinship networks performed, including dispute resolution, crime prevention, poor relief, and education.

These functionalist factors do not, however, fully explain the consistent popularity of kinship hierarchies throughout a millennium of radical political and socioeconomic change. Government sponsorship was not always reliable and often lagged far behind private demand for lineage building, particularly during the Ming and mid-Qing. Social organization and welfare functions, on the other hand, were not the exclusive domain of kinship networks but were also provided by, for example, religious sects and monasteries.[74] There was no necessary correlation between the supply of these functions and the embrace of generational hierarchies. On a more individual basis, the moral premium kinship hierarchies placed on generational seniority benefited lower-income households but limited the influence of straightforward "meritocracies" based on physical, intellectual, sociopolitical, or economic prowess. Most importantly, there could be no argument that age and generational hierarchies were the economically optimal way of lineage organization because even their proponents worried about their lack of meritocracy. This rather tangled bundle of consequences suggests that purely functionalist factors probably would have produced greater geographic and temporal variance in the popularity of kinship hierarchies than actually existed. Functionalist theories do little, in any case, to explain the never-ending outpour of moralistic writings that promoted kinship hierarchies as natural law.

---

[74] *See, e.g.*, DANIEL L. OVERMYER, FOLK BUDDHIST RELIGION: DISSENTING SECTS IN LATE TRADITIONAL CHINA 70 (1976) (highlighting the social organization functions of sectarian popular religion).

In recognizing the importance of normative internalization in establishing basic norms of social ordering and organization, the model constructed here bears some resemblance to the "precommercial ideals" thesis it attempts to replace. There are, however, enormous differences in degree. The model here basically argues for heightened standards of discretion and proof when applying theories of normative internalization to property norms, and for striking the right balance between normative internalization and self-interested negotiation. Property norms themselves, as demonstrated earlier, are usually economically sensitive and malleable. Operating in close proximity to people's core economic interests, particularly in early modern pre-industrial societies, they easily inspire considerations of material self-interest and, therefore, tend to reflect equilibrium outcomes of rational negotiation. However, self-interested negotiation itself follows certain social rules of conduct and can be affected particularly strongly by norms that determine status and authority distribution. This latter kind of norm, which affects economic well-being in less obvious ways, may be a more natural subject for internalization theories. The problem, then, with the "precommercial ideals" thesis is that it jumps too early into cultural internalization without first vetting the possibility of rational negotiation based on individual wealth maximization.

Finally, it must be emphasized that this model does *not* suggest that lower-income households in the Chinese "core" should, in theory, have *dominated* local politics and regulation. Rather, it simply suggests that they were, cumulatively, much more powerful than their English peers and should have won *more* institutional battles that were predominantly fought across class lines. The most that can be said of the "status equalizing" effects of Chinese kinship hierarchies is that they negated *some* of the political advantages of wealth, but to claim that they made wealth completely irrelevant would almost certainly be a serious exaggeration. Nonetheless, one would expect them to make at least some substantial difference in cases where both Chinese and English smallholders were fighting for their most important economic interests.

Redemption of collateralized land was almost certainly one such case. In fact, one could argue that if we could see the institutional impact of Chinese kinship hierarchies *anywhere*, we likely would see it in *dian* redemption, where the stakes for smallholders were probably much higher than the stakes for large landowners. For the former, they risked losing the source of their economic livelihood, indeed at below-market prices, if redemption deadlines were too short, whereas for the latter, even a norm of infinite redeemability would still have preserved, as discussed earlier, much of the economic value of collateralized lending. In other words, the latter probably cared less than the former and probably were willing to invest less of their sociopolitical capital to acquire desirable institutions. Another way to mentally visualize this is to apply the common cognitive assumption of declining "utility returns" to wealth: losing land was a much bigger deal for smallholders than gaining land was for large landowners. Under such circumstances, one would expect to see smallholders gain at least some institutional advantage, assuming that they had at least some sociopolitical capital to spend. This was, as detailed in Chapter 4, largely what happened in North China and the Lower Yangtze. Conversely, the inability of English smallholders to hold the (institutional) fort down even here belies the likelihood that they really had very little sociopolitical capital to speak of.

C Social Norms Theory

The historical "model" discussed in the preceding section has considerable ramifications for the expansive theoretical literature on social norms, usually defined as normative rules made by nonstate actors. Since at least the early 1990s, the study of social norms has gained enormous traction in legal scholarship, particularly within the realm of property. While scholars have proposed a great variety of theories that attempt to explain the emergence and maintenance of social norms, on the most general theoretical level, these theories fall into two large camps that, even today, interact only sporadically. The first, and probably more influential, group follows economic convention in seeing social norms as predominantly the result of rational choice by self-interested actors, usually in repeated games that encourage long-term social cooperation. Thus property norms evolve in response to external shocks that change their cost-benefit effects and are obeyed mainly because individuals or groups find that the net utility outcome of obedience outweighs that of disobedience.[75] The second group,

---

[75] Summarized in Robert C. Ellickson, *Law and Economics Discovers Social Norms*, 27 J. LEGAL STUD. 537 (1998); Richard A. Posner, *Social Norms and the Law: An Economic Approach*, 87 AM. ECON. REV. 365–69 (1997). For a specific empirical example, *see* J. MARK RAMSEYER & ERIC B. RASMUSEN, MEASURING JUDICIAL INDEPENDENCE: THE POLITICAL ECONOMY OF JUDGING IN JAPAN (2003), which applies a political economy methodology to the study of the Japanese judiciary. Their work has been challenged on multiple fronts, including methodological ones. Frank Upham, *Political Lackeys or Faithful Public Servants? Two Views of the Japanese Judiciary*, 30 L. SOC. INQUIRY 421 (2005); JOHN OWEN HALEY, THE SPIRIT OF JAPANESE LAW (2006).

which actually has a far longer history, follows sociological and anthropological tradition in arguing that both the emergence and sustenance of social norms rely primarily on societal internalization of certain cultural and moral values. People usually create and obey norms because they believe them to be inherently just or proper.[76] The study of historical tradition is therefore crucial to understanding such behavior.

Rational-choice analysis of property norm evolution has come a long way since Harold Demsetz's seminal 1967 work, "Toward a Theory of Property Rights."[77] Although Demsetz's proposition that property norms emerge and evolve when the benefits of having a new norm outweigh the costs remains enormously influential, later works have added multiple layers of complexity to this basic assumption. Many have, first of all, attempted to illustrate the precise mechanisms and procedures through which norm evolution takes place, an area where Demsetz was highly ambiguous. They have also incorporated into the model numerous variations in the cost of regime transition, the number and influence of interested parties, information costs, the existence of "rule entrepreneurs," and so on in hopes of mirroring real-life property issues more accurately.[78]

Perhaps most importantly, they have differentiated between cost-benefit analysis at the individual level and calculations of overall group utility, leading to an ongoing debate over whether individual rationality creates norms that benefit the entire group, either under Pareto efficiency or the more relaxed standards of Kaldor-Hicks efficiency. Many public-choice theorists would discard the group-utility dimension altogether, arguing that property norms emerge only if they favor the self-interest of sociopolitically dominant elites. Whether that self-interest promotes overall group utility is largely random.[79] Others have expressed much greater optimism, pointing to the existence of "norm entrepreneurs" within social groups and to the theoretical potential of evolutionary game theory to explain how self-interested negotiation can

---

[76] Amitai Etzioni, *Social Norms: Internalization, Persuasion and History*, 34 L. & Soc. Rev. 157 (2000), at 167–68; Robert D. Cooter, *Book Review: Against Legal Centricism*, 81 Cal. L. Rev. 417 (1993).

[77] Harold Demsetz, *Toward a Theory of Property Rights*, 57 Am. Econ. Rev. 347–59 (1967).

[78] *E.g.*, Jonathan Bendor & Piotr Swistak, *The Evolution of Norms*, 106 Am. J. Sociology 1493 (2001); Gary S. Becker & Kevin M. Murphy, *A Theory of Rational Addiction*, in Accounting for Tastes 50 (Gary S. Becker ed., 1996).

[79] Posner (1996); Russell Hardin, One for All: The Logic of Group Conflict (1995).

produce socially optimal results.[80] For both schools of thought, there are inevitable concerns about how much systematic rationality and strategic planning we can assume about individuals, even political elites – a concern only exacerbated by the rise of behavioral economics.[81]

On the other end of the theoretical spectrum are sociological, anthropological, and psychological studies of norms that place much greater stock in the moral internalization of social behavior.[82] Here social norms are commonly seen as derivative of internalized cultural, ethical, and religious values. Such studies existed long before law and economics scholars "rediscovered" social norms and are far richer in empirical material, but lack clear theoretical paradigms of how values, culture, and norms interact. A few decades ago, the lack of theoretical cohesion prompted some to describe the field as a "swamp."[83] Although some recent works have attempted to reorganize the relevant literature,[84] it still provides few systematic studies on how, precisely, "irrational" values affect norms and law. Certainly they have high-lighted many areas of potential effect, including, for example, the interpretation of legal ambiguities and pluralisms or normative enforcement in the absence of clear sanctions, but such studies, largely by design, rarely attempt to provide testable hypotheses on human behavior. Perhaps more bewildering to law and economics scholars is the tendency of such scholarship to treat social cultures as consolidated "operative engines" without either explaining how culture operates at the individual level or carefully considering whether self-interested rationality could explain away many phenomena they consider

---

[80] Robert C. Ellickson, *The Market for Social Norms*, 3 AMERICAN L. & ECON. REV. 1–49 (2001); Bendor & Swistak (2001).

[81] *E.g.*, Robert E. Scott, *The Limits of Behavioral Theories of Law and Social Norms*, 86 VA. L. REV. 1602 (2000). *See also* PIERRE BOURDIEU, THE LOGIC OF PRACTICE (Richard Nice trans., 1990) (developing a theory of *habitus* that counters rational-choice theories).

[82] *E.g.*, Joseph William Singer, *How Property Norms Construct the Externalities of Ownership* (Working Paper 2008), *available at* http://ssrn.com/abstract=1093341; Eduardo Moisés Peñalver & Sonia K. Katyal, *Property Outlaws*, 155 UNIV. PA. L. REV. 1095–147 (2007); UGO MATTEI, BASIC PRINCIPLES OF PROPERTY LAW 5–6 (2000) (describing property norms as "natural" products of a "spontaneous order"); Stewart MacAulay, *Non-contractual Relations in Business*, 28 AM. SOC. REV. 55 (1963); H. LAURENCE ROSS, SETTLED OUT OF COURT (rev. ed. 1980); David M. Trubek, *Toward a Social Theory of Law: An Essay on the Study of Law and Development*, 82 YALE L.J. 1–50 (1972).

[83] Ellickson (1998), at 549.

[84] Etzioni (2000); Mark C. Suchman & Lauren B. Edelman, *Book Review: Legal Rational Myths*, 21 LAW & SOC. INQUIRY 903–41 (1996).

"cultural."[85] It is worth pointing out that the "precommercial ideals" thesis discussed earlier demonstrates quite vividly both the basic contours of this literature and its main flaws.

There have been several attempts to bridge the divide. Some have proposed a combined "law and socioeconomics" approach, which simply recognizes that some norms are the outcome of functionalist rationality, whereas others are internalized.[86] The basic observation that property norms are a mixture of rational design and internalized mores seems eminently reasonable, but one would ideally also like to know which kinds of norms tend to be rational-choice outcomes and which are more often internalized, not to mention how the two categories interact. One proposed solution to this latter problem is to differentiate between proximate origins and deeper, more systematic ones: changes in social values tend to be the immediate triggers of norm evolution, but the value changes themselves often possess strong functionalist undertones. Demsetz himself noted, for example, that changes in property institutions more often stem from "changes in social mores" than from conscious attempts to address new externality problems, although the long-term viability of new mores does depend on their success in solving those problems.[87] A more recent example is Penalver and Katyal's work on "property outlaws," which notes that whereas property norms reflect "evolving community values," those values themselves are often purposely engineered by discontented parties.[88] Intriguing as these theories may be, their incorporation of normative internalization seems uncomfortably reluctant. The subjection of sociocultural values to functionalist filtering and predetermination leaves very little room for substantive "internalization."

Conceptually, how norms are enforced and obeyed is a separate line of inquiry from how they emerge and evolve, but the patterns of interaction between rational-choice and internalization theories are remarkably similar in both. For the past two decades, law and economics scholars have proposed a wide array of theories on norm enforcement and adherence. The most well known of these highlight the role of esteem sanctions and "signaling" in encouraging adherence

---

[85] Ellickson (1998), at 549–51.

[86] Etzioni (2000); Oliver E. Williamson, *The New Institutional Economics: Taking Stock, Looking Ahead*, 38 J. Econ. Lit. 595 (2000); Mark A. Edwards, *Acceptable Deviance and Property Rights*, 43 Conn. L. Rev. 457, 464–75 (2010); Peñalver & Katyal (2007).

[87] Demsetz (1967), at 350–51.   [88] Peñalver & Katyal (2007).

to norms.[89] Alternatively, pure game theory may also be able to explain norm adherence by assuming the existence of repeated games and evolutionary strategies.[90] In contrast to these rational-choice models, law and society scholars more often highlight the moral and ethical dimensions of norm adherence, noting that many people obey social norms simply because it is "the right thing to do," either because they agree with the norm itself or because they believe in obeying established norms.[91] Unsurprisingly, scholars who have proposed merging economic and sociological theories of norm evolution also tend to support similarly merged approaches toward norm adherence and enforcement, arguing that rational choice and internalization often coexist and mutually complement each other.[92] More ironically, some scholars who distinctly favor rational-choice theories of norm adherence are quite open minded about the importance of internalization in norm evolution: Richard McAdams, for example, emphasizes that norm adherence is largely sustained through the threat of low-cost esteem sanctions, but freely grants that the substantive content of norms may very much depend on commonly shared values and mores.[93]

In recent years, some scholars have explored yet another way to merge rational-choice and internalization theories of norm creation and adherence. They suggest that social norms are actually organized into "pyramids," where "upper level" norms may either shape the procedures and settings under which "lower level" norms are negotiated or directly influence their substantive content.[94] For example, a commitment to political democracy could be a higher-level norm relative to actual legislation produced by the democratic process. Alternatively, in some societies, a shared belief in the basic equality of human beings might be seen as a higher-level norm relative to the establishment of institutional democracy. In either example, the higher-level norms do not actually predetermine lower-level norms, but rather limit the range of possible outcomes and perhaps alter the odds in favor of or against certain outcomes.

---

[89] Eric A. Posner, Law and Social Norms (2000). [90] Bendor & Swistak (2001).
[91] Cooter (1993). [92] Etzioni (2000).
[93] McAdams (1997b); Richard H. McAdams, *Signaling Discount Rates: Law, Norms and Economic Methodology*, 110 Yale L.J. 625, 643–54, 663–68 (2000).
[94] *E.g.*, Amir N. Licht, *Social Norms and the Law: Why Peoples Obey the Law*, 4 Rev. L & Econ. 715 (2008) (citing Hans Kelsen, Pure Theory of Law 193–278 (1989)).

The volume of norms in each level presumably decreases as we move up the pyramid, until only the most durable and foundational values remain in the top levels. Correspondingly, the likelihood that norms are morally internalized increases at higher levels. A supporting contention, drawing heavily on psychological studies of childhood development, is that certain kinds of norms, particularly those governing basic social interactions such as kinship and core religious affinity, are more prone to internalization than explicitly economic norms such as property and contract norms.[95] Most conceivably, this is so because individuals are usually exposed to them at a much younger age, when personal values are still in their formative stage.[96] These constitute, then, the higher-level norms that shape how lower-level economic norms are negotiated.

Intriguing as these theories are, they remain, for the most part, theoretically underdeveloped and empirically untested. The handful of relevant articles has, understandably, focused on outlining the general framework described here rather than proposing falsifiable claims on which norms tend to reside in higher levels, how they actually influence lower-tier norms, and whether these normative paradigms are capable of explaining broader historical trends.

These chapters illustrate how a historical examination of these issues might proceed. The Chinese and English property institutions examined here demonstrate both the theoretical advantages and empirical plausibility of norm pyramids. As noted earlier, neither straightforward normative internalization, in the form of "precommercial ideals of permanence in landholding," nor pure functionalist rationality, which highlights the cooperative nature of rice agriculture, provides an adequate explanation for the stark Sino-English divergence in land pawning and tenancy customs. Rather, this book proposes a model where rationally negotiated property norm outcomes are influenced by morally internalized status-distribution norms. Compared with specific property institutions on land redemption or tenant eviction, these status-distribution norms had a much longer history and occupied a far more prominent position in Confucian intellectual discourse. Central-level legislation, while often outright hostile to *dian* and permanent

---

[95] Robert D. Cooter, *Decentralized Law for a Complex Economy: The Structural Approach to Adjudicating the New Law Merchant*, 144 U. PENN. L. REV. 1643, 1661–62 (1996).

[96] Licht (2008), at 721.

tenancy customs, never wavered in its endorsement and promotion of kinship hierarchies since at least the seventh century *Tang Code*. On the English side, the dependency of social status on landed wealth was also a far more durable norm compared with tightly contested customs of land conveyance and tenancy. It seems reasonable, therefore, to posit these status-distribution norms as "higher level" norms relative to specific property institutions.

4

Kinship, Social Hierarchy, and Institutional Divergence (Empirics)

This chapter is the empirical centerpiece of the book. It substantiates the model in Chapter 3, broken down into three subarguments. First, *dian* redemption customs were the source of considerable social tension and negotiation – predominantly between smallholders and larger landowners. They were therefore far more likely the equilibrium outcome of such negotiation than the institutional manifestation of internalized "norms of permanency in landholding." Second, due in large part to the prevalence of kinship hierarchies, low-income households often occupied positions of considerable sociopolitical authority and dignity. Third, kinship hierarchies and corresponding status distribution patterns significantly influenced the negotiation and enforcement of property norms. A fourth section compares these subarguments with corresponding patterns and trends in English sociolegal history, where tight correlations between status and landed wealth drove property institutions toward the opposite direction of Chinese *dian* customs.

In a fifth section, I discuss the model's applicability to Chinese permanent tenancy (*yongdian*) customs. If kinship networks did indeed provide lower-income households with the kind of sociopolitical capital for which I argue, then we would expect to see their impact in at least a few other major property institutions. I therefore argue that they probably did influence the negotiation of tenancy institutions in the Lower Yangtze and parts of North China and, in fact, probably moved them in tenant-friendly directions. Given the length constraints of this book, the argument will necessarily be abbreviated and somewhat reliant on secondary

Portions of this chapter were published in Taisu Zhang, *Social Hierarchies and the Formation of Customary Property Law in Pre-Industrial China and England*, 62 Am. J. Comp. L. 171 (2014).

scholarship – a full-length treatment would add another three to four chapters – but it nonetheless aims to persuade readers that it is, at the very least, supported by a preponderance of published evidence. Avenues for further substantiation are identified and in many ways preview the research that I intend to provide in future works.

Four major source collections are used here: first, 284 late Qing and Republican-era *dian*-related cases from various court archives, including 202 local civil disputes and 82 provincial or central-level homicide cases; second, around 600 land contracts from the same time frame; third, 12 lineage registries and regulations geographically overlapping with most of the contracts and cases; and, fourth, several major rural surveys conducted by both Chinese and Japanese researchers during the 1930s and early 1940s. On the English side, the arguments derive mainly from the considerable secondary literature on early modern property institutions, kinship, and social status.

A Conflict and Negotiation

The clearest indication that *dian* redemption customs were never really internalized by the Qing rural population is the sheer volume of litigation that arises from related issues. As noted earlier, even after the Qing and Republican governments issued multiple laws and regulations that prohibited redemption after certain periods of time, local magistrates very rarely enforced them, most conceivably out of pragmatic deference to local customs. Their inactivity did not, however, stop landowners from bringing large numbers of redemption-related disputes to their courts, including a substantial number that directly invoked the regulatory and legal year limits on redemption. Magistrates allowed almost all of these to end in mediation, but did often comment, usually informally, on the appropriateness of certain actions.

The overall volume of *dian* disputes is perhaps best illustrated by statistical analysis of a few well-preserved local case archives. Within the geographic regions on which this book focuses, two major legal archives have been unearthed, one at Baodi, Hebei Province, and the other at Longquan, Zhejiang Province.[1] Of these, only the latter is well preserved enough to project a reasonably solid statistical overview. As discussed in Chapter 1, It holds 18,434 cases from 1910 to 1949, including 10,614 civil

---

[1]   The latter is currently housed at the History Department of Zhejiang University and is being edited for publication.

suits and 7,820 criminal cases. Accounting for the loss of case files over time, the average number of civil cases per year probably ranged from 300 to 600 – in a county of roughly 20,000 households – consistent with preexisting estimates of late Qing and Republican county-level caseloads.[2] Within the 10,614 civil suits, 430 stemmed from a dispute concerning *dian* sales, of which 386 focused on whether the *dian* seller should be allowed to redeem. This suggests that perhaps 4 to 5 percent of civil disputes – some fifteen to thirty cases per year – were *dian* related, with over 85 percent of those related directly to redemption disputes.[3] These are sizable numbers by any measure, suggesting that *dian* redemption disputes were one of the most significant sources of social dispute and conflict. If we consider the overwhelmingly strong possibility that the great majority of *dian* redemption disputes were not litigated,[4] it seems fairly safe to assume that *dian* redemption was, in absolute terms, a highly contested and combustible issue.

A more difficult question is how many of the 386 redemption-related cases involved claims by the *dian* buyer that too much time had passed since the original contract for redemption to be allowable. Academic researchers still have only limited access to the full case archive, which makes it highly difficult to retrieve even a majority of these cases. I rely here on a randomly selected sample of sixty-five cases related specifically to *dian* redemption, out of a larger sample of eighty *dian*-related cases.[5] Within these sixty-five cases, twenty-five featured express claims that the *dian* seller's redemption rights had expired after a certain period of time, a ratio of 38 percent. It was, in fact, the single largest reason relied on by unwilling *dian* buyers to reject redemption efforts. The second largest, with fourteen cases, was the claim that the seller had attempted to redeem before the guaranteed-usage period had expired – that is, the redemption request came too early, as opposed to too late in the other twenty-five cases. The remaining twenty-six cases are more diverse, ranging from claims that the original transaction was a permanent sale, not a *dian* sale, to disputes over the proper redemption price, to blatant disregard of redemption requests without stating any reason.

---

[2] *See* HUANG (1996), at 164–67; MACAULEY (1998), at 62.

[3] Longquan Index. Search with keywords "典," "当," "押," and "赎."

[4] Like most other works that have addressed the issue, HUANG (1996) argues that most disputes were handled without interference by local courts and officials in the "informal realm" of local mediation. In this regard, Qing and Republican China were not so different from any modern society, even the "uber-litigious" American populace.

[5] *See* Appendix A, Part I.

Although one cannot directly project these numbers onto the national, or even provincial, level, they do at least demonstrate that *dian* redemption deadlines, or the lack thereof, were in fact a frequently contested issue. Of the twenty-five cases, sixteen involved *dian* contracts that had been made more than thirty years prior to the redemption attempt, the oldest of which was made seventy-two years prior.[6] In at least five of the twenty-five, the *dian* buyer expressly petitioned the magistrate to disregard local customs and enforce government regulations, citing in particular 1917 provincial interpretations of the *Regulations on Clearing Land Tenure*, which, considerably more aggressively than the regulations' original text, banned redemption of *dian* contracts after thirty years.[7] Clearly, some not-insignificant portion of the local population both knew of legal limitations on *dian* redemption and openly preferred them to customary laws that allowed for unlimited redemption.

There is space here only to outline a few cases, but they are very telling. In the case of *Yang Cidian v. Mei Youqi*, Yang's grandfather had *dian* sold land to Mei's grandfather in 1853, which Yang attempted to redeem first in 1921 and then again in 1925.[8] At some point between 1853 and 1921, part of the Mei family migrated south to Fujian Province. The ensuing labor shortage back in Longquan led them to rent the transacted land back to the Yang family. Around 1921, Yang Cidian heard rumors that Mei was contemplating selling his conditional ownership to a third party, probably to take advantage of rising land prices. Fearing future complications and disputes, Yang attempted to redeem the land, citing language in the original contract that allowed him to redeem after seven years from the original transaction – per local custom, he argued, this meant that he could redeem at any time after seven years had passed. The Mei family did not directly contradict this argument but did persuade him to stay his redemption efforts by offering him an additional payment, bringing the transaction price up to current market standards. In 1925, Yang again demanded redemption. When negotiation and attempted communal mediation failed to generate consensus, the case went to court, where Mei asked the judge to reject Yang's interpretation of the contractual language and enforce

---

[6] *Id.*

[7] Longquan M003-01-00038 (1919); Longquan M003-01-00586 (1921); Longquan M003-01-02147 (1920); Longquan M003-01-02160 (1925); Longquan M003-01-15483 (1932) (fifty years).

[8] Longquan M003-01-02160 (1925).

the thirty-year provincial deadline on *dian* redemption. Otherwise, he argued, the regulation would be meaningless. The case ended abruptly after an initial deposition, suggesting that the two sides settled out of court.

The fact pattern in *Yang v. Mei* is quite typical of the sixteen cases mentioned earlier, even if the temporal span – seventy-two years – was unusually long. In the 1924 case of *He Hezheng v. He Zuojian*, for example, He Hezheng attempted to redeem a *dian* sale made in 1892.[9] Citing the thirty-year deadline, He Zuojian asked the court to reject this attempt and declare him the full owner of the property. After a drawn-out litigation process, the parties settled out of court to unknown terms. Similarly, in the 1922 case of *Woman Xu Wu v. Mao Zibao*, Mao attempted to redeem property a female relative had *dian* sold to Xu's father-in-law in 1888, but met with initial rejection.[10] Arguing that too much time had passed since the initial transaction, Xu sued in court for full ownership of the property. Rather than filing a counterclaim, Mao shrewdly asked senior relatives on both sides to intervene and mediate. Xu eventually relented and allowed him to redeem.

There are clear traces in these cases of normative tension between one party's reliance on local custom and communal dispute resolution and the other's appeal to government-issued regulations. Predictably, their preferences correlated directly with their economic interests: the *dian* sellers preferred customary interpretations that would give them virtually unlimited redemption authority, whereas the *dian* buyers came down strongly on the side of state regulations that limited redemption to thirty years. This dichotomy exists in all sixteen cases that involved *dian* transactions of more than thirty years and, rather oddly, even more strongly in two cases that did not. In these latter cases, the *dian* buyers attempted to interpret state laws in ways that – had they been even remotely plausible – would have limited *dian* redemption far more severely than any thirty-year deadline. One argued that he would gain full ownership if the *dian* seller did not redeem within a few weeks after the guaranteed-usage period had expired.[11] The other proposed that the deadline for redemption was actually *two* years after the initial transaction, not thirty.[12] If *dian* buyers were at all sympathetic to "permanency in landholding," many of them certainly did not act like it.

---

[9] Longquan M003-01-00879 (1924). [10] Longquan M003-01-11063 (1922).
[11] Longquan M003-01-00126 (1928). [12] Longquan M003-01-00821 (1926).

Moreover, there is considerable evidence in these cases that *dian* buyers were generally far wealthier than *dian* sellers. Multiple *dian* sellers described their own economic circumstances as "poor," "tight," and "in shambles" while referring to the *dian* buyers as among the "wealthiest households" in the village.[13] While this may simply have been a rhetorical flourish designed to rouse the court's sympathy, the fact that the *dian* buyers in question never contradicted these descriptions, even after ruthlessly attacking the *dian* sellers' moral standing, lends them a fair dose of credibility.

The substantive composition of *dian* disputes brought before Qing County courts did not seem to differ qualitatively from the Republican-era patterns observed here. In, for example, the sample of twenty-six *dian*-related cases from the Baodi, Baxian, and Danxin archives that I use in Chapter 1, whether redemption rights expired after a certain number of years was the main point of contention in nine cases, outnumbering all other causes of dispute.[14] The time span between initial transaction and attempted redemption in these cases ranged from eleven to seventy-seven years, all beyond the ten-year deadline set by the Board of Finance. All nine cases were eventually resolved out of court, generally under terms quite favorable to the *dian* seller.

A much larger spate of *dian* disputes can be found in three private legal archives from the Guangxu era (1875–1908).[15] Each archive collected legal decisions made by one specific official during his term as local magistrate, purportedly to preserve his legal wisdom for future generations to "study and admire." Many Ming and Qing scholar-officials engaged in such self-admiring activity, but these three are, by and large, the best-preserved Guangxu-era collections available today. By some coincidence, all three magistrates served in the Lower Yangtze, within a couple dozen miles – and less than a decade – of each other. Combined, their private archives contain 1,063 cases, including ninety-six *dian*-related cases, fifty-nine of which involved a dispute of redemption. Thirty-four of the fifty-nine

---

[13] *E.g.*, Longquan M003-01-00078 (1946); Longquan M003-01-0642 (1919); Longquan M003-01-00787 (1947); Longquan M003-01-01778 (1945); Longquan M003-01-2543 (1912); Longquan M003-01-16292 (1931).

[14] See discussion in Chapter 1, Section C.

[15] Ni Wangzhong, *Zhuji Yumin Jiyao*, in 10 LIDAI PANLI PANDU [CASES FROM PAST ERAS] 301(Yang Yifan et al. eds., China Soc. Sci. Press, 2005); Sun Dinglie, *Xisizhai Jueshi*, in 10 LIDAI PANLI PANDU (2005), at 499; Zhao Youban, *Liren Pandu Huiji*, in 12 LIDAI PANLI PANDU (2005), at 109.

focused on whether redemption rights could expire.[16] These ratios are reasonably close to what I found in Baodi, Baxian, Danxin, and Republican-era Longquan, clearly suggesting that *dian* redemption deadlines were a significant source of social tension and dispute throughout the late Qing and Republic.

There are, of course, a number of specific empirical caveats in using private case collections. Because the point is to present the magistrate's decision making in a positive light, such collections tend to leave out cases that were not concluded via formal adjudication or court-directed mediation. Moreover, any magistrate who felt comfortable in publishing his own private case archive was, in all likelihood, far more prone to issuing decisions – not to mention far better versed in legal materials – than the average local official who had little or no legal training and relied primarily on professional legal clerks to handle adjudication. All in all, private case collections present a very biased, generally far too positive, view of local judicial behavior.

However, the larger private archives, those that contain several hundred cases within the span of a decade or less, probably did not exclude cases based on the nature of the dispute. All three collections used here belong to this category. Unlike many smaller archives that contain only a few dozen morally complex or "instructional" cases, the vast majority of disputes these collections hold are of the mundane, everyday variety, usually dispatched within a few sentences without recourse to any overarching moral principle. These include petty disputes over trespass, property boundaries, minor frauds, debt collection, inheritance disputes, spousal spats, and, of course, *dian* disputes of all shapes and sizes involving anything from a quarter *mu* (4 percent of an acre) of land to a few dozen *mu*. There is, therefore, no good reason to suspect that these collections significantly misrepresented the relative frequency of *dian*-related litigation.

Widespread social tension over *dian* redemption deadlines also surfaces in a variety of nonlegal sources. The most important of these are Japanese rural surveys ("Mantetsu surveys") of North China, conducted by researchers from the Southern Manchuria Railway Company during the early 1940s, when the Japanese occupation of China was at its zenith.[17] While the researchers visited a large number of villages in Hebei and Shandong, they focused in particular on six villages, four in Hebei and two in Shandong. Unlike some of their earlier forays into rural North China, for

---

[16] *See* Appendix A, Part II.   [17] MANTETSU SURVEYS (1957), vols. 1–5.

this particular set of surveys, the researchers decided to separate themselves from the military – to the extent possible[18] – and attempted to
conduct predominantly academic inquiries into the social and political
institutions that governed everyday life. Apart from collecting economic
data, their research focused largely on interviewing villagers about local
governance, customary law, religious practice, and other aspects of
everyday life.

Under favorable conditions, researchers were able to make four to six
visits to the same village, familiarize themselves with the locals, and discuss
the same topics with villagers from highly diverse socioeconomic backgrounds. Naturally, because they were, after all, foreign researchers in a
conquered land, not all villages welcomed their presence. In at least one
village, locals were so hostile that the researchers had to conduct their
interviews from the local county seat, transporting in a few village elites
from their homes via truck, which naturally made for very poor discussions. Nonetheless, as several prominent historians have pointed out, most
of the surveyed villages were not quite as resistant, and many households
conversed with the research teams quite readily and openly.[19] Moreover,
the richness and scope of this material are virtually unparalleled in early
modern Chinese historical sources, and it would be foolish not to take
advantage, if ideally in conjunction with other sources. The best way to use
them, as Prasenjit Duara has pointed out, is "extensively and intensively,"
that is, to broadly compare the responses of any one villager with that of
other interviewees, covering as much social and economic diversity as
possible.[20]

One particularly salient theme that emerges from such a comparison is
the extent to which villagers from different economic backgrounds quar-
reled over property norms. Given that nearly 90 percent of documented
land mortgagors and sellers during the later 1930s in these villages came
from the bottom half of landholders – whereas only 3 percent belonged to
the top 25 percent – this is highly intuitive.[21] Nonetheless, the interviews
offer a large number of striking anecdotes. In each of the two best-surveyed
villages, Sibeichai and Shajing, researchers surveyed nearly a dozen villagers about what, in their minds, were the customary rules that governed

---

[18] This was sometimes impossible due to the hostility of the villagers. *See* LOUISE YOUNG,
JAPAN'S TOTAL EMPIRE: MANCHURIA AND THE CULTURE OF WARTIME IMPERIALISM
295–97 (1999).

[19] DUARA (1988); HUANG (1985).   [20] DUARA (1988), at 6.

[21] 3 MANTETSU SURVEYS, at 5; 4 MANTETSU SURVEYS, at 218.

dian transactions. In Sibeichai, everyone interviewed agreed that *dian* redemption claims had no deadline but could be made any time after the guaranteed-usage period had expired.[22] At least one of the local landlords complained, however, that such rules made land buying inconvenient and slow, suggesting considerable reluctance toward the customary norm.[23] In contrast, not a single smallholder – specifically, not a single below-average landholder – in any of the surveyed villages ever questioned either the existence or the normative desirability of a norm of infinite redeemability.

On several other normative points, the landlords clashed openly with poorer village political elites over what the proper norms were. The former village chief, who supported a family of ten on around forty-eight *mu* (less than eight acres), argued that *dian* sellers could redeem the property even within the "guaranteed-usage period" and even if they owed additional debt to the *dian* buyer. Moreover, if they ever wished to sell the property permanently, the *dian* buyer would not possess any right of first purchase, but would simply be repaid by the original *dian* seller from the permanent sales proceeds. To summarize, he basically believed that *dian* buyers had no control over the property outside of usage rights until redemption.[24] Several other median or lower landholders agreed.[25] Landlords and wealthier farmers, who made up the great majority of *dian* buyers in this village, disagreed on every point: They did possess a right of first purchase, second only to the *dian* seller's immediate relatives in priority. They could also postpone redemption if the *dian* seller owed them any outstanding debt or if the guaranteed-usage period had yet to expire.[26]

---

[22] 3 MANTETSU SURVEYS (1957), at 166, 172, 176, 246, 273, 312–17. Philip Huang has a different interpretation of the Sibeichai interviews and claims that local customs allowed a separate kind of collateralized transaction, *zhidi jieqian* ("pointing to the land and borrowing money"), that gave the creditor the right to take the collateral outright. HUANG (1985) at 176. His primary evidence for this is a few contracts reproduced in 3 MANTETSU SURVEYS (1957), at 312–13, which state that "if the debtor fails to repay the full loan by the arranged time [note: usually 3–5 years after the original loan], the creditor may do what he pleases with the land." However, on the next page, the interviewee, Zhang Leqing, makes clear that "do what he pleases with the land" simply means that the creditor can now enter the land and farm it while converting the somewhat informal *zhidi jieqian* contract into a more formal *dian* contract. It does *not* mean that he gains full ownership or title and certainly does not mean that the debtor's right of redemption is extinguished. Quite the opposite, the interviewee then states that this right remains valid and can be exercised at any time after the "guaranteed-usage period" stated in the new *dian* contact has passed. 3 MANTETSU SURVEYS (1957), at 314.

[23] *Id.* at 174.   [24] *Id.* at 170–71, 273, 275.   [25] *Id.* at 245, 263.

[26] *Id.* at 165–67, 173–74, 247–48.

Clashes over these diverging interpretations took place in several forums. At the most extreme, when one of the landlords refused to allow the village chief to redeem a piece of property, citing outstanding debt unrelated to the initial transaction, the chief sued in the county court. The lawsuit was ongoing at the time of the interviews. There were also many tense moments in village council meetings and during dispute mediation. By the time the researchers had arrived, many of the landlords had largely resigned themselves to the fact that they were incapable of imposing their interpretation of local custom on the *dian* sellers, complaining that they were "powerless" to persuade or coerce local peasants into abandoning their archaic customs.[27]

In Shajing, social discord existed not only over the comparatively minor issues that villagers disputed in Sibeichai, but also over whether *dian* redemption rights truly were interminable. Most interviewees stated that local custom allowed redemption regardless of time passage since the initial contract,[28] but at least one interviewee, by no coincidence one of the largest landowners in the village, declared that the actual governing principle was the thirty-year limit on *dian* redemptions enacted by the 1929 Republican Civil Code.[29] When asked if they knew about this rule, three of the poorer interviewees – who believed that *dian* redemption had no deadline, that *dian* buyers enjoyed no right of first purchase, and that "guaranteed-usage periods" were not binding – bluntly answered "No."[30]

Three other villages, Houxiazhai,[31] Wudian,[32] and Lengshuigou, resembled Sibeichai more than Shajing, in that all interviewees affirmed the basic rule that *dian* redemption did not have a deadline but disagreed over whether *dian* buyers had a right of first purchase.[33] There was, however, at least one dissenting voice in the remaining village, Houjiaying. There an interviewee declared that "[w]hile the old rule was that redemption could take place at any time, now it must be done within thirty years."[34] This man was a once-wealthy factory owner who possessed some real estate that his deceased brother had *dian* purchased years ago from poorer neighbors, relying on it to maintain a decent standard of living. Considering these circumstances, it is hardly surprising that he both knew of the thirty-year redemption law and attempted to use it to his own advantage. Other

---

[27] Discussed in detail in Section C.   [28] 2 MANTETSU SURVEYS (1957), at 174, 187, 269.
[29] *Id.* at 169.   [30] *Id.* at 269.   [31] Vol. 4.   [32] Vol. 5.
[33] For Lengshuigou, *see* 4 MANTETSU SURVEYS (1957), at 205–06, 214, 222–24, 257. For Houxiazhai, *see* 4 MANTETSU SURVEYS (1957), at 482–85, 508–11. For Wudian, *see* 5 MANTETSU SURVEYS (1957), at 531, 562–63, 578, 583–84.
[34] 5 MANTETSU SURVEYS (1957), at 286.

relatively poor interviewees, when asked about this issue, strongly dis-agreed: "[T]he property is mine even if I *dian* sold it ... and it can be redeemed at any time."[35]

The picture that emerges from this array of sources, cases, and inter-views alike is one of tension and dispute, but not, however, of social chaos in which no operative customary law exists. Despite the large array of cases collected here that involved the *dian* buyer arguing that redemption rights expired after either ten or thirty years, an equally eye-catching trend is that when the great majority of these cases were resolved out of court, these same people almost always agreed to terms quite favorable to the *dian* seller, at least in cases that report the settlement terms. Most often, after further negotiation between senior relatives from both sides, they would simply allow the *dian* seller to redeem.[36] In the other cases, they managed to retain possession of the land, but only after giving the seller an additional payment and sometimes without receiving any promise that redemption was henceforth prohibited.[37] This casts into doubt the strength of their resolve against "backward" or "archaic" *dian* redemption customs that allowed unlimited redeemability, despite the strong language they some-times employed in litigation filings. Their behavior is far more consistent with that of a practical "forum shopper" who attempts to take advantage of the more accommodating property norms provided by the central government, but swiftly conforms to customary norms once social pressure intensifies, than with that of an entrenched dissenter who denies the funda-mental validity of customary law and simply refuses to abide by it.

The resigned complaints of frustrated Sibeichai landlords provide fur-ther support for this interpretation. Even in Shajing and Houjiaying, the few interviewees who proposed overriding traditional custom with the civil code's thirty-year deadline expressed no doubt that local customs did provide for unlimited *dian* redemption. Shajing and Houjiaying were, in any case, the only two villages in a sample of six where such customs appeared to be under any significant challenge. Previous scholarship has, of course, demonstrated that unlimited *dian* redeemability was a staple of customary law throughout North China and the Lower Yangtze.[38]

[35] *Id.* at 266.
[36] See discussion at Chapter 1, Section C; Longquan M003-01-00642 (1919); Longquan M003-01-00787 (1947); Longquan M003-01-01166 (1920); Longquan M003-01-11063 (1922); Longquan M003-01-15821 (1943).
[37] *E.g.*, Longquan M003-01-01283 (1923); Longquan M003-01-05358 (1948).
[38] Another possible piece of evidence that customs protecting infinite *dian* redeemability were both widespread and powerful comes from eighty-two provincial-level homicide

Moreover, despite their numerous complaints against customary norms, these North China landlords continued to make *dian* purchases in apparently large numbers throughout the 1930s and early 1940s. For example, Wang Zuozhou, the largest landlord in the region near Sibeichai Village, made over 100 *mu* worth of *dian* purchases from 1931 to 1941. In general, around 30 percent of arable land in the region was under a *dian* contract when the researchers arrived.[39] Other villages – for which a formal estimate cannot be made – likely had a low figure, but *dian* contracts were a routine part of economic life there, something with which villagers had great familiarity. The surveyors had no trouble collecting multiple sample *dian* contracts from any village.

There is, therefore, strong historical evidence that local communities effectively regulated *dian* transactions via customary law – effective in the sense that not only were customary norms widely obeyed, but also that they did not appear to cripple the market for *dian* sales. That said, these customs were clearly the source of much social contention. This strongly suggests that customary law was, to a large extent, created via negotiation between self-interested and, insofar as their preferred norms correlated strongly with their own economic interests, basically rational parties. Landowners for whom infinite *dian* redeemability was economically inconvenient showed no signs of having internalized any moral ideal of "permanency in landholding," but instead attempted to sidestep those customs by forum shopping in local courts. That they rarely succeeded speaks further to the strength of customary property norms.

cases that involved disputes over *dian* transactions – a sample that covers basically every *dian*-related homicide reported to Beijing from North China and the Lower Yangtze between 1870 and 1910. Selection of cases from the XINGKE TIBEN (First National Historical Archives, Beijing, China), on file with author. Actually, homicide levels were obviously far higher because the wane of central government authority had severely damaged the comprehensiveness of homicide reporting from local officials. Nonetheless, there is no clear reason to suspect that there was any systematic bias in the kinds of disputes that were reported. Of the eighty-two disputes, only eight focused on whether *dian* redemption rights should expire, a far lower ratio than the 35 percent of local *dian* cases, discussed earlier, that focused on this issue. Assuming tentatively that homicides are less likely in disputes that are governed by well-entrenched social norms – compared with, for instance, disputes where the relevant social norms are ambiguous or of uncertain authority – the fact that disputes over *dian* redemption deadlines were apparently less likely to lead to violence than other *dian*-related disputes may suggest that those disputes were governed by more established customs. This actually agrees quite well with the Sibeichai and Shajing interviews, where customs governing *dian* redemption deadlines seemed to generate less social tension than other *dian* customs. Given the somewhat speculative nature of this reasoning, it is only proposed here in a footnote.

[39]   3 MANTETSU SURVEYS, at 5, 177–78.

There were, in fact, multiple social processes and forums through which interested parties could negotiate customary property norms. Lineages and kinship groups were, first of all, no stranger to internal rulemaking, regularly capable of creating highly detailed codes of conduct that covered everything from broad principles of honesty and integrity to the specific norms that determined property inheritance, dispute resolution, and internal governance.[40] Most often, elder kinsmen would simply meet and enact rules for the entire kinship group, although some groups offered lower-ranked members opportunities to weigh in on the deliberations.[41] In Lower Yangtze villages, lineages were often so large that some of the more prominent ones accounted for over half the village's population,[42] making lineage regulations the functional equivalent of local customary law.

Beyond kinship group self-regulation, communal rulemaking was somewhat less structured but no less prevalent. While some villages gave regularized legislative authority to a small group of selected elites, others did not seem to recognize any clear rulemaking procedures. Nonetheless, there were plenty of the opportunities for villagers to propose, debate, and communicate social norms. During the Qing heyday, the emperor often required all villagers to gather once every month to read and discuss certain Imperial edicts, a process called the "local covenant" (*xiang yue*).[43] In practice, the reading of edicts often gave way to more practical discussion and settlement of local affairs, including property and contract norms.[44] More commonly, dispute resolution by village elders provided frequent and procedurally fluid opportunities for villagers to debate, agree on, and enforce proper norms for social and economic conduct. While disputes varied tremendously in the amount of attention they drew, over the long run, the repeated resolution of substantively similar disputes could easily generate sufficient social consensus for norm creation, especially

---

[40] See discussion in Section B.

[41] Also discussed in Section B. On the more democratic rule-making procedures of certain lineages, *see, e.g.*, Lin Ji, *Guomin Zhengfu Shiqi de Lianghu Xin Zuxue yu Xiangcun Zongzu* [*New Lineage Schools and Rural Lineages in Hunan and Hubei during the Republican Era*], (2) JINDAI SHI YANJIU [STUDIES ON EARLY MODERN HISTORY] 117–44 (2004); Li Pingliang, *Jindai Zhongguo de Xinxue, Zongzu yu Difang Zhengzhi* [*New Learning, Lineages, and Local Politics in Early Modern China*], 8(2) ZHONGGUO SHEHUI LISHI PINGLUN [COMMENTARIES ON CHINESE SOCIAL HISTORY] 86–98 (2007).

[42] SUSAN NAQUIN & EVELYN RAWSKI. CHINESE SOCIETY IN THE EIGHTEENTH CENTURY 100-01 (1987); POMERANZ (2000), at 72.

[43] Terada (1998); ROWE (2003); Victor V. Mair, *Language and Ideology in the Written Popularizations of the Sacred Edict, in* POPULAR CULTURE IN LATE IMPERIAL CHINA (David Johnson, Andrew J. Nathan, & Evelyn S. Rawski eds., 1985).

[44] Terada (1998).

when the same handful of elders – the village chief, vice chief, lineage heads, and others who held positions of recognized authority – tended to mediate large percentages of all local disputes.[45]

B Patterns of Status Distribution

Chapter 3 proposed that the relative powerlessness of rural Chinese economic elites derived largely from patterns of status distribution in traditional Chinese communities. This section discusses what those patterns actually were. It argues that status and authority did not correlate strongly with wealth but did correlate strongly with generational seniority in kinship networks. Two sets of sources are marshaled to demonstrate these points: first, lists of village-level political authorities, such as village chief or village councilor, collected from both Japanese and Chinese rural surveys, and second, collections of *dian* contracts from a few North China and Lower Yangtze counties. When matched with demographic surveys from corresponding regions, these collections allow us to identify the basic economic and social circumstances of individuals who were entrusted with positions of authority, including both village leadership positions and the middlemen, guarantors, and arbitrators who handled first-instance disputes over *dian* sales.

Demographic and landholding information on village political elites are, by and large, some of the most reliable data one can extract from the Mantetsu surveys: in all seven villages that provided this information – the six main survey spots and a briefly visited seventh village – researchers were able to confirm the names of village leaders with several different villagers and also collect official registries of village landownership and kinship networks. None of this information relies on the subjective judgment of interviewees, and therefore is considerably "safer" to use than their testimony on local customary practices. A total of 128 elites, covering the great majority of recent village chiefs, their deputies, major lineage chiefs with specified administrative authority, and *jiazhang* ("ten-household chiefs") or equivalent, can be matched with entries in official land registries.[46] Not included in this sample are people who are mentioned only once in the interviews but cannot be found in any village registry.

Quite contrary to what previous and less statistically thorough studies of the Mantetsu surveys have suggested, lower-income households were

---

[45] *E.g.*, Huaiyin Li, Village Governance in North China, 1875–1936 (2005); Duara (1988).

[46] All aggregate statistics discussed here are drawn from data presented in Appendix B.

proportionally represented among the village political elite. Sixty-three of the 128 owned less land than the village average, which was actually higher than the village median due to the existence of a few large landowners in all villages. Nor were the sixty-three all concentrated in "lower tier" positions – *jiazhang* rather than village chief, for example. Of the thirty-two people identified to have been village chief during the past decade, fourteen owned less land per capita than the village average, which suggests a slightly stronger hold over the position by higher-income households than over other positions, but not by much. Moreover, the richest households in the village were absent from these positions of authority surprisingly often. Of the thirty-five largest landowners from the seven villages, five from each, only eight had wielded any formal political authority in recent years. This was, of course, still a considerably higher ratio than the lower-income segments of the population, but nonetheless low enough to suggest that landed wealth was a weak determinant of sociopolitical authority.

On the other hand, the correlation between sociopolitical authority and generational seniority in a large kinship group was extremely strong. 115 of the 128 individuals belonged to a kinship group that accounted for at least 10 percent of all village households, and at least 108 of them belonged to the most senior generation in that group. Only nine people, including the current village chief of Sibeichai and the local militia chief of Lengshuigou, clearly belonged to a younger generation, and all were known as stand-ins for elder relatives, who made most major decisions but preferred not to handle day-to-day operational duties. The generational standings of the other eleven are unclear, but even the most conservative "guesstimate" would surmise that at least half of these people were relatively senior and therefore that around 90 percent of these village political elites belonged to the most senior generation of a relatively large kinship group.

Summary statistics are, of course, often not as revealing as case studies of specific villages. Here again, Sibeichai is the best candidate.[47] Due to the highly detailed coverage of the village, one can extract demographic and landownership information for eighteen of the nineteen individuals who had served in the years leading up to the survey either as village chief, deputy village chief, *lüzhang* (a higher-tier position that presided over several ten-household groups during the 1930s), or *jiazhang* (who presided one ten-household group):

---

[47] The following paragraphs, including the table, are based on 3 MANTETSU SURVEYS (1957), at 12–51.

Village Elites in Sibeichai

Village chief

Zhang Leqing (former)	48 *mu*, household of 10	Head of the Zhang kinship group
Hao Guodong	2 *mu*, household of 6	Nephew of Hao Luozhen (see below)
Hao Qingjun (former)	Unknown, reported to be "very average"	Former head of Hao kinship group no. 1
Hao Yiwei	Over 200 *mu*, household of unknown size	Senior generation of Hao kinship group no. 2

Former *lüzhang* (head of a 30- to 40-person unit)

Hao Luozhuo	4 *mu*, household of 2	Head of Hao kinship group no. 2
Hao Baizi	28 *mu*, household of 14	Senior generation of Hao kinship group no. 1
Hao Luozhen	3 *mu*, rented an additional 62 *mu*, household of 7	Head of Hao kinship group no. 1
Zhao Luohan	23 *mu*, household of 5	Head of Zhao kinship group
Liu Luoliu	25 *mu*, household of about 10	Senior generation of Liu kinship group

Jiazhang (head of a 10-person unit)

Zhao Luoxu	11 *mu*, household of 4	Senior generation of Zhao kinship group
Liu Yuande	10 *mu*, rented an additional 30 I, household of 5	Senior generation of Liu kinship group
Zhao Luofeng	6 *mu*, cotilled another 70 *mu* with other households, household of 8	Senior generation of Zhao kinship group
Liu Luocun (aka Liu Wuzi)	24 *mu*, household of 7	Head of Liu kinship group
Hao Luozhen	See above	
Zhao Luohan	See above	
Xu Laosi	7.5 *mu*, household of 5	Head of Xu kinship group
Hao Luojing	4 *mu*, rented an additional 10 *mu*, household of 8	Senior generation of Hao kinship group no. 2
Hao Luoxi	13 *mu*, rented an additional 34 *mu*, household of 4	Senior generation of Hao kinship group no. 2
Hao Luogeng	20 *mu*, household of 13	Senior generation of Hao kinship group no. 1
Hao Baizi	See above	
Hao Luoxiang	8 *mu*, household of 8	Senior generation of Hao kinship group no. 2

Sibeichai households owned, on average, 1.9 mu per capita and farmed 2.9 mu – over 100 mu were owned by absentee landlords. Twelve of the eighteen village leaders identified earlier were therefore at or below the village average in one category, whereas nine were at or below average in both. These ratios are very similar to the summary statistics for all seven villages described earlier, suggesting decent representativeness. Notably, apart from Hao Yiwei, who had been village chief before Zhang Leqing and reputedly owned over 200 mu in his heyday, none of the eighteen were among the top 10 percent of landowners in the village. If one counts instead the amount of land farmed rather than owned, only Hao Luozhen and Zhao Luofeng belonged in the top 10 percent. Other than Hao Guodong, the current village chief, everyone belonged to the senior generation of a major local kinship group. Five of the eighteen were actually the *zuzhang* ("head") – generally assumed by the most senior member – of their respective kinship groups, a position that, according to several interviewees, was determined solely by inter- and intragenerational seniority. According to Zhang Leqing, the previous village chief, there had traditionally been twelve major kinship groups in the village, two groups of Hao, Zhao, Liu, Xu, and Zhang and one each of Wang and Li. Village censuses show that the two Hao groups accounted for nearly half of the village population by 1940, and their demographic dominance is reflected in the preceding table. Clearly, generational seniority within a large kinship group was a far better indicator of sociopolitical authority in Sibeichai than wealth and was, indeed, perhaps the single most important precondition of high status.

The case of Hao Guodong, a younger-generation village chief whose election apparently bucks this general trend, is not, in fact, a deviation from the norm if we take a closer look. While Hao nominally became village chief after Zhang had retired in disgrace due to his lack of leadership during several fires, it was generally stated, by both Hao himself and others, that he was largely a stand-in for his much more influential uncle, Hao Luozhen, head of the largest kinship group in the village. Hao Luozhen admitted to weighing in on all major policy decisions, but also commented that due to his advanced age and physical frailty, he could not perform all the duties expected of a village chief. Instead, he assumed the lesser roles of *lüzhang* and later *jiazhang*, remaining behind the scenes.

Four other villages, Lujiazhuang, Lengshuigou, Houxiazhai, and Wudian, had power distribution patterns that were largely similar to Sibeichai, allocating the vast majority of authority positions to senior members of large kinship groups without any strong bias toward higher-income households.[48] In the rather extreme case of Lujiazhuang, all ten village leaders who were identifiable on local land registries owned less than fifteen mu, with eight of them owning less than ten mu, the village average. In all four villages, below-average landowners accounted for at least half of the identifiable village leaders, and all four boast at least one recent village chief who was extremely poor: Xing Guanghua in Lujiazhuang, who owned ten mu despite having a large household; Du Fengshan in Lengshuigou, who owned a paltry three mu; Ma Wannian in Houxiazhai, who supported a household of four with only seven mu; and at least four former village chiefs in Wudian who owned less than five mu during their terms. As with Sibeichai, nearly all positions went to senior members of local *daxing* ("large surnames") – kinship groups with a long local history and many member households.

Wudian offers a fairly interesting twist. A few years prior to the survey, the Liangxiang County government attempted to reform the demographic structure of local governance, ordering villages to reelect new village leaders, primarily from the twenty- to forty-year age group.[49] In response, Wudian nominally elected a fresh batch of village leaders comprised almost entirely of the sons of previous leaders, but made sure that actual governance was still handled by their fathers. In the words of one interviewee: "The new leaders are young and have much physical labor to perform, which leaves them no time to handle administrative duties."[50] Some villagers ignored the nominal regime change and continued to refer to the previous generation by their old titles. Given their distinct lack of substantive authority, the younger-generation leaders are not included in the sample of 120 political elites discussed earlier.

The situation in Houjiaying (literally, "Camp of the Hou Family"), on the border between Hebei Province and Manchuria, was much more complex, displaying significant doses of wealth-based social tension. The dominant kinship group there, unsurprisingly the Hou family, happened to include among its senior ranks a small group of fairly wealthy individuals, who argued to the Japanese researchers that their high wealth and seniority should grant them more control over the top leadership positions.[51] They did seem to enjoy some success in this. Of the fifteen people who had been either village chief or deputy village chief in recent years, only six were below-average landowners, whereas five others were among the wealthiest individuals in the village.[52]

---

[48] *See* Appendix B.   [49] 4 MANTETSU SURVEYS (1957), at 555–63.   [50] *Id.* at 558.
[51] 5 MANTETSU SURVEYS (1957), at 1–6.   [52] *Id.* at 5–63.

The dominance of these high-income households did not, however, extend to other positions in village governance. Of the twelve people who had served as *jiazhang*, also known as *dongshi* ("shareholder") or *huitou* in local political terminology, only one was notably wealthy, whereas the other eleven came predominantly from medium- or low-income households, including several less wealthy but comparably senior members of the Hou kinship group. At any given time, these less wealthy politically elites, while a rank below the village chief and deputy village chief, outnumbered them by perhaps ten to two, which made it highly difficult for the wealthy households to dominate local governance. This tension flared up in several parts of the survey, both over the basic requirements for assuming political leadership – the wealthy households insisted that leaders should be wealthy, whereas less affluent interviewees denied this – and, as discussed earlier, over the rules governing *dian* transactions.[53]

Shajing, too, experienced noticeably more wealth-based social tension than the "Sibeichai model" villages.[54] As in Houjiaying, above-average landowners, generally senior members of the Yang and Li kinship groups, dominated the ranks of village chief. At the time of the survey, Yang Yuan had only recently been named village chief over Zhao Shaoting. The economic contrast was sharp: Yang belonged to the top 10 percent of landowners in the village, owning forty mu for a household of five, whereas Zhao owned only sixteen mu and had a household of eight – the average household owned 2.4 mu per capita. Unsurprisingly, Zhao blamed his loss on Yang's economic superiority, although Yang insisted that it was not a factor. Zhao may have had a point. Most former village chiefs were relatively wealthy, including several members of the Li kinship group. The main exception was Yang's predecessor, Du Ruhai, who served for several years as both village chief and deputy *zuzhang* of the Du lineage despite owning barely ten mu while supporting a household of ten. After his death, his son became one of the village's *huishou* ("group head") – basically a *jiazhai* equivalent – and, more importantly, its chief financial accountant. Of the other six identifiable *huishou*, two were also below-average landowners, two led "midlevel" households of around four mu per capita, and two were top-tier landowners who held more than seven mu per capita. All seven *huishou* did belong, however, to the senior generation of their respective kinship groups. In addition, the *zuzhang* of the Yang and Du kinship groups, both below-average landowners, also wielded

[53] *Id.*
[54] 1 MANTETSU SURVEYS (1957), at 89–145, app. 2; 2 MANTETSU SURVEYS (1957), at apps. 2, 3.

considerable administrative authority despite not occupying a formal political post. As in Houjiaying, the situation here was one of tension between higher- and lower-income households, but certainly nothing resembling political dominance by the economically affluent. As in other villages, generational seniority within a sizable kinship group seemed to be a prerequisite for sociopolitical authority.

All in all, the summary statistics presented at the start of this section seem qualitatively accurate. Social status and authority, as measured by occupation of key political positions, correlated far more strongly with generational seniority than it did with wealth. Even in Houjiaying and Shajing, lower-income households occupied sizable portions of local leadership positions, whereas in the other five villages they occupied most positions, including the highest ones. There is, moreover, strong reason to believe that the relatively high wealth-based sociopolitical tension in the former two villages was closely related to the relative instability of their social structure. Of all seven villages surveyed, Shajing displayed by far the most obvious signs of urban migration. A considerable portion of its middle-aged labor force, predominantly members of lower-income households, sought work in nearby Beijing, seriously weakening their influence in village affairs and distorting traditional balances of power within kinship groups. It is all too conceivable that such migration buttressed the political reach and ambitions of higher-income households, who were less likely to seek external employment due to larger landholdings. Houjiaying, however, was unique among the seven villages in its geographic and economic proximity to Manchuria. Many members of the largest kinship groups sought economic opportunity in the relatively underpopulated plains of Manchuria. Of the village's nine wealthiest households, six had, in fact, amassed their initial fortunes in this way. Given the high level of mobility between the village and the northeastern frontier lands, traditional kinship hierarchies were most probably weaker than in the southern parts of North China, where, as in Sibeichai and other villages, kinship groups were more stable and their internal hierarchies more deeply entrenched.

One potential problem lingers: the preceding analysis has largely assumed that political leadership positions were generally objects of social desire and therefore fairly accurate proxies for high social status, influence, and authority. But was this really true? There are at least some scholars who would argue that the richest households actually avoided assuming direct political authority: they thought it would be too burdensome, not to mention entangle them in unwanted sociopolitical controversy, and added little utility to an already fairly decent economic situation. Better to leave the administrative duties and risks to others – particularly lower-income households who sought to supplement their low economic rank with more political authority. Such risk-averse behavior could theoretically intensify during relatively unstable periods such as the Nationalist government's Northern Campaign or the Japanese occupation, when the challenges and potential dangers of political leadership were higher than usual.[55]

There is some evidence of this in at least two villages. A Houxiazhai interviewee noted that, although the Wang kinship group was the wealthiest in the village, many of its senior members avoided becoming village chief, disliking its administrative burdens and sociopolitical exposure.[56] However, their hesitation, to the extent that it existed, did not seem to involve *baozhang* or *jiazhang* positions,[57] which carried much less sociopolitical pressure and, although theoretically less prestigious than village chief, were by no means strictly "subordinate" positions under the chief's direct command. Whatever impact such risk-averse behavior might have had on the preceding analysis is therefore very limited because the sample consists mainly of *jiazhang*-level positions.

Duara has argued that a more systematic retreat from political leadership positions occurred among the Lengshuigou economic elite.[58] The sole piece of evidence for this is an interview with Du Fengshan, the village chief who had served for over two decades despite owning almost no land. Du notes that the village had undergone a political reorganization in recent years, in which fourteen *lüzhang* (a *jiazhang* equivalent) replaced the eight *shoushi* ("chief administrators") who had previously handled basic administration. He then lists from memory the names and landholdings of all twenty-two men and points out that, first, there was no overlap between the two administrations and, second, that he recalls much higher landholding figures for the eight *shoushi* than for the fourteen *lüzhang*.[59] To Duara, this suggests that the village economic elite, as represented by the eight *shoushi*, had consciously chosen to withdraw from political leadership positions due in part to mistrust of the new organizational structure.

There are multiple problems with this argument. Most importantly, Du's recollection is extraordinarily unreliable: no other interviewee ever mentions the eight *shoushi* he lists, and only one of them can be found on

---

[55] DUARA (1988).   [56] 4 MANTETSU SURVEYS (1957), at 18.
[57] There are three senior Wangs of median wealth or above among the *baozhang*. *See* Appendix B.
[58] DUARA (1988), at 169–73.   [59] *Id.* at 170–71.

the village land registry.[60] Moreover, one person actually owned only two mu, not the twenty mu that Du reported.[61] Du's list of the fourteen *lüzhang* was likewise inaccurate. He misstates the names of four people and provides significantly exaggerated landholding numbers for another five.[62] Whether Du was consciously misleading the Japanese is unclear – his advanced age may have impaired his memory – although Lengshuigou was certainly the least cooperative of all surveyed villages. Moreover, while there was no overlap between the fourteen *lüzhang* and the eight *shoushi* that immediately preceded them, one *lüzhang* had in fact been part of an earlier class of *shoushi*. The two classes of *shoushi* also shared only one common member, suggesting that the large volume of personnel turnover was hardly unordinary by traditional standards.[63] All in all, there is no reliable evidence that Lengshuigou economic elites "retreated" in any comprehensive manner. Quite the opposite, some seemed rather eager to assume leadership positions in 1940. According to one interviewee, the village's largest landowner had considerable political aspirations but lacked the necessary sociopolitical status "because he was too young."[64]

Similarly, higher-income households in several other villages were very keen to obtain formal political authority, regardless of rank and public exposure. Houjiaying and Shajing are the best examples: the wealthiest households there were clearly eager to obtain top-level political positions and, in fact, dominated the ranks of village chief and deputy village chief. In Sibeichai, as discussed in the preceding section, the wealthiest landlords openly complained that their sociopolitical status and influence were too weak, and that this damaged many of their core economic interests. Zhang Leqing, the relatively wealthy former village chief, held onto his position until he was forced out by unhappy villagers, strongly suggesting that he valued the position very highly.[65] Moreover, as noted earlier, eight of the thirty-five largest landowners in the seven villages had been village chief or *jiazhang* in recent years, a ratio that, while unspectacular, was nonetheless much higher than the aggregate average. In most villages, political leadership positions were objects of significant allure even for the wealthiest households and, therefore, are reasonably accurate measures of sociopolitical status and influence.

The conclusions drawn here stand in distinct opposition to two previous studies of the Mantetsu surveys, those done by Duara and Philip Huang.

---

[60] *See* 4 MANTETSU SURVEYS (1957), at 1–29, 386–89   [61] Li Fenggui. *Id.* at 387.
[62] *Compare id.* at 25 *and id.* at 386–89.   [63] *Id.* at 25.   [64] *Id.* at 8.
[65] 3 MANTETSU SURVEYS (1957), at 59.

Although neither work gave central importance to the economic backgrounds of village elites, both argued that, in Huang's words, "lineage leaders and village 'councilmen' were generally also the village rich."[66] They rely, however, on highly incomplete surveys of village elite: Huang makes his sweeping argument based on a sample of eighteen people, covering only Shajing and Lengshuigou, whereas Duara uses a list of fifty-five people, mainly current and former village chiefs from Shajing and Houjiaying, but also including the eight phantom *huishou* from Lengshuigou. The overemphasis on Shajing and Houjiaying village chiefs naturally created the illusion that wealthy households dominated leadership positions. The preceding paragraphs have argued, however, that even a more complete survey of political leaders in those two villages would have presented a significantly different picture. Comprehensive coverage of all seven villages demonstrates, of course, that lower-income households were by no means underrepresented among the political elite. Both Duara and Huang also suggest that higher-income households voluntarily withdrew from leadership positions during the 1930s, but, as argued earlier, evidence for such behavior is very thin. More plausibly, one may surmise that, as interviewees from some villages report, the overall wealth of higher-income households had diminished since the late Qing, creating the impression that village political leaders were aggregately poorer.

To be sure, the external framework of village governance did change quite frequently during the Republican era, with *jiazhang* and *lüzhang* systems replacing *huishou* or other traditional positions in many places. This does not, however, imply significant discontinuity in the socioeconomic distribution of political authority. As a detailed study of village governance in Huolu County, Hebei Province, has recently argued, even in the late Qing, economic elites were never able to dominate leadership positions to the exclusion of lower-income households.[67] To the extent that wealthier households were somewhat better represented among such positions, it was because some of their primary duties – tax collection and prepayment – naturally required some level of personal wealth. The selection of higher-income households to these positions was, in fact, preferable for lower-income households and was not sustainable without their support. However, "kinship ties" had long been the single "most important factor" in the selection of village leaders.[68] Both the political strength of lower-income households and the crucial importance of kinship relations

---

[66] HUANG (1985), at 238. *See also* DUARA (1988), at 162, 166, 171.
[67] LI (2005), at 46–59.　　[68] *Id.* at 47.

are reminiscent of the Mantetsu survey results discussed earlier, suggesting considerable continuity between the late Qing and Republican eras, formal institutional reshuffling notwithstanding.

Certain regions of North China were, of course, more economically stratified than others. Joseph Esherick and Kenneth Pomeranz have noted, for example, that resident landlordism was more prevalent in the south-western edge of Shandong Province than in other regions of North China,[69] with large landlords owning perhaps a third or more of all arable land. Whether this meant that they dominated local social and political authority is, however, ambiguous. The main functions that these landlords played in local governance were, according to both Esherick and Pomeranz, organizing and funding local militias – functions that only the rich could fulfill. Otherwise, there is no clear evidence that the ranks of local political elite were forcibly monopolized by higher-income house-holds. Southwestern Shandong villages were highly consolidated, demo-graphically stable, and resistant to government intervention, but this suggests cooperation between rich and poor rather than dominance of one by the other. Kinship groups were also larger and more powerful, which tends to prove, not disprove, the thesis advanced here.

So much for North China. Social organization in the Lower Yangtze was different in several aspects but nonetheless similar in that it revolved around large kinship networks – indeed more so. Unlike North China kinship groups, which owned almost no common property beyond ances-tral worship halls, a small but noticeable fraction of arable land in the Lower Yangtze was owned not by individual households but by lineages (*zongzu*) – commonly understood as kinship groups that collectively owned some property under arrangements quite similar to modern cor-porate holdings.[70] Compared with the kinship groups examined earlier, these lineages were better organized and more populous.[71] Whereas the average North China village might possess several kinship groups, each

---

[69] Joseph Esherick, Origins of the Boxer Uprising 1–37 (1988); Pomeranz (1993), at 101–04.

[70] *See* Teemu Ruskola, *Conceptualizing Corporations and Kinship: Comparative Law and Development Theory in a Chinese Perspective*, 52 Stan. L. Rev. 1599, 1614 at n. 37 (2000).

[71] *See* Kung-Chuan Hsiao, Rural China: Imperial Control in the Nineteenth Century 326 (1960); Huang (1990), at 144–48; Li Wenzhi & Jiang Taixin, Zhongguo Zongfa Zongzu Zhi he Zutian Yizhuang [Lineage Institutions and Common Property in China] 167–77 (2000). This description is substantially different from Kathryn Bernhardt's characterization of Lower Yangtze lineages as predominantly "based in urban centers" and only loosely organized in rural areas. Bernhardt (1992), at 19–21. Bernhardt underestimates the social importance and organization power of rural

consisting of a few dozen households, Lower Yangtze villages were very often dominated by one large lineage operating under published regulations and conduct codes of considerable detail. Political authority and status in geographic communities were therefore virtually inseparable from authority and status within those lineages. The question then becomes: how did lineages allocate status?

The present inquiry focuses mainly on the considerable number of lineage registries that were produced throughout the Ming and Qing, but particularly abundantly in the late Qing and early Republic. While the main function of these registries was simply to preserve as detailed a family tree as possible, they also contained significant information on the use and maintenance of common property, lineage conduct codes, and rules that guided the selection of lineage heads and councilors. In the collection of twelve registries analyzed here, all hail from the Ningbo, Shicang, and Longquan regions of Zhejiang Province, each correlating with a large lineage that dominated at least one village between 1870 and 1930.[72]

lineage groups, which more recent scholarship by mainland Chinese scholars has explored quite extensively. She focuses too exclusively on absentee landlordism and the economic effects of lineage corporate landholding – which were statistically limited due to the low aggregate volume of corporate property – whereas the main function of Lower Yangtze lineages in rural communities, like North China kinship groups, was actually the supply of social and economic order. *See* Zhang Jinjun, *Qingdai Jiangnan Zongzu zai Xiangcun Shehui Kongzhi zhong de Zuoyong* [*The Role of Lineages in the Qing Lower Yangtze*], 34(3) J. ANHUI NORMAL. UNIV. 353 (2006). In any case, while rural Lower Yangtze lineages might have been more "loosely organized" than South China lineages – which, due to very high levels of corporate landholding, naturally demanded higher levels of coordination and administration – they were certainly better organized and more consolidated than North China kinship groups. In fact, even within North China, the regions that bordered the Lower Yangtze possessed notably larger, better organized kinship groups than other regions.

[72] Eight of these are held at the Shanghai Library: NANJIN JIANGSHI MINFANG FAXIANG PU [REGISTRY OF THE MIN BRANCH OF THE NINGBO JIANG LINEAGE] (1890); JIANGSHI ZHIPU [BRANCH REGISTRY OF THE JIANG LINEAGE] (Yu Zhonghuan ed.,1934); SIMING ZHUSHI ZHIPU [BRANCH REGISTRY OF THE ZHU LINEAGE OF SIMING] (Zhu Xiang ed., 1936); XUDETANG YINJIA PU [REGISTRY OF THE YIN LINEAGE OF XUDETANG] (1906); YONGSHANG TUSHI ZONGPU [REGISTRY OF THE TU LINEAGE OF YONGSHANG] (Zhang Meisa ed., 1919); BIANSHI ZONGPU [REGISTRY OF THE BIAN LINEAGE] (Bian Yingshan et al. eds., 1874); YAONAN DINGSHAN FANGSHI ZONGPU [REGISTRY OF THE FANG LINEAGE FROM DINGSHAN, IN YAONAN] (Fang Zheng et al. eds., 1921); DUSHI ZONGPU [REGISTRY OF THE DU LINEAGE] (Du Xizhen ed., 1948). Three, from Longquan County, are held at the Zhejiang University History Department: NANYANG YESHI ZONGPU [REGISTRY OF THE YE LINEAGE OF NANYANG] (Ye Liming et al. eds., 1998); XUSHI ZONGPU [REGISTRY OF THE XU LINEAGE] (Zu Fenglu ed., 1937); GUANCHUAN MAOSHI ZUPU [REGISTRY OF THE MAO LINEAGE OF GUANCHUAN] (late Qing, year unknown).

These lineages shared two basic organizational characteristics. First, *none* of the registries positively identify personal wealth or landholding with higher internal status and authority. At least three, in fact, expressly forbade allocating status based on material affluence, condemning such practices as immoral. The natural order of families was, in their words, one that gave senior members precedence over junior ones (*zhang you you xu*), and any corruption of this principle by materialistic concerns was intolerable.[73] Second, of the eight lineages that published selection criteria for leadership positions, all eight highlight the importance of generational seniority.[74] The Jiang lineage of Ningbo, for example, divided its members into five descent subgroups (*zhi*), each of which sent its most senior member (*fen zun zhe*) – generally the eldest member of the highest generation – to the lineage council. This five-person council wielded authority disproportionate to its size: it arbitrated internal disputes, represented the lineage in external negotiations, managed common property, coordinated labor and resource sharing, and enforced lineage regulations. In this latter task, the council could often count on the backing of the county government, to the point where "bringing offenders to the county court" was listed as the punishment of last resort for particularly grievous violations.[75]

Among members of the same generation, some lineages chose to rank individuals not by age, but by lineal proximity to a descent line of firstborn males extending back to the founding ancestor – the founding ancestor's eldest son, the eldest son's eldest son, and so on.[76] This line of eldest sons (*zongzi*) enjoyed higher status than other members of their generation, regardless of age, and in at least one lineage, all other members were ranked by their lineal proximity to him: his brothers would, for example, have social precedence over his cousins. Such precedence took effect in a variety of ways, usually through more prominent roles in ancestor worship rituals and easier access to lineage leadership positions. In some lineages, although none in our sample, the *zongzi* could succeed his father as lineage head even if some of the father's generation still lived. In such cases,

One, from Shicang village, is held at the Shanghai Jiaotong University History Department: Queshi Zongpu [Registry of the Que Lineage] (Hu Ruixiang ed., 1896).

[73] Jiangshi Zhipu (1934); Dushi Zongpu (1948); Queshi Zongpu (1896).

[74] Nanjin Jiangshi Minfang Faxiang Pu (1890); Jiangshi Zhipu (1934); Siming Zhushi Zhipu (1936); Yongshang Tushi Zongpu (1919); Bianshi Zongpu (1874); Yaonan Dingshan Fangshi Zongpu (1921); Dushi Zongpu (1948); Queshi Zongpu (1896).

[75] Jiangshi Zhipu (1934).   [76] Nanjin Jiangshi Minfang Faxiang Pu (1890).

however, he was always "supported," but also limited, by a group of councilors drawn from the higher generation.[77] For the purposes of this book, at least, these systems are not fundamentally different from straightforward ranking by age, in that they rank lineage members according to criteria that have little discernible correlation with wealth. Previous scholarship on Lower Yangtze lineages suggests, in any case, that straightforward ranking by generation and age gradually replaced *zongzi* systems during the Ming and Qing.[78]

At least two lineages selected councilors on the basis not only of seniority, but also of intelligence and moral reputation.[79] Nonetheless, these supplemented rather than replaced seniority requirements. Councilors were still drawn from the most senior generation physically capable of leadership, but within that generation, intelligence and moral character considerations were balanced with age-based or descent-based seniority. Whether perceived intelligence and moral reputation have any correlation with wealth is ambiguous at best. If anything, considering the strong language in many lineage registries condemning the oppression of poorer relatives by wealthier ones, moral reputation – rather than actual moral behavior – may well have correlated negatively with wealth. In any case, generational seniority remained a basic prerequisite, and as with all other lineages, nowhere is wealth mentioned as a positive factor.

Lower Yangtze lineages were, in this latter regard, noticeably different from the more heavily studied South China, particularly Fujian, lineages. There scholars have identified three major structural categories: "inheritance lineages," which, like the Lower Yangtze lineages described earlier, assigned leadership positions based on generational seniority, without apparent reference to wealth; "control-subordination lineages," where wealthier households dominated poorer ones; and "contractual lineages," usually creations of economic convenience where various loosely households banded together due to shared economic interests, and where organization and leadership were therefore designed to maximize those interests.[80] "Inheritance lineages" were still the most prevalent even in

---

[77] Feng (2005), at 108–11.   [78] *Id.* at 95–96, 111–13, 248–56.

[79] Bianshi Zongpu (1874); Yaonan Dingshan Fangshi Zongpu (1921).

[80] Zheng Zhenman, Family Lineage Organization and Social Change in Ming and Qing Fujian 71–142 (Michael Szonyi trans., Univ. of Hawaii Press 2000). Other major Western studies of South China lineages include David Faure, Emperor and Ancestor: State and Lineage in South China (2007); Michael Szonyi, Practicing Kinship: Lineage and Descent in Late Imperial China (2002); Maurice Freedman, Chinese Lineage and Society: Fukien and Kwangtung (1966).

late-Qing Fujian, but as lineages expanded both demographically and in corporate landholding, the demands for corporate management occasionally concentrated authority into the hands of the most economically capable – and usually the most wealthy – households, creating either a "control-subordination lineage" or a "contractual lineage."[81]

The major difference between South China and the Lower Yangtze was, however, the amount of corporate land owned by lineages. Previous estimates of lineage property show that apart from South China, where it probably exceeded 35 percent of total arable land, corporate landholding was "trivial" in other regions.[82] Even taking South China into account, Republican surveys suggest that nearly 95 percent of arable land in the Chinese core was owned in fee simple, implying that lineage landholdings in other macroregions could not have exceeded a few percentage points. The economic rationales and conditions that sometimes transformed "inheritance lineages" into less egalitarian forms were therefore abundant in South China but largely absent in the Lower Yangtze.

These conclusions are largely consistent with previous scholarship on Lower Yangtze lineages. Scholars who have studied their selection of lineage heads and councilmen have regularly commented on the prevalence of both *zongzi* systems and more straightforward ranking by age, but also note the existence of more meritocratic considerations of intelligence and moral reputation.[83] Compared with studies of South China, examples of intralineage dominance by economic elites rarely appear, if at all. Quite the contrary, throughout the late Qing and early Republic, Lower Yangtze landlords found it difficult to challenge their lower-income kinsmen on issues of land use, rent collection, and tenant eviction despite their strong dislike of existing arrangements.[84] A main socioeconomic function of Lower Yangtze lineages was, in fact, providing social welfare to lower-income households, including regular cash and grain allowances, education, and disaster relief, usually from the agricultural produce and financial returns of corporate property.[85] Unlike the marginal poor relief that Fujian "control-subordination lineages" "symbolically" provided,[86] the social welfare functions of Lower Yangtze lineages were, at least relative to their

---

[81] ZHENG (2000), at 186.   [82] POMERANZ (2000), at 71–72; CHEN (1936), at 34–35.

[83] *See* FENG (2005), at 111–13; Zhang (2006), at 354–56; XU MAOMING, JIANGNAN SHISHEN YU JIANGNAN SHEHUI, 1368–1911 [GENTRY AND SOCIETY IN THE LOWER YANGTZE, 1368–1911] (Beijing: Shangwu Press, 2004).

[84] Rent collection is probably the sharpest example of this. *See* detailed discussion in Section E.

[85] Zhang (2006).   [86] ZHENG (2000), at 185–87.

inherently lower volume of corporate landholding, both statistically significant and meticulously managed, suggesting that their lower-income units wielded considerably greater social influence.

The existence of "control-subordination lineages" and "contractual lineages" in South China does demonstrate, of course, that the normative appeal of Confucian kinship ideals was not immune from erosion by economic factors. It does not, however, imply that such ideals were in anything resembling widespread jeopardy. It would otherwise be difficult to explain the predominance, in both North China and the Lower Yangtze, of kinship groups that adhered closely to them or even the more limited prevalence of "inheritance lineages" in South China. As far as historical evidence can suggest, generational hierarchies were at least the "default state" from which wealth-based forms of lineage organization might mutate given sufficiently compelling socioeconomic circumstances. As Xiao Gongquan argued, based on a variety of ethnographic sources from the late Qing and early Republic, "[a]ge, seniority in generation, and personal ability were as a rule the primary qualifications for clan leadership."[87] "[E]conomic status" could sometimes be "equally decisive,"[88] but its influence was deeply felt predominantly in regions of the country beyond the geographic scope of this book.

C Kinship Hierarchies and Property Norms

The preceding two sections have demonstrated that *dian* customs were the product of self-interested negotiation and that local status distribution correlated far better with "Confucian" kinship hierarchies than with wealth distribution. It remains to show that these behavioral patterns interacted in ways consistent with the model proposed in Chapter 3 – that is, to show that kinship hierarchies affected norm negotiation and enforcement in ways that favored seller-friendly *dian* customs.

This is relatively straightforward for North China, where the Mantetsu surveys provide numerous insights into the roles of village political elites in norm negotiation. First and foremost, village leaders of middling or lower wealth were often quite aggressive in advocating and enforcing these customs against attempted erosion by landlords. The clearest example of this is when Zhang Leqing, former village chief of Sibeichai, engaged in a prolonged battle with local landlord Lin Fengxi over the proper procedure

---

[87] HSIAO (1960), at 326.   [88] *Id.*

for *dian* redemption.[89] Zhang argued, both in intravillage mediation sessions and eventually at the local county court, that his redemption of property under *dian* sale to Lin was only conditional upon repayment of the initial *dian* price.[90] He had later accrued additional debt to Lin, but that was unrelated and immaterial. Lin countered that because he had allowed Zhang to remain on the *dian*-sold property as a rent-paying tenant, and particularly because the additional debt was actually several years of unpaid rent, that debt was too closely tied to the initial *dian* transaction for redemption to be permissible without, at least, full repayment of all outstanding rent.[91] Lin did not attempt to base this argument on any legal authority, but simply argued that this is what local custom "should" be.

Several other local landlords, including some who lived three miles away in the local county seat, voiced their support for Lin,[92] but Zhang and other lower-income village elites were adamant that the no extra conditions should be attached to *dian* redemption other than repayment of the initial sales price.[93] By the time of the interview, the dispute was still ongoing in the county court, but Zhang seemed highly confident that his view would prevail.[94] Lin, meanwhile, seemed resigned that he would be unable to recuperate the outstanding rent before Zhang redeemed, complaining to the researchers that he could not fight the "stubbornness" of villagers who stuck to their "backward customs."[95]

Lower-income village elites advocating seller-friendly *dian* customs is a recurring theme in all six villages that produced detailed interview transcripts. Earlier segments of this chapter have shown that there was a significant amount of tension between higher- and lower-income interviewees over the content of *dian* and tenancy customs. Most disputes were relatively narrow and technical, similar to the Zhang Leqing–Lin Fengxi dispute, but there were, at least in Shajing and Houjiaying, higher-level disagreements concerning the expiration of *dian* redemption rights. As discussed earlier, certain wealthy interviewees suggested superseding traditional customs – which, of course, made *dian* sales infinitely redeemable – with national regulations that banned redemption after thirty years. Naturally, lower-income interviewees rejected this out of hand.

Many of these lower-income individuals were, in fact, members of the village political elite. For example, Li Liangfu, a Lengshuigou village official of middling wealth, seemed to know of the thirty-year legal deadline but

---

[89] 3 MANTETSU SURVEYS (1957), at 170–71, 273–75.　　[90] *Id.*　　[91] *Id.* at 171–74.
[92] *Id.* at 165–67, 177–86, 247–48.　　[93] *Id.* at 245, 263.　　[94] *Id.* at 170–71.
[95] *Id.* at 174.

rejected outright any notion that it should be enforceable in his village.[96] Similar statements were made by Zhao Shaoting, village councilor of Shajing; Hou Dingyi, former village chief of Houjiaying; and Hou Ruihe, also a member of Houjiaying's village administration.[97] Zhang and Hou Ruihe were both below-average landholders, whereas Hou Dingyi was slightly above-average in terms of overall household landholding but probably below average on a per capita basis due to the unusually large size of his household.[98] In the three other villages surveyed, the thirty-year redemption deadline was never openly discussed, but researchers nonetheless encountered middle- or low-income village leaders who expressed preferences for *dian* customs that would allow *dian* sellers to, for example, redeem even before the guaranteed-usage period had expired or reject any right-of-first-purchase claim made by *dian* buyers.[99] Clearly, then, the large number of lower-income individuals on village councils led directly to stronger support for seller-friendly property norms among the political elite.

Many interviewees attested that village officials usually played crucial roles in mediating and settling *dian-* and permanent sale–related disputes and therefore had numerous opportunities in everyday economic life to encourage and perhaps enforce adherence to their preferred institutional norms.[100] The Zhang Leqing–Lin Fengxi dispute also highlights the higher-level forums, including formal litigation and village-wide "policy" debates, in which advocacy and support by sympathetic political elites could be particularly effective at reinforcing customary property institutions. It suggests, moreover, that the less wealthy *dian* sellers often prevailed in such conflicts.

As discussed earlier, intravillage disagreement over *dian* redemption norms was particularly acute in Shajing and Houjiaying. In all other villages surveyed, interviewees basically agreed that *dian* sales were indefinitely redeemable, but disagreed over lesser details: whether, for example, *dian* buyers enjoyed a right of first purchase if *dian* sellers ever decided to permanently sell their property. Sibeichai is perhaps the best example of this. Despite the heated nature of the Lin Fengxi–Zhang Leqing dispute, Lin never claimed that Zhang's redemption rights would expire if too

---

[96] 4 MANTETSU SURVEYS (1957), at 205–06

[97] 2 MANTETSU SURVEYS (1957), at 269; 5 MANTETSU SURVEYS (1957), at 266.

[98] *See* Appendix B.   [99] *See* the discussion at *supra* pp. 130–34.

[100] *E.g.*, 3 MANTETSU SURVEYS (1957), at 29; 4 MANTETSU SURVEYS (1957), at 7, 206–07, 406–07; 5 MANTETSU SURVEYS (1957), at 5–6; 439.

much time had passed since the original *dian* sale. In Shajing and Houjiaying, however, there were at least a few dissenting voices among large
landowners, who argued that *dian* redemption rights should be limited
to a certain period of years, no longer than the thirty years allowed under
Republican law. Poorer households bluntly disagreed, and there is little
evidence that these large landowners really got their way, but at least there
were open disagreements over this issue.

It is therefore rather interesting that Shajing and Houjiaying were also
the only two villages where large landowners were significantly overrepre-
sented, relative to their population share, among the top village leaders.[101]
In Shajing, five of the top eight village leaders (*huishou*), including the only
identifiable village chief, owned significantly more land per capita than the
village average. In fact, four of them, including the village chief, owned
more than twice as much. In Houjiaying, eight of ten identifiable current
and former village chiefs were above-average landholders, including five
people who owned at least three times the average amount, two of whom
were among the village's top five landholders. Additionally, three of five
identifiable vice village chiefs were above-average landholders. Indeed, a
few of Houjiaying's wealthiest households openly demanded that the
selection of villager leaders be based not only on generational seniority
but also on wealth and landholding. In no other village surveyed do above-
average landholders account for more than half of identifiable village
chiefs, vice village chiefs, or *huishou/baozhang*-level officials. Of course,
even in Shajing and Houjiaying, lower-income households still occupied
most of the lower-ranked political positions, but larger landholders did
seem to enjoy a substantial edge in obtaining the top positions. While this
may be pure coincidence – this possibility is hard to rule out in a sample of
only seven villages – one perfectly plausible interpretation is that the
customary right of unlimited *dian* redemption was more secure in villages
where large landholders were politically weaker.

The Lower Yangtze poses somewhat greater empirical challenges. There
are very few sources from the region that directly document the positions
of village or lineage elites in *dian*-related disputes – certainly nothing
approaching the richness of the Mantetsu surveys. Fortunately, there is
much circumstantial evidence to be found not only from the county case
archives discussed earlier, but also from several major collections of land
contracts from the late Qing and early Republic. Combined, they shed

---

[101] *See* Appendix B.

considerable light on who was involved in the deliberation and enforcement of *dian* customs, what their normative standpoints were, and how they advocated those views.

Whether in North China or the Lower Yangtze, relatively few potential *dian* buyers and sellers initiated contract negotiations themselves. Rather, one side would usually ask a middleman to contact the other side, gather both sides' preferences, propose a reasonable compromise, measure the land, and finally, draw up the deed. If any disputes flared up after the contract signing or if either party proposed a change to the terms, the middleman would likewise supervise initial mediation and renegotiation attempts.[102] He was, in modern terms, a mixture of contract lawyer – for both sides – and arbitrator. Given the expansive duties entrusted to middlemen, it was essential that they be of relatively high social status: people who commanded trust and respect within the community and were, consequently, effective at brokering deals and settling disputes.

The argument here is that the great majority of Lower Yangtze *dian* transactions involved middlemen who were senior members of either the *dian* seller's or the *dian* buyer's kinship group. More often than not, these were identical because most people preferred to do business with relatives. In any case, the robust, arguably overwhelming presence of senior kinsmen in *dian* sales strongly suggests that kinship groups were heavily involved in the negotiation and enforcement of proper behavior in these transactions.

These claims rely on data culled from two recently discovered contract collections in Zhejiang. The first is a set of 415 late-Qing land contracts from the Ningbo region, of which 412 were either *dian* sales contracts, redemption contracts, or conversions from *dian* to permanent conveyance.[103] Only three were direct permanent conveyances that had not previously been a *dian* sale.[104] Three hundred and ninety-eight of the 415 were purchased by the largest landowning household in Fenghua County, headed for most of the later nineteenth century by Mao Kunshan and later his son Mao Xiuli. Despite their highly aggressive purchasing of *dian* contracts, neither father nor son had much success in acquiring land

---

[102] *See* HUANG (1996), at 52–58; LI (2005), at 54–55.   [103] NINGBO CONTRACTS (2008).

[104] The three exceptions are *id.*, at nn. 81, 167, 169. As noted in the volume's introduction, contracts designated "mai" were redeemable, and therefore functionally equivalent to what would normally be called a "dian" sale elsewhere. Only contracts that employed the term "juemai" were true permanent sales. There are several examples in the volume of "mai" contracts being coverted–with additional payment–into "juemai" contracts later on, which reinforce this interpretation.

permanently: of the 398 contracts, three were outright permanent sales, while another thirty-two were permanent conveyances converted from *dian* sales. As bad as this ratio is, it might actually have been above average for land purchasers in the region: none of the seventeen purchases made by other parties involved any form of permanent conveyance. Unsurprisingly, *dian* sellers protected their redemption rights quite jealously – and despite their relative wealth, potential land buyers could do little about it.

More importantly, the Ningbo contracts vividly illustrate the influence of kinship ties in land selling. All 415 contracts identify not only the names of their middlemen but also their kinship affinity, if any, with either contracting party – usually the seller. Four hundred and three contracts, or 97 percent, employed at least one relative as middleman.[105] Moreover, of the 389 transactions between members of the Mao lineage, presumably one of the largest in Fenghua, 385 employed *only* fellow lineage members as middlemen, whereas three of the remaining four employed at least one lineage member.[106] The most sought-after middlemen, such as Mao Rongkun, Mao Renli, Mao Youpei, and Mao Shengen, were generally senior members of the lineage, often brokering contracts for their nephews or junior cousins.[107] Commonly, they would head a group of three to five middlemen – all lineage members – and were charged with drafting the final contract. This required, of course, basic literacy, but because literacy rates among men could reach nearly 50 percent in the Lower Yangtze,[108] this was hardly an exceptional distinction. There is no indication that personal wealth enhanced one's perceived fitness to be a middleman – many middlemen, even the most sought after, were themselves previous *dian* sellers, suggesting, as noted earlier, relatively low personal wealth.[109]

The second contract collection is a batch of 140 land sales from Shicang, Songyang County, in Zhejiang Province, spanning the years 1865–1915.[110] One hundred and eight of these, or 77 percent, were *dian*-related transactions. Twenty-five of the 108 were conversions from *dian* to permanent conveyance, suggesting that while it was comparatively far easier to gain permanent ownership of land in Songyang than in Ningbo, in absolute

---

[105] Exceptions are *id.*, at nn. 207, 208, 227, 228, 230, 231, 233, 272, 367, 395, 401, 411.
[106] Exceptions are *id.*, at nn. 333, 338, 392, 411.   [107] *E.g.*, *id.*, at 8, 23, 27, 98.
[108] Evelyn Rawski, Education and Popular Literacy in Ch'ing China 140 (1979).
[109] *E.g.*, Ningbo Contracts (2008), at 82, 87 (showing *dian* selling by Mao Youpei and Mao Rongkun).
[110] Shicang Contracts (2010).

terms, it was nonetheless highly difficult. As in Ningbo, many of the sales were to a single rich household, led in this case by Que Yuqing, which aggressively purchased *dian* parcels but only sporadically obtained permanent ownership over one.

The social composition of middlemen in the Shicang contracts was almost identical to that in the Ningbo collection. Of the 140 transactions, 130, or 93 percent, involved at least one middleman who was related to one of the contracting parties, and the great majority involved at least three.[111] Typically, a senior kinsman of one contracting party, usually the seller, would lead a group of three to ten middlemen, most related to at least one contracting party. Here, too, certain senior members of the locally dominant lineage – in this case, the Que lineage – were in high demand as middlemen, including Que Hansheng and Que Hanliu.[112]

These empirical patterns reinforce, first of all, the arguments advanced earlier that most rural Chinese preferred to entrust positions of influence and authority, as middlemen surely were, to senior members of their kinship group. More importantly, however, they highlight the myriad of everyday venues through which senior lineage members exerted influence on the underlying social norms that governed land transactions. It is imperative to remember here that middlemen were also mediators and arbitrators of first resort in case of dispute and therefore exercised some measure of authority over the contracting parties. Employing senior relatives as middlemen further strengthened such authority and gave them a completely legitimate opening to enforce, or at least advocate for, their understanding of local property norms.

From there it is but a small step to suggest that, because these senior relatives were often quite poor and therefore sympathetic to the interests of similarly situated households, their wide-ranging influence over *dian* transactions probably dampened the ability of higher-income households to obtain their preferred normative and contractual outcomes. One would also expect that this dampening effect was particularly strong on intralineage *dian* sales because the influence of middlemen should have been significantly stronger when they were related to *both* parties. Moreover, as the Ningbo statistics in particular suggest, intralineage sales were much more likely to employ kinsmen as middlemen than interlineage ones, even though a great majority of both do so. Middlemen who were not related to either side probably possessed less authority than those who were because

[111] Exceptions include *id.*, at 15, 16, 73, 107, 131, 133, 147, 167, 168, 209.
[112] *E.g., id.*, at 8, 9.

the reputational costs of ignoring or contradicting them were significantly lower. This created greater potential for extended discord and ruthless bargaining tactics. In, for example, the various Lower Yangtze county cases discussed in Section A, interlineage *dian* sales accounted for a strong majority of disputes,[113] even though, as the preceding paragraphs strongly suggest, intralineage *dian* sales probably outnumbered them by many times. Therefore, if kinship hierarchies affected the negotiation and enforcement of *dian* customs in favor of lower-income households, their effect should have been greater in cases where buyer and seller belonged to the same lineage.

This is precisely what we find in multiple county-level cases from this era. In one particularly telling case from Zhuji County, Zhejiang Province, in 1896, a relatively junior member of the local Zhou lineage attempted to ban a cousin-in-law from redeeming land her husband had conveyed to him five to six years ago.[114] The point of contention was whether the conveyance was a *dian* sale – here termed a *ya* transaction – or a permanent one. After consulting with other community members, the magistrate decided that the debate was immaterial: "[A]t the time of the transaction, the parties clearly should have understood that, because they were relatives, not only was a *dian* sale certainly redeemable, but there was also no reason why a permanent sale would not be . . . In any case, [the defendant] is [the plaintiff's] senior cousin-in-law . . . so why does he not treat her according to reason and moral responsibility?" This was not an isolated incident: the magistrate makes similar statements in at least three other cases, ruling that people who sold land to fellow lineage members could exercise redemption or additional payment rights even if the original transaction was supposedly a permanent sale.[115]

The magistrate cites no clear authority for his claim that nominally permanent sales between relatives were essentially no different from *dian* sales, but unless we assume incredible ignorance of central laws and regulations, he was probably aware that it ran against every legal authority ever published on the issue.[116] Moreover, it seems unlikely that he believed that this was some universal moral commandment that basic decency required – the steps he took to reach the conclusion, including meeting with outside parties, indicate that he was persuaded of its applicability under certain circumstances, not that he came in with a priori moral faith in it. This strongly suggests that the claim derived from his understanding

---

[113] *See* Appendix A, Part II.   [114] 10 Lɪᴅᴀɪ Pᴀɴʟɪ Pᴀɴᴅᴜ (2005), at 443.
[115] *Id.* at 403–04, 449, 484.   [116] *See* DQLL, at §§ 95–03, 95–07.

of local customary practices, probably brought to his attention by the community members with whom he consulted.

He was hardly alone in making these observations of customary law. It appears also in three cases decided by another Lower Yangtze magistrate, who commented that *dian* buyers were expected to show greater leniency for low-income kinsmen, to the point where normal permanent sales could become redeemable.[117] The vast majority of *dian* sellers probably would have appreciated this extra concession, especially if, as argued earlier, the selling of property was usually a last resort in times of extraordinary financial need. All this suggests, as argued earlier, that middlemen were often sympathetic toward the economic interests of lower-income relatives and could act on that sympathy more strongly in cases where the transacting parties were kinsmen.

Finally, among the large number of case files in the Longquan archives that ended in outside mediation, some actually recorded the outcomes of that mediation. The eighty-case sample discussed earlier includes eight of these, all of which, coincidentally, involve claims by the *dian* buyer that the seller's redemption rights had expired over time.[118] It is quite telling, especially in light of preceding paragraphs, that senior lineage members were actively involved in all eight mediation processes and that all eight *dian* sellers were granted considerable rights over the property under dispute despite the passage of anywhere from fifteen to forty-one years. Five were allowed to redeem outright, whereas the other three were allowed to charge additional payments of up to 100 percent of the original sales price. It certainly seems that the involvement of lineage members and the generally sympathetic treatment of *dian* sellers were strongly related.

All in all, there is much evidence, from both North China and the Lower Yangtze, that kinship hierarchies affected norm negotiation and enforcement in ways that favored seller-friendly *dian* customs. In other words, the status distribution patterns explored in Section B had much impact on the rationalistic negotiation processes highlighted in Section A. Those status distribution patterns themselves, as discussed in Chapter 5, were in large part the product of societal internalization of "Confucian" kinship norms. They demonstrate, therefore, how a narrowly defined set of social organization mores can shape the negotiation of property and contract norms that themselves possess little to no inherent moral content.

---

[117] 12 LIDAI PANLI PANDU (2005), at 303, 397.   [118] See discussion at Chapter 1, Section C.

D Comparisons

But do Chinese kinship norms also explain the institutional *divergence* between Chinese and English property customs? I argue, of course, that they do. This blanket statement can again be broken down into three subarguments. First, English property norms, like Chinese ones, were largely the product of self-interested maneuvering and negotiation. Their comparatively weaker protection of lower-income households reflected, in all likelihood, the weaker bargaining power of such households in norm negotiation. Second, substantial landed wealth was generally a prerequisite for high social status and public service in rural England, which dramatically concentrated sociopolitical authority in the hands of large landowners. Third, kinship networks were *far* less expansive and influential in English society than in China and, consequently, were of marginal significance in status distribution and norm negotiation. Ultimately, the reach and influence of "Confucian" kinship hierarchies in China were indeed distinct factors that substantially explain the Sino-English divergence in property regulation.

Preexisting scholarship provides largely consensual support for all three subarguments. The first has been particularly uncontroversial. As noted in previous chapters, studies of early modern English land norms have generally highlighted the highly aggressive, even ruthless manner in which large landlords attempted to reshape property norms in their favor.[119] Especially in the sixteenth and seventeenth centuries, the wide array of unilateral enclosures, tenant evictions, rent and fee manipulations, and default seizures that wealthy households employed to accumulate and consolidate land clashed intensely with what lower-income households saw as normatively appropriate. Even after 1700, when general social hostility toward enclosures had ebbed, issues such as gleaning rights and inheritance procedures remained highly contentious between higher- and lower-income households.[120] Even the comparatively few studies that do not overtly emphasize the role of wealth-based conflict in shaping property norms readily portray the process of norm

---

[119] THE BRENNER DEBATE (1987); KERRIDGE (1969), at 36–37; Hoyle (1990), at 7–12, 17–18; Hoyle (1987) at 24, 29–36.

[120] Peter King, *Legal Change, Customary Right, and Social Conflict in Late Eighteenth-Century England: The Origins of the Great Gleaning Case of 1788*, 10 LAW & HIST. REV. 1 (1992).

creation as one conducted by largely rational parties who knew precisely where their economic interests lay.[121]

Self-interested rationality was therefore a foundational aspect of norm creation in both Chinese and English society, but rational negotiation led, as discussed throughout this book, to radically different outcomes. The striking thing about English property norms is not merely that they treated lower-income households less leniently than Chinese norms, but also that they became progressively less lenient over time. The normative position of small tenants, for example, deteriorated quite severely during the sixteenth and seventeenth centuries as large landowners hacked away at traditional customs that shielded copyholders and leaseholders from enclosures, rent and fee adjustments, and outright evictions.[122]

Mortgage laws and customs underwent a similar transformation. As discussed in Chapter 2, during the twelfth and thirteenth centuries, it was still possible to establish "living gages" in which the debtor did not face any fixed deadline to redeem. By the fifteenth century, however, this debtor-friendly instrument had fallen into disuse, replaced almost completely by "mortgages" ("dead gages") that required repayment within a fixed term and would strip away the debtor's right of redemption on default. The deterioration of the debtor's institutional position accelerated during the sixteenth and seventeenth centuries. An increasing number of local customs cut down on repayment windows, to the point where mortgage contracts generally demanded redemption within a year of the original transaction. Moreover, both custom and common law increasingly allowed the creditor to simply seize full ownership of the land on default, even if the initial mortgage sum fell far short of its full value. Clearly, property norms leaned ever more toward wealthy, land-accumulating, households throughout the early modern era.

This brings us to point two. Even during the sixteenth century, when wealth disparity was not nearly as severe as in the eighteenth century, large English landowners enjoyed one distinct advantage over their Chinese peers: they possessed a near monopoly on formal sociopolitical authority within local communities. Surveys of English localities during the sixteenth

---

[121] *See, e.g.*, Rab Houston, *Custom in Context: Medieval and Early Modern Scotland and England*, 211 PAST & PRESENT 35 (2011); and Andy Wood, *The Place of Custom in Plebeian Political Culture: England, 1550–1800*, 22 SOC. HIST. 46 (1997).

[122] THE BRENNER DEBATE (1987); KERRIDGE (1969), at 36–37; Hoyle (1990), at 7–12, 17–18 (placing the start of conscious landlord encroachment at around 1550).

and seventeenth centuries have repeatedly shown that leadership positions – churchwardens, surveyors, overseers, and most importantly, membership among the "gentry" – were universally filled by men of substantial landed wealth.[123] Scholars have traditionally argued, in fact, that landed wealth was *the* central determinant of status and that higher levels of landownership directly "dictated" higher social and political status.[124] Some recent studies have tempered this argument, demonstrating that other factors, including a consistent commitment to public service or long-term residency in the community, were comparably important.[125] However, they continue to emphasize that "above average" landed wealth was at least a prerequisite for high status and, moreover, that other factors displayed considerable correlation with wealth. Because larger landowners generally had more settled residency patterns and stronger records of public service, the status effects of these factors could often be indistinguishably conflated. In any case, a sociopolitical situation such as that in Sibeichai, where most village leaders, including many of the highest ranked, were actually *below*-average landholders, would have been unthinkable in early modern England.

Why larger English landowners enjoyed this monopoly has no simple explanation. To some extent, it was buttressed by sociopolitical reorganization after the Black Death, in which the "the upper orders of English society drew together into a more cohesive government" to combat the social disorder created by the death of perhaps half the country's population.[126] The large expansion in state power weakened, on the one hand, hereditary hierarchies between lords and subjects, but on the other hand, because the state delegated local authority exclusively to the landed classes, it also excluded lower-income households more completely from positions of power. However, significant wealth-based stratification certainly predated the Black Death[127] and, moreover, was generally discussed in highly moralistic terms – for example, the nobility and gentry were referred to by influential clergyman William Harrison as "those whome their race and blood or at least their vertues doo make noble and knowne" – that suggested at least some degree of internalization.[128] Most plausibly, moralistic internalization and state promotion went hand in hand. In any case,

---

[123] WRIGHTSON (2003); French (2000) at 86.   [124] WRIGHTSON (2003) at 43.
[125] French (2000).
[126] ROBERT C. PALMER, ENGLISH LAW IN THE AGE OF THE BLACK DEATH 1348–1381, at 1 (2001).
[127] *Id.*   [128] WRIGHTSON (2003) at 27.

the status dominance of higher-income classes predated widespread land-lord encroachment on traditional customary rights by over a century and was almost certainly an important precondition. The comparison with China, where relatively egalitarian status distribution seriously stunted the institutional preferences of higher-income households, could not be more vivid.

There remains, for the sake of logical completeness, the issue of whether kinship networks influenced status distribution in England. In short, not significantly. Macfarlane's influential yet controversial work on "English individualism" is probably the first item that comes to mind on this subject,[129] but more systematic studies in recent years have largely confirmed his basic findings – that economic transactions were usually made without any hindrance or input from kinsmen and that individual landowners were generally free to buy, sell, or mortgage land without substantial interference from either their kinship groups or traditional feudal hierarchies of landownership.[130] Many, perhaps most landowners preferred to keep their property within the family if pos-sible, but "no one would deny that ... they had the right to buy and sell land without reference to their kin."[131] Individual households, not the kinship groups, made fundamental social and economic decisions. For most nonnobility, the most "vital social bonds" in their lives were "not with an extended kinship group,"[132] but rather with fellow community members. Theirs was a highly mobile society in which most personal relationships were cultivated on mutual interest rather than inherited, and where wealth, correspondingly, was the most, perhaps only reliable bellwether of sociopolitical status.

Ultimately, the relative egalitarianism of *dian* institutions is paradoxic-ally best explained by the prevalence and influence of kinship hierarchies in rural communities. Even when compared with the widely hailed "individualism" and equality of early modern English institutions, Chinese kinship and property norms encouraged greater status mobility and, consequently, afforded stronger protection to lower-income house-holds. English law and custom may have done away with most feudal indentures by the seventeenth century, but continued to embrace wealth-based inequality as a matter of both status distribution and substantive property law. In comparison, by overriding wealth-based status inequality

---

[129] Macfarlane (1978).   [130] Cressy (1986); French & Hoyle (2003).
[131] French & Hoyle (2003), at 621.   [132] Wrightson (2003), at 59.

with "Confucian" kinship hierarchies, Chinese social norms actually promoted substantive socioeconomic equality.

Thus far my analysis has focused clearly and unapologetically on social norms or customary law. Official laws and regulations simply mattered far less on the Chinese land market than communally negotiated customs, and indeed were usually superseded outright if the two came into conflict. Even in England, the main normative issues examined here – for how long could a mortgagor retain the right of redemption and whether landlords could evict or modify fees against the tenants' wishes – were regulated primarily by custom rather than by statute or precedent. The common-law courts certainly contributed to the efficacy of mortgage default as a land acquisition tool, but chiefly by harshly enforcing customary redemption deadlines, not by setting the deadlines themselves. The primacy of customary law is true, in fact, of most economic activities in early modern China and England, due largely to the weakness of Qing local governance and the inaccessibility of English royal courts.[133]

This does not mean, however, that the state can simply be ignored. As Chapter 5 will discuss, the state probably played some substantive role in the proliferation of kinship hierarchies in late Imperial China. Likewise, the consolidation of sociopolitical power by the English landed classes benefited from state expansion after the Black Death. If legal authorities often took a back seat to social norms in the direct regulation of land transactions, they were certainly more visible in promoting the status distribution norms that underlay those norms. For the Qing and Republican governments, this created some uncomfortable paradoxes: property customs created under the influence of state-sponsored kinship norms often contradicted, indeed overrode, official laws and regulations. The early modern English state behaved more consistently: both its status redistribution efforts and its forays into substantive property regulation favored higher-income households. This contrast was not, however, due to any difference in the composition of officials – wealthy families dominated government ranks in both countries. More likely, it was due to differences in sociolegal culture, in what were internally understood to be proper norms of status distribution and institutional deference.

---

[133] On the difficulties involved with using common-law or equity courts in early modern England, *see* Richard Ross, *Commoning of the Common Law: The Renaissance Debate over Printing English Law, 1520–1640*, 146 UNIV. PENN. L. REV. 323–461 (1998).

E Permanent Tenancy: An Additional Example of Kinship Hierarchies at Work?

As discussed in Chapter 3, collateralized lending is an especially convenient place to observe the institutional impact of Chinese and English rural social hierarchies. The legal stakes for smallholders were extremely high, largely because tighter redemption windows dramatically increased the likelihood that they would lose their land, whereas the stakes for larger landowners, who could still profit from acquiring collateral even if the norm was infinite redeemability, were considerably lower. We would expect, therefore, that the social status differences between Chinese and English smallholders really could have had some significant institutional impact here – as opposed to other potential sociopolitical settings in which the stakes were also extremely high for large landowners and may therefore have motivated them to "win at all costs," regardless of the social status of smallholders. This is, as argued earlier, exactly what happened.

That said, it would nonetheless be quite odd if collateralized lending was the *only* place where such an impact was observable. The sweeping (one is tempted to use "paradigmatic") differences between Chinese and English social hierarchies described in this book would presumably have influenced most corners of socioeconomic life. This influence may be difficult to observe, perhaps because economic elites were still somewhat more powerful than smallholders in the Chinese countryside – just not nearly as dominant as they were in England – or perhaps because the interests of large and smaller landholders were not always, or even often, in conflict. Even so, another major example or two would clearly be desirable, and this section attempts to provide one by outlining the model's likely applicability to tenancy institutions in North China, the Lower Yangtze, and England.

It should be emphasized that this is a supplementary exercise, and perhaps not even a logically necessary one. The qualitative links between kinship hierarchies and *dian* institutions discussed in this chapter are neither strengthened nor weakened by the existence of an additional application of the model. If no such application existed, it would simply beg the additional question of "what made *dian* institutions special" rather than invalidate the entire model. The model's applicability to *dian* and mortgage institutions stands on its own.

For this reason, and also because a fully detailed treatment would likely double the length of this book with terrible effects for readability, the treatment that follows will necessarily be abbreviated. It is truly the *outline* of an argument based more on secondary sources than on primary ones. Fortunately, the secondary literature on tenancy institutions is much more extensive than the literature on collateralized lending, but even so, I make no claim here that this is a conclusive argument. It is a somewhat in-depth preview of future research, perhaps to be taken up immediately after the conclusion of the present project. The goal is to establish plausibility rather than probability – although hopefully the discussion that follows can go a bit beyond that.

The system of permanent tenancy, in general terms, allowed tenants to actually "own" usage rights over a piece of land and not be subject to random eviction by the landlord. In this sense, they owned the "topsoil" of the land, whereas the landlords owned the "subsoil."[134] "Topsoil" owners were essentially entitled to remain on the land as long as they paid rent – or, most commonly, even if they did not, as long as unpaid rent did not exceed the land's full value. Landlords could not increase the rent without the tenant's consent and could not charge any additional fees. The practice became popular during the Ming and eventually came to be the dominant form of tenancy in some macroregions during the Qing, most notably the Lower Yangtze and South China, where it probably accounted for well over half of rented land in the early twentieth century.[135] By at least the early Qing, most permanent tenants had also gained the right to sublease, transfer, or even *dian* sell their "topsoil" rights, which effectively created a bipartite land market, one for "topsoil" and one for "subsoil."[136]

One might wonder if the landlord was compensated for his loss of control through higher rents, but this was likely not the case: rent levels generally fell between 40 and 50 percent of annual produce for both permanent and nonpermanent tenants in the later-nineteenth-century

---

[134] Pomeranz (2008), at 131; YANG (1988), at 92–93; ZHOU & XIE (1986), 290–92.

[135] Pomeranz (2008), at 132; CHEN SHUZHU, ZHEJIANG SHENG TUDI WENTI YU WU.ER. JIANZU [THE LAND ISSUE IN ZHEJIANG PROVINCE AND THE MAY 2ND TAX REDUCTION MOVEMENT], 283–84 (1996); LI WENZHI & JIANG TAIXIN, ZHONGGUO DIZHU ZHI JINGJI LUN [ON CHINA'S LANDLORD-BASED ECONOMY], 292–94 (2005). A 1949 study by Muramatsu Yujii, cited in Mi-chu Wiens, *Lord and Peasant in China: The Sixteenth to Eighteenth Centuries*, 6 MODERN CHINA 29 (1980), gives a lower figure (one-third to two-fifths) even for Jiangnan, but this was quite likely affected by wartime disruptions. For the late-nineteenth-century estimate, *see* Han Hengyu, *Shilun Qingdai Qianqi Diannong Yongdian Quan de Youlai ji qi Xingqi* [*On the Origins and Nature of the Permanent Tenancy Rights of Early Qing Tenant Farmers*], 1 QINGSHI LUNCONG [COLLECTED ESSAYS ON QING HISTORY] 38 (1979).

[136] BERNHARDT (1992), at 25.

Lower Yangtze.[137] A similar situation existed across South China. In fact, many, possibly most, tenants had actually been able to secure fixed rents (rather than fixed percentages of produce) by the nineteenth century, which means that actual rent burdens – and the "real" intake by landlords – plummeted during the sharp inflation of the 1890s and early 1900s to well below 30 percent of produce. This begs the question: why were landlords willing to accept these constraints on their legal powers?

The answer lies in the specific circumstances under which permanent tenancies were created. As Philip Huang, Pomeranz, and others have argued, most permanent tenancies existed where the bargaining power of the tenand to-be was strong and that of the potential landlord was limited.[138] First, and perhaps foremost, they were created via contractual arrangement in crisis or postcrisis eras, during which the population shrank, and good tenants were therefore difficult to find. For example, major waves of Lower and Middle Yangtze permanent tenancy contracts were granted during and immediately after the mid-seventeenth-century Qing conquest and again during the Taiping Rebellion, when landlords were often unable to man their land and needed extra concessions to attract tenants. A second way to obtain "topsoil" ownership was through the reclamation of wasteland. Under such circumstances, the landlord himself was presumably in no position to effectively reclaim and therefore had to supply extra economic incentives for the tenant to do so.

Finally, a significant number of permanent tenancies were created in conjecture with *dian* or permanent land sales – more often the former. In such cases, a smallholder would *dian* sell his land under the condition that he would be allowed to remain on it as tenant.[139] Most often the rent would not count toward the repayment of the loan, but rather provided the financial incentive for the creditor to issue the loan. For *dian* sellers at least, the incentive to pursue such an arrangement was fairly clear: it allowed them to enjoy at least some of the profits of the collateralized land rather than losing it altogether until they managed to redeem. It also created a scenario where the *dian* seller could have taken advantage of the institutional and social advantages he enjoyed in the *dian* sale context to push for more favorable terms as tenant. Given that, as argued earlier, *dian* sellers were able to marshal considerable sociopolitical capital to create

---

[137] *E.g.*, Fang Xing, *Qingdai Qianqi de Fengjian Dizu Lü*, 1992(2) Zhongguo Jingjishi Yanjiu 61, 65.

[138] Huang (2001); Pomeranz (2008), at 131–33.

[139] Hayashi Megumi, Chu Shi Konan noson shakai seifo kenkyu (1953), at 150–60.

highly protective *dian* customs, it is easily conceivable that they might have pressed their advantage to further secure a right of permanent tenancy – if the seller so desired – over all *dian* collateral. There are indeed, as discussed below, documentable cases where such "institutional piggybacking" likely occurred. This does not imply, of course, that piggybacking was always, or even often, successful (or desirable), but it does seem to have been the norm in some parts of the Lower Yangtze and North China.[140]

Beyond these circumstances – there may have been others, but these are the three major categories – landlords tended to resist the creation of permanent tenancies, or at least would have charged abnormally high rents for them. Even so, the spread of permanent tenancy throughout the Lower Yangtze in particular was more or less an irreversible trend, driven by the simple reason that, once granted, permanent tenancies were extraordinarily difficult to take back.

This was not for lack of effort. As the years passed, many landlords began to realize that they could derive significantly greater profits – more on this in Chapter 6 – from hands-on management of their land than from rents.[141] Even though the supply of wage labor was somewhat depressed due to the ability of smallholders to retain some control over their plots for very long periods of time, wages were low enough to make managerial farming highly attractive. In addition, the growing prevalence of fixed rents substantially depressed the real income of many landlords during times of high inflation – most notably the final fifteen years of the Qing.[142]

These considerations fueled landlord hostility toward preexisting permanent tenancy rights and incentivized many landlords to attempt, when possible, to extinguish them, or at least to impose higher rents. The former could come in the form of legal actions to expel a tenant for unpaid rent – the Longquan archives, for example, contain several dozen such cases – or simply an expulsion by force.[143] Barring an attempt to formally expel the tenant, some landlords tried to unilaterally increase rents, claiming that the archaic rent levels paid by many permanent tenants no longer reflected the monetary value of the land's actual productivity. Needless to say, tenants were rarely willing to surrender their rights without a fight. As a number of scholars have documented, the socioeconomic tension between landlords

---

[140] HAYASHI (1953); for North China, *see* discussion of *dian xiaozuo* practices in the Mantetsu surveys below.

[141] Chapter 6, Section B.

[142] On Late-Qing inflation, *see* Broadberry, Guan, & Li (2014); Ma & Chu (2013).

[143] Longquan Dang'an Hebian Mulu; search for 抗租.

and tenants boiled over into significant peasant rent resistance movements multiple times during the later eighteenth and nineteenth centuries and again during the Republican era.[144]

From time to time, the landlords seemed to have the government on their side. The *Qing Code* had little to say about this issue, but provincial authorities tended to be quite aggressively hostile to permanent tenancy: the Fujian, Jiangxi, and Jiangsu governments all issued, at multiple points after mid-dynasty, prohibitions against the practice.[145] By the end of the dynasty, central legal reformers had soured on the system enough that they attempted to eliminate the notion of truly *permanent* tenancy nationwide and imposed, in the draft Civil Code of 1911, a limit of fifty years on all tenancies.[146]

Despite all this, the landlords never really seemed to gain the upper hand. Peasant rent resistance was effective enough that fairly few landlords were able to obtain the higher rents they desired, let alone eliminate significant numbers of permanent tenancies. The fact that late Qing and Republican landlords, particularly those in the Lower Yangtze, actually began to seek the state's assistance in combating permanent tenancy is a particularly telling development. As Kathryn Bernhardt documents in some detail, Lower Yangtze landlords were traditionally reluctant to allow state involvement in tenancy disputes, perhaps because it posed potential challenges to their own authority.[147] Nonetheless, by the post-Taiping era, and especially by the Republican era, things had become bad enough that many landlords were openly petitioning the state for assistance.[148] Apart from supporting the legal changes described in the preceding paragraph, they also seemed somewhat more willing to sue delinquent tenants in county courts, generating a moderate wave of such cases in late-nineteenth- and early-twentieth-century case archives.[149]

But even with government support, landlords were apparently unable to shake the socioeconomic prevalence of permanent tenancy. Cases from the 1930s and 1940s suggest that the practice was still widespread in the Lower Yangtze. Moreover, the Republican government seemed to acknowledge that the half-hearted crackdown of previous regimes had largely failed by "reinstating" permanent tenancy in the Civil Code of

---

[144] *Id.*; Li Wenzhi, Mingqing Shidai Fengjian Tudi Guanxi de Songjie [The Loosening of Feudal Land Relations in the Ming and Qing] (2007); Bernhardt (1992); Evelyn S. Rawski, Agricultural Change and the Peasant Economy of South China (1972).
[145] Yang (1988), at 115. [146] Huang (2001), at 99–118.
[147] Bernhardt (1992), at 40–41. [148] Bernhardt (1992), at 165–72.
[149] Huang (2001) at 114–18; Longquan Dang'an Hebian Mulu; search for 佃 and 租地.

1929 , which formally recognized *yongdian* ("permanent tenancy") as the "right to cultivate or to raise livestock permanent on the land of another person by paying a rent."[150]

A common assumption in the preexisting academic literature is that permanent tenancy was primarily a southern – Lower Yangtze and South China, in particular – institution and that it was economically insignificant in North China.[151] This may have been somewhat true as a general matter, but there were probably many exceptions: The Mantetsu surveys, for example, document at least one village, Sibeichai, where permanent tenancy was by far the most important form of tenancy, indeed covering almost a third of the village's arable land, and three other villages where it was fairly commonplace but where precise statistical estimates are impossible.[152] In Sibeichai, the most prevalent form of tenancy was what the surveyors called "*dian* tenancy," in which a *dian* seller remained on the collateralized land as tenant and paid a fixed rent to the landlord/creditor until he was able to redeem in full. This was, of course, more or less the same way that many Lower Yangtze and South China permanent tenancies were created. Under the Sibeichai version of "*dian* tenancy," the tenant/ debtor could not be removed from the land as long as the *dian* contract was still in effect – in fact, not even when he had failed to pay rent for over two years. Given that these *dian* contracts were, by custom, infinitely redeemable, this essentially created a full permanent tenancy in which the landlord could, in general, neither unilaterally raise rents nor evict the tenant.[153] The vast majority – well over 95 percent – of *dian* contracts led to such an arrangement. Cumulatively, they accounted for, at the time of the survey, 627 of the 2,074 mu of arable land in the village, or 30.2 percent. Even in cases where tenancy was not tied to any underlying *dian* contract, some interviewees speak of a kind of tenancy contract that granted some form of permanent tenancy. These did not specify any term of years and, in general, ended with the declaration that "the landlord shall not have the right to take back the land, but the tenant may terminate the tenancy" (*xu ci bu xu shou*). The economic scale and institutional framework of this latter kind of tenancy are somewhat unclear, but both tenants and landlords acknowledged its existence.[154]

In three other villages, Houxiazhai, Houjiaying, and Shajing, the surveyors found evidence of similar tenancy relationships, but were unable to

---

[150] REPUBLICAN CIVIL CODE Art. 842.   [151] Pomeranz (2008), at 132.
[152] 3 MANTETSU 1; 2 MANTETSU 177; 4 MANTETSU 151; 5 MANTETSU 181–83.
[153] 3 MANTETSU 213, 241.   [154] 3 MANTETSU 186–93, 241–42.

calculate their scale.[155] There is no reason to think that it was nearly comparable to what they found in Sibeichai, which is, in many ways, highly unusual among North China villages in terms of tenancy. Whereas most estimates of the percentage of North China land under tenancy come out in the 10 to 30 percent range, in Sibeichai, the figure was around 60 percent, of which half were "*dian* tenancies."[156] The other half consisted of normal fixed-year tenancies in which the landlord could remove the tenant after a number of years, generally no more than a decade. Apart from Sibeichai, no other village in the survey fell out of the normal range, indicating that tenancy as a whole, and specifically "*dian* tenancies," were of rather limited economic significance. Nonetheless, they did seem to exist in many, perhaps most, localities and could occasionally be of considerable importance. In other words, permanent tenancy was not merely a southern phenomenon – although it was certainly more economically important in southern macroregions – but was instead at least a somewhat national one.

The parallels between this summary of permanent tenancy practices and the history of *dian* redemption norms covered in Chapter 1 are fairly striking: both were highly prevalent – permanent tenancy was probably less prevalent overall in North China and the Lower Yangtze than infinite *dian* redemption, but nonetheless was the dominant form of tenancy in, at least, the southern macroregions – customary economic institutions that favored the interests of poorer households over larger landowners. Both eventually drew some institutional opposition from nineteenth- and early-twentieth-century state authorities but were probably able to maintain their socioeconomic dominance in the face of that. In both cases, the Republican state eventually recognized that such opposition was ineffective and fruitless and therefore ceded ground to customary norms in the Civil Code of 1929.

The parallels become even more remarkable when we throw in the English comparison. For many scholars, particularly those who agree – in whole or in part – with the "Brenner thesis," the most important theme in the early modern history of English land law was the increasingly dire circumstances faced by tenants. The closest analogy to permanent tenancy one can find in early modern English tenancy institutions is probably the copyhold, especially copyholds of inheritance.[157] Established by manorial custom rather than the common law, such tenancies usually

---

[155] 2 Mantetsu 177; 4 Mantetsu 151; 5 Mantetsu 181–83.
[156] Esherick (1981); 3 Mantetsu 1.   [157] Hoyle (1990), at 1, 7–12, 17–18.

had no fixed term; paid only a nominal rent; could be inherited, sold, mortgaged, or subleased just as freehold land; and were not subject to direct evictions. Although the lack of substantive rent makes any comparison with any form of commercial tenancy rather tenuous, these were, to most peasants, the most secure form of nonfreehold ownership available.

Creation of copyholds, however, had slowed to a trickle during the fifteenth and sixteenth centuries and had largely vanished by the seventeenth century.[158] Quite the opposite, landlords encumbered by copyholds were busy attempting to revoke copyhold rights throughout the early modern era, usually by raising inheritance and conveyance fees to exorbitant levels or even by raising rents outright.[159] This is what some historians refer to as the "first enclosure movement," as distinguished from the Parliament-driven enclosure movement that emerged in the later eighteenth century. Copyholders who converted their holdings into leasehold land under such pressure became tenants in the modern Anglo-American sense: they held only for a fixed term of years and could not pass the tenancy to their heirs without the landlord's express approval. Courts of equity occasionally offered some legal relief to pressured copyholders, usually by blocking arbitrary increases in fees or rent, but were beyond the financial and physical reach of most copyholders.[160] Overall, the early modern era saw English property institutions move away from tenancy security – something that Qing and Republican landlords certainly coveted but could never quite manage.

While this basic institutional narrative, at least in broad strokes, has been accepted by most scholars, there has been vociferous debate over its economic significance. This was, in fact, the core of the famous "Brenner debate" that drew enormous amounts of attention from historians, sociologists, and political scientists alike in the 1970s and 1980s – in which Robert Brenner and some supporters argued that landlord enclosure was responsible for the rise of large managerial farms in early modern England, while their opponents denied that causal link.[161] Later studies, based on

---

[158] *Id.*; Gray (1963).

[159] BRENNER DEBATE, at 10–63; KERRIDGE (1969), at 36–37; Hoyle (1990) (placing the start of conscious landlord encroachment at around 1550).

[160] ALEXANDER SAVINE, COPYHOLD CASES IN THE EARLY CHANCERY PROCEEDINGS: -1902 (1902); KERRIDGE (1969); GRAY (1963).

[161] BRENNER DEBATE (1987).

more systemic surveys of available evidence, offered some support to Brenner but also argued that it was seriously incomplete: landlord enclosure was likely a major cause of managerial farming, but it was nonetheless one among several and may not have been as significant as some other causal mechanisms, particularly tenant-driven land consolidation.[162] For the purposes of our present discussion, however, the institutional narrative of landlords rolling back tenant rights is what matters, not the economic consequences of that narrative.

To summarize, Chinese and English tenancy institutions diverged dramatically over the two centuries or so prior to industrialization. Chinese tenancy institutions remained strongly protective of tenant interests, whereas English ones became – under severe pressure from landlords – much harsher toward tenants. This is, in broad strokes, the same divergence that occurred between *dian* institutions and English mortgage institutions. In England, both sets of institutions came to favor the interests of large, wealthy landholders, whereas in China, they remained consistently "egalitarian," in the sense that they favored, in large part, the interests of poorer rural households.

The question then becomes: can the same model that I have applied to the *dian*-mortgage divergence also apply in the tenancy context? Is there a plausible argument to be made that Chinese kinship hierarchies also empowered lower-income households to negotiate for, and often obtain, favorable tenancy institutions? The remainder of this section makes the case that there is.

Previous scholarship has generally attempted to explain permanent tenancy in essentially the same way that it attempted to explain *dian* redemption: by appealing to "precommercial" ideal that peasants could gain close to full ownership of a piece of land by investing their labor, especially when the land was previously uncultivated. Landlords were compelled to respect such claims by social values that prioritized subsistence and survival – and therefore the rights of smallholders over large landlords.[163] And yet this argument is at least as tenuous – if not more so – as when it was made in the *dian* context. Not only is the evidence provided extremely thin, but there really is, as argued earlier, very little reason to believe that Chinese social attitudes toward landed property were any more "precommercial" or "premodern" than whatever sentimental attachment historical or contemporary American or European landowners felt toward

---

[162] Hoyle (1990). [163] HUANG (2001), at 203–05. *Cf.* BUOYE (2000) for criticism.

their land.[164] All across the country, rural Chinese households sold, mortgaged, and subleased land regularly, displaying fairly high levels of economic aggression and sophistication.

None of this is to deny that permanent tenants did have strong attachments to their rented land or even that, in many cases, the depth of that attachment might have exceeded what pure "rational economic choice" would have predicted, but only to argue that such attachment did not rise to the level of a widely embraced societal custom that could have dissuaded landlords from seeking higher rents or eviction. As with *dian* institutions, the sheer amount of documentable social tension and conflict over permanent tenancy would seem to decisively rebut any claim that there were general communal "ideals" preventing landlords from acting against tenants.

In fact, social conflict over permanent tenancy was arguably more dramatic and disruptive than tensions over *dian* redemption. Whereas, in the latter context, the primary evidence of intravillage disagreement was the occasional legal suit and some oral histories of local dispute collected in targeted rural surveys, in the former context, we actually have – as noted earlier – abundant evidence of tenancy-related disputes boiling over into violent conflict between tenants and their landlords, some of which required formal military intervention by provincial authorities.

Take, for example, the Suzhou region. In the mid-nineteenth century alone, it experienced two significant incidents of severe tenant-landlord conflict, each involving over a hundred tenant families and extensive acts of looting and rioting. First, in 1846, a large number of households in Zhaowen County rose up to protest attempted rent increases by absentee landlords.[165] When negotiations broke down, the tenants – perhaps emboldened by an 1842 incident in which famine-year looting of wealthier households went largely unpunished – organized a series of riots, raiding landlord granaries and even residences across several nearby towns. At this point the county government attempted to intervene, first through mediation and then through armed intervention by local militia. When its efforts failed to bear fruit, formal military intervention became necessary, eventually bringing the protests to an end after a two-week campaign. The

---

[164] There has been no shortage of articles arguing that landownership is a deeply psychological thing in Western societies. *See, e.g.,* Margaret Jane Radin, *Personhood and Property*, 34 STAN. L. REV. 957 (1982).

[165] ZHENG GUANGZU, YIBAN LU ZASHU[MISCELLANEOUS ESSAYS FROM THE YIBAN RECORDS] chap. 7 (Zhongguo Book Store ed., 1990).

protest ringleaders were put in custody, but in the end, the planned rent increases were also abandoned. A somewhat similar incident happened in Wujiang County in 1852 when negotiations between local landlords and tenants over the adoption of a fixed rent – the landlords wanted more flexibility, whereas the tenants insisted on a flat rate – boiled over into prolonged conflict.[166] While there was never any single incident that rose to the scale of the Zhaowen riots, raids against landlord-owned granaries happened on and off for nearly three years until the county magistrate finally managed to engineer an agreement, the terms of which are unfortunately not known.

If we turn our sights instead to less intense forms of conflict, the Lower Yangtze Qing and Republican case collections examined earlier – including both the Longquan Archives and an assortment of private case collections – contain numerous permanent tenancy-related cases, most often in the form of actions against delinquent tenants, most to recover unpaid rent and some to evict the tenant entirely. In fact, it was an even larger source of litigation than *dian* redemption, accounting for around 1,000 of the some 17,000 cases in the Longquan Archives.[167] Without going through all of these one by one – something that is impossible within the constraints of this project – there is unfortunately no way to know how many of these involved permanent tenancies, but it is probably safe to say that many were, given that permanent tenancy was, by the Republican era, the dominant form of tenancy in southern Zhejiang. A preliminary survey of a subset of 100 cases yields six cases in which a landlord explicitly sought to evict a permanent tenant. In all six cases, unpaid rent was cited as one reason for litigation, but in no case did the total delinquency add up to more than a fraction of the land's total value – recall that the customary Lower Yangtze practice was that eviction was only permissible if unpaid rent had exceeded the total value.[168] In at least two cases, the landlord also argued – echoing the late Qing and early Republican attempts to ban permanent tenancy – that he was entitled to evict the tenant simply because the tenancy had exceeded half a century.[169] In one other case,

---

[166] Lı Lı Xu Zhı [Additional Gazetteer of Lı Lı] (Guangxu edition) chap. 12 (1899); Ke Wuchi, Louwang Yongyu Ji [Record of the Fish that Escaped the Net] 15 (Zhonghua Shuju Press, 1959); Bernhardt (1992), at 63–66.

[167] Longquan Dang'an Hebian Mulu, search for 佃 and 租地.

[168] Longquan Archives M003-01-04941; M003-01-09131; M003-01-09612; M003-01-01317; M003-01-14243; M003-01-01787.

[169] Longquan Archives M003-01-01317; M003-01-14243.

the landlord apparently sought to increase rents and, when faced with tenant resistance, sued to evict.[170]

None of these cases received a final decision, and they were presumably settled out of court. We can only guess at the content of those settlements, but given that permanent tenancy remained the dominant form of tenancy in southern Zhejiang throughout the Republican era, it is hard to imagine that landlord eviction attempts succeeded with any regularity. Nonetheless, there is fairly good reason to believe that Longquan landlords occasionally attempted to challenge customary practices. Looking across the wide range of violent conflict between Lower Yangtze landlords and tenants in the later Qing, one can reasonably suspect that, in this regard, they probably had much in common with multiple generations of landlords across the entire macroregion.

Landlord-tenant conflicts were, as a general matter, less prevalent in North China, if only because tenancy was not nearly as economically significant there. Nonetheless, in places where we know it was – Sibeichai, in particular – social tensions over customary tenancy law were, unsurprisingly, a significant theme of local life. As noted earlier, permanent tenancy in Sibeichai was essentially an institutional add-on to *dian* sales, which meant, of course, that tension over permanent tenancy was often folded into disputes over *dian* redemption. For example, when speaking about the Zhang Leqing–Lin Fengxi *dian* redemption dispute discussed in Section C, Lin, echoing some of the other landlords, complained that landlords should have, in general, stronger remedies against tenants who fail to pay rent on time. Because Zhang Leqing was essentially renting his own land – which had been *dian* sold to Lin – Lin felt that he had very limited power to enforce rent payment and found this frustrating.[171] Wang Zanzhou, the largest landlord in Sibeichai, actually went quite a bit further than that and proposed that landlords should have the right to expel tenants if unpaid rent accumulated to some unspecified level and, if the tenancy was based on a *dian* sale, to force a sale of the collateralized land and collect the unpaid amount from the proceeds.[172] Naturally, this claim was fiercely disputed by the tenants, particularly Zhang Leqing, who argued that no amount of unpaid rent could allow the landlord/*dian* buyer to expel the tenant or touch the underlying *dian* sale.[173] Wang, apparently wary of tenant resistance, admitted that despite his belief that he did possess these rights, he had never actually exercised them.[174]

---

[170] Longquan Archives M003-01-01787.   [171] 3 MANTETSU 174.   [172] *Id.*, at 224–26.
[173] *Id.*, at 186–93, 213.   [174] *Id.*, at 242.

Simply put, there is very little evidence, if any, that rural communities in *any* core Chinese macroregion shared any "precommercial ideal of permanency in landholding," whether in the *dian* context or in the permanent tenancy context. Quite the opposite, they were constantly reexamined and renegotiated and the source of much social argument and dispute. In this regard, they shared much in common with English property institutions, which, as noted earlier, have commonly been portrayed as one of the most significant sources of social tension and conflict in early modern England.

But if so, can we also explain the relative institutional success of Chinese tenants vis-à-vis their English counterparts by appealing to their collectively greater sociopolitical status under gerontocratic kinship hierarchies? Time and length limitations preclude an in-depth, qualitative examination of this issue within the corners of this book, but a preliminary survey of available circumstantial evidence nonetheless suggests that the answer could very well be "Yes." Kinship networks and their internal power relations clearly played a major role in the negotiation of tenancy institutions, and it seems very possible – perhaps likely – that the presence of high-status but low-income seniors in Lower Yangtze and North China villages had a significant impact on the outcomes of these negotiations.

Permanent tenancy relations came in two forms: those between local landlords and tenants and those between an absentee landlord and a local tenant. As a number of scholars have argued, in the Lower Yangtze, the latter gradually overtook the former over the course of the Qing, until, by the early nineteenth century, it was clearly the dominant form in most localities.[175] But even after most major landlords had moved away from the villages in which they owned land, they still tended to conduct rent collection and renegotiation via the kinship networks to which they belonged. In many places, the *yizhuang* institution – which formerly had been a kind of lineage-owned and -managed corporate property that provided welfare blankets to the lineage's poorer members – became the nexus of tenancy negotiations: the landlord's closest relatives would manage his rented properties, collect rent, and renegotiate terms with tenants.[176] It bears repeating

[175] Wu Tao, *Qingdai Jiangnan de Yitian Liangzhu Zhi he Zhudian Guanxi de Xin Geju*, 2004(5) JINGDAI SHI YANJIU 137; BERNHARDT (1992).

[176] Zhang Yan, *Qingdai Jiangnan Shouzu Jigou Jianlun* [*A Brief Discussion of the Rent-Collection Institutions in the Qing Lower Yangtze*], 1990(4) HANGZHOU SHIFAN DAXUE XUEBAO [ACADEMIC JOURNAL OF THE HANGZHOU NORMAL UNIVERSITY] 135; MURAMATSU Yūji, KINDAI KŌNAN NO SOSAN – CHŪGOKU JINUSHI SEIDO NO KENKYŪ [TENANCY IN THE EARLY MODERN LOWER YANGTZE: RESEARCH ON CHINESE LANDLORD INSTITUTIONS] 679–740 (1970).

here that many, arguably most, Lower Yangtze villages were dominated by one or two major lineages and that most households preferred to do business with their relatives before looking outside. This meant that the majority of tenancy relations in these villages were established between members of the same lineage and therefore that the *yizhuang* nexus was really an intralineage institution that helped to mediate tenancy-related disputes between different branches of the same extended family. In other words, the landlord, despite being physically absent from the village, still relied on – and was therefore subject to – his kinship-based social structure.

Unsurprisingly, then, several scholars have argued that kinship ties and hierarchies still wielded a fair amount of influence over the business conduct of landlords.[177] This was especially true of middling and smaller landlords, who generally maintained closer ties with their ancestral home-town and often retained residences in them. Such cases were common in North China – in Sibeichai, for example, most landlords lived within less than a day's commute from the village, some only a couple of miles away – but also existed in significant numbers in the Lower Yangtze, even in the late nineteenth century. For some of these landlords, local lineage ties were constraining enough that they desired to lessen their reliance on them, instead employing professional, urban-based rent collectors. Such strategies often backfired, in that they could provoke tenant resistance and actually *lower* rent yields, but in any case, their mere existence strongly suggests that lineage networks often worked *against* the economic interest of landlords.

For Lower Yangtze landlords who resided in major urban centers – such cases were rare in North China – reliance on *yizhuang* institutions and lineage networks to collect rent tended to be inconvenient, not least because they owned land in many villages, most of which they had no kinship ties to. Instead, they employed professional rent managers, who often had local agents but did not rely on lineage networks for collection, dispute resolution, or the renegotiation of terms.[178] In such cases, although local lineages were unable to place any significant normative pressure on

---

[177] Wu (2004); Zhang (1990); Muramatsu (1970); Yamana Hirofumi, *Shinmatsu Konan no Giso ni Tsuite* [*Late Qing charity estates in the Jiangnan area*], 62 Tayo Gakuho [East Asian Studies] 99 (1980).

[178] Natsui Haruki, Chūgoku kindai kōnan no jinushi sei kenkyū [A Study of Landlord Institutions in the Early Modern Lower Yangtze] (2001); You Jianxia, *Suzhou de Dizhu yu Nongmin* [*Landlords and Peasants in Suzhou*], *in* 3 Suzhou Wenshi Ziliao [Literary and Historical Documents from Suzhou] 57 (1990); Muramatsu Yūji, *A Documentary Study of Chinese Landlordism in the Late Ch'ing and Early Republic Kiangnan*, 29 Bull. Schl. Ori. Afr. Stud. 566 (1966).

the landlords, they nonetheless provided crucial institutional support for tenant resistance. At the minimum, they supplied social networking and helped to create a consolidated local front against "oppressive" outsiders. Even these basic functions relied on the support and authorization of lineage elites, which were intuitively much easier to obtain if some elites shared, or at least deeply sympathized with, the tenants' economic interests. As a general matter, tenant resistance tended to be driven by less affluent households, which, of course, had the most to lose from rent increases or evictions. Wealthier tenants could absorb these shocks more easily and were therefore often unsure – on the margins – whether they were worth fighting for, especially when the act of resistance was not without its significant economic and political risks.[179] At the same time, tenant resistance obviously would be much more effective if the village or lineage could act as a whole. There was, in other words, a "free-rider problem" not unlike what scholars have observed in modern labor union organization or, more generally, in almost any kind of social movement.

In theory, seniority-based internal hierarchies should have helped to resolve such free-rider problems in favor of poorer tenants. Because such a system allowed poorer tenants to occupy senior positions of leadership within the lineage or village, it also enabled them to push, often quite effectively, for collective action even when wealthier tenants were less enthusiastic. Contrast this with a scenario where poorer tenants were largely excluded from the local political elite. Rousing wealthier tenants to action would likely be a far more difficult task under such circumstances, unless they were otherwise inclined – perhaps due to economic self-interest, perhaps due to emotional solidarity – to join the resistance movement. Seniority-based kinship hierarchies could have given lower-income tenants an avenue to compel resistance participation by wealthier tenants, thereby boosting the strength of their resistance and the likelihood of success.

For example, in both the Zhaowen and Wujiang rent riots, a collection of the poorest tenant households was able to persuade or force nearly their entire lineage into participating in the resistance movement despite the initial reluctance of other lineage members.[180] Several organizers of the Zhaowen riots apparently enjoyed relatively prominent positions within

---

[179] The reluctance of wealthier tenants is documented in, for example, *Bing wei Chengjing Difang Yanban Kangzu Shi* [*A Report on Measures to Enforce Strict Local Penalties Against Rent Resistance*], in SUISHOU JILU [RECORDS OF CONVENIENCE] (held at Changshu Municipal Library, 1891). For general discussion on collective action problems in rural Qing society, *see* Terada (1998).

[180] ZHENG GUANGZU (1990), at chap. 7; KE WUCHI, LOUWANG YONGYU JI [Record of the Fish that Escaped the Net] 15 (Zhonghua Shuju Press, 1959).

their respective lineages and were able to persuade the overseers of local ancestral temples – generally the most senior members of the lineage – to help them organize, including by allowing worship and prayer events in which lineage ancestors were presumed to have given their blessing to the riots.[181] Similarly, in the Sibeichai rent disputes documented in the Mantetsu surveys, Zhang Leqing's senior status in the village helped him to rally a large number of tenant households to his cause.[182] This created the perception among some landlords that they were facing resistance from the entire village rather than from a few scattered tenants, which, in turn, significantly boosted their willingness to accept the tenants' demands.

It goes without saying that the preceding discussion amounts only to a preliminary sketch of a historical argument. The point here, once again, is simply to create a prima facie case for the possibility – probably a strong possibility – that kinship hierarchies affected tenancy disputes and negotiations in a pro-tenant fashion. At the very least, it offers a plausible and coherent interpretation of secondary sources and historical narratives – much more so than the major preexisting theory, which argues for "precommercial ideals" of permanency in landholding. In other words, there is a decent likelihood that the basic model advanced here and in Chapter 3 can apply beyond the *dian* context and explain at least one other important set of property institutions.

A fuller argument – something that I intend to pursue in the near future – would be fairly straightforward. It would rely on a set of archival material similar to what this chapter has drawn on, including local cases, tenancy contracts, private writings, and local surveys. The basic contours of the argument were already established earlier in this chapter. First, permanent tenancy was constantly renegotiated between households, or groups of households, possessing divergent interests. The types of institutional arrangements a household desired largely depended on its economic standing and incentives. Second, the outcome of these negotiations was substantially affected by the relative sociopolitical status of the interested parties and specifically by kinship hierarchies. As noted earlier, this would likely be a simpler argument to make than the one made herein about *dian* redemption, if only because tenancy-related disputes were more likely to trigger serious social tension, in which the dynamics of conflict and negotiation were easier to follow than in the lower-key disputes over *dian* institutions.

---

[181] ZHENG GUANGZU (1990), at chap. 7.   [182] 3 MANTETSU 170–74, 245, 263.

What, exactly, would be the significance of this? One could make a strong argument that *dian* redemption and permanent tenancy, combined, actually accounted for most of the property institutions that incited significant amounts of rich-poor tension. In general, early modern smallholders, whether in China or in England, preferred property institutions that provided the following: secure, largely private ownership and usage; the ability to sell and collateralize land when needed; the right to devise their property to heirs; minimal risk of losing the land permanently due to economic duress; and relatively favorable tenancy institutions in case they had to rent. Large landowners, too, generally benefited from the first two items, thereby creating a strong social consensus in their favor. The third item, inheritance rights, created complicated socioeconomic problems that are probably best left to a future project. In any case, the primary battle lines concerning inheritance rights were rarely drawn across rich-poor divisions.[183] The latter two items, however, tended to be major focal points of wealth-based social tension – and Chinese smallholders "won" on both points far more regularly than their English peers. Therefore, simply by covering collateral redemption and tenancy, the model presented here already can explain the comparative outcomes of arguably *most* early modern property-related disputes between rich and poor.[184] In fact, even if it were only capable of explaining collateral redemption, that would still be a very significant slice of the pie.

As a theoretical matter, there is a good argument to be made that the set of socially contested landed property institutions, particularly in early modern economies, was often much smaller than commonly assumed. As several property theorists have argued, societies – whether early modern

---

[183] There were, as a number of scholars have argued, significant disagreements over property institutions between different kinds of families – those with multiple male heirs and those without, those with female claimants and those without, and so on. For example, families with multiple heirs often attempted to dodge the customary (and legal) rule of equal division between male heirs in the hope of keeping the family estate in one piece and thereby preserving its economies of scale. There was indeed some correlation between the wealth of the family and the likelihood of it possessing multiple male heirs, but the correlation was by no means strong enough to unite large land-owners against the default norm – or smallholders in favor. William Lavely & R. Bin Wong, *Family Division and Mobility in North China*, 34 Comp. Stud. in Soc. & Hist. 439–63 (1992). Gender-related issues, however, simply display no significant connection to wealth distribution. Kathryn Bernhardt, Women and Property in China, 960–1949 (1999).

[184] See also Huang (2001) chaps. 5–7, for a similar treatment: the three major property-related issues that Huang identifies are *dian*, permanent tenancy, and debt, with significant amounts of overlap between *dian* and debt.

or modern – have a tendency to consensually adopt certain "core features": privately owned and used, relatively secure, and alienable real property rights centered on the right of exclusion.[185] Not only is there little variation from society to society on these issues, but there is also fairly little disagreement within local communities. They can become issues of severe class-based contention when a small section of wealthy households owns most of the property in a society,[186] but this was rarely a perpetual condition in the early modern era. Instead, a far more common trend, as seen across Western Europe, Japan, and perhaps a number of British colonies, was for landholding to go from relatively equitable to severely disparate.[187] In the earlier phases of this process at least, smallholders were much less concerned with weakening the private ownership rights of large land-owners than they were with protecting their own – both against outright trespass and against transaction losses such as the foreclosure or seizure of collateralized land. As argued both earlier and in Chapter 6, China essentially remained in this "earlier phase" throughout its pre-industrial history largely because its smallholders were so successful at securing favorable *dian* institutions. The more successful they were at this, the less contentious private land ownership was. In other words, rich-poor conflict in many early modern economies tended to focus on what many would consider the "details" of property law – and particularly on collateral redemption and tenancy – rather than on the "core principles." Moreover, it was precisely those "details" that would determine, over the long run, whether smallholders could sustain their economic position or fall prey to the expansion of large estates.

It bears repeating that the model presented here does *not* predict that Chinese smallholders should have won *all* their institutional battles against

---

[185] *E.g.*, Yun-chien Chang & Henry E. Smith, *An Economic Analysis of Civil versus Common Law Property*, 88 NOTRE DAME L. REV. 1 (2012).

[186] *E.g.*, ALEXANDER CHAIANOV, THE THEORY OF THE PEASANT ECONOMY (David Thorner, Basile Kerblay, & R.E.F. Smith eds., 1986).

[187] For England, *see* Beckett (1984), at 1. For Japan, *see* SMITH (1959); A. BOOTH & R. M. SUNDRUM, LABOUR ABSORPTION IN AGRICULTURE: THEORETICAL ANALYSIS AND EMPIRICAL INVESTIGATIONS 145 (1985); Osuma Saito, *Land, Labour and Market Forces in Tokugawa Japan*, 24 CONTINUITY & CHANGE 169, 173–74 (2009); T.J. Byres, *The Agrarian Question, Forms of Capitalist Agrarian Transition and the State: An Essay with Reference to Asia*, 14 SOCIAL SCIENTIST 3 (1986). For British colonies, *see* Ewout Frankema, *The Colonial Roots of Land Inequality: Geography, Factor Endowments, or Institutions?*, 63 ECON. HIST. REV. 418 (2010).

their richer neighbors. As noted in Section B, the most we could expect is that kinship hierarchies gave smallholders *some* political capital – much more than their English counterparts, who had extremely little, but almost certainly not enough to overwhelm larger landowners. As much as lineage regulations claimed to prohibit wealth-based conferral of status, it still seems more than likely that landed wealth carried significant sociopolitical benefits. The political aggression of large landowners in Republican-era Houjiaying, for example, seems to speak to this.[188] At a societal level, therefore, the model simply predicts that Chinese smallholders had the ability to "win" more often – on issues that were highly important to them – than their English counterparts, but certainly not that they won *all the time*.

Furthermore, as argued in Chapter 3, if it is possible to observe this effect *at all*, we would expect to observe it in such things as *dian*-mortgage redemption and tenancy. For smallholders, these were about as close to life-or-death issues as an institutional issue could possibly get: they wielded enormous influence over whether smallholders would lose their fundamental source of livelihood. In comparison, these issues were not nearly quite as life or death for larger landowners, who, as argued earlier, stood to benefit economically from *dian* purchases or land rentals even if they conceded things like infinite redeemability or permanent tenancy to smallholders. In other words, these were issues that were of virtually unsurpassed importance to smallholders but were quite compromisable for larger landholders. If Chinese smallholders were unable to convert their seniority-based capital into institutional "victories" here, it is hard to imagine where else they could have done better. Similarly, the fact that English smallholders gradually surrendered even these vital interests – and soon descended into landlessness as a result – speaks volumes about their relative sociopolitical weakness.

---

[188] 5 Mantetsu Surveys (1957), at 1–6.

5

Kinship Hierarchies in Late Imperial History

To complete the analysis of *dian* customs, this chapter considers how "Confucian" kinship hierarchies came to be embedded in Chinese society in the first place. The question must be asked for the sake of logical completeness. This book attempts to explain structural economic divergence between pre-industrial China and England via institutional differences in land collateralization and then to explain those institutional differences by analyzing the power dynamics within Chinese kinship hierarchies. Although this book obviously cannot ask "why" questions for each additional explanatory factor – it has to stop somewhere – it seems appropriate and necessary to explain at least why kinship hierarchies are a good place to stop.

As alluded to repeatedly in previous chapters, the primary reason is that kinship hierarchies are at least partially the product of widespread moral internalization by the Chinese population, whereas the immediate causes of farming patterns or property institutions were largely rationalistic and functionalist. As discussed later in Chapter 6, the relative lack of managerial farming was the result of farmers maximizing their perceived self-interest under institutional constraints, whereas the institutional constraints themselves were the product of "rational," self-interested negotiation based on preexisting social distributions of status and rank. In comparison, purely functionalist factors – whether political or economic demand – do not seem to explain why kinship hierarchies were so widespread and powerful in Qing and Republican China. Therefore, even if the analysis ends at kinship hierarchies, it would nonetheless illustrate the need, as discussed in the Introduction, to "reculturalize" global economic history.

By and large, the claim that kinship hierarchies were sustained by society-wide moral internalization is uncontroversial among historians. Most scholars who study lineages or kinship networks in Ming and Qing society probably would be willing to accept that filial piety, obedience to elders, extended ancestor worship, and close association with one's extended family were values deeply ingrained within the Chinese psyche. They will emphasize, of course, that these values interacted with, were reinforced by, and could even be overridden by pragmatic economic and political circumstances in fairly complex ways, but few would doubt that, at some level, most Chinese truly *believed* in their moral legitimacy. Feng Erkang probably speaks for many when he states that Qing society adhered "piously" to the "collectivist" ideal that "one should make their ancestors proud" by closely adhering to Confucian moral values.[1]

Yet, for all their rhetorical force, these are, to the critical academic eye, still *assumptions*. No one, to my knowledge, has bothered to systematically argue – with an eye toward potential counterarguments – that kinship hierarchies were indeed internalized by the Chinese populace. Perhaps this is so because the point seems obvious to most specialists. But then again, they have also been shielded, for the most part, from skeptical questioning by social scientists who adhere more to a rational-choice view of social institutions, and who would be profoundly unhappy with being told that "we just know it is." This book, however, attempts to engage directly and extensively with the social sciences and hence must take seriously the hypothetical concerns these scholars might raise. In doing so, it presents perhaps the first systematic *argument* for the widespread internalization of kinship hierarchies.

Section A of this chapter explains why we need to move further back in time, well beyond the late Qing and Republican time frame that previous chapters have adhered to, to examine how, and why, kinship hierarchies became a dominant mode of social organization. Section B traces their rise during the Song through Qing dynasties, examining socioeconomic, political, and value-based narratives. Due to its significantly longer time sweep, this section inevitably relies far more heavily on preexisting academic studies than any other part of this book.

---

[1] FENG (2005), at 12. *See also* FAURE (2007), at 6 (discussing how Zhu Xi's Neo-Confucianism was "put into practice" by South China lineage building); ZHENG (2000), at 286 (describing lineage organizational principles as an "ethics"); LI & JIANG (2000), at 57–63, 111–17 (discussing possible changes in the "lineage ethics" of the Chinese population). Both Faure and Zheng emphasize that lineages pragmatically adapted their organizational principles and worship rituals to suit socioeconomic needs and local conditions and that the ideological position of the Confucian elite was by no means binding over their actions, but both also take very seriously the idea that norms of kinship and social behavior did constitute an ethical discourse that went beyond mere materialist advancement of economic and political interest. In other words, moral internalization of cultural norms and language stood side by side with – and, of course, interacted with and mutually influenced – more pragmatic concerns.

A Moving Back in Time

The analysis here expands significantly beyond the late Qing and early Republican time frame to which previous chapters have adhered. This is a matter of logical necessity. Based simply on evidence drawn within that time frame, it is impossible to persuasively rule out either a fully functionalist explanation for kinship hierarchies or one that allows for moral and cultural internalization. In fact, one could make the stronger claim that the *only* way to effectively differentiate between those two theoretical possibilities is via a *longue durée* analysis of Chinese kinship networks, reaching back at least to the early Second Millennium.

This deserves some elaboration. From a purely theoretical point of view, there are three possible explanations for the social dominance of kinship hierarchies in Qing and Republican China. Two are largely "functionalist," in that they focus on the pragmatic utility of kinship hierarchies: First, they served the political or economic interests of the country's highest political elite and were therefore encouraged as a matter of state policy. Second, they conveyed substantial political or economic benefits on those who self-organized into kinship networks and therefore spread "organically" from the bottom up. The third, nonfunctionalist possibility is that kinship hierarchies were morally internalized on a large scale and therefore spread simply because people believed, independent of any pragmatic calculation, that they were a morally desirable or "natural" means of social organization.

Common sense indicates that all three mechanisms probably coexisted to some extent. In fact, many probably would be satisfied with the basic statement that all three were "important" and then move on. Such statements may well be true, but they are nonetheless unsatisfying in an analytical sense. The more pertinent and far more difficult question is whether any of them were *necessary conditions* for the social dominance of kinship hierarchies. Questions about necessary or sufficient historical conditions are understandably unpleasant to many historians – in fact, despite the robust literature on late Imperial lineages, apparently no one has seriously addressed these questions – but perhaps there are more comfortable ways to ask this question. For example, are there any fundamental characteristics of Qing and Republican kinship hierarchies that can *only* be plausibly explained by one or more of these mechanisms?

The problem, however, with focusing exclusively on the later Qing and Republic, as the previous chapters have done, is that evidence from that era alone cannot answer the necessity question, however it is framed. This is primarily so because the rectitude of kinship hierarchies was rarely challenged in local sources – whether in county-level case archives, rural surveys, or lineage registries – making it extremely difficult to unearth the social rationales that sustained their predominance. Although some urban intellectual elites, particularly during the Republican era, did challenge the social and moral foundations of kinship hierarchies, their abstract arguments had little impact on rural social life, where the pace of change was much slower.

Consider, for example, what the Mantetsu surveys and lineage registries examined in Chapter 5 reveal about the basic state of kinship networks in the later nineteenth and early twentieth centuries: they existed almost everywhere but varied in size and amount of commonly held property. Correspondingly, in the great majority of North China and Lower Yangtze villages, they exerted significant influence on the allocation of status, rank, and sociopolitical authority but varied in how successfully they excluded other social ranking mechanisms, particularly ranking by landholding and wealth. In Houjiaying and Shajing, for example, wealth was clearly a more important determinant of political stature than in Sibeichai and the other four villages surveyed. Some of Houjiaying's wealthiest households went so far as to opine that they should, by rule, enjoy higher political stature than poorer households, whereas economic elites in other villages expressly disowned the notion that wealth should convey political advantages. Likewise, wealthy households could obtain some measure of sociopolitical dominance in certain South China lineages but rarely did so in the Lower Yangtze.

Despite some dispute in Houjiaying over the role of wealth in determining sociopolitical stature, Mantetsu interviewees generally agreed that age and generational seniority were crucially important determinants of status and rank. In fact, no one expressly challenges this assertion. Even the Houjiaying interviewees who argued that wealth should matter only argued that it should *matter*, not eliminate ranking by seniority altogether. They seemed to envision some hybrid system where both factors were balanced – perhaps a system that, in crude mathematical terms, quantified and compared the status benefits conveyed by seniority and wealth and allocated overall social rank based on a weighted sum of those two factors. In Lower Yangtze lineage registries, including those drafted during the Republican era, ranking by age and generational seniority – and, depending on the type of lineage, by lineal proximity to the original ancestor – was usually espoused as a form of natural law, the morally ideal form of social organization to which all kinship networks should aspire.

In addition, formal legal challenges to the sociopolitical dominance of kinship networks were virtually nonexistent. This is certainly not to say that the courts never processed cases in which people were accused of disrespecting their elder kinsmen – "disrespecting one's superiors" (*fanshang*) was a rare but certainly existing category of accusations in both Qing and Republican case archives – but rather that the accused in such cases almost never argued that seniority-based kinship hierarchies were unjustifiable or undesirable. Instead, they made factual defenses: that they did not disrespect the accuser in any form, that the accuser was not actually related and therefore did not deserve that kind of respect, that their actions were merely mild retaliations against far greater oppression by the accuser, and so on.[2] *Fanshang* accusations were, in any case, quite rare.[3] Presumably they were highly embarrassing for everyone involved and therefore usually dealt with privately.

During the Qing, of course, formal legal challenges to the sociopolitical superiority of elder kinsmen over younger ones were categorically impossible, seeing as the *Qing Code* itself expressly upheld the inviolability of such hierarchies.[4] The various criminal codes instituted during the Republican era, including the 1928 Republican Criminal Code, recognized fewer kinship-based inequalities but continued to dictate that crimes were aggravated if committed against a senior kinsmen.[5] Lawmakers seemed to understand that kinship hierarchies remained deeply ingrained in China's social structure and that the public legitimacy of the legal system would benefit from some express recognition of them.

By and large, these observations are consistent with previous scholarship on nineteenth- and early-twentieth-century kinship networks, most of it produced in mainland China.[6] The long-standing consensus among

---

[2] *See, e.g.,* Longquan M003-01-14737 (1920); M003-01-9857 (1912); M003-01-13283 (1949).

[3] Searching for "犯上" in the Longquan Index yields only six results out of 18,434 cases. The same search in the Xingke Tiben electronic archives in the First National Historical Archives in Beijing yielded twenty-nine homicide cases nationally between the years 1870 and 1910.

[4] 8 ZHONGGUO FAZHI TONGSHI (1999), at 208, 256–57, 508.   [5] Liu (2012).

[6] English-language studies of Republican kinship networks are surprisingly rare. There are frequent and substantial references to the social role of kinship networks' most social and economic histories (many of which are cited below) – which is hardly surprising considering the fundamental role they played in basic sociopolitical organization – but there are few studies devoted specifically to the study of Republican lineage structures. Notable exceptions include Evelyn S. Rawski, *The Ma Landlords of Yang-chia-kou in Late Ch'ing and Republican China, in* KINSHIP ORGANIZATION IN LATE IMPERIAL CHINA, 1000–1940, at 245 (Patricia Ebrey & James Watson eds., 1986), and Rubie S. Watson, *Corporate Property and Local Leadership in the Pearl River Delta, 1898–1941, in* CHINESE LOCAL ELITES AND PATTERNS OF DOMINANCE 239 (Joseph Esherick & Mary Rankin eds., 1990), both of which stress the continual social influence – arguably dominance – of major local lineages in Republican South and Northwest China.

mainland historians, even after several waves of new scholarship during the past decade, is that although some kinship networks did indeed adjust their organizational structures in the face of changing economic and political circumstances, the basic predominance of traditional age and generational hierarchies was never fundamentally challenged. Moreover, kinship networks retained most of their social clout during the first third of the century and, despite some signs of gradual decline, remained the dominant form of rural social organization even in the later 1940s.

Feng Erkang and Chang Jianhua, for example, find that kinship networks retained much of their social position in local life throughout the nineteenth and early twentieth centuries and that the great majority of kinship networks continued to uphold traditional hierarchies and leadership structures during the Republican era.[7] In a separate study, Feng suspects that kinship networks exercised comparatively less control over individual members and were therefore somewhat "in decline," but the decline was a very slow and uneven one, largely concentrated in areas where the Communist Party exercised considerable power or where wars had forced massive emergency migration.[8] He finds little evidence of decline in the Lower Yangtze and South China until the 1940s and not until the late 1930s in North China – and even then, only the occasional piece of anecdotal evidence. To be sure, even during the 1910s and 1920s, some lineages "democratized" their political structure to a limited extent, allowing all lineage households to participate in certain decisions, but even these somewhat more "enlightened" lineages retained the basic inequalities between elder kinsmen and younger ones.[9] In fact, Feng demonstrates that the early twentieth century was in fact an era of high enthusiasm about consolidating existing lineages and building new ones, if the massive amount of new lineage registries compiled during this period is any indication.[10] On the issue of generational hierarchies, at least these new lineages were not qualitatively different from their Qing predecessors, even as they grappled with the ideological and moral implications of nationalism and republicanism.

Other studies on early-twentieth-century kinship networks generally agree that they retained most of their social vitality until very late in the Republican era, regardless of whether they were "destined to collapse" under the Communist regime. Xu Yangjie, for example, believes that

---

[7] FENG ERKANG ET AL., ZHONGGUO ZONGZU SHI [HISTORY OF CHINESE LINEAGES] 318–25 (2009).

[8] FENG (2005), at 262–70.   [9] *Id.* at 271–72, 277–82.   [10] *Id.* at 288–313.

whatever attack kinship networks suffered during the Republican era was superfluous and immaterial, and it was not until the Communist Revolution that they were "fundamentally destroyed."[11] Likewise, Wang Huning finds that traditional kinship networks remained a "powerful restraining force" on social revolution throughout the Republican era.[12] Chen Zhiping also finds that South China kinship networks were extremely adaptable and resilient despite rapidly changing sociopolitical circumstances.[13] As Tang Lixing demonstrates through a quantitative study of Lower Yangtze lineages, the demise of kinship networks was not the product of "natural evolution," but rather the specific result of Communist social revolution – and even early Communist attempts at overthrowing traditional rural social hierarchies during the late 1920s and early 1930s were, as Li Ji demonstrates, largely unsuccessful.[14] In Yang Wanrong's opinion, this was so because the "economic and political foundations" of kinship networks continued to exist in the Republican era.[15]

The main arena in which traditional kinship hierarchies were under serious attack was the world of urban intellectual elites and, less frequently, high politics. No historian of this era is unfamiliar with the often virulent rhetoric that Liu Shipei, Wu Yu, Chen Duxiu, Hu Shi, and others employed against "oppressive" and "backward" kinship hierarchies.[16] Chen Duxiu argued, for example, that kinship hierarchies "had four serious consequences: First, they damaged the development of personal independence

---

[11] Xu Yangjie, Zhongguo Jiazu Zhidu Shi [A History of Lineage Institutions in China] 459 (1992).

[12] Wang Huning, Dangdai Zhongguo Cunluo Jiazu Wenhua [Lineage Culture in Contemporary Chinese Villages] 52 (1991).

[13] Chen Zhiping, Jin 500 Nian lai Fujian de Jiazu Shehui yu Wenhua [Lineage Society and Culture in Fujian over the Past 500 years] (1991).

[14] Tang Lixing, *20 Shiji Shangbanye Zhongguo Zongzu Zuzhi de Taishi – Yi Huizhou Zongzu wei Duixiang de Lishi Kaocha* [*The Trends in Chinese Lineage Organization in the First Half of the 20th Century – A Historical Study on the Lineages of Huizhou*], 34(1) J. Shanghai Normal Univ. 103 (2005); Lin Ji, Changjiang Zhongyou Zongzu Shehui ji qi Bianqian: Ming Qing zhi 1949 Nian [The Lineage Society of the Middle Yangtze Region and Its Evolution: From the Ming and Qing to 1949] (1999).

[15] Yang Wanrong, *Shilun Minguo Shiqi Nongcun Zongzu de Bianqian* [*On the Evolution of Rural Lineages in the Republican Era*], 2002(2) Guangdong Soc. Sci. 103.

[16] Hu Shi, 2 Hu Shi Jingpin Ji [The Best Writings of Hu Shi] 355 (1998); Wu Yu, Wu Yu Wen Lu [Selected Writings of Wu Yu] 1-6, 15 (1927); Chen Duxiu, Chen Duxiu Wenzhang Xuanbian – Dong Xi Minzu Genben Sixiang zhi Chayi [Selected Papers of Chen Duxiu – On the Fundamental Difference between Eastern and Western Peoples] (1984); Zhao Yancai, *Lue Lun Liu Shipei de Jiazu Zhidu Sixiang ji qi Lunli Jindai Hua Guan* [*A Brief Study of Liu Shipei's Thought on Lineage Institutions and the Early Modernisation of Ethics*], 2004(11) Xueshu Yanjiu [Academic Research] 89.

and dignity; second, they obstructed personal free will; third, they impaired equality before the law; fourth, they encouraged a habit of reliance, which retarded individual productivity."[17] The only solution, he claimed, was to "replace China's kinship-based ideology with individualism."[18]

Chen's hostility toward kinship hierarchies was shared by some highly influential intellectuals and perhaps by quite a few urban student organizations.[19] Other equally influential intellectuals, however, strongly disagreed, as did, apparently, most politicians. Liang Qichao, for example, argued that the construction of a modern, nationalist sociopolitical identity was not necessarily inconsistent with traditional kinship hierarchies.[20] Quite the opposite, filial piety toward one's parents could be expanded into patriotism toward one's country in much the same way that traditional Confucian moralists advocated expanding filial piety into loyalty to one's ruler. Cai Yuanpei, perhaps China's premier advocate of educational reform, also proved fairly conservative when it came to kinship hierarchies. He believed that large lineages were an ideal form of social organization and that obedience to one's elders was required as a matter of both individual morality and social utility.[21]

Politicians and military leaders, too, rarely expressed significant hostility toward traditional kinship relations. During the late-Qing debates surrounding the drafting of new criminal and civil codes, Shen Jiaben and Yang Du argued, without much success, against enshrining kinship hierarchies into the new law codes – Yang was especially vocal in arguing that family loyalties should not trump national ones – but stopped far short of suggesting that the hierarchies themselves were unjustifiable.[22] Major Republican political leaders, including Sun Yat-sen, Chiang Kai-shek, and many others, were often quite willing to adopt Liang Qichao's belief in the basic compatibility between kinship hierarchies and nationalism. Sun, for example, firmly believed that traditional kinship

---

[17] CHEN (1984), at 98.   [18] *Id.*

[19] For a general summary, *see* Yuan Hongtao, *Zai "Guojia" yu "Geren" Zhijian – Lun 20 Shiji Chu de Zongzu Pipan [Between "Country" and "Individual" – On the Criticism of Lineages in the Early 20th Century]*, 119 TIANFU XINLUN [NEW OPINIONS FROM SICHUAN] 119 (2004).

[20] LIANG QICHAO WENXUAN [SELECTED WRITINGS OF LIANG QICHAO] 110–12 (Xia Xiaohong ed., 1992)

[21] CAI YUANPEI, GUOMIN XIUYANG ER ZHONG [TWO WRITINGS ON CITIZEN CHARACTER] 37–40 (1999).

[22] Wu Zhihui, *Qingmo "Li Fa zhi Zheng" de Pingjia yu Qishi [Evaluating and Learning from the Late-Qing "Ritual and Law" Debates]*, 2013(26) RENMIN LUNTAN [PEOPLE'S FORUM], *available at* http://paper.people.com.cn/rmlt/html/2013-09/11/content_1311789.htm.

networks were ideal building blocks for a "greater union" at the national level.[23] Chiang, once in power, went a step further and attempted to consolidate his own lineage in much the same way that high-level degree holders would often build lineages in the Qing.[24] Few, if any, key political players during the "Nanjing decade" were openly hostile to the social influence that traditional lineages continued to wield. Quite the opposite, many government officials, perhaps most, actively belonged to large lineages themselves and benefited enormously from the social connections they provided.[25] Certainly the Nanjing government never made any attempt to challenge the social legitimacy of kinship hierarchies. Quite the opposite, its major pieces of legislation, as discussed earlier, continued to recognize and support them.

The Nanjing government did attempt, of course, to expand its authority over local affairs, at least relative to the highly laissez-faire approach taken by the Qing state, but there is very little evidence that its reform agenda significantly weakened the sociopolitical importance of kinship networks. Previous social histories of North China, many focusing also on the Mantetsu surveys, suggest that local state authorities were rarely successful in their attempts to dismantle traditional power relations and "cultural nexuses."[26] When, for example, Hebei provincial authorities attempted to shake up village politics by implementing an age limit for political service in certain localities, most leadership positions were simply passed down to the sons of previous leaders, who continued to make policy decisions vicariously.[27] State policy did have a significant impact on local economic development, ecological change, and legal culture, but those impacts were made largely within the institutional confines of local lineages, religious groups, and other networks.[28] Studies of the rural Lower Yangtze have

---

[23] Sun Zhongshan Xuanji [Selected Works of Sun Yat-sen] 616–22 (Beijing People's Press ed., 1981).

[24] *See* Qi Pengfei, Jiang Jieshi Jiashi [The Family History of Chiang Kai-shek] (2007).

[25] The most famous, of course, are the Jiang, Song, Kong, and Chen families – often referred to as the "four major lineages" of Republican politics. Beyond these, there were large numbers of less prominent lineages that nonetheless wielded major influence in national or provincial politics. On the family connections and social stratification of midlevel Republican technocrats, *see* Xu Xiaoqun, Chinese Professionals and the Republican State: The Rise of Professional Associations in Shanghai, 1912–1937, at 21–78 (2001).

[26] Duara (1988); Li (2005).

[27] This was in Wudian village. *See* 5 Mantetsu Surveys (1957), at 531, 562–63, 578, 583–84.

[28] *E.g.*, Pomeranz (1993).

generally reached similar conclusions.[29] It really was not until the later 1940s, and not until the Communists had risen to national prominence, that China experienced serious and systematic challenges to the local hegemony of traditional kinship networks

The fact that the local sociopolitical status of kinship hierarchies was largely secure during the nineteenth and early twentieth centuries makes it very difficult, however, to weed out the precise reasons for their vitality. Such analysis is almost always easier when a social institution is contested – *dian* redemption norms are a good example – simply because controversy usually forces people to openly identify their preferences and defend them. Court documents and other evidence of deep social discord are often the key, as they were throughout the earlier chapters of this book, to understanding why a certain institution survived or failed. Lack of localized controversy, however, lends itself to multiple interpretations, none of which are unambiguously correct.

The most obvious interpretation is that kinship hierarchies were so widely internalized as a fundamental moral principle that beyond a relatively limited circle of urban intellectuals, they were very rarely questioned or challenged. There is, in fact, a large body of evidence that could easily be construed as supporting this interpretation: Nearly all lineage registries speak of age- and generational-based seniority as essentially a form of natural law, carrying indisputable moral authority.[30] Taken at face value, these documents seem to indicate that vast portions of the Chinese population had indeed internalized kinship hierarchies into their core value system.

The problem, of course, is that moral writings often can be the by-product of more pragmatic and material calculations. It would not necessarily be surprising if most advocates of kinship hierarchies had some economic or political interest in doing so. The argument that China's political and economic elites promoted "Confucianism" to enhance their dominance over the masses is, for example, exceedingly old and influential in mainland China.[31] Western scholars, well versed in Bourdieuian

---

[29] HUANG (1990). *See also*, BERNHARDT (1992), at 161–88 (arguing that Kuomintang intervention into local governance in the Lower Yangtze fell far short of its design and that the state's relationship with traditional local elites was mainly one of cooperation), XU (2008), at 115–48 (drawing a similar conclusion for legal reform efforts in rural Jiangsu).

[30] This characterization applies to every lineage registry cited in Chapter 5, Section B.

[31] These arguments are summarized in LI ZEHOU, ZHONGGUO XIANDAI SIXIANG SHI LUN [ON THE INTELLECTUAL HISTORY OF MODERN CHINA] (2008); WANG HUI, XIANDAI ZHONGGUO SIXIANG DE XINGQI [THE RISE OF MODERN CHINESE THOUGHT] (2008); Chen (2000).

theories of cultural reproduction,[32] have also displayed, in past decades, considerable fondness for such ideas.[33] Although previous chapters in this book have strived to debunk this argument – if anything, kinship hierarchies tended to promote the sociopolitical stature of lower-income households – the fact remains that large segments of the social sciences treat the notion of widespread moral internalization with deep skepticism, especially if more functionalist explanations cannot be entirely ruled out. "Mainstream ideologies serve the ruling classes" is perhaps the most common example, applied not only to Confucianism in China but also more broadly as a general theory of cultural change.[34]

Even if we reject the "ruling classes" moniker and its obvious Marxist undertones, the belief that, over time, religious beliefs or value systems are shaped by external economic and political circumstances is nonetheless fairly commonplace among historians and social scientists. One recent study argues, for example, that communities select religious beliefs based largely on the information costs of economic transactions and levels of communal trust: communities with low information costs tend to adopt individualistic, "behavior based" religions such as Protestantism, whereas those with high information costs usually adopt "ritual based" religions such as Catholicism or perhaps any of the Asian religions.[35] One need not agree with this particular thesis to appreciate that for many scholars, using moral internalization to explain social institutions is a last resort, employed only when rationalist explanations are deficient.

It is possible, in fact, to piece together a rationalist explanation for the resiliency and strength of kinship hierarchies during the late Qing and Republic. As discussed in previous chapters, kinship hierarchies were

---

[32] Pierre Bourdieu, The Field of Cultural Production: Essays on Art and Literature (1993).

[33] Chapter 4, Section B, cites to a wide array of examples. For a criticism of the overuse of "reproduction" theories in Chinese historiography, *see* Benjamin A. Elman, *The Failures of Contemporary Chinese Intellectual History*, 43 Eighteenth-Century Stud. 371 (2010).

[34] For discussion and critique of these traditionally Marxist ideas, *see* Marvin Harris, *Cultural Materialism, in* Encyclopedia of Cultural Anthropology 277 (David Levinson & Melvin Amber eds., 1996); Nicholas Abercrombie & Bryan S. Turner, *The Dominant Ideology Thesis*, 29 British J. Sociology 149 (1978).

[35] Gilat Levy & Ronny Razin, *Rituals or Good Works, Self and Social Signaling in Religious Organizations* (London School of Economics, Working Paper, July 2011). For research in a similar vein, *see, e.g.,* J.D. Huber, *Religious Belief, Religious Participation, and Social Policy Attitudes Across Countries* (Columbia University, Working Paper, 2005); R. Benabou & J. Tirole, *Willpower and Personal Rules*, 112 J. Pol. Econ. 848 (2004); L. Iannaccone, *Introduction to the Economics of Religion*, 36 J. Econ. Lit. 1465 (1998).

surprisingly egalitarian in their distributions of status, rank, and political authority: lesser landholders, as a group, tended to enjoy higher status and rank relative to their wealth, whereas larger landholders enjoyed relatively less. We would expect, therefore, that average and below-average land-holders would favor the ranking-by-seniority system employed in most kinship networks, whereas the largest landholders would dislike it. If, for example, 5 percent of a village occupied political leadership positions at any given time, and if rank and status were conveyed, as they were in England, on the basis of landed wealth, then perhaps the top 10 to 20 percent of landholders might have a realistic chance to obtain one of those positions, whereas the great majority of households would be shut out completely. If, however, kinship hierarchies dominated village social life, then most households, depending on how many seniors they possessed, might occupy a slot at some point. The question then becomes why larger landholders would agree to such an arrangement rather than insisting on a "natural meritocracy" based on economic prowess.

If we look only at the nineteenth and twentieth centuries, at least, the answer may well be that the social cost was simply too high. Because kinship hierarchies were of such fundamental importance to sustaining the social status of smallholders, any open challenge against them would conceivably trigger very rigorous retaliation by lower-income households. Considering that large numbers of senior smallholders had already obtained relatively high status and rank by the start of this period, the costs imposed by such retaliation may well have been high enough to override the institutional and economic costs imposed on larger landhold-ers under preexisting kinship hierarchies.

In fact, if higher-income households felt that the costs of challenging kinship hierarchies were too high, then perhaps it may even have been in their interest to advocate and support such hierarchies. Such advocacy would boost their social prestige and reputation among smallholders, which could often generate extensive material benefits in the long run. In other words, if kinship hierarchies were already embedded enough that large numbers of people both benefited from and resolutely supported them, then perhaps the large volume of moralistic advocacy we see in lineage registries or private writings may simply have been strategic behavior by self-interested individ-uals, rather than evidence of widespread moral internalization. Neither possibility can be conclusively ruled out based simply on the nineteenth- and twentieth-century sources currently available to historians.

The rationalist explanation depends, however, on the assumption that lower-income households were collectively powerful from the start of the period. Otherwise, there would have been little incentive for larger land-holders to compromise their own sociopolitical power to appease them. In other words, kinship hierarchies are self-reinforcing, in that they strengthen the social groups that have the strongest incentive to sustain them. All that this means, however, is that it can be difficult to challenge social hierarchies once they are already embedded – hardly a surprising conclusion. The far more interesting question is how they became embedded in the first place. But that inquiry can only be pursued in earlier times, when kinship networks were still developing and spreading rather than already established as a dominant social institution.

B A (Short) *Longue Durée* History of Chinese Kinship Networks

Depending on geographic region, the emergence and entrenchment of kinship networks and hierarchies within the general population occurred anywhere from the tenth to the eighteenth century, and scholars vary tremendously in the start and end dates of their narrative. They generally agree that prior to the Song Dynasty, the great majority of large, organized kinship networks, some organized according to strict Confucian hierarchies, others less so, belonged to major aristocratic houses that dominated the central government – in other words, they were limited in number and were largely concentrated in major urban centers.[36] It was not until the tenth or eleventh century that they began to trickle down, with limited and somewhat reluctant government approval,[37] into the general population, generally in the form of extended ancestor worship and the construction of strict social hierarchies based on age and family line. The chronology becomes much murkier during the following five centuries. If the number of surviving lineage genealogies is any indication, private lineage formation seemed to speed up during the twelfth century in both North China and the Lower Yangtze and then again after the Mongol occupation ended in the fourteenth century.[38] By at least the fifteenth and sixteenth centuries, expansive kinship hierarchies were highly prevalent in North China and the Lower Yangtze and had begun to emerge en masse

---

[36] This general narrative is summarized in FENG ET AL. (2005), at 164–289; INOUE TOHRU, ZHONGGUO DE ZONGZU YU GUOJIA LIZHI [CHINA'S LINEAGES AND RITUAL INSTITUTIONS OF THE STATE] (Qian Hang trans., 2008); XU (1992); CHANG JIANHUA, ZONGZU ZHI [A HISTORY OF LINEAGES] (1998); KE CHANGJI, ZHONGGUO GUDAI NONGCUN GONGSHE SHI [RURAL COMMUNES IN CLASSICAL CHINESE HISTORY] (1988) (presenting a historical periodization of lineage development).

[37] See the discussion in Section B(ii).   [38] FENG ET AL. (2005); INOUE (2008).

in South China as well.[39] By at least the early eighteenth century, they were clearly a cornerstone of social life in North China, the Middle and Lower Yangtze, South China, and even the relatively underdeveloped northeastern frontier.[40]

This long social history is punctuated by state legislation and edicts in the fourteenth, sixteenth, seventeenth, and eighteenth centuries that either allowed or encouraged extended ancestor worship by commoners, but as explained below, such actions tended to react to preexisting social trends rather than stimulate or immediately precede any substantial private lineage-building activity. In other words, like most premodern social history, it is extremely difficult, if not impossible, to put precise years or even decades on the macro-level time line just provided. The endpoint of that time line, at least, is fairly clear: by the comparatively well-documented eighteenth and nineteenth centuries, extended kinship hierarchies were clearly a fundamental organizational principle in most Han-dominated regions.

While this basic macronarrative has been retold numerous times in the academic literature, as discussed earlier, almost no preexisting work has attempted to systematically analyze, far less prove, the causes behind the spread of kinship hierarchies. At most, scholars have identified several factors that hypothetically contributed to the process. First, there was significant "bottom-up" demand among local literati and major families to form more cohesive kinship networks. Second, from time to time, the central government would encourage lineage formation through favorable financial policies or straightforward moral exhortation. Third, the rise and spread of "Song-Ming Neo-Confucianism" may have stimulated the widespread moral internalization of kinship hierarchies as a fundamental social value. The following subsections evaluate these hypotheses one by one, ultimately arguing that the basic historical chronology of kinship hierarchies is, in all likelihood, inexplicable if the third factor – widespread moral internalization – did not exist.

i "Bottom-Up" Demand

Few would question that the first factor played a crucial role. In the end, the decision to form kinship networks had to be made and executed – willingly – by local communities and households, not by increasingly

---

[39] FAURE (2007); SZONYI (2002); ZHENG (2000); JOSEPH P. McDERMOTT, THE MAKING OF A NEW RURAL ORDER IN SOUTH CHINA (Vol. 1) (2014).
[40] *See* ISETT (2007).

remote central policymakers and not by the moralistic urgings of Confucian scholars. The more challenging question is to what extent the latter two factors affected that decision, whether by shaping economic and political incentives or by imposing a sense of moral propriety.

During the Northern Song, a substantial share of lineages was created by new generations of high-level degree holders and officials – Fan Zhongyan, and the lavish estate he bequeathed to his extended family, is by far the most famous example[41] – who hoped to enshrine their historical legacy through the creation of common ancestor lineages endowed with significant corporate landholding, but as time passed, kinship networks became somewhat more "plebian" in their origin.[42] The percentage of the population that held high-level degrees fell quite severely after the Song and then plunged again from the Ming to the Qing. Moreover, even in the Ming and Qing, a fairly small number of lineages in a few geographically concentrated regions supplied a large majority of all high-level degree holders,[43] which meant that the shrinking quota was distributed very unevenly. At the same time, organized kinship networks were spreading rapidly across the country, eventually becoming the dominant mode of social organization by the eighteenth century.[44] Inevitably, an increasing number, probably a significant majority, of these kinship networks had to operate without any substantive ties to a *jinshi* degree holder or even a *juren*.

Correspondingly, rationales for creating kinship networks tended to "descend" from concerns over one's historical legacy to more straightforward calculations of socioeconomic utility. In any macroregion, self-organizing into large kinship networks conveyed some fairly obvious and significant advantages: resource sharing, labor pooling, better information sharing, and a stronger capacity for collective action – all leading to higher economic productivity, more orderly social life within the group, and stronger responses to external challenges, whether from intrusive state

---

[41] *See* Wang Shanjun, *Fanshi Yizhuang yu Songdai Fanshi Jiazu de Fazhan* [*The Fan Philanthropic Estate and the Development of the Fan Lineage in the Song Dynasty*], 2004(2) Zhongguo Nongshi [Agricultural History of China] 89.

[42] This process is discussed in, among other works, Beverly J. Bossler, Powerful Relations: Kinship, Status, and State in Sung China (1996); Hymes (1986); Hilary J. Beattie, Land and Lineage in China: A Study of T'ung-Ch'eng County, Anhwei, in the Ming and Ch'ing Dynasties (1979); Hartwell (1982), at 365.

[43] Elman (2000); Elman (1991), at 1, 14–15.

[44] Or earlier. In Huizhou, for example, they had become the dominant form of organization by the middle to late Ming. McDermott (2014).

agents or other social entities. In particular, once a few established kinship networks had emerged in a region, the pressure intensified on other households to form their own kinship networks or else be at a considerable disadvantage in all dimensions of social and economic life.

Take, for example, the Chen lineage of Shunxi, a relatively mountainous county in the heart of Zhejiang.[45] The "first ancestor" of this lineage was a merchant, Chen Yuqiu, from Wenzhou, who moved to Shunxi around 1570. He was apparently drawn to the rich forest in the area and soon started a lumber business. To pool capital and squeeze out local competitors – most notably the initially more populous Li surname that moved to Shunxi shortly after Chen Yuqiu's arrival – his descendants attempted to keep as much as possible of the family fortune in one piece and maintained close economic ties with one another across multiple generations. A lineage registry was maintained throughout the Ming and even during the turbulent Ming-Qing transition, until it was formally published and distributed from the Qianlong era onward. Various lineage regulations, some dealing primarily with economic relations between kinsmen, were drafted through the years and eventually collected in this publication. The effectiveness of these organizational measures can be seen in the lineage's steady economic rise: within a few generations of Chen Yuqiu's death, his descendants had established a virtual monopoly over the area's increasingly profitable lumber trade and had relegated all other major surnames to rice agriculture.[46] By the late Ming and early Qing, the various branches of the lineage could pool together enough educational resources, possibly in the form of a lineage school, to produce a fairly steady string of lower-level degree holders, which significantly boosted the lineage's local sociopolitical stature. By 1723, it had become wealthy enough to construct a new ancestral worship hall, establishing itself as arguably the most prominent lineage in the county.

The creation and rise of the Chen lineage had nothing to do with the philanthropy or moral conviction of a *jinshi* or *juren*. Once the lineage had entered into a position of socioeconomic strength, it attempted to buttress its political standing by investing in education and examination preparation, but examination success was clearly the result, not the cause, of lineage building. Instead, like most other lineages that sprouted up during

---

[45] ZHOU ZHUWEI ET AL., ZHEJIANG ZONGZU CUNLUO SHEHUI YANJIU [A SOCIAL STUDY OF LINEAGE VILLAGES IN ZHEJIANG] 91–163 (2001).

[46] *Id.* at 91–99, 104–06. LIU SHAOKUAN, MINGUO PINGYANG XIANZHI [COUNTY GAZETTEER OF REPUBLICAN-ERA PINGYANG], at *Jianzhi Zhi Yi* [*The First Chapter on Construction and Establishments*] & *Shihuo Zhi San* [*The Third Chapter on Commerce*] (Shanghai Bookstore ed., 1993).

the Song, Yuan, and Ming, it emerged via a grassroots process in which related households bonded together for economic and social gain and specifically to compete with other local surnames.[47]

These basic driving forces were deeply influential not only in core provinces such as Zhejiang, Jiangsu, and Shandong but also in most frontier regions – where they were arguably even stronger, due to the greater challenges that settlers faced in securing economic subsistence and basic social order. southern Chinese lineages, which emerged in a few geographically concentrated waves during the sixteenth and seventeenth centuries, are perhaps the best example of this. As multiple historians have demonstrated, more than anything else, concerns about social and economic welfare – the desire to strengthen one's economic security and to deter against hostile behavior by local officials, outlaws, and other residents – drove the formation of lineages in Fujian and Guangdong.[48]

The overarching concern with socioeconomic welfare is reflected particularly vividly in the way that many lineages played fast and loose with their claimed ancestral heritage. There are, for example, numerous examples in South China of previously unrelated households coming together to form a brand new lineage. In one particularly notorious incident from eighteenth-century Fujian, the Li, Chen, Su, Zhuang, and Ke families of Xiamen came together to form a new lineage called the Bao, which immediately prompted a group of rival families to form another new lineage called the Qi.[49] The compelling socioeconomic advantages of lineage formation were sufficient to persuade both groups to set aside any reservations they might have harbored toward falsifying their ancestral heritage. In comparison, the construction of imaginary ancestors who once held prominent government positions – an extremely widespread practice among South China lineages and even those in the Lower Yangtze and North China – seems almost tame and unremarkable.[50] Clearly, genealogies could be manipulated and falsified with surprising ease, which speaks to the deep pragmatism that drove the formation of many, probably most, kinship networks during the Ming and Qing.

---

[47] See also the process of lineage creation documented in McDermott (2014), which also broadly follows these lines.

[48] Faure (2007); Szonyi (2002).

[49] Ng Chin-Keong, Trade and Society: The Amoy Network on The China Coast, 1683–1735, 31 (1983).

[50] Ruskola (2000), at 1636–45; Chow Kai-wing, The Rise of Confucian Ritualism in Late Imperial China: Ethics, Classics, and Lineage Discourse 77 (1994).

It should be noted that the social and economic conditions that facilitated the large-scale creation of kinship networks were, by and large, a post–Song Dynasty phenomenon. Historians have long argued that until the Northern Song, state authorities – whether it was the central government, local military commanders, or major aristocratic houses – exercised fairly tight control over local affairs.[51] This was reflected, in part, in tax burdens that were collected not only in agricultural produce or textiles but also in labor owed to government projects. Such a tax regime assumed a relatively immobile society in which the state could control and monitor the whereabouts of most individuals. The deep penetration of governmental authority into local social and economic life both curtailed the necessity to form private kinship networks and also limited whatever practical functions they could have performed.

Correspondingly, it was not until rapid population growth and commercialization during the Song began to severely limit the state's political reach that kinship networks really took off as a form of private social organization. The decline of large aristocratic houses during the Northern Song allowed a wide array of kinship networks and social organizations to assume more prominent roles in local governance.[52] If we see the Song as the dividing line between the fairly immobile and somewhat feudal "ancient China" and an increasingly commercialized and decentralized "modern" or "early modern" China,[53] then powerful local kinship networks were functionally attractive – not to mention tolerated and supported by the central government – only in the latter. They were, essentially, a form of social capital that filled the gaps left by a retreating state.

But while socioeconomic utility may explain the emergence and proliferation of kinship *networks*, it cannot explain why, by at least the later Ming, most of them had adopted either an internal *hierarchy* based on age and generational seniority or a *zongzi* system that combined the privileging of the founder's patrilineal descendants with ranking by age and generation. Probably by the late Ming, and certainly by the Qing, the former system

---

[51] Hartwell (1982); Miyakawa Hisayuki, *An Outline of the Naito Hypothesis and its effects on Japanese Studies of China*, 14 FAR EASTERN QUARTERLY 533 (1955).

[52] *See* BOSSLER (1996); HYMES (1986); INOUE (2008), at 18–26; KE (1988); Wang Shanjun, *Songdai Zongzu Zhidu de Shehui Zhineng ji Qi dui Jieji Guanxi de Yingxiang* [*The Social Functions of Song Lineages and Their Effects on Class Relations*], 1996(3) HEBEI DAXUE XUEBAO [ACADEMIC J. OF HEBEI UNIV.] 15.

[53] VALERIE HANSEN, THE OPEN EMPIRE: A HISTORY OF CHINA THROUGH 1600, at 3–14 (2000); Hartwell (1982).

was firmly predominant in most core macroregions.[54] If straightforward socioeconomic efficiency was the driving concern, then neither system would have been optimal. Quite simply, both were so deeply nonmeritocratic that it is very difficult to positively assess their material functionality. While one may quibble about whether age and experience often lead to wisdom or whether ranking by patrilineal proximity promoted structural stability and therefore political specialization, the unavoidable fact is that there were vastly more effective ways of guaranteeing that the most capable people were in charge. Educational level, economic success, popular support, and moral reputation – any of these would have been a more reasonable proxy for leadership qualities than age or patrilineal proximity.

There are, in fact, many signs that some kinship networks were concerned about the amount of meritocracy within their internal governance structures. Many, if not most, kinship networks gave exalted status to people who held *juren* or *jinshi* degrees.[55] Others, when ranking individuals of comparable seniority, relied on proxies such as "possessing a good reputation among relatives" or "known for good sense and integrity."[56]

Neither of these mechanisms, however, did much to challenge straightforward ranking by age and generation over the long run. After the Ming, and especially during the Qing, higher-level degrees were extraordinarily hard to come by.[57] Consequently, at any given time, the great majority of kinship networks possessed no living *juren* or *jinshi*. Considerations of social reputation, however, were generally subsumed within the age hierarchy and only used, if at all, to differentiate between people of comparable seniority.[58] However we look at it, the vast majority of local kinship networks were organized around nonmeritocratic principles.

Of course, meritocracy is not always equivalent to socioeconomic efficiency. There are a number of potentially overriding concerns, especially political stability and the cost of leadership transitions: Pure meritocracy tends to create frequent leadership changes and may cause

---

[54] FENG (2005), at 95–96, 111–13, 248–56; ZHU YONG, QINGDAI ZONGFA YANJIU [STUDIES ON LINEAGE RITUALS IN THE QING] (1987).

[55] CH'U (1962), at 168–80.

[56] *E.g.*, NANJIN JIANGSHI MINFANG FAXIANG PU (1890); SIMING ZHUSHI ZHIPU (1936); YONGSHANG TUSHI ZONGPU (1919); BIANSHI ZONGPU (1874); YAONAN DINGSHAN FANGSHI ZONGPU (1921).

[57] Elman (1991), at 14–15; SOMMER (2000), at 8 ("By the eighteenth century, all but a tiny percentage of the population could be considered free commoners").

[58] This is true of all lineage regulations cited at p.147.

significant inefficiencies if the cost of transitioning is high – which, in fact, is often true of meritocratic selection, given the considerably subjectivity and room for disagreement involved in evaluating "merit."[59] In comparison, the *zongzi* system does at least limit the frequency of transitions, whereas pure ranking by age is a far more objective, simpler, and therefore low-cost way of selecting leaders. Even so, this suggests at most that kinship hierarchies may have had some redeeming qualities and falls far short of showing that they were, by any measure, consistently more efficient than meritocratic selection.

The truly curious thing about Chinese kinship hierarchies was, in the end, their uniformity and consistency across highly diverse geographic, economic, and social terrain: during the late Ming, Qing, and Republic, a period of some 500 years, they were the predominant organizational principle almost everywhere, whether wheat or rice growing, silk or cotton producing, mountainous or flat, humid or arid, densely or sparsely populated, interior or frontier. It is not terribly difficult to imagine a scenario where kinship hierarchies were a socioeconomically optimal institution, but this does nothing to explain their near-universal appeal in late Imperial China. A society-wide phenomenon deserves a society-wide explanation. As the preceding paragraphs show, however, the strongly nonmeritocratic nature of kinship hierarchies makes it extremely difficult to argue that they were almost always, or perhaps even frequently, socioeconomically optimal.

Quite the opposite, the long-term socioeconomic consequences of gerontocratic social ordering in late Imperial China were very likely negative. As argued earlier, its predominance helped to create and sustain a set of property institutions that were distinctly hostile to land accumulation by the economic elite. Over time, this most probably led to somewhat lower agricultural productivity, but more importantly, it cut off entrepreneurial families from a crucial source of capital accumulation and may very well have contributed to China's very slow pace of industrialization in the late nineteenth and early twentieth century. At a more micro level, there is evidence from South China that a substantial minority of lineages that had amassed considerable common property – property that was owned by the lineage rather than any specific household – in the eighteenth and nineteenth centuries became so concerned about the nonmeritocratic nature of their leadership selection, and presumably about the negative financial

---

[59] Zhang (2008).

consequences this generated, that they eventually switched to a model where the wealthiest households in the lineage were solely responsible for managing the common property.[60] This suggests that the economic cost of ineffective leadership was often high, which may explain why, in China's traditional core regions – North China and the Lower and Middle Yangtze – lineage ownership of common property was actually very limited. In addition to all this, grumbling about incompetent leadership and persistent factional discord between different lineage branches were apparently commonplace in North China villages where seniors dominated village politics,[61] which further suggests that seniority-based social hierarchies could themselves be a significant source of leadership turnover and regime transition costs. This makes sense when we consider the unpredictability, especially in an era where life expectancy was only around forty years, of which households or lineage branches would possess the greatest numbers of seniors.

As noted earlier, if we limited our analytical time frame to the late Qing and early Republic, we could plausibly argue that the longevity of non-meritocratic hierarchies derived simply from path dependency. That is, it was very difficult to force lower-income households to surrender status and authority already afforded to them under traditional kinship hierarchies, partially because that status and authority increased their bargaining power. But this self-sustaining circle was clearly nonexistent during the Song and Yuan, when extended kinship networks were still a novelty among commoners – in frontier regions such as South China, of course, they remained relatively rare even in the late Ming and early Qing. In fact, for much of the Song, Yuan, and early Ming, large numbers of smaller landowners and tenants still lived under fairly feudal conditions of personal bondage to large landlords,[62] which suggests that, if nothing else, their social clout and influence probably were very limited. In other words, social path dependency does not explain why the Chinese population chose that path in the first place – indeed, over multiple centuries and in tremendously diverse ecological conditions. If lower-income households received most of their social status from kinship hierarchies, then one has to wonder why wealthier households would agree to their establishment in the first place, especially when the socioeconomic efficiency of kinship hierarchies was, at best, ambiguous.

---

[60] ZHENG (2000). The fact that traditional kinship hierarchies could be eroded by economic concerns does not imply that economic forces were also responsible for their establishment.
[61] Mantetsu surveys, especially of Sibeichai and Houjiaying.   [62] McDermott (1984).

The two most plausible explanations, as discussed earlier, are political incentives issued by the central government and widespread moral internalization of related values. But was it one of the two or both? The remainder of this chapter argues that, in all likelihood, it was both, but the political prodding of the central government alone was probably insufficient.

ii State Policy

The interaction between government policy and the private establishment of "Confucian" lineages during the Song, Ming, and Qing is probably a familiar subject to most late Imperial historians. Throughout these dynasties, the central government maintained criminal codes – the *Song Criminal Code* (*Song Xingtong*), the *Great Ming Code* (*Da Ming Lü*), the *Great Qing Code* (*Da Qing Lü*), and so on – that, as discussed earlier, afforded unequal legal status to senior and junior relatives and enforced basic norms of "filial piety" (*xiao*): the same crime, whether it was assault, insult, bringing an illegal lawsuit, or homicide, was punished far more severely when committed by a junior relative against a senior relative than vice versa. In addition, failing to provide for one's parents when they entered old age was a serious crime, as was establishing a separate household when one's parents were still alive or failing to observe proper funeral procedures on their death. For the most part, these were straightforward continuations of earlier dynastic legal codes, going as far back as the Han Dynasty and quite possibly earlier.[63]

Compared with earlier dynasties, however, the Song government and its successors were increasingly willing to recognize and sometimes encourage the private establishment of extended kinship hierarchies by officials who possessed no hereditary title and, in later dynasties, by commoners. Pre-Song governments generally displayed little interest in promoting – or even allowing – the establishment of kinship networks with clearly delineated rank and command structures beyond a very narrow circle of hereditary nobility or high-level officials.[64] Although "untitled" officials and commoners were expected, as elaborated in the penal codes, to respect their parents, grandparents, and close senior relatives such as first uncles and aunts, this says nothing about whether they should subsume their socioeconomic decision making within a systematic hierarchy of kinsmen

---

[63] *See* the summary provided at ZHANG JINFAN (1997), at 113–35.
[64] FENG ET AL. (2009), at 93–163.

or, indeed, whether they should create any kind of expansive kinship network. There is a profound difference between simply demanding that I not assault or insult a senior relative – or that I provide for my parents in their old age – and regulating the permissible or ideal size of one's extended family or, for that matter, encouraging my senior relatives to regulate and monitor my everyday economic activity. Penal codes, whether before the Song or after, generally did the former but not the latter two.

There was, however, a fairly profound shift during the Northern Song in the state's nonpenal regulation of ancestor worship rights and lineage building. Prior to the eleventh century, untitled officials and commoners were generally prohibited from engaging in systemized ancestor worship beyond their father and grandfather.[65] This prevented them from worshipping together with anyone except the households of their direct brothers and first cousins. Apparently, central authorities preferred that commoner family networks remain small, unorganized, and without the kind of social authority that could realistically obstruct government power.[66]

In 1041, however, the Song government tentatively allowed all government officials, including those without any hereditary title, to engage in systemized ancestor worship "according to ancient rituals."[67] At the time, what "ancient rituals" actually meant was left undefined, but it nonetheless sent a clear message that the government was interested in loosening the traditional aristocratic monopoly over large-scale ancestor worship and extended kinship hierarchies. By 1108, following intense lobbying by officials from the Ministry of Rituals, a clearer set of regulations had been issued, which allowed all officials of the third rank or higher to worship five generations of ancestors, officials of the eighth to fourth ranks to worship three generations of ancestors, and all other officials and commoners to worship two generations – that is, one's father and grandfather.[68] In effect, this allowed all higher-ranked officials, regardless of aristocratic title, to create state-sanctioned extended kinship networks many times larger than the basic network of brothers and first cousins, but theoretically kept lower-ranked officials and commoners under much tighter control. The construction of ancestral worship halls needed special permission from the emperor, and only a handful were authorized throughout the Song.[69]

---

[65] *Id.*, at 170–71; Ye Mengde, 1 Shilin Yanyu [Sparrow Sounds of the Rock Forest] 8 (Zhonghua Shuju ed., 1984).

[66] Li & Jiang (2000), at 27–32.   [67] Feng et al. (2009), at 170.

[68] Song Shi [The Official History of the Song], chap. 109 (Li Zhi no. 12), *available at* http://gj.zdic.net/archive.php?aid=7760.

[69] Feng et al. (2009), at 171.

This basic legal framework went largely unchanged until the fourteenth century. The Khitan, Jurchen, and Mongols, when and where they conquered Song territory, generally displayed little interest in revising or regulating "Han" ancestral worship rituals.[70] Not until the early Ming did the ruling government make serious changes to the system. In 1384, following a series of petitions by local county magistrates, all commoners received the right to worship three generations of ancestors, which expanded their formally recognized kinship networks by several times, while all officials, regardless of rank, could worship four – and only four – generations.[71] Essentially, the worship rights of commoner and lower-ranked officials were expanded, but those of officials of the third rank and higher actually shrunk.

The most radical change in Ming government policy came in 1536, when, driven by Xia Yan, then head of the Ministry of Rituals, the Ming Court authorized all commoners and officials to worship up to five generations.[72] Moreover, an unpublished internal document apparently *required* all ranked officials to construct ancestral worship halls, in which, for officials below the third rank, up to four generations of ancestors could be permanently worshipped – the fifth, most distant generation could only be worshipped during the Dongzhi and Lichun festivals.[73] Officials of the third rank and above could permanently worship all five generations. Commoners, however, were still formally forbidden from constructing ancestral halls. But even so, the central government had clearly warmed up to the idea of large-scale social organization through extended kinship hierarchies.

By the early Qing, the central government had gone from merely permitting the formation of large commoner kinship networks to actively promoting them. Both Kangxi and Yongzheng issued several edicts that praised both the emergence of extended kinship networks and their

---

[70] *Id.* at 171–72.

[71] Chang Jianhua, *Mingdai Zongzu Cimiao Jizu Lizhi ji Qi Yanbian* [*The Evolution of Ancestor Worship Practices in Ming Dynasty Lineages*], 2001(3) NANKAI XUEBAO [ACADEMIC JOURNAL OF NANKAI UNIV.] 60.

[72] Xia Yan, *Ling Chenmin De Ji Shizu Li Jiamiao Shu* [*A Petition Asking that All Subjects Be Allowed to Worship their Founding Ancestors*], in GUIZHOU WENJI [WRITINGS OF GUIZHOU], chap. 11 (1574, Microfilm, Peking University Library); ZHU GUOZHEN, HUANG MING DAZHENG JI [A COLLECTION OF RIGHTEOUS WRITINGS IN AN ERA OF A BENEVOLENT EMPEROR], Chapter 28, Section 2 (Qilu Shushe ed., 1997). *But see* INOUE (2008), at 122–26, for skepticism on whether Xia Yan's proposal was really implemented by official decree.

[73] JI HUANG ET AL., QINDING XU WENXIAN TONGKAO [OFFICIAL SEQUEL TO THE EXEGESIS OF HISTORICAL DOCUMENTS], chap. 115 (1784, microfilm, Zhejiang Univ. Library).

close adherence to "proper" Confucian norms of seniority and status.[74] Yongzheng, in particular, encouraged people to think of their extended family as one "body," in which the most senior members coordinated and regulated the movements of everyone else.[75] To further incentivize the creation of extended kinship hierarchies, the Qing government regularly granted symbolic economic favors – money to construct a commemorative stele, a few bundles of tapestry, and so on – to kinship networks that displayed particularly "virtuous" behavior: "five generations living under one roof," an unusually filial man who closely observed the wishes of elder relatives, or a "chaste" widow who refused to remarry after her husband's death. In the Lower Yangtze, such commemorative grants numbered in the tens of thousands during the eighteenth and nineteenth centuries. Between 1825 and 1830 alone, nearly 5,000 people in four Jiangsu Province counties had received some sort of reward for filial piety or chastity. In Wujiang County, by the early nineteenth century, the government had constructed fifty steles in honor of lineages that had a recognized tradition of filial piety and another seven to honor those that were known for female chastity.[76]

At the same time, the government ramped up its legal efforts to recognize and protect lineage corporate property both against intrusion from outsiders and also against embezzlement from within the lineage. Embezzlement of lineage common property was punishable by either temporary incarceration for minor offenses or permanent banishment for major ones.[77] Moreover, if a lineage leader committed a criminal offense, whatever economic penalty the government imposed would not touch on any common property he was managing.[78] Effectively, the lineage had acquired some degree of legal personhood.

The Qing government's enthusiasm for private lineage formation – which was distinctly higher than that of the Song and Ming governments – may have had something to do with its unique political circumstances. Being a conquest dynasty, the Qing constantly struggled with the issue of ethnic tension, and its Manchu rulers were keen to find ways of pacifying their

---

[74] QINDING DAQING HUIDIAN SHILI [OFFICIAL APPLICATIONS OF THE DAQING HUIDIAN], chap. 397 (Shangwu Press ed., 1909).

[75] *Id. See* Chang Jianhua, *Lun* Shengyu Guangxun *yu Qingdai de Xiaozhi* [*On the* Shengyu Guangxun *and the Use of Filial Piety as a Governing Tool in the Qing*], 1988(1) NANKAI SHIXUE [NANKAI UNIV. HISTORICAL STUD.] 35, *available at* http://wenku.baidu.com/view/e85a377102768e9951e7385c.html, for analysis.

[76] FENG (2005), at 52.   [77] QINDING DAQING HUIDIAN SHILI (1909), at chap. 755.

[78] FENG (2005), at 54.

predominantly Han population.[79] Vigorously embracing "Confucian" virtues such as filial piety or at least conveying such a message to the Han-dominated regions of the empire was one potentially effective way of doing this. In addition, the Qing also took perhaps the most laissez-faire approach to local governance of any unified dynasty during the Second Millennium, keeping its bureaucratic apparatus, not to mention examination degree quotas, at a very small size despite rapid population growth.[80] Encouraging the formation of self-regulating kinship hierarchies may simply have been a way to compensate for the government's own administrative limitations.

Given all this, is it plausible to argue that the embrace of Confucian kinship hierarchies by most private kinship networks during the Second Millennium was simply a direct response to legal or economic incentives provided by the government? That is, did people form kinship hierarchies because they coveted state approval or feared state sanctions? It should be pointed out immediately that this does *not* amount to asking, "Did kinship hierarchies proliferate completely independently of the state?" – several major recent studies have labored to demonstrate that they did not and that southern Chinese lineages were keenly aware of, and deftly reacted to, the political circumstances surrounding them.[81] Rather, I ask the narrower question of whether lineages were built *because the state encouraged it.*

In short, probably not. First of all, the Song and Ming governments never actively embraced the idea that commoners should be forming their own extended kinship hierarchies. Rather, they seemed merely to permit it – indeed, rather grudgingly – and their regulatory efforts generally fell far behind the actual proliferation of private ancestor worship in local social life. The Song government, as discussed earlier, never allowed lower-level officials and commoners to worship more than two generations of ancestors, and expressly forbade them from constructing ancestor worship halls.

Local documents indicate, however, that not only did considerable numbers of local lineages worship far more than two generations of ancestors, but many of them had constructed private worship halls.[82] For example, in the early twelfth century, the famed poet Li Lü, who had never held any examination degree, constructed what was nominally a "pavilion"

---

[79] *See* Rowe (2009), at 11–62.
[80] On the limited size and reach of the Qing bureaucracy, *see* Ch'u (1962); Reed (2000); Watt (1972); Rowe (2009), at 31–62. On examination degree quotas, *see* Elman (1991).
[81] Most notably, Faure (2007); Szonyi (2002).
[82] Examples are drawn from Feng et al. (2009), at 172–76.

beside his father's grave that provided all the normal functions of an ancestor worship hall. A similar trick was employed by the Wang lineage of Ningbo during the later twelfth century and recorded by the prominent scholar Lou Yue. Toward the end of the Song, Huang Zhongyuan, of Putian in Fujian Province, constructed a private worship hall despite never having held an official post and proceeded to worship a whopping thirteen generations of ancestors in it.

Private worship of distant ancestors continued to expand at a brisk pace throughout the Song, Yuan, and early Ming, often coupled with the construction of worship halls.[83] Thus, when the Ming government finally allowed commoners to worship five generations of ancestors in 1536, it was simply belatedly recognizing and legitimizing what had long been an extremely common social practice. Even then, the government refused to legally permit commoners to construct worship halls but continued to turn a blind eye to the vast numbers of private worship halls that were being built across the country.

All this suggests that, in their interaction with private demand for building extended kinship hierarchies, pre-Qing Imperial governments usually played a reactionary role rather than an active one. Whether in 1108, 1384, or 1536, Imperial decrees came as responses to persistent lobbying and pleading from scholar-officials who believed that the old ancestor worship regulations had become outdated and overly restrictive and that the overwhelming private demand for extended ancestor worship rights needed to be placated.

It is not difficult to understand why the Imperial government was often reluctant to extend ancestor worship rights to commoners: people who have exclusive privileges are rarely eager to share them with others. But perhaps more importantly, such extension amounted, effectively, to a conferral of social authority and privilege from the central political elite to commoners and would erode their control over local affairs. Essentially, the larger and better organized local kinship networks were, the greater was their potential threat to state authority. The very compelling counterargument to all these concerns was, of course, that state power in localities would shrink inevitably – population growth, commercialization, and increasing migration saw to that – that people would worship multiple generations of ancestors and form large kinship hierarchies regardless of whether the state formally allowed them to, and therefore that the state might as well boost its

---

[83] LI & JIANG (2000), at 35–71; INOUE (2008), at 26–74.

public legitimacy and popularity by granting extended worship rights. The tension between these opposing ideas nicely explains why Song and Ming governments were constantly playing catch-up to the private proliferation of large and tightly organized kinship hierarchies.[84]

The Qing government, as discussed earlier, was significantly more active in promoting private establishment of kinship hierarchies – most plausibly due to its unique political circumstances and governing ideology. But even it harbored considerable reservations and concerns about the "overempowerment" of local lineages vis-à-vis central government authority. In 1726, Yongzheng issued an edict stating that in areas where the dominant local lineage had more than 100 members and where the more conventional *baojia* system was ineffective, the lineage should elect a *zuzheng* to serve as its go-between with the government.[85] The *zuzheng* would wield formally recognized arbitration and policing powers and could rely on local magistrates to help enforce his decisions. The rationale seemed to be that this would allow the state to more effectively harness the organizational capacities of local lineages. Within a few decades, however, it had become abundantly clear that formally delegating power to *zuzheng* tended to erode, not reinforce, the state's local authority, in that it simply emboldened lineages to further expand the scope of their self-governance. By 1789, Qianlong had decided to abolish the position entirely, stating that *zuzheng* were rarely "people who observed the public interest and obeyed the laws."[86] Clearly, local lineages had grown too powerful – even by the relatively lax standards of the Qing – for comfort.

But even if we ignore these tensions, it would nonetheless be hard to believe that state advocacy and encouragement had much to do with the continued proliferation of kinship hierarchies during the Qing. First and

---

[84] INOUE (2008), at 106–07, 123–24; HAMASHIMA ATSUTOSHI, MINDAI KOUNAN NOUSON SHIAKAI NO KENKYU [RESEARCH ON MING DYNASTY JIANGNAN RURAL SOCIETY] (1982); Chang Jianghua, *Yuandai Muci Jizu Wenti Chutan* [*A Preliminary Study on Yuan Dynasty Ancestor Worship Practices*], *in* ZHONGGUO SHEHUI WENHUA SHI DUBEN [THE CHINESE SOCIAL AND CULTURAL HISTORY READER] 260 (Liu Yonghua ed., 2011); Xu Huailin, *Chenshi Jiazu de Wajie ji "Yimen" de Yingxiang* [*The Disintegration of the Chen Lineage and the Influence of the "Yimen"*], 1994(2) ZHONGGUO SHI YANJIU [STUD. CHINESE HIST.] 56 (discussing the Song government's role in limiting lineage development); XU (2004), at 72–77, 84–95 (discussing Ming and Qing efforts to curb local gentry lineages).

[85] 19 QINGCHAO WENXIAN TONGKAO [COMPREHENSIVE STUDY OF QING HISTORICAL DOCUMENTS] 5031 (Zhejiang Guji Press ed., 1988).

[86] 25 QING SHILU [TRUE RECORDS OF THE QING] 1097, 1101 (Zhonghua Shuju ed., 1986).

foremost, the government was probably not powerful enough to do much more than nudge forward a preexisting social trend of such magnitude. As discussed in previous chapters, historians now believe that the Qing state, even more so than previous dynasties, exercised little authority beyond the county level – it had very limited manpower, extremely tight finances, and a highly questionable ability to enforce laws and regulations. Correspondingly, local communities tended to regulate themselves in most areas of socioeconomic life. Customary law, rather than formal law, governed the use and transfer of property in most regions. Similarly, scholars have generally found that guilds, not government officials, regulated most aspects of commerce and business in core macroregions.[87]

Perhaps reflecting the state's limited capacity, the material incentives it offered to "virtuous" lineages were by and large symbolic, conveying some prestige but no significant economic or political benefit. It is hard to imagine them having more than a peripheral impact on the private creation of kinship hierarchies: how many people would organize and enforce an extended kinship hierarchy mainly to win bundles of silk or money for a stele? Certainly these things could provide a nice additional incentive, but in all likelihood not a very large one. In fact, the social dominance of large kinship networks was already very much secure by the early Qing, at least in core regions such as the Lower Yangtze and North China. It was still a work in progress in the frontier regions of Fujian or Guangdong, but the state's administrative capacity was even weaker there than in core macroregions[88] and therefore even less likely to have been a major driving factor.

For all these reasons, it seems unlikely that late Imperial state activity – whether the passive permissiveness of the Song and Ming governments or the more active stance taken by the Qing government – really did much to directly stimulate the spread of kinship hierarchies. People built kinship networks because it suited their local socioeconomic interests, with or without additional incentives provided by the state. Moreover, they adhered to Confucian seniority hierarchies not because the state pushed them to – or even because it conferred any material socioeconomic benefit – but because, in all likelihood, they thought it was morally appropriate.

---

[87] Moll-Murata (2008).
[88] *See* ROBERT MARKS, TIGERS, RICE, SILK, AND SILT: ENVIRONMENT AND ECONOMY IN LATE IMPERIAL SOUTH CHINA 226–48 (2006); SUSAN MANN, LOCAL MERCHANTS AND THE CHINESE BUREAUCRACY, 1750–1950 (1987); FAURE (2007).

iii Values and Moral Internalization

The preceding two subsections have argued that socioeconomic and political incentives alone cannot satisfactorily explain the rapid proliferation of large kinship hierarchies during the later Imperial dynasties. The inadequacy of functionalist explanations suggests that kinship hierarchies were also sustained by some form of moral internalization, wherein people justified seniority-based inequality through moral reasoning rather than through calculations of socioeconomic welfare or political interest: To some extent, they had to think it was "the right thing to do" regardless of the material consequences. Of course, reaching a conclusion via the exclusion of alternatives is never terribly satisfying. The remainder of this chapter attempts to compensate by providing some "positive" evidence that widespread moral internalization among the general population had probably occurred as early as the Southern Song.

Basically, this relies on both the volume and uniformity of late Imperial private writings on kinship relations and ancestor worship. As many have observed, there was an explosion, relative to immediately preceding eras, of such writings in the Southern Song and again in the Ming and Qing.[89] Virtually all these writings speak of the basic principle that senior relatives possessed higher social stature than junior ones in highly moralistic tones – in fact, *only* in highly moralistic terms. The same was largely true, of course, of most late Qing and even Republican-era writings on kinship. But whereas, as discussed in Section A, one could semiplausibly argue that pragmatic incentives drove the moralistic tone of these later writings, it is much harder to justify similar skepticism toward Song, Yuan, and Ming documents, which were written in eras where the social dominance of large kinship networks was yet a work in progress and, therefore, where the pragmatic incentives were much weaker.

As with most discussions of late Imperial social morality, the major Song Neo-Confucian scholars – Zhang Zai, Cheng Yi, Zhu Xi, and so on – are a good place to start. Zhu Xi, of course, zealously promoted the establishment of large, private kinship networks organized according to traditional Confucian seniority principles and published his own "Family Rituals" as

---

[89] *See, e.g.*, Feng et al. (2009), at 195–208; Li & Jiang (2000), at 32–35; Bossler (1998) (focusing on the proliferation of eulogies in the Song); Fei Chengkang et al., Zhongguo de Jiafa Zugui [Family and Clan Regulations in China] 14–25 (1998); Xu (1992); Zhu (1987).

an example of how this should be done.[90] His Northern Song predecessors were often not quite as thorough but nonetheless believed that "privileging elders" (*zun gaonian*) was a fundamental principle of human morality. Zhang Zai and Cheng Yi both argued that it was the natural order of things and that divergence from it would lead to societal decay and collapse – whereas adherence would bring peace and prosperity.[91] Similar statements also appear in abundance in the writings of Zhou Dunyi, Shao Yong, Lu Jiuyuan, and Chen Liang.[92] Despite their otherwise deep and sometimes irreconcilable philosophical differences, virtually all major figures in Song Neo-Confucianism apparently agreed that seniority hierarchies among kinsmen was not something to be disputed.

Although Neo-Confucianism often had a somewhat tenuous relationship with the Song government – at certain points during the Southern Song, the government attempted to crack down on private teachings of Neo-Confucian doctrine – the two sides did agree, at least, on the basic principle that seniority within a kinship network should correlate with higher status and authority. The state may not have always appreciated the philosophical twists and turns that Neo-Confucian scholars applied to this principle, but at no point did it question the principle itself. Its enshrinement in all manners of legal codes and regulations is but one indication of this. Furthermore, virtually all top-level scholar-officials who left some written record – including relatively uncontroversial figures such as Fan Zhongyan but also many individuals, such as Wang Anshi and Sima Guang, who were otherwise entrenched political enemies[93] – at some point found it necessary or desirable to declare their firm belief in the social utility of extended kinship networks organized according to Confucian hierarchies and principles. In fact, as discussed earlier, most Song officials

---

[90] Zhu Xi, Jiali [Family Rituals] (Wang Yanjun & Wang Guangzhao eds., Shanghai Guji Press, 1999).

[91] Zhang Zai Ji [Collected Writings of Zhang Zai] 258–59 (Zhonghua Shuju ed., 1978); 2 Er Cheng Ji [Collected Writings of Cheng Hao and Cheng Yi] 350–52 (Zhonghua Shuju ed., 1981).

[92] Qiu Hansheng, *Songmin Lixue yu Zongfa Sixiang* [*Song-Ming Neo-Confucianism and Lineage Rituals and Thought*], 1979(11) Lishi Yanjiu [Hist. Stud.] 63.

[93] On Fan Zhongyan, *see* Bian Guofeng, *Fan Zhongyan Zongzu Fuli Sixiang Yanjiu* [*A Study on Fan Zhongyan's Thoughts on Lineage Welfare*] (M.A. Thesis, Jilin Univ., 2004). On Wang Anshi, *see* Shi Yingying, *Wang Anshi Jingxin yu Jingshi Sixiang Lunshu* [*On Wang Anshi's Ideology of "Heart-Cultivation" and "Social Cultivation"*] (Ph.D. Thesis, Pengjia Univ., 2011). On Sima Guang, *see* Ma Jialu, *Sima Guang Shehui Sixiang Tanxi* [*An Exploration of Sima Guang's Social Thought*] (M.A. Thesis, Qingdao Univ., 2009).

deeply coveted the opportunity to establish their own extended kinship networks, which were then almost always organized around either seniority or *zongzi* principles.

So much, then, for Song intellectual and political writings. But even if we descend into the much more diverse world of nonacademic private writings – for example, personal eulogies and short essays that celebrated the unveiling of private ancestral worship halls, both of which survive in significant numbers – the largely unconditional acceptance of kinship hierarchies continues to be a basic theme.[94] The style and narrative focus of eulogies and commemorative essays changed considerably from the Tang to the Song and underwent further changes during the Song, but the praising of individuals for filial obedience to elder relatives remained largely consistent.

Buddhism and Daoism did, of course, compete with Confucianism, sometimes violently, for political and social influence during much of the First Millennium, but by the Song they had largely retreated from the realm of high politics and sought out a more peaceful coexistent in local religious and cultural life.[95] In fact, large numbers of Buddhist monasteries and Daoist temples were more than happy to host large-scale ancestral worship events in the absence of private worship halls.[96] Many established long-term relationships with local kinship networks in which the kinship networks purchased a "permanent" worship place in the monastery or temple and would assemble there at regular intervals. For a fee, the monks and priests would provide religious services at these events, including the maintenance of incense burners and the recital of certain texts. As far as historical research has shown, since at least the eleventh century, neither religion substantively obstructed the proliferation of ancestor worship and kinship hierarchies, whether in writing or in practice.

Despite the radical social, economic, and political changes that occurred in the centuries following Song collapse, the aforementioned observations could basically be made of any late Imperial dynasty. While Ming and Qing scholars may have preferred a less metaphysical style than Zhou Dunyi or Zhang Zai,

---

[94] *See* sources cited at pp. 209–10.

[95] *See* RICHARD VON GLAHN, THE SINISTER WAY: THE DIVINE AND THE DEMONIC IN CHINESE RELIGIOUS CULTURE (2004); JACQUES GERNET, BUDDHISM IN CHINESE SOCIETY: AN ECONOMIC HISTORY FROM THE FIFTH TO THE TENTH CENTURIES (Franciscus Verellen trans., 1995); BAREND TER HAAR, THE WHITE LOTUS TEACHINGS IN CHINESE RELIGIOUS HISTORY 16–63 (1992); VALERIE HANSEN, CHANGING GODS IN MEDIEVAL CHINA, 1127–1276 (1990).

[96] FENG ET AL. (2009), at 178–81.

they nonetheless shared their basic conviction that inequality and some measure of sociopolitical dominance between senior and junior relatives was simply the natural order of things. For all their philosophical differences, Wang Yangming echoed Zhu Xi very closely when he wrote that "the different statuses of senior and junior relatives" had been a fundamental and self-evident natural principle since the age of Yao and Shun.[97]

Even scholars who expressly challenged the Neo-Confucian mainstream generally embraced these basic "human principles" (*renlun*): Gu Yanwu, Huang Zongxi, and Wang Fuzhi during the Ming-Qing transition and any number of "Hanxue" advocates during the Qing.[98] The famed – and in some modern intellectual circles, revered – intellectual Li Zhi, who relentlessly accused most Neo-Confucian scholars of being thorough "fakes,"[99] vehemently rejected large swathes of the late Ming social order and ended his life as a solitary monk, nonetheless endorsed filial piety as a desirable moral principle. It is quite telling that even after denouncing a wide range of inequalities in Ming society, ranging from the disdain for merchants in mainstream Confucian ideology, to the political privileging of Confucianism over Buddhism and Daoism, to the higher sociopolitical status occupied by examination degree holders, Li expressed firm support for probably the most fundamental and important one.[100] In fact, it really was not until the early twentieth century that serious intellectual skepticism toward kinship hierarchies began to emerge among the intellectual elite, but by then kinship hierarchies were so deeply entrenched in Chinese society that, as discussed earlier, such skepticism did relatively little to dent their social dominance until the Communist era.

Private writings on kinship norms proliferated rapidly, of course, as extended kinship networks gradually became the predominant form of social organization. In particular, an increasing number of kinship networks began compiling genealogies and internal regulations, which were

---

[97] Wu Tianxia, *Chuantong Xiaodao de Chuancheng yu Yanbian [The Inheritance and Evolution of Traditional Filial Piety]* (M.A. Thesis, Shaanxi Normal Univ., 2008) (demonstrating the basic continuity between Zhu and Wang in their ideas on filial piety and kinship hierarchies).

[98] Zhou Qirong, *Rujia Lijiao Sichao de Xingqi yu Qingdai Kaozheng Xue [The Rise of Confucian Ritualism and Evidential Scholarship of the Qing]*, 2011(3) NANJING SHIDA XUEBAO [ACADEMIC J. NANJING NORMAL UNIV.] 7. For a more general survey, *see* LU BAOQIAN, QINGDAI SIXIANG SHI [INTELLECTUAL HISTORY OF THE QING] (2009).

[99] PAULINE C. LEE, LI ZHI, CONFUCIANISM, AND THE VIRTUE OF DESIRE (2012).

[100] These writings are summarized at Shi Jiaoyu, *"Yiduan" Li Zhi de Chuantong Sixiang [The Traditional Thought of the "Heretic" Li Zhi]*, 16(2) CHONGQING ZHIYE JISHU XUEYUAN XUEBAO [J. CHONGQING TECH. INST.] 78 (2007).

natural venues for philosophical and moral discussion on social hierarch-ies.[101] Given that virtually all these lineages adopted some form of seniority hierarchy, it is utterly unsurprising that many, perhaps most, of them, echoing the more prominent scholars and officials discussed earlier, expressly declared it some sort of natural law that reached back into the distant past: "[Our lineage regulations and genealogy] are drafted," declared one Yuan lineage, "so that our descendants may recognize the gravity and wisdom of ancient ways, and reject the cynicism of contem-porary society."[102] An early Ming genealogy claimed that traditional Confucian hierarchies were "heavenly moral principles" (*tianlun*) and that those who violated them "would be annihilated by the heavens, and abandoned by men."[103] Similar language, if not quite as ominous, was epidemic in Yuan, Ming, and Qing genealogies.

The "wisdom of ancient ways" did not necessarily hold absolute author-ity in all circumstances. For example, by the early Qing, most lineages had expressly rejected the classical *zongzi* system in favor of more straightfor-ward ranking by age and generation, arguing that the former scheme was outdated and practically impossible to sustain. Nonetheless, on simpler issues, such as sustaining individual inequalities between senior and junior relatives (with perhaps some exception made for members of the *zongzi* line), few lineages displayed any doubts about their consistency with "ancient wisdom" or indeed with "the way of heaven."

Ultimately, despite facing different, sometimes dramatically different, socioeconomic and political conditions during the Second Millennium, the moral discussion of kinship hierarchies remained basically consistent in tone and content. People generally assumed that their moral legitimacy was self-evident, which suggests, especially in the absence of satisfying rationalistic or functionalist explanations, that the rise of extended kinship hierarchies was inseparable from the deep moral sway that they held over the Chinese, or at least the Han Chinese, population. Widespread moral internalization may not have been a sufficient condition – after all, it may well have existed for some of the First Millennium as well – but all evidence points to it being a necessary one.

In the end, where was the Chinese state in all this? As discussed earlier, the political authorizations and material incentives periodically issued

---

[101] Fei et al. (1998), 17–25.   [102] Feng et al. (2009), at 203 (citing Chen Gao).
[103] Fang Xiaoru, Xunzhi Zhai Ji [Writings from Xunzhi Villa] 34 (Xu Guangda ed., Ningbo Press, 2000).

probably did fairly little to spur the spread of extended kinship hierarchies. Nonetheless, the state may have been considerably more competent in shaping moral discourse than in shaping local sociopolitical institutions. As with any society, the most prominent intellectuals and scholars were disproportionally influential in late Imperial social discourse, but also tended to have closer ties to the state than other sectors of society, even the literate ones. One can see this in the fact that most lineages afforded special positions of honor to members who held high-level examination degrees, even though, by at least the mid-Ming, the great majority of them probably had no *juren* or *jinshi* among their ranks. In other words, the moral and intellectual prestige of these elite scholars considerably outpaced their actual economic or political presence in local affairs. Many, perhaps most, of these elite minds *were* state officials and shared a similar moral language due to their examination preparation. In this context, the mostly unwavering state support for Confucian moral ideals, and particularly the state's formal endorsement of Zhu Xi's Neo-Confucianism from the mid-Yuan to the Ming, becomes intellectually and morally significant even if the state's actual regulatory capacity was in steep decline.

As David Faure and others have demonstrated, Ming and Qing lineages were quite keen to adopt the ritualistic practices, organizational principles, and moral language of state authorities and higher gentry, believing that it conferred social legitimacy and prestige.[104] Despite the existence of popular Buddhism and Taoism, they looked, first and foremost, to elite – and state – practice to determine what was proper and right, although those elites were, in fact, quite wary about granting them extended worship rights. In other words, the "moral example" that the state set helped to drive the internalization of Confucian rituals and social hierarchies, whereas the "real" political and economic incentives it provided were much less of a factor.

Even so, the state's ideological interaction with the population it ruled over, especially in the Ming and Qing, was mostly one of discourse, persuasion, and setting "moral examples," not coercion or even material incentivizing. Most accurately, it was probably a process of commoners wanting to emulate the moral rituals and language of intellectual and political elites, indeed often without the express approval of the elites themselves. This explains, for example, why the Song and Ming grants of extended ancestral worship rights were always seen as playing catch-up to

---

[104] FAURE (2007); SOMMER (2000).

social reality. In any case, no Second Millennium dynastic government made any serious attempt to prevent private ancestor worship. One imagines that if it had tried, it probably would have fared no better than the Qing government's failed attempts to regulate *dian* redemption. Nonetheless, the fact that there was an elite example to aspire to, and that state activity clearly helped to sustain and legitimize that example, was of great significance. Even the most laissez-faire government can hold considerable moral prestige and authority.

6

Property Institutions and Agricultural Capitalism

Previous chapters have focused on explaining the institutional differences between pre-industrial Chinese and English collateralized borrowing institutions. Along the way, I discussed the microeconomic incentives created by these institutions and, in a few places, made passing mention of their broader macroeconomic effects – specifically, how they affected economic inequality and disparity in landholding. This chapter examines these macroeconomic consequences in greater detail. Primarily, it argues that customary *dian* redemption rules had a major impact on the concentration of landed capital and the fundamental structure of Chinese agricultural production. Basically, by shielding smallholders from losing their land under conditions of economic duress, *dian* norms clogged the flow of landed capital from lower economic classes to higher ones. While this helped to sustain an unusually equitable distribution of landed wealth, it also hampered the capital accumulation necessary for agricultural capitalism. In comparison, land purchases by larger landholders from smallholders fueled, to a large extent, the ascension of capitalist agriculture in England, leading to greater economies of scale and sharp increases in labor productivity.

To understand this argument, one must first remember that, as discussed earlier, the stereotypical socioeconomic identity of the average Chinese *dian* seller and English mortgagor was a small landholder of limited means, whereas the great majority of *dian* buyers and mortgagees were significantly wealthier. Chapter 3 explored this issue from the perspective of an individual landholder – when and how he would want to sell

Portions of this chapter were previously published in Taisu Zhang, *Property Rights in Land, Agricultural Capitalism, and the Relative Decline of Pre-Industrial China*, 13 SAN DIEGO INT. L.J. 129 (2011).

or collateralize land – but there is an equally interesting macro-level narrative to be told. On the English side, the sixteenth and seventeenth centuries were a time of massive wealth and land concentration, from smallholders, both tenants and lesser yeomen, into the hands of large capitalist farmers. The process, especially in its earlier stages, relied heavily on land acquisition via sales or mortgage defaults, driven on the supply side by falling grain prices and shrinking agricultural profit margins.[1] Such trends were not unique to England – French landholding underwent a similar wave of engrossment and concentration at roughly the same time.[2]

Certainly, as many historians would caution, sixteenth-century lords and gentry also conveyed property to tenants with some regularity, but these tended to be upgrades of copyhold land to freehold status, usually because the copyholder's property rights had become so secure that the landlord had effectively lost control over them, and not actual conveyances of new land.[3] Shortly thereafter, landlords began clamping down on the creation of new copyholds, instead of moving toward at-will tenancy. At the same time, England saw the number of landed gentry and capitalist farmers skyrocket, aided enormously by the increase of land under private ownership, which made it even easier for larger landowners to engross freehold property via purchase or mortgage.[4] By the later eighteenth century, many noble houses and higher gentry had themselves become highly indebted and prone to mortgaging land to newly ascendant merchants, traders, and bankers, but for much of the previous two centuries, the wealthier landed classes were firmly in expansion mode against their poorer neighbors and tenants.

Although China did not experience any comparable flood of land engrossment, its overall pattern of land transaction was nonetheless from poorer households to wealthier ones. As noted in previous chapters, most historians believe that Qing and Republican *dian* sales were predominantly made by relatively impoverished households under great

---

[1] See J.V. Beckett, *The Decline of the Small Landowner in Eighteenth- and Nineteenth-Century England: Some Regional Considerations*, 30 AGRI. HIST. REV. 97, 98–100 (1982) (summarizing existing literature).

[2] See Philip T. Hoffman, *Taxes and Agrarian Life in Early Modern France: Land Sales, 1550–1730*, 46 J. OF ECON. HIST. 37, 40 (1986), for comparisons with France.

[3] Hoyle (1990); Hoyle (1987).

[4] Hoyle (1990); Hoyle (1987); Lawrence Stone, *Social Mobility in England, 1500–1700*, 33 PAST & PRESENT 16–55 (1966).

financial stress.[5] This observation has fueled a long tradition of Marxist history that sees such transactions as essentially a form of economic exploitation by landlords and wealthy farmers. Some suggest, in fact, that most *dian* sellers were so poor that they were never able to redeem their land and, instead, eventually had to permanently convey it at a discounted price.

While this latter point is *highly* questionable – the enormous number of redemption-related disputes in local courts strongly suggests otherwise, as do Republican-era survey data indicating that less than 15 percent of *dian* sales eventually became fully owned by the creditor – the basic consensus that most *dian* sellers were poor is probably correct. In two North China villages that were extensively surveyed by Japanese researchers in the early 1940s, for example, around 85 percent of households that had conditionally sold land during the later 1930s possessed less land than the village average, and nearly 40 percent possessed less than a third of that average.[6] In contrast, less than 3 percent of *dian* sellers belonged to the top 25 percent of landowners.

On the purchaser side of the transaction, the most active players seemed to have been relatively well-off landholders who employed some wage labor. The best statistical data on this come from an academic survey of Qingyuan County, Hebei, from 1934 to 1936.[7] It indicates, among other things, that around 70 percent of buyers in local *dian* sales were either "middle farmers" or "rich farmers."[8] In fact, around 20 percent of both "middle farmer" and "rich farmer" households in Qingyuan engaged in at least one *dian* sale during the surveyed period, whereas very few "poor farmers" did the same.[9] The survey does not define these categories, but we can calculate some rough quantitative boundaries based on average landholding statistics. Average "middle farmer" households tilled around thirty *mu* – about 50 percent higher than the village median – while average "rich

---

[5] *See* HUANG (2001), at 73; HUANG (1990), at 106; MACAULEY (1998), at 230; Zelin (1986), at 515. Qing officials generally assumed that conditional sales were done out of a pressing and unavoidable need for cash. *See* Lin & Zhang (2003).

[6] 3 MANTETSU SURVEYS, at 5; 4 MANTETSU SURVEYS, at 218.

[7] I draw on two sources of published data: Zhang Peigang, *Qingyuan de Nongjia Jingji* [*The Agricultural Economy of Qingyuan*], 7 SHEHUI KEXUE ZAZHI [J. OF SOC. SCI.] 1 (1936); Shi Zhihong, *20 Shiji San Sishi Niandai Huabei Pingyuan Nongcun de Tudi Fenpei ji Qi Bianhua* [*Land Distribution and Change on the North China Plain in the 1930s*], 2002(3) ZHONGGUO JINGJISHI YANJIU [STUD. ON CHINESE ECON. HIST.] 3.

[8] Calculated using transactional statistics at Zhang Peigang (1936), at 8, 16, and demographic data at Shi Zhihong (2002), at 5–6.

[9] Zhang Peigang (1936), at 8, 16.

farmer" households managed around ninety *mu*.[10] Given that the average nineteenth-century North China household could only farm twenty to thirty *mu* without outside help,[11] this suggests that most land-purchasing "middle farmers" and probably *all* "rich farmers" employed at least some wage labor.

Dian selling in the Lower Yangtze followed a broadly similar pattern. Although agricultural surveys of the region do not provide the kinds of statistical data available from North China surveys, scholars do have access to several sets of contract archives that offer equally compelling evidence. In these collections from late Qing- and Republican-era Zhejiang, the great majority of *dian* sales were bought up by the same handful of households from a wide assortment of sellers, mostly within their own lineage. This clearly suggests that a few relatively wealthy households were aggressively acquiring land from numerous poorer ones.[12]

Under these basic conditions, the provision of strong *dian* redemption rights in Chinese customs had the cumulative effect of dampening the flow of land from smallholders to wealthier households, whereas the tightening of mortgage redemption rights in England had largely the opposite effect. The remainder of this chapter argues that this explains why English agriculture had become predominantly "capitalist" or "managerial" by 1700, whereas Chinese agriculture remained household-based and of limited scale throughout the Qing and Republican eras. Both negative and positive proofs are offered: I argue that previous attempts at explaining the relative lack of "managerial farming" in China are inadequate, but more importantly, I then test my explanation and its primary theoretical derivatives against existing data on land transaction volume, landowner-ship patterns, and labor-to-land ratios.

Apart from its obvious connection to the academic literature on Sino-European economic divergence, this exercise also relates to some important debates within law and economics theory. One of the most significant trends in law and economics over the past two or three decades has been

---

[10] Shi Zhihong (2002), at 5–6.

[11] Based on figures at HUANG (1985), at 70 (thirty *mu* seems to be an upper limit, whereas most households could farm perhaps fifty *mu* mainly with their own labor – suggesting that the average household could farm around twenty-five *mu* with its labor).

[12] NINGBO CONTRACTS (2008) (showing Mao Kunshan *dian*-purchasing land from over 100 different sellers), 3 SHICANG QIYUE (showing Que Yuqing *dian*-purchasing land from over fifty sellers).

the study of nonlegal "social norms,"[13] to which the various land customs examined in this book certainly belong. While scholars have, as outlined in Chapter 3, provided ample evidence that communities are generally capable of creating their own "social norms" without state-driven legal influence and, moreover, that these norms frequently outrank formal laws in their practical importance,[14] they have vigorously debated whether "norms are likely to promote social welfare"[15] – with "social welfare" often defined in terms of overall economic efficiency. Scholars such as Robert Ellickson, James Coleman, and Robert Cooter have expressed general optimism on this point, at least for "closely knit" communities where people share information about each other,[16] whereas Eric Posner, Russell Hardin, Richard McAdams, and others argue the contrary.[17]

The Chinese land customs examined here were generally created and maintained within a few adjacent villages that, in all likelihood, qualify as closely knit communities. By preventing the widespread development of managerial farming, however, these customs impeded, rather than pro- moted, economic efficiency. While it would be folly to "refute" the optimists based on this one historical example, its scope and significance do present an empirical challenge to their theories that should not be overlooked. The natural follow-up question here would be why Chinese localities adhered to these macroeconomically inefficient customs in the first place – despite persistent government efforts to eliminate them and despite the fact that they did considerable economic damage to many of the richest and most entrepreneurial landowners – but that issue is left to Chapters 4 and 5.

Section A surveys the extent of managerial farming in England and China. The differences in scale, as will be seen, are fairly dramatic. Section B examines existing explanations for this contrast, arguing that they are generally unsatisfactory. In particular, the evidence suggests that managerial farming in both North China and the Lower Yangtze enjoyed

---

[13] Ellickson (1998), at 537, 542.

[14] A review of the relevant literature can be found in Ellickson (1998) and Etzioni (2000), at 157.

[15] Richard H. McAdams, *Comment: Accounting for Norms*, Wisc. L. Rev. 625, 635 (1997).

[16] James S. Coleman, Foundations of Social Theory 249–58 (1990); Robert C. Ellickson, Order without Law: How Neighbors Settle Disputes 167 (1991); Robert D. Cooter, *Structural Adjudication and the New Law Merchant: A Model of Decentralized Law*, 14 Int'l Rev. L. & Econ. 215, 224–26 (1994).

[17] Eric A. Posner, *Law, Economics, and Inefficient Norms*, 144 U. Pa. L. Rev. 1697 (1996); Hardin (1995); McAdams (1997b).

higher productivity than household-based production and, moreover, that it generated higher profits than other land-usage arrangements – renting out to tenants, for example. In other words, it made economic sense for relatively wealthy peasants to pursue managerial farming. Their general inability to do so suggests the existence of institutional obstacles. Section C elaborates how the *dian*-mortgage comparison avoids the empirical problems with previous explanations and tests its main theoretical derivatives against an array of economic data from the late Qing and early Republic.

A Managerial Farming in Early Modern China and Europe

First, a conceptual note: the attractiveness of "managerial farming" – or "capitalist farms," as they have sometimes been called – as an academic concept derives mainly from its statistical flexibility and clarity. A "managerial farm" is simply one that employs wage labor for *most* of its everyday operations.[18] There is, generally speaking, no need to artificially and clumsily construct a numerical "lower bound" for absolute size or profitability, which would inevitably fail to account for at least some individual circumstances. Equally important, this focuses the analysis directly on the actual scale of farming and economic operations rather than on the sometimes misleading debate over Chinese *landownership* patterns. After all, in terms of economic productivity, a 100-mu plot that is rented out to ten separate tenants is hardly any different from ten plots of ten *mu*, each farmed by one household. Finally, we might note that managerial farms can also exist in open-fields agriculture.[19] In fact, by the early eighteenth century, more than half of open-fields agriculture in southern England was capitalist.[20] Agricultural capitalism is not logically tied to "enclosure," nor as ideologically charged.

After several decades of debate,[21] scholars have reached, at least, a rough consensus on the chronology of English managerial farming. By 1700, small-scale managerial farming predominated throughout the south, especially in the vicinity of London. Although household production still predominated in the much poorer northwest, the transition to

---

[18] ALLEN (1992), at 56–57.

[19] Note that even in English open-fields agriculture, land was privately owned for most of the year – this was a necessary condition for the development of capitalist farms. *See* Ellickson (1993), at 1390.

[20] ALLEN (1992), at 73, tbl. 4–4.   [21] *Id.*, at 2–5.

managerial farming was nonetheless well underway, with nearly half the farming population employed as full-time wage laborers.[22] Whereas most scholars would agree that this transition generated some increase in agricultural productivity – in certain cases, very reluctantly[23] – the classic theory that such increases led to English economic divergence from continental Europe is much more questionable. Recent studies show, for example, that the richer regions of France, particularly the Paris Basin, also experienced a strong shift toward small-scale managerial farming after 1550. By the early eighteenth century, Paris Basin farmers could generally amass enough land to enjoy low-level economies of scale.[24] In any case, these narratives indicate that the sixteenth and seventeenth centuries marked the basic transition from household to managerial farming in both countries.

Chinese agriculture is an entirely different story. As a number of scholars have noted, large aristocratic or gentry estates farmed by bonded labor still accounted for a substantial share of Song and Ming agriculture,[25] but the inability of such estates to adapt to deepening commercialization and market integration had all but wiped them out by the eighteenth century. Despite deep and sweeping changes in Qing economic historiography over the past few decades, the old notion that Qing agriculture relied predominantly on household-level smallholdings remains largely unchallenged. Of course, scholars *have* periodically debated the extent of landownership concentration, but this only means that large landlords may have *owned* a higher percentage of total land than previously assumed, not that they *farmed* a higher percentage. Higher concentration of ownership could simply have reflected a higher level of tenancy. Joseph Esherick's 1981 essay, for example, argues that "landlords" and "rich peasants" owned around 56 percent of arable land in early Republican China – other scholars place this figure at closer to 35 to 40 percent – but nonetheless concedes that around 42 percent of this was rented out in small parcels.[26] As discussed below, much of this

---

[22] Shaw-Taylor (2008), at 16–18.   [23] ALLEN (1992), at 17–19, 218–27.

[24] PHILIP HOFFMAN, GROWTH IN A TRADITIONAL SOCIETY: THE FRENCH COUNTRYSIDE, 1450–1815, at 143–49, 162–64 (1996) (arguing that although managerial farming boosted productivity, tenants in the Paris Basin could easily assemble large farms, whereas the same cannot be said of the southwestern and eastern provinces).

[25] McDermott (1984); CHINESE CAPITALISM 1522–1840 (Xu Dixin & Wu Chengming eds., Li Zhengde et al. trans., 2000), at 22–43.

[26] Esherick (1981), at 387, 397, 405.

was due to necessity: most landowners did not own large, concentrated plots but instead owned dozens to hundreds of small and scattered ones, few exceeding five *mu*. This probably forced them to rent their land out in these small parcels because farming everything themselves would have been a logistical nightmare.

Of course, even if we focus on landownership and not usage, and even if we adopt Esherick's fairly controversial estimates, it turns out that Chinese landownership in the eighteenth and nineteenth centuries was nonetheless significantly more diversified than early modern English landownership. "Landlords" and "rich peasants" comprised, by most estimates, around 10 percent of China's population and owned 40 to 55 percent of the land.[27] In comparison, the English royalty, nobility, and gentry, which together comprised somewhat less than 10 percent of the population, owned around 70 percent of total land in 1690, 75 percent in 1790, and 80 percent by 1873.[28] Moreover, contrary to the clear trend toward land concentration in England, Chinese land distribution remained basically stable – if not more diversified – throughout the nineteenth and early twentieth century despite several major natural and political disasters that should have created significant economic duress for poorer households. Nonetheless, the focus in this chapter remains on land usage patterns because they are more directly connected to economic productivity. There the contrast between the two countries multiplies in degree.

Given the significant regional variation in Chinese agriculture, national-level statistics are of fairly limited analytical use. A better approach would be to look at individual agricultural regions, where ecological conditions, crops, and farming techniques are more uniform. For conceptual clarity, I will employ William Skinner's physiographic macroregions[29] and, as discussed in the Introduction, focus on "North China" and the "Lower Yangtze." In John Lossing Buck's 1937 statistical report, these two macro-regions are roughly equivalent to the "winter wheat-kaoliang area" and the "Yangtze rice-wheat area."[30] Provincial boundaries mean very little in these subdivisions: northern Jiangsu, for example, belongs to North China, whereas southern Jiangsu belongs to the Lower Yangtze.

---

[27] Esherick's own estimates fall toward the higher end of this range. The studies he critiques fall toward the lower end.

[28] Beckett (1984) at 1.

[29] The City in Late Imperial China chap. 1 (G. William Skinner ed., 1977).

[30] John L. Buck, Land Utilization in China: A Study of 16,786 Farms in 168 Localities, and 38,256 Farm Families in Twenty-two Provinces in China, 1929–1933, at 27 (1937).

Philip Huang's 1985 book remains the most comprehensive agrarian study of North China. Drawing from Buck's research, the Mantetsu database, the 1937 Guomindang Land Commission reports, and various regional surveys conducted during the 1920s and 1930s, several scholars have estimated that hired labor accounted for around 17 percent of total labor input, with about half of that coming from managerial farms that relied on wage labor for most of their production.[31] Accounting for the managerial farmers' own household labor, managerial farms incorporated approximately 9 percent of North China's labor input. Since labor input per *mu* on the largest northern farms was, according to Buck's surveys, 80 to 85 percent of the median,[32] managerial farms probably occupied about 11 percent of total farmland. This agrees with the Mantetsu data, which found that 9.1 percent of the surveyed area was under managerial farming.[33] A crude calculation based on Esherick's data[34] suggests a slightly higher figure: "landlords" cultivated (as opposed to rented out) approximately 10 percent of total farmland, whereas "rich peasants" cultivated another 18 to 20 percent. The Land Commission reports, which found that farms exceeding 100 *mu* in size accounted for 10 percent of total farmland, seem to confirm these estimates.[35] Assuming that nearly all landlords *and* some of the wealthiest "rich peasants" ran managerial farms, the total would probably be close to 15 percent of total farmland – somewhat higher than Huang's estimate of 10 percent but still low enough to suggest that household-level smallholdings were predominant.

Existing studies on the Lower Yangtze are much more chaotic. Since Huang's 1990 book, the most common opinion seems to be that managerial farming was virtually nonexistent in this region: Wage labor accounted for less than 5 percent of total labor input and, in any case, was

---

[31] HUANG (1985), at 80–81; LI (1998); MAZUMDAR (1998), at 237.

[32] JOHN L. BUCK, THE CHINESE FARM ECONOMY 47, 53 (1930).

[33] See Mantetsu survey data compiled in HUANG (1985), at 313–20.

[34] Esherick provides two kinds of data: first, provincial calculations on the total amount of land that landlords and rich peasants respectively owned (O1 and O2); second, provincial calculations on the total amounted of rented land (R). He also notes that on the national level, landlords accounted for around 85 percent of total rented land, whereas rich peasants accounted for the remaining 15 percent. These percentages are largely derived by data from Shandong, so applying them in the North China (roughly Hebei and Shandong) context seems somewhat reasonable. Thus a very crude calculation would put the amount of land that landlords farmed at O1 − 85% · R, while the amount of land that rich peasants farmed would be O2 − 15 percent · R. Esherick (1981), at 397, 402–05.

[35] TUDI WEIYUANHUI, QUANGUO TUDI DIAOCHA BAOGAO GANGYAO 27 (1937).

concentrated on rich peasant holdings that were too small to be considered managerial.[36] Huang bases his estimates on two sources: Buck's data and a 1949 survey by the East China Military Administration Committee. This latter source indicates that 4 percent of rural households were "agricultural laborers," but this figure includes only *landless* households.[37] Wage laborers who owned *any* amount of land, however small, were apparently excluded. However, Huang's interpretation of Buck's data is somewhat surprising: by Buck's own calculation, hired labor accounted for 15 percent of the Lower Yangtze's total labor input.[38] This does not include northern Jiangsu, which more properly belongs to North China.

The 15 percent figure may, in fact, be the more plausible one, even if Buck's survey is somewhat biased in favor of large farms.[39] By most estimates, the average nineteenth-century Lower Yangtze household could only cultivate around eight *mu* of grain – double-cropped – and two *mu* of mulberries without the aid of hired labor.[40] A detailed 1929 survey of three Wuxi villages[41] seems to support this assertion: nearly all farms that exceeded ten *mu* employed a substantial amount of wage labor, generally for no less than 100 labor-days per year. Of the three farms that exceeded twenty *mu*, wage labor accounted for more than 60 percent of total labor input on two and for nearly 50 percent on the third. This suggests that most farms larger than twenty *mu* were probably managerial. According to a 1920s study of southern Jiangsu, such farms occupied around 4.5 percent of total farmland in all surveyed counties, whereas farms that exceeded fifteen *mu* accounted for another 32 percent.[42] All in all, while the scale of managerial farming was considerably smaller in the Lower Yangtze than in North China, it did, at least, exist. Wage labor, too, was probably much more important than Huang suggests.

---

[36] *See, e.g.,* Huang (1990), at 58–60; Mazumdar (1998), at 237.

[37] Huadong Junzheng Weiyuanhui, Jiangsu Sheng Nongcun Diaocha 13, 29–30, 62–64 (1952).

[38] Buck (1937), at 293.

[39] This bias is well known, but a quantitative adjustment does not seem possible. *See* Esherick (1981); Randy Stross, *Numbers Games Rejected*, 10(3) Republican China 1 (1985).

[40] Li (1998), at 136–38, 140.

[41] The data have been compiled into charts in Bell (T. 1992), at 207, 226–29, 232–39.

[42] Survey results are compiled at Li Bozhong, *"Rengeng Shimu" yu Mingqing Jiangnan Nongmin de Jingying Guimo* [*"Ten mu Per Person" and the Scale of Jiangnan Agriculture in the Ming and Qing*], 1996(1) Zhongguo Nongshi [Chinese Agricultural Hist.] 1, 6.

Still, when compared with eighteenth-century English farming, even the North China figures seem miniscule. Nor was agriculture in other Chinese macroregions noticeably more concentrated: Buck's data suggest that in no region did wage labor account for more than 25 percent of total labor input.[43] Sucheta Mazumdar's study of Guangdong also indicates that smallholdings were the predominant norm.[44] Perhaps even more interesting, the level of land concentration in China could sometimes experience mild but prolonged *declines*, as it apparently did between 1703 and 1771 and between 1870 and 1940.[45] There was, ultimately, a real and fairly drastic difference between China and Western Europe in the scale of agricultural production. But why?

B Existing Explanations

Existing explanations fall into two general categories – economic and institutional. The former argues that managerial farming simply made no economic sense in China either because it generated no increase in productivity, involved too much risk, or, somewhat more plausibly, it was relatively unprofitable for most individual households.[46] Either argument would imply that the *economic demand* for managerial farming was low. In comparison, institutional explanations argue that legal or customary obstacles would have prevented the creation of managerial farms *even had demand been high*. Scholars have recently explored at least two different mechanisms for this. Some argue that certain Chinese customs *restricted* the free alienation of land – that is, landowners found it difficult to convey land even if they wanted to.[47] Others claim that the problem was not with rights of alienation but with rights of exclusion – large landlords were unable to expel their tenants and, therefore, could not consolidate their holdings into managerial farms.[48] Older works, especially some pre-1950 Japanese writings, have also focused on differences between Chinese and

---

[43] BUCK (1937), at 293.   [44] MAZUMDAR (1998).

[45] For 1703 to 1771, see the data chart at LI WENZHI, MINGQING SHIDAI FENGJIAN TUDI GUANXI DE SONGJIE [THE LOOSENING OF FEUDAL LAND RELATIONS IN THE MING AND QING] 58 (2007). For 1870 to 1940, *see* Ramon Myers, *Land Distribution in Revolutionary China*, 8(5) THE CHUNG CHI J. 62 (1969).

[46] LI ET AL. (1983), at 215–17; HUANG (1990), at 58–76; XU & WU (2000), at 158–61.

[47] *See, e.g.*, HUANG (1990), at 107–08; MAZUMDAR (1998), at 217–30. *See also* the discussion at POMERANZ (2000), at 70–72.

[48] The clearest argument to this is effect is made by Brenner & Isett (2002).

English inheritance norms, particularly the institution of primogeniture, which supposedly made managerial farming more prevalent by helping households keep their landholdings in one piece.

Although recent developments in European economic history have questioned whether farms consistently become more productive as they increase in size, the key comparison in that particular debate has been between *smaller managerial farms and larger ones*, not between *household-size farming and managerial farming.*[49] The classical argument that small-scale managerial production is, at the very least, more productive than household production remains largely unchallenged. In any case, existing data on North China and the Lower Yangtze do seem to agree with this orthodoxy. For example, Buck's surveys show that farms of all sizes generated nearly identical per-mu yields but also that larger farms operated on less labor input. The labor input per *mu* on "large farms" was less than 80 percent of that on "small farms" and around 85 percent of that on "medium farms."[50] Labor productivity increased, therefore, as farms became larger. When we factor in the more efficient use of farm animals and tools on larger farms – by Buck's estimate, the average farm animal tilled over twice as much land on large (but not necessarily managerial) farms than on small ones[51] – the productivity differences become even more pronounced.

This should not be surprising because managerial farms generally enjoy several important efficiency advantages over household-based farms. First, they usually can manage their labor input more effectively. By laying off or hiring workers as circumstances demand, they are better able to match labor input with the size of their land holdings and seasonal variations in

---

[49] *See, e.g.,* Charles Sabel & Jonathan Zeitlin, *Historical Alternatives to Mass Production: Politics, Markets and Technology in Nineteenth-Century Industrialization,* 108 Past & Present 133 (1985). For a survey of more theoretical writings, *see* Matthew Gorton & Sophia Davidova, *Farm Productivity and Efficiency in the CEE Applicant Countries: A Synthesis of Results,* 30 Agricultural Econ. 1 (2004).

[50] Buck (1937), at 273, 276; Buck (1930). Pomeranz raised several concerns at a 2011 American Historical Association panel discussion, "Property Rights and Economic Development in the Qing" (January 9, 2011), about whether managerial farming really boosted labor productivity in the Lower Yangtze. I have yet to see, however, any substantive evidence to the contrary. The most conservative figures, drawn from Buck (1930) and reaffirmed by Pomeranz himself in *Land Markets in Late Imperial and Republican China* (2008), at 118–19, still suggest that large, predominantly managerial farms enjoyed a 13 percent labor productivity edge even in the Yangtze Delta.

[51] Buck (1937), at 277. *See also,* Huang (1985), at 144–45.

production conditions. Moreover, as discussed below, their larger size facilitates coordinated investments in the land that can improve its overall productivity, often through optimizing irrigation, roads, and the use of animals and fertilizer. While it is also possible for several smaller farms to effectively make these investment decisions by cooperating among themselves, consolidating the smaller patches under more unified ownership helps to internalize and reduce the transaction, organization, and coordination costs involved.[52] Generally speaking, it is usually possible to gain some economies of scale through managerial farming, which tends to increase your productivity, regardless of the kind of crop or the ecological conditions.

The main factors that may render managerial farming less productive than household production are the management or supervision costs involved: by employing labor and managerial help, a larger farm naturally increases the need for planning and oversight. In some cases, these costs may be so high that they negatively affect productivity, but as we discuss later, such scenarios were exceedingly unlikely in nineteenth- and early-twentieth-century China.

A somewhat more complicated issue is whether managerial farming was *profitable* enough to attract individual landowners, even if they were more *productive*. Several scholars, most notably Li Wenzhi and Huang, have argued that the cost of hired labor was so high in the Yangtze Delta that landowners made larger profits by leasing out their land than by consolidating it into managerial farms. Li, for example, relies on late-nineteenth-century missionary surveys to suggest that leasing out was 35 percent more profitable than managerial farming in southern Jiangsu and nearly three times as profitable in northern Zhejiang.[53] Relying on both Li's estimates and a somewhat uneven collection of Qing farming guides, Huang reaches similar conclusions.[54]

These are empirically questionable claims. As Li himself admits, the missionary data relied heavily on a few scattered case studies, "might be numerically inaccurate," and "are generally of limited trustworthiness."[55] Huang adds fairly little to Li's empirical basis: the farming guides he examines come either from the early Qing, when labor was considerably scarcer, or from the wheat-producing areas of Jiangsu, which do not belong to the Lower Yangtze. All in all, they seem to drawing very broad

---

[52] Ronald H. Coase, *The Nature of the Firm*, 4 ECONOMICA 386 (1937).
[53] LI ET AL. (1983), at 215–17.   [54] HUANG (1990), at 58–76.
[55] LI ET AL. (1983), at 216.

conclusions from extremely limited data. In fact, recent estimates of Lower Yangtze wages from 1750 to the early twentieth century would lower Li's wage figures by 30 to 55 percent, or by six to sixteen taels of silver.[56] Using these more conventional estimates, managerial farming becomes more profitable than leasing by at least 60 percent in southern Jiangsu and equally profitable in Zhejiang.

Assuming for the moment that Li's figures are largely accurate and representative, they would imply that very few Lower Yangtze households had any incentive to employ wage labor. In particular, while Li's estimates focus on the cost of year laborers, a quick calculation based on his sources indicates that day laborers were comparably unprofitable. If we assume that a ten- to fifteen-mu plot required 120 to 150 days of wage labor per year,[57] that the average year laborer worked around 200 days each year, and that, as Buck's surveys indicate, Lower Yangtze day labor was roughly 25 percent more expensive than year labor on a daily basis, then the cost of day labor would have been 72 to 92 percent of a year laborer's wages.[58] Using Li's missionary data, leasing out would still have been 27 to 33 percent more profitable than employing day laborers in southern Jiangsu and more than 2.5 times as profitable in northern Zhejiang.

The problem with this picture is that wage labor was, in fact, fairly important to the Lower Yangtze economy. As I argued earlier, managerial farms occupied around 4.5 percent of total farmland, whereas nearly 40 percent of households employed some form of wage labor. All in all, wage labor accounted for perhaps 15 percent of total agricultural labor input. These are fairly significant numbers and strongly suggest that wage labor could not have been nearly as prohibitively costly as Li and Huang

---

[56] The 1750 estimates come from POMERANZ (2000), at 319–20 (estimating an upper-limit wage of around twelve taels). Robert Allen et al. argue, in *Wages, Prices, and Living Standards in China, 1738–1925: in comparison with Europe, Japan, and India* 51, Oxford University, Department of Economics Working Paper No. 316 (2007), that the nominal agricultural wage basically remained stable (or declined slightly) from 1750 to the nineteenth century and largely confirm Pomeranz's estimates. Li's wage estimates, when converted to silver taels, suggest an annual agricultural wage of around twenty-eight taels for southern Jiangsu and around eighteen taels for Zhejiang.

[57] Bell (1992).

[58] This calculation uses data presented in BUCK (1937) at 328, and assumes that the average year laborer worked around 200 days, following HUANG (1985), at 81. If we change the 200-workday assumption, then the 25 percent figure would change, but the ultimate figures on relative profits would not, because the workload of year labor is not a variable in the calculation.

believed. The fact that roughly two-fifths of households were willing to employ some form of wage labor is particularly significant. For Li's data to make much sense, we would have to assume that most of these households were financially irrational. Given that most Lower Yangtze households farmed significantly less than ten *mu*,[59] any household that wished to rent out its excess land probably would have encountered a healthy supply of eager potential tenants. Why, then, were so many households willing to employ wage labor? Unless we are willing – and there is really no reason why we should be – to assume *widespread* economic irrationality,[60] then Li's data were either inaccurate or unrepresentative. Apparently, the employment of wage labor was profitable enough to attract a *very* significant portion of rural households.

Li and Huang's arguments are, in any case, strictly limited to the Lower Yangtze. As both scholars readily admit, quite the opposite was true of North China, where managerial farming was considerably more profitable than leasing out.[61] This explains, in Huang's opinion, why managerial farming was relatively "prevalent" there, occupying roughly 10 percent of total farmland, compared with (by my estimates) only 4.5 percent in the Lower Yangtze. Whatever the merits of this argument, it is logically unhelpful for the present analysis. It still concedes that smallholding predominated in North China, which is all the more puzzling if managerial farming generated both higher productivity *and* higher profits.

This indicates, at the very least, that labor prices were not too high for managerial farming. But were they too low? A few scholars, such as Zhao Gang and Martin Heijdra, have also suggested that population growth

---

[59] By the mid-nineteenth century, the average Lower Yangtze household farmed around seven *mu*, split seven to three between rice and mulberries. Various existing estimates and figures are compiled in Brenner & Isett (2002), at 620.

[60] Empirical studies of peasant economic behavior indicate that most Qing households were eager to maximize their income and, moreover, were both rational and informed enough to make good decisions toward this end. *See* Bell (1992). While certain elite families were probably wealthy and politically ambitious enough to break out of this wealth-maximizing mentality, focusing instead on national examinations and political ties, even the majority of gentry households depended on landholding and economic affluence for their social status – a trend that started in the Song Dynasty. *See, e.g.,* BEATTIE, (1979); HYMES, (1986); BEVERLY J. BOSSLER, POWERFUL RELATIONS: KINSHIP, STATUS, AND STATE IN SUNG CHINA (1996). Given these academic developments, anyone who wishes to argue that Chinese peasants and farmers eschewed profit-maximizing behavior must bear the burden of the proof.

[61] LI ET AL. (1983), at 215–17; HUANG (1990), at 69–72.

might have made managerial farms less profitable.[62] The basic rationale here is that population growth drove down labor prices, making investment in capital less attractive. But there is no reason why a managerial farm must be capital intensive. It could very well be labor intensive yet still gain a productivity boost simply from more efficient management of the labor supply and economies of scale in existing capital investments.[63]

One concern here is that farms with more intensive labor input might be harder to supervise, which leads to the broader question of whether managerial farms were generally too costly to supervise in the Chinese core – a potential moral hazard problem. Such arguments are rarely seen in the existing academic literature, only indirectly raised by Martin Heijdra,[64] but they deserve to be considered nonetheless. Moral hazard issues can be triggered where the employee earns a fix wage and not a percentage of the revenue, but his employer cannot efficiently monitor or control his behavior. The more hired labor a farm requires, assuming that farm size remains stable, the higher unit supervision costs become.

When applied to China, however, such concerns seem largely unnecessary because most nineteenth-century farms in the Chinese core, even managerial ones, would have been small enough to monitor on a daily, even hourly, basis. Generally speaking, because most plots above twenty *mu* in Jiangnan were managerial, it would have taken less than ten minutes to walk around the basic managerial farm. A managerial farm in North China would have been considerably larger but still small enough to circle in twenty to thirty minutes.[65] Another variable to consider is geographic segregation: arable land might be too naturally scattered to manage cheaply. But this clearly was not true of North China and the Lower Yangtze, which had reasonably concentrated and flat farmland.[66]

---

[62] ZHAO (2006), at chap. 5; *see also*, Heijdra (1998) at 417, 525–26, although Heijdra discusses the Ming, not the Qing, and seeks to explain the decline of sharecropping, not economies of scale.

[63] This certainly does not mean that Chinese farms made no capital investments – quite the opposite, as discussed in some detail below, they made many, which further calls into question the arguments made by Zhao Gang and Heijdra. On the importance of labor-intensive production in global economic history, *see* Kaoru Sugihara, *Labour-Intensive Industrialisation in Global History*, Kyoto Working Papers on Area Studies No. 1 (2007), *available at* www.cseas.kyoto-u.ac.jp/edit/wp/Sugihara_WP_Web_081018.pdf.

[64] Heijdra (1998), at 525–26.   [65] HUANG (1985), at 70.

[66] HUANG (1985), at 53–66; HUANG (1990), at 21–43.

Chinese agriculture did require enormous amounts of labor, perhaps ten to fifteen times more per acre than English farming in the rice areas, but if English farmers found 100- or 200-acre managerial farms doable on a regular basis,[67] then it seems highly unlikely that a twenty-mu (three-acre) rice paddy created too much supervision cost to manage effectively. Our question here is *not* why Chinese farms were not managerial on the scale of English farms, but rather why, for the most part, they were not managerial *at all*. Labor intensity and the corresponding supervision costs might explain why China did not have huge farms of several hundred *mu*, but they cannot explain why China also lacked smaller managerial farms of a few dozen *mu*, especially when, as noted earlier, even these smaller farms enjoyed notably higher labor and animal productivity.[68]

A final economic explanation to consider is the theory of risk sharing, which would argue that landowners with surplus land may tend to prefer a secure rent over a riskier crop yield.[69] This theory also runs into empirical difficulties here. Generally, we expect smaller landowners, who own less capital and are therefore more at risk from economic fluctuations, to display stronger risk-aversion tendencies than larger landowners.[70] In Qing China, however, we have shown that smaller households that owned some surplus land but not enough for managerial farming employed wage labor regularly. This suggests that risk sharing was probably not a prevalent priority for those who could afford managerial farming.[71] All things considered, economic considerations do not seem capable of explaining China's lack of managerial farming.

---

[67] Shaw-Taylor (2008), at 4–6.

[68] For a theoretical treatment of these issues, *see* Mukesh Eswaran & Ashok Kotwal, *A Theory of Contractual Structure in Agriculture*, 75 AM. ECON. REV. 352, 359–60 (1985). According to this influential model, as long as management costs are low, rational landowners will employ wage labor whenever their own managerial abilities outpaced those of their employed workers. Because, as discussed earlier, labor and animal productivity were notably higher on managerial farms than on household-sized ones, we may reasonably assume that this latter condition was met. In any case, sharecropping has been in steady decline in China since at least 1500. Kang Chao, *Tenure Systems in Traditional China*, 31 ECON. DEV. & CULT. CHANGE 295 (1983).

[69] Heijdra (1998), at 525–26.

[70] *See* Luigi Guiso & Monica Paiella, *Risk Aversion, Wealth and Background Risk*, 6 J. OF EURO. ECON. ASS. 1109 (2008) ("We find that risk aversion is a decreasing function of the endowment").

[71] *See* Chao (1983), at 312 ("There seems to be no strong statistical evidence to suggest that distribution of tenurial contracts was based on the consideration of risk factors").

It must be noted, however, that many of the wealthiest landowners in the Lower Yangtze chose to become "absentee landlords" instead of managerial farmers, renting their holdings to tenants while living in urban centers, preferring the comforts of urban life and the political and commercial opportunities it offered.[72] However, such opportunities were largely limited to the highest echelon of landowners.[73] The vast majority of rural landowners and tenants regularly acted to maximize their *agricultural* profits, which, as I have argued, would have encouraged managerial farming, not rent collecting.

There is, in fact, some reason to suspect that even absentee landlords might have shared these preferences – that they rented out their holdings due to necessity, not choice. As analyzed in detail below, the landholdings of these large landlords were usually so scattered that managerial farming was not possible. Instead of owning several large plots, most large landowners seemed to have owned dozens to hundreds of small and unconnected plots, which could not efficiently support managerial farming unless consolidated. I argue below that this was not by choice – rather, they were unable to purchase land in more efficient patterns. The prevalence of absentee landlordism among these large landowners does not, therefore, speak to the relative profitability of tenancy versus managerial farming. Rather, this latter option was inaccessible due to external factors.

All in all, the fact that economic incentives actually favored the creation of managerial farms suggests that we should be looking for institutional obstacles. One approach, as Robert Brenner and Christopher Isett have advocated as recently as 2002, is to emphasize that landlords lacked strong rights of exclusion against their tenants.[74] Lower Yangtze tenants, for example, frequently enjoyed "permanent tenancy" (*yong dian*) rights, which protected them against both outright exclusion and rent increases as long as they paid their rents. As several scholars have pointed out, this was necessarily a customary right because provincial laws frequently attempted to ban *yong dian* practices, albeit generally without success.[75] In practice, local communities were apparently willing to enforce customary rights of permanent tenancy throughout the Qing and early Republican eras. This prompts Brenner and Isett to argue that Chinese landlords were

---

[72] Madeleine Zelin, *China's Economy in Comparative Perspective, 1500 Onward, in* ASIA IN WESTERN AND WORLD HISTORY 474 (Ainslie Embree & Carol Gluck eds., 1997), *available at* www.upf.edu/materials/huma/central/abast/zelin.htm.

[73] Landlords probably constituted less than 5 percent of total population. Esherick (1984), at 405.

[74] Brenner & Isett (2002).   [75] *See, e.g.*, YANG (1988); HUANG (2001), at 107–08.

therefore unable to create large, consolidated plots that were capable of supporting managerial farming. In comparison, British landlords had stronger exclusion powers and were consequently able to consolidate their property.

This is very likely an important piece of the puzzle, but it is also incomplete. The main problem is that, even in England, the exclusion of tenants was simply not the primary means of creating managerial farms. The general consensus among English economic historians is that the initial creation of large farms during the sixteenth century was tenant driven instead of landlord driven.[76] In addition, even when landlords became the main force in the seventeenth and eighteenth centuries, they used *both* purchases and exclusions to increase farm size.[77] Thus the principal mechanism by which plot size increased was probably the combining of adjacent farms via either outright purchase or the closing of mortgages rather than exclusion through rent manipulation or outright enclosure.[78] Chinese landlords may well have possessed weaker exclusion rights, but this, by itself, does not completely explain why China had less managerial farming. We must still ask whether relatively richer peasants were unable to purchase enough land from their poorer neighbors or even from large landlords in need of cash to create managerial farms. Moreover, even if Chinese landowners had possessed strong rights of exclusion, the highly scattered nature of their landholdings probably would have prevented them from creating efficient managerial farms via exercising those rights. They most likely would have needed to consolidate their holdings into a few continuous fields, which again demonstrates that the ability – or inability – to transact is arguably more central to our inquiry than the ability to exclude.

Given the importance of land transactions in the creation of English managerial farms, explanations that emphasize rights of alienability would seem to be a logical necessity. Nonetheless, these have so far encountered their own share of objections. Existing accounts focus mainly on the existence of lineage-based obstacles to alienability. Huang and Mazumdar, for example, argue that local customs in both the Lower Yangtze and South China dictated that potential land sellers first offer their property to lineage

---

[76] *E.g.* Hoyle (1990), at 2, 14; P. Glennie, *Distinguishing Men's Trades: Occupational Sources and Debates for Precensus England, in* HISTORICAL GEOGRAPHY RESEARCH SERIES 1, 33 (1990). More generally, *see* Shaw-Taylor (2008).

[77] ALLEN (1992), at 14–15.

[78] For the importance of mortgages in land transaction, *see* Clay (1981); ALLEN (1992), at 15.

members and neighbors.[79] Some South China customs actually *prohibited* selling land to outsiders unless lineage members consented.[80] In addition, lineage-owned land, which may have occupied as much as 35 percent of arable land in Guangdong, was simply inalienable.[81] Combined, these observations suggest that landowners would have found it difficult to convey land even if they wanted to and, therefore, that obtaining large plots was difficult. However, English laws and customs seemed to impose fewer restrictions on free alienation. Legal historians have long agreed that by at least the fifteenth century, royal and local courts expressed distinct hostility toward inalienable rights in land, mainly by recognizing and creating methods to break entail.[82]

Although such simple theories of inalienability are attractive in their clarity, a more comprehensive survey of the existing data suggests that they cannot adequately explain China's relative lack of managerial farming. First, lineages in the Lower Yangtze and South China were generally so large that a "one must offer first to kinsmen" rule or even a "one can *only* offer to kinsmen" rule would nonetheless have allowed many potential buyers to compete for most plots.[83] Second, although lineages owned a fair amount of "corporate land" in South China, their holdings were miniscule in other regions, including the Lower Yangtze and North China.[84] Buck's surveys, for example, find that 93 percent of arable land in China was owned by individual households in "fee simple."[85] In any case, no one has made any effort to apply these arguments to North China, where lineage power was considerably weaker. Finally, a survey of Medieval English borough and manor customs shows that certain localities gave family members and intestate heirs a "right of first purchase" that was not noticeably different from the Lower Yangtze customs.[86] We do not know, at this point, whether such local customs were prevalent in sixteenth- and seventeenth-century England, but should at least proceed with caution when arguing that lineage-based inalienability was unique to China.

Kenneth Pomeranz has, more recently, suggested another way of measuring the economic effects of such customary restrictions.[87] If, in fact, they

---

[79] HUANG (1990), at 108; MAZUMDAR (1998), at 226–31; POMERANZ (2000), at 70.
[80] MAZUMDAR (1998), at 217–30.   [81] POMERANZ (2000), at 71–72
[82] For a short but authoritative summary, *see* BAKER (1990), at 318–21.
[83] This point is made in NAQUIN & RAWSKI (1987) at 100–01, and POMERANZ (2000), at 72.
[84] CHEN HAN-SENG, LANDLORD AND PEASANT IN CHINA 34–35 (1936).
[85] BUCK (1930), at 192.   [86] *See, e.g.,* 21 PUBLICATIONS OF THE SELDEN SOCIETY 66–68.
[87] Pomeranz (2008), at 118–19.

constituted a significant barrier to the free transaction of land, we would expect that as individual households fluctuated in size, they would "have had a hard time adjusting the amount of land they worked to the amount of labor they possessed."[88] We should expect to find, therefore, large differences in labor input per *mu* figures between different size classes and, more importantly, considerable variance between farms of the same class. Such differences should be particularly acute among small and medium-sized farms, which were generally not large enough to employ wage labor. Buck's surveys indicate, however, that this was not the case. If labor input per *mu* on small farms was set at 100, then it was consistently around 95 on medium-sized farms, and around 80 on large farms, with very little variance within each class.[89] Land productivity was nearly identical for all size classes. These data suggest that customary restrictions on land alienability probably placed no significant burden on free land transaction and that most households were able to keep up with their labor supply fluctuations.

Finally, we should probably address the somewhat ancient thesis that differences between Chinese and English inheritance laws made managerial farming more prevalent in England. This thesis seems to have originated in certain pre-1950 Japanese treatises[90] but has received minimal academic attention in recent years, perhaps because of its obvious empirical and logical problems. The basic idea is that due to the existence of primogeniture and entail, English landowners were able to keep their holdings in one piece from generation to generation, while Chinese landowners, who customarily gave all their sons equal inheritance rights, more often split up their holdings into smaller pieces.[91] This empirical description is, first of all, much too simplistic. The extremely widespread use of wills, trusts, and various "entail breaking" instruments in England since at least the fifteenth century allowed landowners to secure land for younger sons despite primogeniture and entail,[92] whereas Chinese cultural and

---

[88] *Id.*   [89] Buck (1937).

[90] *See, e.g.,* Nagano (2004). *See also,* Albert Feuerwerker, *Economic Trends, 1912–1949, in* 12 Cambridge History of China 28, 76 (John K. Fairbank & Dennis Twichett eds., 1983) (discussing the impact of family division on Chinese farm size); Lavely & Wong (1992), at 439, 448.

[91] Nagano (2004).

[92] The ineffectiveness of entail is discussed in G. R. Rubin & David Sugarman, Law, Economy, and Society, 1750–1914: Essays in the History of English Law 39 (1984). The most famous statement on these issues is, of course, Macfarlane (1978).

customary norms that promoted lineage solidarity often discouraged sons from disintegrating family property.[93]

But even if we disregard all these complications, the lack of primogeniture in China would nonetheless have very little logical bearing on the prevalence of managerial farming – although it may have more to say about raw capital accumulation in the form of absolute plot size. The rationale here is straightforward: a family that possesses both a managerial farm and multiple male heirs, who constitute the bulk of the household labor supply, would only create a number of smaller managerial farms if it engaged in household division. For example, a managerial farm with two male heirs and four hired laborers, if it underwent household division, would create two managerial farms with one owner and two laborers each. In fact, given that larger farms generally enjoyed higher labor productivity, the new farms probably would have to employ *additional* labor to match their old output, making them even more managerial. However, if family division led to the creation of two nonmanagerial farms, then logically the original undivided farm could not have been managerial either, possibly because the increase in household population outpaced the accumulation of land – which again suggests that the difficulty of purchasing land was the main obstacle to the spread of managerial farming. The total amount or percentage of Chinese farmland under managerial farming should not, therefore, decrease simply because of household division. The prevalence of managerial farming depends on the *ratio* of household labor to plot size and not simply on absolute plot size itself.

C Testing a New Theory

This does not mean, however, that we should give up on seeking an institutional explanation altogether. As discussed at the outset of this chapter, I propose the following: the availability of infinitely redeemable *dian* sales in Chinese society made landowners much less willing to engage in permanent transactions. In *dian* sales, however, the eventual probability of permanent alienation was radically lower than in an English mortgage.

---

[93] *See, e.g.*, the Qing dynasty case discussed in Bobby K.Y. Wong, *Dispute Resolution by Officials in Traditional Chinese Legal Culture*, 10 MURDOCH UNIV. ELECTRONIC J. OF LAW no.2, at §8, *available at* www.murdoch.edu.au/elaw/issues/v10n2/wong102_text.html (2003). The official was applauded for preventing family division, even though the brothers were within their rights to seek it.

Combined, these factors made land accumulation over the long run a fairly difficult and slow process, too slow, in fact, for the widespread buildup of managerial farms. The supply of permanent sales was too low to effectively sustain large-scale land accumulation. If, however, affluent peasants attempted to create managerial farms through *dian* sales, they would have to shoulder the risk that land redemption, something beyond their control, could swiftly lead to the farms' disintegration. It was not, therefore, that managerial farms were necessarily harder to create in China – after all, the supply of *dian* sales was, by any measure, quite large – but rather that they fell apart more easily. Over the long run, this prevented managerial farms from occupying a more prominent place in Chinese agriculture.

In comparison, as scholars have argued for some time, irrevocable sales and fixed-term mortgages generated a steady stream of permanent alienations from smaller landholders to larger ones in early modern England, which eventually led to the widespread creation of managerial farms.[94] As discussed earlier, the harshness of mortgage redemption rules, in particular, aided this process in two ways. First, it led to much larger volumes of mortgage default and, consequently, automatic transfer of land from debtor to creditor. Second, it scared away many potential mortgagors and, for those who needed the cash anyway, forced them to sell land outright. This significantly increased the supply of permanent sales, leading to very active land markets during the sixteenth and seventeenth centuries[95] and making it much easier to accumulate land – securely, unlike in *dian* sales – for large-scale farming.

While the English side of this story is fairly well documented, the Chinese side has yet to be substantively developed in the existing literature. The remainder of this chapter attempts to do so by verifying three derivative hypotheses: if *dian* redemption norms indeed had the limiting effect I described earlier, we would expect to find that, first, enterprising Chinese peasants who wished to purchase land usually had to rely on *dian* sales; second, *dian* sellers tended to exercise their redemption rights; and third, obtaining permanent ownership of land was therefore highly difficult. I test these hypotheses against an array of data on land transaction volume, landownership patterns, and labor-to-land ratios largely garnered from the Republican-era economic surveys and Qing contract archives used in previous chapters.

---

[94] *See* discussion on p.238.   [95] Hoyle (1998).

The first hypothesis is easily confirmed. Historians have known for some time that *dian* sales were by far the most important means of transacting land in Qing and Republican China. The Japanese survey data cited in the preceding paragraph speaks clearly to this effect. Moreover, virtually everyone who has conducted research on mainland Chinese contract archives confirms that *dian* sales tend to vastly outnumber irrevocable ones, generally by ratios of nine to one or more: Yang Guozhen and Cao Xingsui have done this for Fujian and parts of Jiangsu, whereas Huang has made somewhat vaguer but basically parallel claims for North China.[96] The several Zhejiang contract archives I use in this study, primarily from Ningbo and Shicang, tell a similar tale.[97]

This is a straightforward consequence of the extremely favorable conditions that customary law afforded *dian* sellers. As discussed in Chapter 3, most pre-industrial landholders had little economic incentive to permanently sell land unless they absolutely had to, usually because of debt, but occasionally also because of migration. Moreover, *dian* purchases offered creditors enough economic benefits – free use of the land for at least a couple of years – that they could actually command most of the land's full market value: around 70 percent in North China and up to 80 percent in the Lower Yangtze.[98] There were, of course, some outliers – Madeleine Zelin has unearthed at least one Middle Yangtze case in which the *dian* sales price was only 25 percent of the full value[99] – but they were few in number. For most landowners who needed to finance an upcoming wedding, funeral, or some other contingency, *dian* sales probably met their cash needs almost as well as a full-value but irrevocable sale.

The second hypothesis – that *dian* sellers tended to exercise their redemption rights – is almost certainly true as a qualitative manner, although it is likely impossible to precisely estimate how frequently *dian* sales became permanent. For example, previous chapters have clearly established that *dian* sellers were highly protective of their customary rights of infinite redemption. It seems rather unlikely that they would have cared so much about this issue – which was, as argued previously, one of the major sources of rich-poor tension in rural North China and the Lower Yangtze – if most of them ended up permanently selling away the collateral

---

[96] Yang Guozhen (1981), at 31; Cao Xingsui, Jiu Zhongguo Sunan Nongjia Jingji Yanjiu [Research on the Rural Economy of Southern Jiangsu in Old China] 31 (1996); Huang (1990), at 106.

[97] *See* Ningbo Contracts (2008); Shicang Contracts (2010).

[98] Huang (1985), at 176; McAleavy (1958), at 406; Macauley (1998), at 231.

[99] Zelin (1986), at 516.

anyway after a couple of years. It is especially hard to imagine how such customs could have survived well into the Republican era despite both entrenched opposition from creditors and express hostility from the state if people rarely exercised their redemption rights in practice.

Both the North China survey data and the Lower Yangtze contract archives discussed in previous chapters support this deduction. A Japanese accounting of the Mantetsu survey data and other rural surveys from Republican North China suggests that within the permanent land-holdings of an average North China household, only 5 percent came from transactions, whereas the other 95 percent was inherited.[100] In comparison, at any given point in time, some 10 percent of rural land was likely under a *dian* sale, with most of that coming from transactions made in the preceding one to three years.[101] This suggests that the average duration of a *dian* sale was likely in the range of two to six years, which corroborates the testimony of several Mantetsu interviewees that *dian* sales were commonly redeemed after three to five years.[102] But if only 5 percent of land permanently changed hands over the course of a generation – around twenty years – then clearly the considerable majority of *dian* sales were redeemed by the original owners. Otherwise, assuming that around 10 percent of land entered and exited a *dian* transaction every five years or so, then at least some 15 to 20 percent of land would permanently change hands over twenty years.

A separate batch of anecdotal evidence comes from a series of state-sponsored surveys conducted in Baoding between 1930 and 1957. These surveys attempt to measure the frequency of both *dian* sales and permanent alienations in the region, but provide reliable statistical data for only one village, Gushang, in Qingyuan County.[103] There the number of *dian* sales is only measured for 1930 and 1936, but for both years they were around twice as high as permanent transactions.[104] Given that the total number of permanent transactions includes both *dian* sales that became permanent and straight-up permanent sales, it is more likely than not that less than half of *dian* transactions in any given year became permanent. In any case, the small survey sample makes it impossible to reliably project these figures onto even the regional level,

---

[100] NAGANO (2004), at 121–23.   [101] *Id.*

[102] *E.g.*, 3 Mantetsu 224–42; 4 Mantetsu 203–07; 5 Mantetsu 229–46.

[103] Shi Zhihong (2002), at 4, 14.

[104] *Compare id.* at tbl. 19 *with id.* at tbl. 22 (as Shi observes on p. 14, data on land transactions are only available for Gushang village. We can assume, therefore, that the data in both table 19 and table 22 come from this one village).

but when combined with the survey statistics discussed in the preceding paragraph, they do suggest that most North China *dian* sales were eventually redeemed.

As noted in Chapter 1, when a Lower Yangtze *dian* sale became permanent via a *juemai* and *zhaojia* procedure, addendums were generally added to the original contract documenting the terms of this procedure. This gives us a crude measure of how many *dian* sales eventually became permanent. In both the Ningbo and Shicang archives, only a fraction of *dian* contracts contains such addenda – less than 10 percent in Ningbo and around 25 percent in Shicang.[105] Even accounting for the possibility of damage to the contract collections over time – a somewhat curious and therefore unlikely kind of damage in which the addendum was lost but the original contract was not – this indicates that few *dian* sales in those localities became permanent. When or whether they were redeemed is impossible to pinpoint simply because there was generally no addendum to a redeemed *dian* contract. Instead, the buyer would simply return his copy of the contract to the seller. Without more detailed information on how, and from which sources, the contract archives were assembled, it is impossible to know more about the eventual fate of these transactions. At the very least, however, the mere fact that few contracts became formally permanent suggests that redemption was actively pursued by most *dian* sellers.

This leaves, in any case, the third hypothesis – that permanent land purchasing was so difficult that larger landholders often, if not usually, failed to acquire permanent ownership over economically optimal amounts of land. In this particular aspect, our *dian* sales–based explanation shares considerable common ground with existing theories of land inalienability, which, as discussed earlier, suggested that lineage first-purchase rights posed inefficient obstacles to free alienability. Their other empirical problems aside, they, too, sought to demonstrate that the market for permanent transactions was too small. The claim that permanent land purchasing was, for large landholders, inefficiently difficult would seem to follow naturally from the first and second hypotheses – that the great majority of transactions were *dian* sales and that a considerable majority of *dian* sales were likely redeemed – but because our discussions of those hypotheses was qualitative rather than quantitative, they cannot support an

---

[105] *See* discussion at Chapter 4, Section C.

automatic inference of the third hypothesis. Instead, the third hypothesis needs to be empirically demonstrated in separate terms.

Some scholars have attempted to argue that the market for permanent sales was inefficiently slow by emphasizing that the vast majority of transactions were small. This is undoubtedly true, but its usefulness is limited without reliable data on frequency. Another issue is how to interpret the size of transactions. They were small in absolute terms, but so was the average Chinese farm. In the Gushang survey, the average transaction between 1930 and 1936, before the Japanese invasion triggered significant social upheaval, was around five *mu*.[106] This seems to agree with other sources from North China, all of which indicate that the vast majority of permanent transactions were between one and ten *mu*.[107] Private contract collections from the Lower Yangtze suggest that most permanent transactions were somewhat smaller, usually between one-half and five *mu*.[108] In addition, Mazumdar has estimated that most permanent transactions in Guangdong also fell into one- to ten-mu range, with roughly a four-mu average.[109] Considering that one *mu* was only one-sixth of an acre, these figures would naturally seem miniscule to anyone familiar with English land transactions. However, if we remember that the great majority of North China farms were less than twenty-five *mu* and that most Lower Yangtze farms did not exceed ten *mu*, then these figures seem much more substantial. If, for example, a North China household who farmed fifteen *mu* sold off a third of its holdings, we must consider that a fairly drastic measure. All in all, these figures mean very little until we

[106] Shi Zhihong (2002), at 14.

[107] 6 Mantetsu Surveys, at 406–20; Jing Su & Luo Lun, Qingdai Shandong Jingying Dizhu Jingji Yanjiu [Economic Analysis of Qing Managerial Landlords in Shandong] 65–68, 98–102 (1984).

[108] Bernhardt (1992), at 17; *see also* contracts from Anhui, Zhejiang, and Jiangsu in Tiancang Qiyue (2001), at nn. 1–17, 19–21, 23–26, 99, 138, 239, 240, 244, 275, 471, 506, 587–906, 928. All of these are officially recognized "red contracts" and are all contracts for permanent sale. See especially the series of purchases by one Hong Ruoci from Anhui, in items 812–906. Between 1727 and 1760, he made these ninety-five transactions with fifteen different parties, with the great majority of purchases falling between 0.4 and 1.5 *mu*. The small size of each purchase can be deceptive: some sellers would sell him several parcels in rapid succession (e.g., Hong Jincheng at 848, 849, 857, 858, 866, 868) and would thus end up transferring seven to eight *mu* to him – a fairly large parcel by Lower Yangtze standards – within a year. This demonstrates, again, the need to know the identity of the transacting parties before drawing conclusions.

[109] Mazumdar (1998), at 231–32.

have better evidence on *who* sold *how much* at *what frequency*. This seems unlikely for the foreseeable future.

If a direct measurement of transaction volume remains elusive for now, is there any way to compensate? One solution is to take a harder look at landholding patterns – that is, the actual outcomes of transactions. If landowners purchased real property in patterns that were clearly disadvantageous to them, then it seems reasonable to assume that obtaining permanent rights to land was highly difficult and that the demand for permanent transactions outpaced supply.

Somewhat predictably, we only have decent information on the landholding patterns of large landlords, but these are nonetheless quite suggestive. Lower Yangtze landlords very rarely possessed large and contiguous tracts of land, instead owning a large number of tiny patches dispersed over several counties. For example, a Guangxu-era landlord in Yuanhe owned several hundred segregated plots in forty different polders, while a Pinghu landlord living in the later Qianlong era owned numerous unconnected parcels spread out over 60 percent of the county.[110] Likewise, in 1903, the Zhang family of Zhe County, southern Anhui, owned sixty-three unconnected plots spread over ten different villages, none larger than three *mu*.[111] We can also try to understand this from a different angle: according to Mantetsu surveys, over 80 percent of arable land in one 1940 Shanghai village was owned by eighty different outsiders, each possessing an average of six *mu*.[112] Tenancy was, of course, much less prevalent in North China, but the existing data still suggest that large landlords in Hebei and Shandong rented out more land than they managed themselves: roughly 17 percent of total arable land fell into the former category compared with 10 to 15 percent in the latter.[113] Within this 17 percent, holdings were apparently just as scattered as they were in the Lower Yangtze. The Meng family of Jiujun, for example, rented out 600 *mu* to at least ninety tenant families, generally in separated plots spread across four or five villages.[114]

---

[110] BERNHARDT (1992), at 17 ("Absentee landlords seldom possessed contiguous tracts of property, owning instead tiny parcels dispersed over a broad area, frequently over several counties").

[111] TIANCANG QIYUE (2001), at no. 908. *See also* the discussion on Hong Ruoci at *supra* note 108: his ninety-five purchases can be separated into at least seventeen unconnected plots, each no larger than seven to eight *mu*.

[112] HUANG (1990), at 107.

[113] The 17 percent figure is calculated based on Esherick (1981), at 397. The 10 to 15 percent figure was discussed earlier.

[114] JING & LUO (1984), at 98–102.

It is hard to imagine why any landlord would have preferred to scatter his holdings to such an extent. It made rent collection and account keeping exceedingly difficult and, moreover, severely limited the landlord's economic flexibility: renting out large and consolidated bundles to rich tenants, which often generated greater rent security, was rarely possible. Some landlords may have wished to geographically diversify their holdings to safeguard against natural disasters, but this hardly justifies the extreme dispersion we find in both North China and the Lower Yangtze. It might have made more sense to own medium-sized parcels in a handful of villages than to own one big plot, but further intravillage or intrapolder separation into numerous tiny parcels probably provided no additional ecological security. Most villages, especially in the Lower Yangtze, were small and consolidated enough to ensure that its various segments experienced similar ecological conditions.

Chinese landowners were also notoriously unwilling to pay official land and property taxes, so could the scattering of holdings simply have been a tax- evasion technique? Lower Yangtze landlords, in particular, were known for *registering* their holdings in hundreds of small parcels, each under a different name, to confuse tax collectors,[115] but that hardly justifies *actually* breaking up one's holdings into hundreds of tiny, unconnected plots – which is what we see here. What really confuses the tax collector is the registration of land under different names, but that can occur with or without actual segregation of land. This latter action does very little to aid the former and would simply add to logistical confusion. All things considered, the severe scattering of landlord property was probably not by choice, which suggests that even the largest landlords found it highly difficult to permanently purchase real property. Because the supply of permanent transactions was very low, potential purchasers could not afford to be as selective as they would ideally prefer.

On a somewhat separate note, because landlords could not easily create large and contiguous farms, it made much more sense to rent out their property in its natural, segregated state than to manage it themselves. This explains why Lower Yangtze landlords, despite owning a fairly high percentage of arable land, generally failed to establish managerial farms.

---

[115] Madeleine Zelin, The Magistrate's Tael: Rationalizing Fiscal Reform in Eighteenth Century Ch'ing China 245 (1992).

To summarize, all three hypothesis laid out earlier are supported by empirical data. This strongly suggests that the existence of *dian* sales was indeed a strong limiting factor on the creation of managerial farming. Compared with preexisting inalienability theories that emphasize lineage first-purchase rights, my proposed explanation highlights the different *incentives* in English and Chinese land markets rather than the different *restrictions*. Its empirical advantages should be fairly obvious by now, but one point deserves particular mention: as discussed earlier, Pomeranz has pointed out that labor input per *mu* figures in both North China and the Lower Yangtze were fairly consistent between and within different size classes. This suggests that contrary to traditional inalienability theories, lineage restrictions on land alienability probably placed no significant burden on free land transaction. However, this statistical situation makes excellent sense in my *dian* sales–based explanation: relatively easy access to indefinitely redeemable *dian* sales meant that farmers could efficiently adjust their landholdings to accommodate short-term fluctuations in household labor supply – but also that such adjustments often failed to accumulate over the long run. Thus labor input ratios could remain relatively stable even while richer peasants generally failed to amass enough land for managerial farms.

One might also question the rationality of creating managerial farms on conditionally held land. The productivity advantage of at least some Qing and Republican managerial farms came from the fact that they could coordinate certain capital investments more efficiently than household-size farms – Chinese agriculture may not have been capital intensive, but it certainly was not capital free. In particular, irrigation, the use of roads, the creation of raised banks for fruit trees, and the long-term maintenance of fertilizer were all more efficient on managerial farms, which helps to explain how they maintained land productivity despite using less labor and fewer animals. This was true both in North China[116] and in Jiangnan.[117] Other forms of long-term capital investment include tools or animals that worked better on larger farms – a farmer would only buy these things if he could reasonably assume that the size of his farm would remain stable for a prolonged period. Because these all involved making

---

[116] JING & LUO (1984), at 130–41; HUANG (1985), at 139 (Huang claims to disagree, at p. 153, with this point mainly because managerial farms did not have a higher crop yield than household farms, but that does little damage to Jing and Luo's main points).
[117] LI (1998), at 62–68.

permanent or semipermanent investments, farmers would be hesitant to pursue them on conditionally held land that could be redeemed at any time.

Without these permanent improvements, however, both the productivity and profitability of managerial farms would be diminished. In fact, several scholars argue that permanent capital investments were one of the *main* reasons why managerial farms enjoyed higher productivity and therefore that to remove them would be to lose the point of managerial farming.[118] The validity of this argument depends on whether these capital investments were cheap enough relative to labor to merit widespread use in pre-industrial China. If they were, then it would indeed make little sense to create a managerial farm on conditionally held land. If they were not, then affluent peasants could conceivably choose to create a labor-intensive managerial farm via conditional purchases. The problem there, as I have just explained, would be that the purchases could be redeemed, which shortened the farms' life spans and prevented them from becoming a more prominent force in the economy.

Ultimately, this chapter has argued for a property rights–based approach to the Sino-English divergence in agricultural production. Whereas harsh rules on mortgage redemption and conditional fee reversion facilitated the tenant-driven creation of managerial farms in sixteenth- and seventeenth-century England, the existence of infinitely redeemable conditional sales in Qing and Republican China diminished landowners' incentive to permanently sell land and thereby obstructed the creation of managerial farms. The macroeconomic "problem" with Chinese property norms, therefore, was not that they were too rigid, but rather that they were too flexible and accommodating toward sellers. This may well have generated important benefits for social stability and cohesion, but over the long run, it lead Chinese agriculture onto a fundamentally different path than English agriculture.

This analysis does, of course, generate a multitude of follow-up questions. Most importantly, what, precisely, was the broader economic significance of managerial farming? Such farms did enjoy somewhat higher agricultural productivity, but as noted in the Introduction, whether this can explain Europe's industrial and manufacturing advantage remains a complex matter of great contention. The precise scale and significance of the productivity boost constitute one issue, but one must also consider the

---

[118] JING & LUO (1984), at 130–41; LI (1998), at 62–68.

effects of managerial farming on overall labor mobility, proto-industrial concentration of capital, and so on. Although it is impractical to tackle these issues full on in this chapter – a few extra thoughts are presented in the Conclusion – they are, in the end, what gives the agrarian structural divergence examined here much of its historical significance. Here the relative lack of managerial farming in China is an endpoint, something that needs to be explained. Within the broader literature on Sino-European economic divergence, however, it is one of several possible starting points. I do, at least, demonstrate that laws and institutions are highly important to any serious study of Chinese or English economic history – but perhaps in less obvious ways than many scholars have previously assumed.[119]

---

[119] Some have used the example of China's recent economic boom to argue that traditional Western notions of "private property" may not be necessary for robust economic growth. *See* Frank Upham, *From Demsetz to Deng: Speculations on the Implications of China's Growth For Law And Development Theory*, 41 N.Y.U. J. INT'L L. & POL. 551 (2009); Donald C. Clarke, *Economic Development and the Rights Hypothesis: The China Problem*, 51 AM. J. OF COMP. L. 89 (2003); Tom Ginsburg, *Does Law Matter for Economic Development? Evidence from East Asia*, 34 L. & SOC'Y REV. 829 (2000). A closer inspection of their arguments suggests that these scholars are arguing that we need to change our idea of what constitutes an efficient property rights regime, not that "property rights do not matter." My arguments here agree with this sentiment.

Conclusion

The longevity of *dian* redemption customs in Qing and Republican China is more than a little counterintuitive, especially if we consider how much our understanding of Chinese economic history has changed over the past two decades. Under the new "paradigm," the Qing economy was highly commercialized and market based, land was increasingly commoditized, and individual households were, by and large, rational and aggressive in their pursuit of material wealth. But despite all that, a customary legal institution that was not only economically inefficient on multiple levels, but was in fact deeply disliked by the wealthiest segments of society, somehow remained firmly entrenched throughout the political upheaval and rapid economic change of the nineteenth and early twentieth century. In comparison, the broad themes of early modern English history seem more "natural," especially from a Marxist or Neo-Classical Economic perspective. From the sixteenth century onward, large landholders were able to establish property institutions that further enhanced their economic interests and, in so doing, eventually fueled the rise of agricultural capitalism.

These diverging narratives only make sense – or so I have argued – if we remember that in some fundamental sense, China was a "Confucian" society where status was arguably more a matter of seniority than of wealth, whereas England was a far more individualist one in which status and wealth were tightly connected. Chinese society provided for substantially more equitable distributions of social status between rich and poor, whereas English society concentrated both sociopolitical power and material wealth in a relatively small class of landholders. These were "cultural" differences, in that they derived from sociomoral values that, especially on the Chinese side, were broadly "internalized" by a large part of the population. The chain of causation runs, therefore, from cultural norms, to patterns of status distribution, to property institutions, and to macroeconomic outcomes.

This suggests that, at least to the extent that institutional differences mattered economically – the focus here has been their effect on agricultural capitalism – we should seriously consider "reculturalizing" our understanding of global economic history and particularly the Sino-English comparison. Although big "Weberian" cultural paradigms have lost much of their appeal, the reluctance to overapply cultural factors to economic history does not mean that they should not be applied at all. It only means that we should be judicious in applying them, perhaps when conventional economic analysis has been attempted and found insufficient.

Legal institutions, in particular, are more properly seen as human constructs that bridge complex sociopolitical considerations and value commitments with the more spontaneous and straightforward decisions made in everyday life, than as monolithic starting points for economic analysis. As discussed in Chapter 4, even the most strident rational-choice theorists regularly allow that cultural and moral internalization can play a major role in shaping social norms and institutions. In fact, if we take the idea that people tend to pursue their self-interest seriously, then the creation of almost any economic or political institution will eventually boil down to how a community or polity chooses among competing interests. That decision, in turn, depends heavily on how sociopolitical status is allocated within this collection of individuals – and, as the example of Confucian kinship hierarchies demonstrates, the criteria for status allocation are often heavily laden with cultural values and ideological undertones. It may take a few twists and turns, but value-based considerations do tend to lurk in the background of institution building and lawmaking.

It is possible, of course, to sidestep these concerns if institutional differences are simply not a crucial component of the economic narrative, but increasingly few scholars are willing to make this assertion. Within the realm of Chinese economic history, at least, there seems to be a significant trend in recent years toward the embrace of institutional economics. Most scholars who have entered the field – Isett, Faure, and Ma, for example – during the last decade lean distinctly in that direction.[1] In fact, Pomeranz himself has recently begun to complement his past

---

[1] Isett (2007); Faure (2006), Ma (2008).

emphasis on natural resource constraints and New World colonies with the idea that tenancy institutions played a crucial role in deepening China's relative decline.[2] Although it may be an exaggeration to call this a budding consensus, especially when almost everyone seems to emphasize different institutional factors, there does, at least, seem to be a growing sense that "institutions mattered." But if institutions mattered, then cultural factors, particularly those related to status distribution, probably did as well.

This book inevitably has its share of historiographic and theoretical "loose ends": questions about how, precisely, the relatively limited case study it presents fits into a number of broader academic debates. The "reculturalizing global economic history" theme developed earlier and in the Introduction is but one of these broader debates, and even it begs the additional question of whether, and to what extent, this study really affects our understanding of China's broader relative decline. Did the Sino-English divergence on agricultural capitalism – the endpoint of my economic analysis – really matter for the broader divergence in living standards, productivity, and, eventually, industrialization between the two countries? The Introduction offered a few thoughts on this question, but only in a preliminary way.

The remainder of this Conclusion provides a somewhat more detailed response, along with thoughts on two additional issues of some contemporary significance. First, how does this book's balancing act between cultural values and economic rationality relate to theoretical debates in behavioral economics and social norm theory? Second, does the historical account presented here have anything to contribute to our general understanding of "Confucianism" – defined as either an interconnected collection of sociopolitical discourses based on Confucian classics or a more concrete set of social, cultural, and political institutions? The latter issue, in particular, touches on an increasingly visible debate in mainland Chinese intellectual and political circles on the historical legacy and modern applicability of the "Confucian" state and its social norms.

---

[2] Kenneth Pomeranz, *Ten Years After: Responses and Reconsiderations*, 12(4) HISTORICALLY SPEAKING 20, 23 (2011) ("Institutional factors, particularly the widespread prevalence of long-term tenancy arrangements and tenant ownership of topsoil/cultivation rights (which itself became a tradable commodity), made it possible for [the low number and general impoverishment of agricultural laborers in China] to endure").

AGRICULTURAL CAPITALISM IN GLOBAL ECONOMIC
HISTORY

The role of agricultural capitalism in "the Rise of the West" has gone
through some fairly dramatic academic ups and downs over the past few
decades. As recently as the 1980s, economic historians were in broad
agreement that the advent of managerial farms was critical to England's
economic rise.[3] They presumably paved the way to enormous gains in
productivity – whether land, labor, or total factor productivity – which
then supplied the surplus wealth necessary for investment in technology
and eventual industrial takeoff. By and large, this was a straightforward
Marxist narrative: the removal of peasants from farmland, either
through coercion or under conditions of economic duress, led to both
capitalist production relations and the accumulation of economic capital, spurring the emergence of large-scale capital-intensive manufacturing with highly specialized wage labor and eventually leading to full-
scale industrialization.

This narrative was mirrored on the Chinese side by arguments that
China's failure to produce large-scale managerial farming helped to keep
its agricultural production in an "involutionary" Malthusian trap, in which
population growth led to decreasing returns on labor investment and long-
term productivity decline.[4] Most historians who studied the issue bought
into some version of this argument, although, as discussed in Chapter 3,
they disagreed about why managerial farming did not emerge. For scholars
such as Robert Brenner, China was, in its lack of agricultural capitalism,
fundamentally similar to continental European economies such as France,
which were also purportedly unable to move peasants off the land and were
therefore stuck in a small-scale, low-productivity mode of agriculture.[5]

For much of the past two decades, however, these narratives have been
under assault from several angles. Perhaps the most successful has been the
dismantling of the belief that England was somehow unique among European countries in possessing managerial farms. Studies of the Paris Basin
in the eighteenth century, for example, reveal managerial farming on a
level comparable to that in southern England.[6]

[3] ALLEN (1992), at 2–5, 18–19 (summarizing the field prior to 1992).
[4] *E.g.,* MAZUMDAR (1998); HUANG (1990); HUANG (1985); ELVIN (1973); RAMON
H. MYERS, THE CHINESE PEASANT ECONOMY; AGRICULTURAL DEVELOPMENT IN
HOPEI AND SHANTUNG, 1890–1949 (1970).
[5] Brenner & Isett (2002).   [6] HOFFMAN (1996).

The fact remains, however, that there was a real difference between England and China in this regard. Here, critics have tried a different line of attack – that managerial farming actually did very little to boost land productivity in either country. Robert Allen argues, for example, that the lion's share of land productivity growth in England occurred before the rise of managerial farms as a direct result of the innovations carried out by individual yeomen.[7] To the extent that labor productivity leapt after the formation of large farms, it was only because they obtained the same agricultural output with less labor. Pomeranz, among others, makes a similar argument for the Chinese economy.[8]

Even if true – and some scholars, notably Peer Vries, remain skeptical[9] – these arguments fail to demonstrate that agricultural capitalism was economically irrelevant. They show, perhaps, that neither economy's gross agricultural output benefited much from managerial farming and, therefore, that any talk of an "agricultural surplus" feeding investment into other sectors of the economy is questionable. That said, the "agricultural surplus" theory is only one of several hypothetical benefits of managerial farming. Even Allen would acknowledge that managerial farming did lead to substantial gains in labor productivity.[10] He would also temper this admission by insisting that farm labor was not removed voluntarily from managerial farms – and therefore the process was neither market based nor Pareto efficient and indeed might have involved huge transaction costs that would have canceled out any short-term gain in labor productivity – but the fact remains that labor productivity was around 25 percent higher on Chinese managerial farms than on household plots,[11] and some 10 to 30 percent on English managerial farms.[12] In addition, no matter how high the transaction costs might have been, they were a one-time occurrence, whereas the productivity benefits were forward looking.

More importantly, moving labor off-farm essentially forced much of it into manufacturing, allowing businesses to hire at lower wages. Allen has devoted considerable energy over the years to criticizing the notion that labor migration from the English agricultural sector provided a major boost to manufacturing and industrialization, with varying levels of success. His earliest attack focused on migration from the South Midlands to London and other urban centers. Whereas scholars traditionally believed the demographic flow was substantial, Allen argued that it "fell sharply"

---

[7] ALLEN (1992); ALLEN (2009).   [8] POMERANZ (2000), at 73.   [9] Vries (2010).
[10] ALLEN (1992).   [11] BUCK (1937), at 273, 276.   [12] ALLEN (1992), at 150–70.

after 1750.[13] But this is an extremely odd claim, as his data show that net emigration increased by over 100 percent from 1701–1751 to 1801–1831, from less than 60,000 to over 110,000, despite the latter period's shorter time frame.[14] In fact, emigration as a percentage of total population also increased from the former period to the latter. The only decline came in emigration as a percentage of natural population increase, but it is unclear why this should matter for our assessment of labor supply to the industrial sector. Before 1750, of course, even Allen admits that the emigration from southern agricultural regions was "exceptionally high."[15]

His more recent work argues that higher labor costs were actually beneficial for English industrialization, in that they forced entrepreneurs to invest in capital-intensive technologies,[16] but even so, this hardly implies that entrepreneurs did not also welcome the extra inflow of labor generated by capitalist agriculture. After all, even the most capital-intensive businesses needed reasonably priced labor to generate profits and grow. It is telling that even by Allen's own estimates, the ratio between worker income and food prices in London – that is, what he calls "real income" – fell sharply during the eighteenth century, precisely in the several decades preceding English industrial takeoff.[17]

One could at least hypothesize, therefore, that the labor surplus generated by the emergence of managerial farms helped English wages achieve the "right balance" between incentivizing investment in capital and allowing entrepreneurs to build businesses of reasonable size and profitability. Allen would likely disagree with this idea: in a relatively recent paper, he argues that by the early nineteenth century, the percentage of the English workforce still in agriculture, around 40 percent, was too low to supply any significant labor surplus to the cities.[18] But clearly this number only reflects the agricultural population well after managerial farms had already done their damage – indeed, well after the main socioeconomic conditions for industrialization were in place. Of course, his arguments are but the most recent reincarnation of a long academic debate over the merits of higher wages in Western Europe, one that, after several decades, remains empirically inconclusive.[19]

On the Chinese side, whether lower manufacturing wages would have significantly boosted proto-industrial growth and urbanization is likewise an unresolved question. Certainly there is considerable evidence, mainly anecdotal, suggesting that Lower Yangtze manufacturing business owners

---

[13] *Id.*, at 241.   [14] *Id.*, at 239–43.   [15] *Id.*, at 241.   [16] ALLEN (2009).   [17] *Id.*
[18] Allen (2000) at 1.   [19] Summarized in POMERANZ (2000), at 50–54.

would have preferred lower wages – don't they always? – and that the labor supply there may actually have been too low for efficient industrial expansion in the nineteenth century. Furthermore, the debate between Jack Goldstone, among others, and Pomeranz on whether Chinese manufacturing would have benefited substantially from a larger influx of female labor has reached no clear conclusion.[20] Goldstone's primary argument, one that Pomeranz questions but does not quite categorically disprove, was that male labor in the textiles industry was too expensive relative to the stay-at-home female spinners who produced lower-quality but much lower-priced clothing and that this militated against the building of factories. In other words, gender norms that obstructed female labor mobility harmed China's industrial development. If so, then, at least in theory, the textile industry would also have benefited from a large influx of male labor, created by the displacement of agricultural laborers via capitalist agriculture.[21]

Even more importantly, the emergence – or the lack thereof – of managerial farming may have had important consequences for capital accumulation. Many economic historians and sociologists have long believed that significant levels of capital accumulation were necessary, although not sufficient, for industrial takeoff, especially for the capital-intensive model of industrialization that Western European countries generally followed.[22] Recent studies continue to explore this possibility through macroeconomic modeling. The basic logic is simple: even in economies with relatively low labor costs, such as Meiji Japan,[23] industrialization required immense investment in technology and infrastructure, and therefore also required the emergence of entrepreneurs with significant material wealth, whether in the form of currency, land, or other physical goods. For countries with higher labor costs such as England,

---

[20] Summarized in *id.*, at 98–106.

[21] *See also*, FRANCESCA BRAY, TECHNOLOGY AND GENDER: FABRICS OF POWER IN LATE IMPERIAL CHINA (1997), which basically comes down in support of Goldstone's arguments.

[22] Recent writings on this topic include Robert C. Allen, *Engels' Pause: Technical Change, Capital Accumulation, and Inequality in the British Industrial Revolution*, 46 EXPLORATIONS IN ECON. HIST. 418 (2009); Nico Voigtländer & Hans-Joachim Voth, *Why England? Demographic Factors, Structural Change and Physical Capital Accumulation during the Industrial Revolution*, 11 J. ECON. GROWTH 319 (2006); Oded Galor & Omer Moav, *Das Human-Kapital: A Theory of the Demise of the Class Structure*, 73 REV. ECON. STUD. 85 (2006).

[23] This led to the proposal of a "labor-intensive" theory of industrialization by some Japanese scholars. *See, e.g.*, Sugihara (2007).

massive capital accumulation was even more essential. Land, in particular, was generally the most important form of economic wealth in pre-industrial societies and the preferred source of collateral for large credit transactions.

Whatever else it did not provide, managerial farming was a highly effective way of concentrating landed capital into the hands of economically active entrepreneurs. Concentration of wealth alone does little to stimulate investment if the wealthiest segments of society assign a low priority – as they sometimes do in highly stratified aristocracies – to maximizing the economic earning power of their wealth. Agricultural capitalism, to the contrary, tended to match landed wealth with people who both cared about wealth maximization and were comparatively capable of doing so, at least in the rural context. Whether this created a virtuous chain reaction in which rural capital concentration in early modern England fed urban capital concentration is presently unclear, but the idea certainly seems intuitively appealing. A number of people, ranging from Peter Mathias to Allen himself, have suggested that rural landed wealth supplied much of the "savings" necessary for urban industrialization.[24]

Despite this recognition, scholars have rarely highlighted rural capital concentration as a significant factor in global economic divergence, perhaps because they assume that most other major economies, including China, Japan, and the Middle East, also had similar – perhaps even higher, given the traditional assumptions about "despotic" Oriental societies – levels of land concentration and economic inequality. It is hard to think of capital accumulation as a significant obstacle to economic development because, as some have argued, achieving high levels of capital accumulation really was not a difficult thing to accomplish in most commercialized economies.[25]

But this is not necessarily true. As we have seen, even if measured by pure landownership, land distribution in China was significantly more equitable than in England. Moreover, large portions of landlord property were, in fact, held by tenants under permanent tenancy, especially in the Lower Yangtze and South China, and therefore of comparatively limited economic value to their owners.

---

[24] Peter Mathias, The First Industrial Nation (1969); Allen (2009).

[25] Jan de Vries, The Economy of Europe in an Age of Crisis, 1600–1750, at 210–35 (1976) (demonstrating that large-scale capital accumulation existed in most European economies, regardless of pace of industrialization).

In addition, because *dian* redemption norms clogged the supply of permanent land sales, land was not always – or, in the case of larger landowners, perhaps not even often – held or owned by those who were most motivated to and capable of maximizing its value. Due to the high difficulty of purchasing land, those who owned large amounts of it often benefited from strong political connections or other "unfair" advantages. In other words, the land market was an uneven and inefficient playing field that probably failed to match economic resources with their most effective users on a fairly regular basis. Optimal use of land, whether as a means of production or as a source of capital, could not be assumed. All things considered, there is much reason to doubt that China possessed economically meaningful rural capital accumulation at anything near the English or Western European level.

Once again, whether this translated to comparative capital shortages in the manufacturing sector is a matter of open debate. There were, however, substantial signs that the manufacturing sector did suffer from capital shortages. Most records we have of manufacturing shops show businesses of limited production capacity and balance sheets.[26] As noted earlier, some have argued that professional textile producers were often unable to compete with household-based female weavers,[27] which suggests, among other things, that these producers had trouble acquiring sufficient economies of scale, whether in their use of labor or in their use of machinery.

Moreover, many businesses in textiles, tea, and salt production were joint-stock ventures, indicating that single families or lineages were often unable to muster sufficient capital. While joint-stock businesses could function quite well under good macroeconomic conditions, they tended to fall apart at any substantial sign of political or economic turbulence.[28] Limited liability was generally unavailable to Chinese investors, which made them highly risk averse and prone to flight.[29] This actually strengthened their bargaining power, allowing them to demand higher profit shares and greater management powers in return for their investment. These conditions also drove up the cost of credit, creating hostile financial conditions for entrepreneurs.

---

[26] SHIROYAMA (2008); LINDA GROVE, A CHINESE ECONOMIC REVOLUTION: RURAL ENTREPRENEURSHIP IN THE TWENTIETH CENTURY (2006); ALBERT FEUERWERKER, CHINA'S EARLY INDUSTRIALIZATION: SHENG HSUAN-HUAI AND MANDARIN ENTERPRISE (1958); Brenner & Isett (2002).

[27] POMERANZ (2000), at 98–106.   [28] ZELIN (2005); Zelin (2004b) at 230.

[29] Zelin (2004b); Kirby (1995).

European legal historians will point out that limited liability was generally not available to private English businesses until the mid-nineteenth
century, well after the advent of industrialization.[30] The difference between
that and the Chinese situation, however, is that most English businesses
may not have needed outside investment to obtain desirable economies of
scale or sufficient capital. The massive concentration of landed capital in
the hands of entrepreneurial households – something that China had much
less of – may have helped individual business owners to avoid altogether
the capital constraints that forced Chinese entrepreneurs into fragile joint-
stock arrangements.

Large swathes of the previous paragraphs are, of course, speculative, but
the point here is not to prove anything conclusively. Rather, it is simply to
argue that preexisting scholarship cannot rule out these possibilities and
that, put together, they offer a fairly compelling case for why agricultural
capitalism, or the lack thereof, may have had major consequences for
English and Chinese economic history – even if Pomeranz, Allen, and
others are right about land productivity. In other words, no one knows for
sure right now, so we should keep talking about it.

CULTURE, RATIONAL CHOICE, AND SOCIAL NORMS

By attempting to incorporate both rational choice and cultural elements
into institutional analysis, this book is perhaps stepping into an academic
minefield. There are few academic issues more inflammable in contemporary social sciences than whether, and to what extent, we should assume
that individuals make economically rational decisions. Behavioral economists, cognitive scientists, and their allies in other fields have been quick to
declare "victory" over their rational-choice foes,[31] but then again, the vast
majority of empirical studies on economic trends, politics, and legal institutions that one comes across on a day-to-day basis continue to apply the
old assumptions of individual rationality, often with a complexity that
would boggle the average human mind.[32]

---

[30] Harris (2009).
[31] *E.g.*, Russell B. Korobkin, *What Comes after Victory for Behavioral Law and Economics?*,
UCLA School of Law, Law-Econ Research Paper No. 11–10 (March 15, 2011), *available
at* http://ssrn.com/abstract=1787070.
[32] In the latest issue of the *American Economic Review* (vol. 103, no. 7), seven of nine articles
that had significant empirical content applied models derived from rationalistic assumptions of human economic decision making. Only one, Benjamin R. Handel, *Adverse
Selection and Inertia in Health Insurance Markets: When Nudging Hurts*, 103 Am. Econ.

To the fullest extent possible, this study has tried to avoid making assumptions about human institutional and economic behavior. When it argues that Chinese landholders preferred property institutions that benefited their perceived economic self-interest, it is making an empirical statement based on available data, not a theoretical conjecture. The same applies to its analysis of kinship hierarchies and norm negotiation. The only actual "assumption" it makes about individual behavior is that, when households make major decisions about land and labor utilization – whether to pursue managerial farming or rent extra land out, for example – they generally tried to maximize their material wealth. This is a fundamental analytical premise of Chapter 3 and, admittedly, is not specifically proven with any empirical data. That said, there have been fairly systematic studies on household-level economic behavioral in Qing and Republican rural China that do, in fact, argue that the vast majority of households attempted to maximize their own wealth.[33] Moreover, even the most ardent behavioral economists would probably have little objection to the very basic statement that when consciously making a decision on, of all things, *farmland and labor utilization*, most households were willing and able to do the simple math and choose the path of highest returns. This hardly amounts to a sweeping endorsement of perfect individual rationality.

One can, in fact, glean some empirical support for a theory of bounded and imperfect rationality from the previous chapters. In the Chinese context, at least, even though individual landholders generally pursued property institutions that made the most sense for them, the end result was a set of land redemption norms that generated considerable macroeconomic inefficiency. One could easily construe this as proof that individual welfare and group welfare do not always converge, but it is also possible to see this as a short-term versus long-term interest decision. If – and with all the usual historiographic warnings against doing "counterfactual history" in mind – the removal of unlimited *dian* redeemability could have sparked deep-reaching structural improvements in the Chinese economy, then it is at least possible that, at some point, there would be a significant positive-feedback effect on the welfare of lower-income

REV. 2643 (2013), expressly applied behavioral assumptions. The final paper, Ori Heffetz & Matthew Rabin, *Conclusions Regarding Cross-Group Differences in Happiness Depend on Difficulty of Reaching Respondents*, 103 AM. ECON. REV. 3001 (2013), makes no use of models.

[33] *E.g.*, Bell (1992).

households. In other words, over the long run, smallholders might have been better off under harsher *dian* redemption norms even if many of them lost their land in the process, in much the same way that English industrialization did, in the end, confer higher living standards on the proletariat.

Needless to say, it is *highly* unlikely that Chinese smallholders were actually capable of calculating these long-term payoffs, even if – and this is a very big "if" – they did exist. Even the most highly educated Qing and Republican rural residents had no knowledge of modern economic theory, and probably would have had no success in tackling the macroeconomic issues surrounding capitalism and industrialization that have puzzled economic historians for so long. If so, the fact that their powers of long-term utility calculation were limited would actually fit very well into a theory of bounded rationality. These are, of course, mere conjectures at this point, but they raise some reasonably interesting questions for future research.

A separate and more concrete theoretical implication of the historical account presented herein is that it may indeed be possible to identify "pyramids of norms" or even Weberian "cultural paradigms" in legal and quasi-legal institutions. As discussed in Chapter 4, the "pyramids of norms" thesis has, in recent years, been circulated as a possible bridge between pure rational-choice accounts of social norm creation and culture-based sociological accounts.[34] To quickly summarize, it argues for a hierarchical relationship between norms in which a few higher-tier norms, created via long-term internalization of core religious or cultural values – this is where the concept of "cultural paradigms" conceivably comes in – set the parameters within which lower-tier norms are rationally negotiated over shorter time frames. Presumably, lower-tier norms would be more numerous and diverse and would address issues that are more explicitly economic in nature.

Ideally, this thesis should do more than simply highlight the limits of rational-choice theories. By narrowly defining the content and scope of internalized values – identifying, for example, the specific psychological and social settings in which moral internalization commonly occurs – and by laying out the precise mechanisms through which they affect calculations of self-interest, the theory aspires to provide an empirically testable account of how cultural factors shape social norms. It hopes to

---

[34] *See* discussion in Chapter 4, Section C.

solve, therefore, what some social scientists have called "Sen's paradox," referring to Amartya Sen's call for theories of socioeconomic behavior that both "bring in something outside individual choice behavior" and also avoid speaking of "society's 'preferences'" in such aggregate terms that no empirically testable model of individual decision making can emerge.[35] At the moment, however, this remains very much a work in progress. Considering the emphasis on empirical testability, a particularly pressing challenge is to rigorously demonstrate the existence of real "pyramids."

It is not difficult to see the makings of a rudimentary "norm pyramid" in the relationship between "Confucian" kinship hierarchies and *dian* institutions: kinship hierarchies were the "higher tier" "cultural" norm that defined the parameters within which self-interested parties negotiated "lower tier" property norms. Moreover, the vast majority of Chinese were exposed to, indeed, indoctrinated with, kinship hierarchies from infancy, whereas they usually did not confront or grapple with property institutions until early adulthood.

There are obvious dangers in generalizing too much based on one specific example – especially one that covers only a small subset of Qing and Republic customary law – but the thematic similarities are hard to ignore. At some point in the future it may be worthwhile to consider whether "Confucian" kinship hierarchies also had a hand in shaping other institutional peculiarities of Qing and Republican society. As discussed in this book, permanent tenancy norms are an obvious candidate. In fact, because kinship hierarchies effectively leveled, to a significant extent, the political playing field between rich and poor households, any institution that may have incited class-related tensions is a theoretical possibility: anything related to tenancy and credit transactions, for example, but also numerous institutions related to water use, land reclamation, trespass, and corporate management. Whatever the results – and regardless of whether it makes any sense to speak of a "Confucian" paradigm in Chinese economic institutions – this book does share with "pyramid" theorists a fundamental methodological interest in conceptualizing cultural norms as measurable analytical units influencing socioeconomic behavior in predictable and observable patterns.

---

[35] Amartya Sen, *Internal Consistency of Choice*, 61 Econometrica 495, 498 (1993).

"CONFUCIANISM"

Whatever qualms historians may have about the term "Confucianism," it is, and will probably continue to be, a central concept in modern Chinese political discourse, constantly being redefined and attached to any number of social and political causes. Since at least the early twentieth century, Chinese intellectuals have viciously attacked what they perceived as "feudal" (*fengjian*) norms of "Confucian" hierarchy, which purportedly led to moral bankruptcy and the ruthless oppression of lower-income classes by a combination of large landowners, merchants, literati gentry, and perpetually corrupt government officials.[36] Despite – or perhaps because of – the deep politicization of these ideas, they remain tremendously influential in the Chinese academic world even today, enjoying deep support among both self-identified Marxists and liberals.[37] At the same time, they also continue to have surprising traction with Western intellectuals, many of whom have yet to advance substantively beyond the Weber and Wittfogel stereotypes of "Confucianism" as either fundamentally "irrational" or "despotic."[38]

More recently, however, a major debate has erupted in Chinese intellectual and political circles over whether these traditional perceptions of "Confucianism" miss the mark. Driven by some combination of nationalism, cultural conservatism, and genuine intellectual admiration, a growing number of scholars and state officials have voiced support for the "revival" of "Confucianism" as a mainstream sociopolitical ideology that could offer a viable alternative to what they derisively refer to as "full-scale Westernization" (*quanpan xihua*).[39] For these people, "Confucianism" represents – as an ideal type but also as a central part of China's past – both a meritocratic state of public service–oriented intellectual elites and a stable, "harmonized" social order. Correspondingly, they seek to downplay the notion that China was "outcompeted" by Western countries during the eighteenth and nineteenth centuries, instead preferring to see the "rise of

---

[36] Two of the most influential summaries of this intellectual mainstream are Li (2008) and Wang (2008).

[37] Chen (2000) (summarizing the general consensus); Weifang He, *The Judicial System and Governance in Traditional China*, in The Rule of Law: Perspectives from the Pacific Rim 91 (Mansfield Center for Pacific Affairs ed., 2000) (laying out a typical "liberal" stance on this issue).

[38] *See* discussion in Chapter 4, Section B.

[39] For a basic introduction to these ideas, *see* the essays in The Renaissance of Confucianism in Contemporary China (Fan Ruiping ed., 2011).

the West" as a brutal process that derived primarily from imperialist aggression and exploitation. Short of that, they certainly would downplay any suggestion that "Confucianism" had much to do with China's relative decline.

Naturally, this has aroused the ire of many others from both sides of the traditional socialist-liberal ideological divide, who accuse these Neo-Confucian proponents of, among other things, unwarranted historical revisionism, if not flat-out lying.[40] Considering the massive amounts of historical baggage that the term "Confucianism" carries in modern Chinese sociopolitical discourse, it was probably inevitable that this debate would come to hinge, at least partially, on how people understand the historical legacy of Confucian institutions and norms. If it seems somewhat odd that a major social debate in a self-avowed secular and materialist society should turn so much on perceptions of history, we should remember that post–Cultural Revolution China has become highly nationalist and that the perceived past is of fundamental importance to its sociopolitical self-identity.[41]

These debates are not always, and perhaps not even usually, won by the side that has the better historical argument. Nonetheless, to the extent that either side cares about historical accuracy and not merely for the sake of twisting it to suit their own purposes, this book offers some important nuggets of information.

First, especially when compared with corresponding English norms, "Confucian" kinship hierarchies in both North China and the Lower Yangtze promoted, not suppressed, the cumulative sociopolitical status of lower-income households. Regardless of how one understands the concept of "Confucianism" – whether as a collection of interconnected sociopolitical discourses or as a set of more concrete social, cultural, and political institutions – it is, as argued in Chapter 6, impossible to escape the conclusion that strict ordering by generational seniority within an extended kinship network was an unambiguously "Confucian" or perhaps "Neo-Confucian" ideal. The closer real-life kinship networks in Qing and Republican China resembled this ideal, the stronger was their egalitarian

---

[40] *E.g.*, Deng Xiaomang, Rujia Lunli Xin Pipan [A New Critique of Confucian Ethics] (2010); Fang Keli, Xiandai Xin Ruxue yu Zhongguo Xiandaihua [Modern Neo-Confucianism and China's Modernization] (1997). Deng is one of the leading liberal-leaning philosophers in China, whereas Fang is an avowed Marxist.

[41] *See* Prasenjit Duara, Rescuing History from the Nation: Questioning Narratives of Modern China (1997).

effect on social status distribution: the comparison between Lower Yangtze and South China lineages is particularly illuminating.

Interestingly, none of this exonerates "Confucian" kinship hierarchies from accusations of serious economic inefficiency. Under their influence, Chinese property institutions afforded significantly greater protection to smallholders. Unfortunately, however, the egalitarianism of *dian* and tenancy customs deepened the relative underdevelopment of Chinese capitalism – whereas the harshness of English land customs toward smallholders and tenants was actually a long-term economic asset. It may have taken a rather convoluted path, but once more one arrives at the old conclusion that "Confucian" sociocultural institutions damaged China's economic development.

Even so, this is hardly the old "feudal backwardness" story rehashed. At least within the historical confines of *dian* institutions and agricultural capitalism, "Confucian" kinship hierarchies essentially engineered a trade-off between status equality and economic efficiency. That is to say, both sides of the mainland Chinese "Confucian revival" debate have significant portions of their historical narratives wrong. At risk of stating the very obvious, history has a way of being more complex than contemporary political arguments are usually comfortable with.

It seems oddly appropriate to end with a quote from the *Analects*, purportedly made by Confucius himself: "I hear that rulers of states and heads of families fear inequality, but not poverty; they fear instability, but not scarcity of people."[42] This would seem to capture the political and economic tradeoffs of Qing and Republican kinship hierarchies particularly succinctly. But if the cost of poverty and relative economic decline was arguably a century-long entanglement with foreign imperialism, domestic strife, and ideological turmoil, then perhaps even the old master himself would have wondered whether status equality was really worth it.

---

[42] Jin Liangnian, *Lun Yu Yi Zhu* [Interpretation and Commentary of the *Analects*] 196 (Shanghai Guji Press, 1995) (passage 16.1). Some online versions of the *Analects* have this passage as "[they] fear inequality, but not scarcity of people; they fear instability, but not poverty." *See, e.g.*, Analects, Quan Xue Net, www.quanxue.cn/ct_rujia/LunYu/LunYu16.html (last visited December 31, 2013).

APPENDIX A: List of *Dian*-Related Cases

Cases related to *dian* redemption are listed in bold type. Cases involving claims by the *dian* buyer that the seller's redemption rights had expired are marked with @.

Part I Longquan Legal Archives, Zhejiang University

(Sorted by Archive Document Number) Cases involving *dian* transactions of more than thirty years are marked with an asterisk (*).

M003-01-00034 (1947) @
M003-01-00038 (1919) @*
M003-01-00044 (1948)
M003-01-00078 (1946) @
M003-01-00116 (1918)
M003-01-00126 (1928) @
M003-01-00191 (1931)
M003-01-00199 (1940)
M003-01-00277 (1941)
M003-01-00536 (1942)
M003-01-00549 (1926) @*
M003-01-00586 (1921) @*
M003-01-00642 (1919) @*
M003-01-00769 (1940)
M003-01-00787 (1947) @
M003-01-00821 (1926) @
M003-01-00847 (1920)
M003-01-00851 (1944)

M003-01-00872 (1927)
M003-01-00879 (1924) @*
M003-01-00915 (1941)
M003-01-00938 (1943)
M003-01-00956 (1942)
M003-01-01095 (1946)
M003-01-01119 (1919) @*
M003-01-01166 (1920) @
M003-01-01193 (1931)
M003-01-01229 (1926)
M003-01-01283 (1923) @*
M003-01-01412 (1944) @
M003-01-01480 (1933)
M003-01-01698 (1926) @*
M003-01-01778 (1945)
M003-01-01791 (1915)
M003-01-01923 (1937)
M003-01-01941 (1918)
M003-01-02104 (1923)
M003-01-02147 (1920) @*
M003-01-02160 (1925) @*
M003-01-02262 (1927) *
M003-01-02269 (1944)
M003-01-02484 (1927)
M003-01-02537 (1947)
M003-01-02543 (1912) @*
M003-01-02564 (1918)
M003-01-02553 (1926)
M003-01-02633 (1944)
M003-01-02715 (1942)
M003-01-02756 (1931) @*
M003-01-02781 (1921) @*
M003-01-02790 (1943) @*
M003-01-02792 (1930)
M003-01-03064 (1920)
M003-01-03427 (1946)
M003-01-03478 (1918)
M003-01-03653 (1948)
M003-01-04662 (1941)

M003-01-04738 (1924)
M003-01-04960 (1947)
M003-01-05358 (1948) @*
M003-01-06049 (1949)
M003-01-06251 (1931)
M003-01-06436 (1927)
M003-01-06546 (1922)
M003-01-06719 (1944)
M003-01-07697 (1935)
M003-01-10732 (1932)
M003-01-11063 (1922) @*
M003-01-11205 (1921)
M003-01-12468 (1944)
M003-01-14125 (1942)
M003-01-14275 (1944)
M003-01-14334 (1945)
M003-01-14772 (1941) @
M003-01-15067 (1932)
M003-01-15080 (1945)
M003-01-15483 (1932) @*
M003-01-15821 (1943) @
M003-01-16217 (1930)
M003-01-16292 (1931)

Part II *Lidai Panli Pandu* Cases

Ni Wangzhong, *Zhuji Yumin Jiyao*

This collection does not provide citation information other than page numbers (each corresponding to a single case in *Lidai Panli Pandu*, vol. 10). For example, "473" refers to the (only) case that is entirely on page 473, while "473–74" refers to the (only) case that spans pages 473 and 474. No case exceeds two pages. Disputes between relatives are marked with an asterisk (*).

313 @*
315 *
320–21 *
324 *

331 @*
332
336 *
344 @*
346 @*
348–49 @*
359 @*
375 *
377
380 *
386 *
393
403–04 @
410 @*
424 *
426
443 @*
446–47 *
449 @*
473 *
473–74 *
476–77 @
484 @*
487 @
490–91 @

Sun Dinglie, *Xisizhai Jueshi*

Citation system is identical to the preceding one. Disputes between relatives are marked with an asterisk (*).

510
511–12
514
524
546
565–66 @
571 @*
581 *

585
592–93
602 @*
644
647

Zhao Youban, *Liren Pandu Huiji*

This collection does not provide citation information other than page numbers (in *Lidai Panli Pandu*, vol. 12). For example, "398" refers to the only case entirely on page 398, 398–99 refers to the (only) case spanning pages 398 and 399, whereas "398(1)" refers to the first case on a page with more than one case. Disputes between relatives are marked with an asterisk (*).

114(2) *
115–16
123(1)
128–29 @
132–33
136–37 *
138(2) *
142–43 @*
143 *
146–47
152
156 @
165–66 @
166–67
169(1)
172
178(1) *
212
215
216(1) @
222(2) *
224(1) *
239(1) *
245–46 @
250(2)

258(2) @
260–61
261(1)
271(1)
278(1) @*
303–04 @*
309
312 @
315(2)
320–21 @
321 @
328(2)
331(1) @
334(2) *
338(2)
342(2)
345(2) *
347–48
348(2)
363(2) *
365–66
376–77 @
380–81 *
388(2) @
393–94
397(1) @*
397(2) @*
400(1)
402–03

APPENDIX B: List of Political Elites from Seven North China Villages

Sources

1. Chugoku Noson Kanko Chosa [Investigation of Rural Chinese Customs] 89–145, app. 2 (Committee for the Publication of the Rural Customs and Practices of China ed., Iwanami Shoten Press 1958)
2. Chugoku Noson Kanko Chosa apps. 2, 3
3. Chugoku Noson Kanko Chosa 27–51, app. 3
4. Chugoku Noson Kanko Chosa 1–29, 353–83, 385–89, 397–417, 555–63
5. Chugoku Noson Kanko Chosa 1–55, 63, 179–82, 406–31

Name	Landholding (number of *mu*/ household size, if available)	Belonging to the senior generation of a major lineage (as identified by villagers)? (Y/N)	Position (current or former)
Sibeichai (median landholding per person: 2 *mu*)			
Zhang Leqing	48/10	Y	Village chief
Hao Guodong	2/6	N	*Id.*
Hao Qingjun	"Very average"	Y	*Id.*
Hao Yiwei	200+/?	Y	*Id.*
Hao Luozhuo	4/2	Y	*Lüzhang* (闾长)
Hao Baizi	28/14	Y	*Id.*
Hao Luozhen	3/7	Y	*Id.*
Zhao Luohan	23/5	Y	*Id.*
Liu Luoliu	25/10	Y	*Id.*
Zhao Luoxu	11/4	Y	*Jiazhang* (甲长)
Liu Yuande	10/5	Y	*Id.*
Zhao Luofeng	6/8	Y	*Id.*

(*continued*)

(*continued*)

Name	Landholding (number of *mu*/ household size, if available)	Belonging to the senior generation of a major lineage (as identified by villagers)? (Y/N)	Position (current or former)
Liu Luocun (Wuzi)	24/7	Y	*Id.*
Xu Laosi	7.5/5	Y	*Id.*
Hao Luojing (Luoping)	4/8	Y	*Id.*
Hao Luoxi (Luoji)	13/4	Y	*Id.*
Hao Luogeng	20/13	Y	*Id.*
Hao Luoxiang	8/8	Y	*Id.*

Shajing (median landholding per person: 2.5 *mu*)

Yang Yuan	40/5	Y	Village chief
Li Ruyuan	76/7	Y	*Huishou* (会首)
Zhang Rui	110/18	N	*Id.*
Du Xiang	11.5/10	Y	*Id.*
Zhao Tingkui	14/10	Y	*Id.*
Yang Ze	35/5	Y	*Id.*
Yang Run	11/5	Y	*Id.*
Zhang Yongren	46/13	Y	*Id.*
Li Xiufang	50/9	?	*Xinminhui* Officer
Yang Yongcai	18/8	Y	Councilor/head of kinship group
Du Chun	4/5	Y	*Id.*
Zhang Wentong	110/18	Y	*Id.*
Yang Zheng	40/5	Y	*Id.*
Zhao Shaoting	16/8	Y	Councilor/village chief candidate

Lujiazhuang (median landholding per household: 10 *mu*)

Xing Guanghua	10	Y	Village chief
Chen Jirong	1.6	Y	*Lüzhang*
Xing Dawen	7	Y	*Id.*
Chen Dianxiang	13	Y	*Id.*
Yang Fenglin	8	Y	*Id.*
Yang Jinglin	8	Y	*Jiazhang*
Chen Jifu	14	Y	*Id.*
Xing Mingyun	10	N	*Id.*
Sun Riwen	3.3	Y	*Id.*

Name	Landholding (number of *mu*/ household size, if available)	Belonging to the senior generation of a major lineage (as identified by villagers)? (Y/N)	Position (current or former)
Chen Qingzhang	4.2	?	*Id.*
Yang Jinghe	2.7	Y	*Id.*

Lengshuigou (median landholding per household: ~13 *mu*)

Du Fengshang	3	Y	Village chief
Ren Fushen	27	Y	*Jiazhang*
Li Liangfu	17.8	Y	*Id.*
Ren Fuyu	27	Y	*Baozhang* (保长)
Zhang Zengjun	27	?	*Id.*
Li Yongxiang	16	Y	*Id.*
Li Fengkun	17	Y	*Id.*
Li Xiangling	80(?)	Y	*Shoushi* (*id.* as *Lüzhang*)
Ren Dexuan	50(?)	Y	*Id.*
Li Wenhan	50(?)	Y	*Id.*
Li Fenggui	2	Y	*Id.*
Yang Hanqing	80(?)	Y	*Id.*
Yang Lide	30(?)	Y	*Id.*
Wang Weishan	40(?)	Y	*Id.*
Li Fengjie	70(?)	Y	*Id.*
Cheng Zhensheng	6	Y	*Lüzhang*
Yang Liquan	10	Y	*Id.*
Li Changhai	3	Y	*Id.*
Li Xingchang	17	?	*Id.*
Li Defu	20	Y	*Id.*
Li Zonglun	13	Y	*Id.*
Liu Xi'en	13	Y	*Id.*
Li Yongmao	14.5	Y	*Id.*
Ren Fuzeng	40	Y	*Id.*
Ren Furun	1	Y	*Difang* (地方)
Son of Yang Qingyun	3	N	Head of local militia

Houxiazhai (median landholding per person: 3.6 *mu*)

Ma Fengxiang	43/10	Y	*Difang*
Wu Yuheng	30/?	Y	*Baozhang* (same as village chief in this village)

(*continued*)

(*continued*)

Name	Landholding (number of *mu*/ household size, if available)	Belonging to the senior generation of a major lineage (as identified by villagers)? (Y/N)	Position (current or former)
Ma Wannian	7/4	Y	*Id.*
Wang Qinglong	30/?	?	*Id.*
Wu Yulin	36/11	Y	*Id.*
Wang Baotan	50/?	?	*Id.*
Li Pu	30/?	?	*Id.*
Li Shengtang	22/7	Y	*Jiazhang*
Wei Jinsheng	28/7	?	*Id.*
Wang Baojun	35/11	Y	*Baozhang*, head of kinship group
Wang Lianzhi	6/2	Y	Head of kinship group
Wang Junling	24/5	Y	*Id.*
Ma Zhongting	30/14	Y	*Id.*
Wu Xiangzhong	27/8	Y	*Id.*
Wu Zhide	33/6	Y	*Id.*
Wang Qingyun	7/2	Y	*Id.*
Ma Xinggang	17/4	Y	*Id.*
Wang Zhende	10/2	Y	*Id.*
Wei Jizhou	11/4	Y	*Id.*

Houjiaying (median landholding per household: 25 *mu*)

Name	Landholding	Belonging	Position
Hou Junliang	10	Y	Head of largest kinship group
Hou Dingyi	50, but supports household twice as large as average	Y	Village chief
Hou Quanwu	80	Y	*Id.*
Hou Yintang	70+	Y	*Id.*
Hou Rongkuan	25	Y	*Id.*
Liu Zixin	100+	Y	*Id.*
Hou Dasheng	40	Y	*Id.*
Hou Xianyang	150	Y	*Id.*
Hou Changzan	35	Y	*Id.*
Hou Baotian	25	Y	*Id.*
Hou Yuanguang	98	Y	*Id.*
Hou Yonghe	35, but supports household three times as large as average	Y	Vice village chief

Name	Landholding (number of *mu*/ household size, if available)	Belonging to the senior generation of a major lineage (as identified by villagers)? (Y/N)	Position (current or former)
Hou Xichen	30	Y	*Id.*
Kong Ziming	20	Y	*Id.*
Hou Tingwu	35	Y	*Id.*
Xiao Huisheng	25	Y	*Id.*
Hou Zhende	10	?	*Jiazhang*
Liu Wanchen	10	?	*Id.*
Hou Ruiwen	<10	?	*Id.*
Hou Yuanzhao	Possibly landless	Y	*Id.*
Ye Runting	"Below average"	Y	*Id.*
Hou Ruihe	13	N	*Xiangding* (a lower-level village official on the level of *Jiazhang*)

Wudian (median landholding per household: ~15 *mu*)

Name	Landholding	Belonging	Position
Zhang Qilun	20	Y	Village chief
Zhao Xianzhang	10–15	Y	*Id.*
Zhao Kai	10	Y	*Id.*
Pei Zhenyu	30	Y	*Id.*
Guo Ru	5–6	Y	*Id.*
Father of Jia Zhenheng	3–4	Y	*Id.*
Guo Kuan	70	Y	*Id.*
Yang Wenhai	3–4	Y	*Id.*
Zhang Wenzhong	3–4	Y	*Id.*
Pei Shun	No. 1 landowner	Y	Vice village chief
Zhang Wenhui	Landless	Y	*Id.*
Li Yongyu	30	Y	*Id.*
Guo Zhongsheng	70	N	*Jiazhang*
Li Rong	31	N	*Id.*
Zhao Xiang	10	N	*Id.*
Hui Zhen	20	N	*Id.*
Yu Duo	30	Y	*Id.*

Note: Lengshuigou landholding data marked with (?) are highly unreliable.

Individuals on the List Who Were among Top Five Landowners in Their Respective Villages

Sibeichai: Hao Luozhen, Zhao Luofeng
Shajing: Zhang Rui
Lujiazhuang: none
Lengshuigou: Li Xiangling, Yang Hanqing
Houjiaying: Hou Xianyang, Liu Zixin
Wudian: Guo Kuan, Pei Shun

Bibliography

Primary Sources

13 Edward I., Statute of Westminister II (1285)

23 Henry VIII 8 c.6 (Eng.) (1531)

27 Edward III st. ii., c.9 (1353)

Analects, Quan Xue Net, www.quanxue.cn/ct_rujia/LunYu/LunYu16.html (last visited December 31, 2013)

Backs v. Gayer (1684), 1 Vern 258

Bamfield v. Bamford (1675), 73 Publications of the Selden Society 183

Baodi County Archives

Baxian County Archives

Bianshi Zongpu [Registry of the Bian Lineage] (Bian Yingshan et al. eds., 1874)

Bing wei Chengjing Difang Yanban Kangzu Shi [*A Report on Measures to Enforce Strict Local Penalties Against Rent Resistance*], *in* Suishou Jilu [Records of Convenience] (held at Changshu Municipal Library, 1891)

Blacklock v. Barnes (1725), Sel. Cases of the King 53

Blackstone, William. Commentaries on the Laws of England (Univ. of Chicago Press, 1979)

Bracton, Henry de. De Legibus et Consuetudinibus Angliae (Samuel E. Thorne trans., 6 vols., 1970)

Buck, John L. Land Utilization in China: Statistics (1937)

Burgess v. Wheate (1750), 1 Eden 177, 96 English Reports 67

Cai Yuanpei, Guomin Xiuyang Er Zhong [Two Writings on Citizen Character] (1999)

Chen Duxiu, Chen Duxiu Wenzhang Xuanbian – Dong Xi Minzu Genben Sixiang zhi Chayi [Selected Papers of Chen Duxiu – On the Fundamental Difference between Eastern and Western Peoples] (1984)

Christopher Corbet's Case (1579), 2 Anderson 134, 1 Co. Rep. *83b

Chugoku Noson Kanko Chosa [Investigation of Rural Chinese Customs] (Committee for the Publication of the Rural Customs and Practices of China ed., Iwanami Shoten Press 1958)

Collier v. Walters (1873), Law Reports 17 Equity 252

Da Qing Lü Li [The Great Qing Code] (1905)

Danxin County Archives

Duchess of Hamilton v. Countess of Dirlton (1654), 1 Ch. Rep. 165

Dushi Zongpu [Registry of the Du Lineage] (Du Xizhen ed., 1948)

Emmanuel College, Cambridge v. Evans (1625), 1 Chancery Reports 10

Er Cheng Ji [Collected Writings of Cheng Hao and Cheng Yi] (Zhonghua Shuju ed., 1981)

Faling Jilan [Edited Collection of Laws and Regulations] (Sifa Bu ed. 1917)

Fan Zengxiang, Fanshan Pipan [Decisions and Orders from Fanshan] (Shanghai Guangyi Bookstore ed., 1915)

Fang Xiaoru, Xunzhi Zhai Ji [Writings from Xunzhi Villa] (Xu Guangda ed., Ningbo Press, 2000)

Glanvill, Ranulf de. Tractatus de Legibus et Consuetudinibus Regni Angliae (G.D.G. Hall ed., 1965)

Gloucester Cathedral, Historia et Cartularium: Monasterii Sancti Petri Gloucestriae (William Henry Hart ed., 1863)

Guanchuan Maoshi Zupu [Registry of the Mao Lineage of Guanchuan] (late Qing, year unknown)

Guizhou Wenji [Writings of Guizhou] (1574, Microfilm, Peking University Library)

Hu Shi, 2 Hu Shi Jingpin Ji [The Best Writings of Hu Shi] (1998)

Huadong Junzheng Weiyuanhui, Jiangsu Sheng Nongcun Diaocha (1952)

Ji Huang et al. Qinding Xu Wenxian Tongkao [Official Sequel to the Exegesis of Historical Documents] (1784, microfilm, Zhejiang Univ. Library)

Jiangshi Zhipu [Branch Registry of the Jiang Lineage] (Yu Zhonghuan ed.,1934)

Jin Liangnian, Lun Yu Yi Zhu [Interpretation and Commentary of the Analects] 196 (Shanghai Guji Press, 1995)

Jindai Zhongguo Shiliao Congkan (Shen Yunlong ed., Taibei, 1966)

Ke Wuchi, Louwang Yongyu Ji [Record of the Fish that Escaped the Net] 15 (Zhonghua Shuju Press, 1959)

Law of Property Act 1925, 15 & 16 George V. c.20

Li Li Xu Zhi [Additional Gazetteer of Li Li] (Guangxu edn.) chap. 12 (1899)

Liang Qichao Wenxuan [Selected Writings of Liang Qichao] (Xia Xiaohong ed., 1992)

Lidai Panli Pandu [Cases from Past Eras] (Yang Yifan et al. eds., China Soc. Sci. Press, 2005)

Littleton, Thomas de. Littleton's Tenures in English § 332 (Eugene Wambaugh ed., 1903

Liu Shaokuan, Minguo Pingyang Xianzhi [County Gazetteer of Republican-Era Pingyang] (Shanghai Bookstore ed., 1993)

Longquan County Archives

Longquan Dang'an Hebian Mulu [Index of Collected Archives from Longquan] (December 5, 2011) (unpublished index, on filed with the Zhejiang University History Department)

Manning v. Burgess (1663), 1 Ch. Cas. 29

MINGDAI LÜLI HUIBIAN [COLLECTED LAWS AND PRECEDENTS OF THE MING] (Huang Zhangjian ed., 1979)

MINSHANGSHI XIGUAN DIAOCHA BAOGAOLU [RESEARCH REPORT ON CIVIL AND COMMERCIAL CUSTOMS] (Sifa Xingzheng Bu ed., 1930)

NANJIN JIANGSHI MINFANG FAXIANG PU [REGISTRY OF THE MIN BRANCH OF THE NINGBO JIANG LINEAGE] (1890)

NANYANG YESHI ZONGPU [REGISTRY OF THE YE LINEAGE OF NANYANG] (Ye Liming et al. eds., 1998)

Newcombe v. Bonham (1681), 1 VERN 7 (Ch.), 1 VERN 214, 1 VERN 232, 2 VERN 264

PUBLICATIONS OF THE SELDEN SOCIETY, vol. 18 (1904)

PUBLICATIONS OF THE SELDEN SOCIETY, vol. 21 (1906)

QINDING DAQING HUIDIAN SHILI [OFFICIAL APPLICATIONS OF THE DAQING HUIDIAN] (Shangwu Press ed., 1909)

QING SHILU [TRUE RECORDS OF THE QING] (Zhonghua Shuju ed., 1986)

QINGCHAO WENXIAN TONGKAO [COMPREHENSIVE STUDY OF QING HISTORICAL DOCUMENTS] (Zhejiang Guji Press ed., 1988)

QINGDAI GE BUYUAN ZELI: QINDING HUBU ZELI (QIANLONG CHAO) [REGULATIONS OF QING BOARDS AND MINISTRIES: IMPERIAL BOARD OF FINANCE REGULATIONS (QIANLONG ERA)] (Fuchi Shuyuan ed., 2004)

QINGDAI NINGBO QIYUE WENSHU JIJIAO [QING CONTRACTS FROM NINGBO] (Wang Wanying ed., Tianjian Guji Press 2008)

QIU HUANG, FUPAN LUCUN [RECORDINGS OF MAGISTRATE DECISIONS], *in* 1 MING QING FAZHI SHILIAO JIKAN [COLLECTION OF LEGAL MATERIAL FROM THE MING AND QING] 371 (National Library of China ed., 2008)

QUESHI ZONGPU [REGISTRY OF THE QUE LINEAGE] (Hu Ruixiang ed., 1896)

Roscarrick v. Barton (1672), 1 CH. CAS. 216

SAVINE, ALEXANDER. COPYHOLD CASES IN THE EARLY CHANCERY PROCEEDINGS: -1902 (1902)

Seton v. Slade (1802), 7 Ves. 265, 32 Eng. R.; Mortgagees Legal Cost Act, 58 & 59 Victoria c.25 (1895)

SHICANG QIYUE [SHICANG CONTRACTS] (Cao Shuji ed., Zhejiang Univ. Press 2010)

SIMING ZHUSHI ZHIPU [BRANCH REGISTRY OF THE ZHU LINEAGE OF SIMING] (Zhu Xiang ed., 1936)

SONG SHI [THE OFFICIAL HISTORY OF THE SONG]

Stamp v. Clinton (1615), 6 Co. REP. Pt. XI *46b, 1 ROLL 95, 101

Statement of Choke, J. (1466), YEAR BOOK 7 Edward IV 12a, pl. 2

Statement of Counsel (1535), YEAR BOOK 27 Henry VIII. 29 pl. 20

SUN ZHONGSHAN XUANJI [SELECTED WORKS OF SUN YAT-SEN] (Beijing People's Press ed., 1981)

TIANCANG QIYUE WENSHU CUIBIAN (Hugh T. Scogin & Zheng Qin eds., 2001)

TUDI WEIYUANHUI, QUANGUO TUDI DIAOCHA BAOGAO GANGYAO (1937)

Vavasour J. & Townshend J. (1497), YEAR BOOK 13 Henry VII (Easter Term) fol. 24

Wade's Case (1602), 5 Co. Rep. 114

Walsingham's Case (1573), 2 PLOWDEN 547, 75 ENGLISH REP. 805

WANG YOUHUAI, QIANGU BEIYAO [ESSENTIALS OF FINANCE AND GRAIN] (1893)

WU YU, WU YU WEN LU [SELECTED WRITINGS OF WU YU] (1927)

XUDETANG YINJIA PU [REGISTRY OF THE YIN LINEAGE OF XUDETANG] (1906)

XUSHI ZONGPU [REGISTRY OF THE XU LINEAGE] (Zu Fenglu ed., 1937)

YAONAN DINGSHAN FANGSHI ZONGPU [REGISTRY OF THE FANG LINEAGE FROM DINGSHAN, IN YAONAN] (Fang Zheng et al. eds., 1921)

YE MENGDE, SHILIN YANYU [SPARROW SOUNDS OF THE ROCK FOREST] (Zhonghua Shuju ed., 1984)

YONGSHANG TUSHI ZONGPU [REGISTRY OF THE TU LINEAGE OF YONGSHANG] (Zhang Meisa ed., 1919)

ZHANG ZAI JI [COLLECTED WRITINGS OF ZHANG ZAI] (Zhonghua Shuju ed., 1978)

ZHENG GUANGZU, YIBAN LU ZASHU [MISCELLANEOUS ESSAYS FROM THE YIBAN RECORDS] chap. 7 (Zhongguo Book Store ed., 1990)

ZHONGGUO JINDAI SIXIANG JIA WENKU: BAO SHICHEN JUAN [COLLECTED WORKS OF EARLY MODERN CHINESE THINKERS: BAO SHICHEN] (Liu Ping & Zheng Dahua eds., 2013)

ZHONGHUA MINGUO MINFA DIAN [CIVIL CODE OF THE REPUBLIC OF CHINA] (1929)

ZHU GUOZHEN, HUANG MING DAZHENG JI [A COLLECTION OF RIGHTEOUS WRITINGS IN AN ERA OF A BENEVOLENT EMPEROR] (Qilu Shushe ed., 1997)

ZHU XI, JIALI [FAMILY RITUALS] (Wang Yanjun & Wang Guangzhao eds., Shanghai Guji Press, 1999)

Secondary Sources

Abercrombie, Nicholas & Bryan S. Turner. *The Dominant Ideology Thesis*, 29 BRITISH J. SOCIOLOGY 149 (1978)

ACEMOGLU, DARON & JAMES A. ROBINSON. WHY NATIONS FAIL: THE ORIGINS OF POWER, PROSPERITY AND POVERTY 117 (2010)

Acemoglu, Daron, Simon Johnson, & James Robinson. *The Rise of Europe: Atlantic Trade, Institutional Change, and Economic Growth*, 95 AM. ECON. REV. 546 (2005)

Ackerman, James M. *Interest Rates and the Law: A History of Usury*, ARIZ. ST. L.J. 61 (1981)

Alford, William P. *The Inscrutable Occidental: Roberto Unger's Uses and Abuses of the Chinese Past*, 64 TEXAS L. REV. 915 (1986)

Allee, Mark. *Code Culture, and Custom: Foundations of Civil Case Verdicts in a Nineteenth-Century County Court*, in CIVIL LAW IN QING AND REPUBLICAN CHINA 122 (Kathryn Bernhardt & Philip C.C. Huang eds., 1994)

Allen, Robert C. *Economic Structure and Agricultural Productivity in Europe, 1300–1800*, 3 EURO. REV. ECON. HIST. 1 (2000)

ALLEN, ROBERT C. ENCLOSURE AND THE YEOMAN: THE AGRICULTURAL DEVELOPMENT OF THE SOUTH MIDLANDS 1450–1850 (1992)

Allen, Robert C. *Engels' Pause: Technical Change, Capital Accumulation, and Inequality in the British Industrial Revolution*, 46 EXPLORATIONS IN ECON. HIST. 418 (2009)

ALLEN, ROBERT. THE BRITISH INDUSTRIAL REVOLUTION IN GLOBAL PERSPECTIVE (2009)

Allen Robert et al. *Wages, Prices, and Living Standards in China, 1738–1925: in comparison with Europe, Japan, and India*, Oxford University, Department of Economics Working Paper No. 316 (2007).

BAKER, J.H. AN INTRODUCTION TO ENGLISH LEGAL HISTORY (3d ed. 1990)

BEATTIE, HILARY J. LAND AND LINEAGE IN CHINA: A STUDY OF T'UNG-CH'ENG COUNTY, ANHWEI, IN THE MING AND CH'ING DYNASTIES (1979)

Becker, Gary S. & Kevin M. Murphy, *A Theory of Rational Addiction, in* ACCOUNTING FOR TASTES 50 (Gary S. Becker ed., 1996)

Beckett, J.V. *The Decline of the Small Landowner in Eighteenth- and Nineteenth-Century England: Some Regional Considerations*, 30 AGRI. HIST. REV. 97 (1982)

Beckett, J.V. *The Pattern of Landownership in England and Wales, 1660–1880*, 37 ECON. HIST. REV. 1 (1984)

BEDDOES, W.F. A CONCISE TREATISE OF THE LAW OF MORTGAGE (2d ed., 1908)

Bell, Lynda S. *Farming, Sericulture, and Peasant Rationality in Wuxi County in the Early Twentieth Century, in* CHINESE HISTORY IN ECONOMIC PERSPECTIVE 207 (Thomas G. Rawski & Lillian M. Li eds., 1992)

Benabou, R. & J. Tirole, *Willpower and Personal Rules*, 112 J. POL. ECON. 848 (2004)

Bendor, Jonathan & Piotr Swistak, *The Evolution of Norms*, 106 AM. J. SOCIOLOGY 1493 (2001)

BERNHARDT, KATHRYN. RENTS, TAXES, AND PEASANT RESISTANCE: THE LOWER YANGTZE REGION, 1840–1950 (1992)

BERNHARDT, KATHRYN. WOMEN AND PROPERTY IN CHINA, 960–1949 (1999)

Bian, Guofeng. *Fan Zhongyan Zongzu Fuli Sixiang Yanjiu [A Study on Fan Zhongyan's Thoughts on Lineage Welfare]* (M.A. Thesis, Jilin Univ., 2004)

BODDE, DERK & CLARENCE MORRIS. LAW IN IMPERIAL CHINA (1967)

BOOTH A. & R. M. SUNDRUM. LABOUR ABSORPTION IN AGRICULTURE: THEORETICAL ANALYSIS AND EMPIRICAL INVESTIGATIONS (1985)

BOSSLER, BEVERLY J. POWERFUL RELATIONS: KINSHIP, STATUS, AND STATE IN SUNG CHINA (1996)

BOURDIEU, PIERRE. THE FIELD OF CULTURAL PRODUCTION: ESSAYS ON ART AND LITERATURE (1993)

BOURDIEU, PIERRE. THE LOGIC OF PRACTICE (Richard Nice trans., 1990)

Bourgon, Jerome. *Uncivil Dialogue: Law and Custom Did Not Merge into Civil Law under the Qing*, 23 LATE IMPERIAL CHINA 50 (2002)

BRAY, FRANCESCA. TECHNOLOGY AND GENDER: FABRICS OF POWER IN LATE IMPERIAL CHINA (1997)

Brenner, Robert & Christopher Isett. *England's Divergence from China's Yangtze Delta: Property Relations, Microeconomics, and Patterns of Development*, 61 J. OF ASIAN STUD. 609 (2002)

Britannica Online Encyclopedia (Academic Version), Social Status, www.britannica.com/EBchecked/topic/551450/social-status (last visited July 1, 2012)

BROAD, JOHN. TRANSFORMING ENGLISH RURAL SOCIETY: THE VERNEYS AND THE CLAYDONS, 1600–1820 (2004)

Broadberry, Stephen, Guan Hanhui, & Li Daokui. *China, Europe and the Great Divergence: A Study in National Accounting*, Working Paper, London School of Economics (2014)

Buck, John L. Land Utilization in China: A Study of 16,786 Farms in 168 Localities, and 38,256 Farm Families in Twenty-two Provinces in China, 1929–1933 (1937)

Buck, John L. The Chinese Farm Economy (1930)

Buoye, Thomas. Manslaughter, Markets and Moral Economy: Violent Disputes over Property Rights in Eighteenth Century China (2000)

Bush, M.L. The English Aristocracy: A Comparative Synthesis (1984)

Byres, T.J. *The Agrarian Question, Forms of Capitalist Agrarian Transition and the State: An Essay with Reference to Asia*, 14 Social Scientist 3 (1986)

Cantor, Paul & James Kraus. *Changing Patterns of Ownership Rights in the People's Republic of China: A Legal and Economic Analysis in the Context of Economic Reforms and Social Conditions*, 23 Vand. J. Transnat'l L. 479, 483 (1991)

Cao, Xingsui. Jiu Zhongguo Sunan Nongjia Jingji Yanjiu [Research on the Rural Economy of Southern Jiangsu in Old China] (1996)

Chaianov, Alexander. The Theory of the Peasant Economy (David Thorner, Basile Kerblay, & R.E.F. Smith eds., 1986)

Chang, Jianghua. *Yuandai Muci Jizu Wenti Chutan [A Preliminary Study on Yuan Dynasty Ancestor Worship Practices]*, in Zhongguo Shehui Wenhua Shi Duben [The Chinese Social and Cultural History Reader] 260 (Liu Yonghua ed., 2011)

Chang, Jianhua. *Lun Shengyu Guangxun yu Qingdai de Xiaozhi [On the Shengyu Guangxun and the Use of Filial Piety as a Governing Tool in the Qing]*, 1988(1) Nankai Shixue [Nankai Univ. Historical Stud.] 35, *available at* http://wenku.baidu.com/view/e85a377102768e9951e7385c.html

Chang, Jianhua. *Mingdai Zongzu Cimiao Jizu Lizhi ji Qi Yanbian [The Evolution of Ancestor Worship Practices in Ming Dynasty Lineages]*, 2001(3) Nankai Xuebao [Academic Journal of Nankai Univ.] 60

Chang, Jianhua. Zongzu Zhi [A History of Lineages] (1998)

Chang, Yun-chien & Henry E. Smith. *An Economic Analysis of Civil versus Common Law Property*, 88 Notre Dame L. Rev. 1 (2012)

Chao, Kang. *Tenure Systems in Traditional China*, 31 Econ. Dev. & Cult. Change 295 (1983)

Chaplin, H.W. *The Story of Mortgage Law*, 4 Harv. L. Rev. 1 (1890)

Chen Shuzhu, Zhejiang Sheng Tudi Wenti yu Wu.Er. Jianzu [The Land Issue in Zhejiang Province and the May 2nd Tax Reduction Movement] (1996)

Chen, Albert H.Y. *Towards a Legal Enlightenment: Discussions in Contemporary China on the Rule of Law*, 17 UCLA Pac. Basin L.J. 125 (2000)

Chen, Peipei. *Qingdai Falü Tequan Yanjiu [A Study of Legal Privileges in the Qing]* (2007) (unpublished M.A. thesis, Anhui University), *available at* http://cdmd.cnki.com.cn/Article/CDMD-10357-2007193110.htm

Chen, Zhiping. Jin 500 Nian lai Fujian de Jiazu Shehui yu Wenhua [Lineage Society and Culture in Fujian over the Past 500 years] (1991)

Chinese Capitalism 1522–1840 (Xu Dixin & Wu Chengming eds., Li Zhengde et al. trans., 2000)

CHINESE HISTORY IN ECONOMIC PERSPECTIVE (Thomas G. Rawski & Lillian M. Li eds., 1992)

CHOW, KAI-WING. THE RISE OF CONFUCIAN RITUALISM IN LATE IMPERIAL CHINA: ETHICS, CLASSICS, AND LINEAGE DISCOURSE (1994)

CH'U, TUNG-TSU. LOCAL GOVERNMENT IN CHINA UNDER THE CH'ING (1962)

Chua, Amy L. *Markets, Democracy, and Ethnicity: Toward a New Paradigm for Law and Development*, 108 YALE L.J. 1 (1998)

CIVIL LAW IN QING AND REPUBLICAN CHINA (Kathryn Bernhardt & Philip C.C. Huang eds., 1994)

Clarke, Donald C. *Economic Development and the Rights Hypothesis: The China Problem*, 51 AM. J. OF COMP. L. 89 (2003)

Clay, Christopher. *Property Settlements, Financial Provision for the Family, and Sale of Land by the Greater Landowners, 1660-1790*, 21 J. BRIT. STUD. 18 (1981)

Coase, Ronald H. *The Nature of the Firm*, 4 ECONOMICA 386 (1937)

COLEMAN, JAMES S. FOUNDATIONS OF SOCIAL THEORY (1990)

Cooter, Robert D. *Book Review: Against Legal Centricism*, 81 CAL. L. REV. 417 (1993)

Cooter, Robert D. *Decentralized Law for a Complex Economy: The Structural Approach to Adjudicating the New Law Merchant*, 144 U. PENN. L. REV. 1643 (1996)

Cooter, Robert D. *Structural Adjudication and the New Law Merchant: A Model of Decentralized Law*, 14 INT'L REV. L. & ECON. 215 (1994)

Cressy, David. *Kinship and Kin Interaction in Early Modern England*, 113 PAST & PRESENT 38 (1986)

DAVIS, RALPH. THE INDUSTRIAL REVOLUTION AND BRITISH OVERSEAS TRADE (1979)

DE VRIES, JAN. THE ECONOMY OF EUROPE IN AN AGE OF CRISIS, 1600–1750 (1976)

DE VRIES, JAN. THE FIRST MODERN ECONOMY: SUCCESS, FAILURE, AND PERSEVERANCE OF THE DUTCH ECONOMY, 1500–1815 (1997).

DE VRIES, JAN. THE INDUSTRIOUS REVOLUTION: CONSUMER DEMAND AND THE HOUSEHOLD ECONOMY, 1650 TO THE PRESENT (2008)

DELURY, JOHN & ORVILLE SCHELL. WEALTH AND POWER: CHINA'S LONG MARCH TO THE TWENTY-FIRST CENTURY (2013)

Demsetz, Harold. *Toward a Theory of Property Rights*, 57 AM. ECON. REV. 347 (1967)

DENG, XIAOMANG. RUJIA LUNLI XIN PIPAN [A NEW CRITIQUE OF CONFUCIAN ETHICS] (2010)

DUARA, PRASENJIT. CULTURE, POWER AND THE STATE: RURAL NORTH CHINA, 1900–1942, (1988)

DUARA, PRASENJIT. RESCUING HISTORY FROM THE NATION: QUESTIONING NARRATIVES OF MODERN CHINA (1997)

DUKEMINIER, JESSE & JAMES E. KRIER, PROPERTY (5th ed. 2002)

Edwards, Mark A. *Acceptable Deviance and Property Rights*, 43 CONN. L. REV. 457 (2010)

Egalitarianism (Stanford Encyclopedia of Philosophy), http://plato.stanford.edu/entries/egalitarianism/ (last visited March 7, 2013)

Ellickson, Robert C. *Law and Economics Discovers Social Norms*, 27 J. LEGAL STUD. 537 (1998)

ELLICKSON, ROBERT C. ORDER WITHOUT LAW: HOW NEIGHBORS SETTLE DISPUTES (1991)

Ellickson, Robert C. *Property in Land*, 102 YALE L.J. 1315 (1993)
Ellickson, Robert C. *The Cost of Complex Land Titles: Two Examples from China* (Yale Law & Econ. Research Paper no.441, 2011), *available at* http://papers.ssrn.com/sol3/papers.cfm?abstract_id=1953207
Ellickson, Robert C. *The Market for Social Norms*, 3 AMERICAN L. & ECON. REV. 1 (2001)
ELLIOTT, MARK C. THE MANCHU WAY: THE EIGHT BANNERS AND ETHNIC IDENTITY IN LATE IMPERIAL CHINA (2001)
ELMAN, BENJAMIN A. FROM PHILOSOPHY TO PHILOLOGY: INTELLECTUAL AND SOCIAL ASPECTS OF CHANGE IN LATE IMPERIAL CHINA (1984)
Elman, Benjamin A. *Political, Social, and Cultural Reproduction via Civil Service Examinations in Late Imperial China*, 50 J. ASIAN STUD. 1 (1991)
Elman, Benjamin A. *The Failures of Contemporary Chinese Intellectual History*, 43 EIGHTEENTH-CENTURY STUD. 371 (2010)
ELMAN, BENJAMIN. A CULTURAL HISTORY OF CIVIL EXAMINATIONS IN LATE IMPERIAL CHINA (2000)
ELMAN, BENJAMIN. ON THEIR OWN TERMS: SCIENCE IN CHINA (2005)
ELVIN, MARK. THE PATTERN OF THE CHINESE PAST (1973)
Esherick, Joseph W. *Number Games: A Note on Land Distribution in Prerevolutionary China*, 7 MODERN CHINA 387 (1981)
ESHERICK, JOSEPH. ORIGINS OF THE BOXER UPRISING (1988)
Eswaran, Mukesh & Ashok Kotwal. *A Theory of Contractual Structure in Agriculture*, 75 AM. ECON. REV. 352 (1985)
Etzioni, Amitai. *Social Norms: Internalization, Persuasion and History*, 34 L. & SOC. REV. 157 (2000)
Fang Xing, *Qingdai Qianqi de Fengjian Dizu Lü*, 1992(2) ZHONGGUO JINGJISHI YANJIU 61
FANG, KELI. XIANDAI XIN RUXUE YU ZHONGGUO XIANDAIHUA [MODERN NEO-CONFUCIANISM AND CHINA'S MODERNIZATION] (1997)
Fang, Qiang. *Hot Potatoes: Chinese Complaint Systems from Early Times to the Late Qing*, 68 J. ASIAN STUD. 1105 (2009)
FAURE, DAVID. CHINA AND CAPITALISM: A HISTORY OF BUSINESS ENTERPRISE IN MODERN CHINA (2006)
FAURE, DAVID. EMPEROR AND ANCESTOR: STATE AND LINEAGE IN SOUTH CHINA (2007)
FEI, CHENGKANG, ET AL. ZHONGGUO DE JIAFA ZUGUI [FAMILY AND CLAN REGULATIONS IN CHINA] (1998)
FENG, ERKANG ET AL. ZHONGGUO ZONGZU SHI [HISTORY OF CHINESE LINEAGES] (2009)
FENG, ERKANG. 18 SHIJI YILAI ZHONGGUO JIAZU DE XIANDAI ZHUANXIANG [THE MODERN TURN OF CHINESE LINEAGES SINCE THE 18TH CENTURY] (2005)
FEUERWERKER, ALBERT. CHINA'S EARLY INDUSTRIALIZATION: SHENG HSUAN-HUAI AND MANDARIN ENTERPRISE (1958)
Feuerwerker, Albert. *Economic Trends, 1912–1949, in* CAMBRIDGE HISTORY OF CHINA 28 (John K. Fairbank & Dennis Twichett eds., 1983)
FRANK, ANDRE GUNDER. REORIENT (1998)
Frankema, Ewout. *The Colonial Roots of Land Inequality: Geography, Factor Endowments, or Institutions?*, 63 ECON. HIST. REV. 418 (2010)

FREEDMAN, MAURICE. CHINESE LINEAGE AND SOCIETY: FUKIEN AND KWANGTUNG (1966)

French H.R. & Richard Hoyle. *English Individualism Refuted and Reasserted: The Case of Earls Colne (Essex), 1550–1750*, 56 ECON. HIST. REV. 595 (2003)

French, H.R. *Social Status, Localism and the "Middle Sort of People" in England, 1620–1750*, 166 PAST & PRESENT 66 (2000)

GARDELLA, ROBERT PAUL. HARVESTING MOUNTAINS: FUJIAN AND THE CHINA TEA TRADE, 1757–1937 (1994)

GERNET, JACQUES. BUDDHISM IN CHINESE SOCIETY: AN ECONOMIC HISTORY FROM THE FIFTH TO THE TENTH CENTURIES (Franciscus Verellen trans., 1995)

Ginsburg, Tom. *Does Law Matter for Economic Development? Evidence from East Asia*, 34 L. & SOC'Y REV. 829 (2000)

Glennie, P. *Distinguishing Men's Trades: Occupational Sources and Debates for Pre-census England, in* HISTORICAL GEOGRAPHY RESEARCH SERIES 1 (1990)

GOLDSTONE, JACK. WHY EUROPE? THE RISE OF THE WEST IN GLOBAL HISTORY (2008)

Gorton, Matthew & Sophia Davidova. *Farm Productivity and Efficiency in the CEE Applicant Countries: A Synthesis of Results*, 30 AGRICULTURAL ECON. 1 (2004)

GRAY, CHARLES MONTGOMERY. COPYHOLD, EQUITY, AND THE COMMON LAW (1963)

Greif, Avner & Guido Tabellini. *Cultural and Institutional Bifurcation: China and Europe Compared*, 100(2) AM. ECON. REV.: PAPERS & PROC. 1 (2010)

Greif, Avner. *Cultural Beliefs and the Organization of Society: A Historical and Theoretical Reflection on Collectivist and Individualist Societies*, 102 J. POL. ECON. 912 (1994)

GROVE, LINDA. A CHINESE ECONOMIC REVOLUTION: RURAL ENTREPRENEURSHIP IN THE TWENTIETH CENTURY (2006)

Guiso, Luigi & Monica Paiella. *Risk Aversion, Wealth and Background Risk*, 6 J. OF EURO. ECON. ASS. 1109 (2008)

GUO, JIAN. DIANQUAN ZHIDU YUANLIU KAO [VERIFYING THE ORIGINS OF DIAN INSTITUTIONS] (2009)

HABERMAS, JÜRGEN. THE POSTNATIONAL CONSTELLATION: POLITICAL ESSAYS (M. Pensky, Trans., 2001)

Haley, John O. *Law and Culture in China and Japan: A Framework for Analysis*, 27 MICH. J. INT'L L. 895 (2006)

HALEY, JOHN OWEN. THE SPIRIT OF JAPANESE LAW (2006)

HAMASHIMA, ATSUTOSHI. MINDAI KOUNAN NOUSON SHIAKAI NO KENKYU [RESEARCH ON MING DYNASTY JIANGNAN RURAL SOCIETY] (1982)

Han Hengyu. *Shilun Qingdai Qianqi Diannong Yongdian Quan de Youlai ji qi Xingqi [On the Origins and Nature of the Permanent Tenancy Rights of Early Qing Tenant Farmers]*, 1 QINGSHI LUNCONG [COLLECTED ESSAYS ON QING HISTORY] 38 (1979)

Handel, Benjamin R. *Adverse Selection and Inertia in Health Insurance Markets: When Nudging Hurts*, 103 AM. ECON. REV. 2643 (2013)

HANSEN, VALERIE. CHANGING GODS IN MEDIEVAL CHINA, 1127–1276 (1990)

HANSEN, VALERIE. THE OPEN EMPIRE: A HISTORY OF CHINA THROUGH 1600 (2000)

HAN-SENG, CHEN. LANDLORD AND PEASANT IN CHINA (1936)

HARDIN, RUSSELL. ONE FOR ALL: THE LOGIC OF GROUP CONFLICT (1995)

HARDING, ALAN. A SOCIAL HISTORY OF ENGLISH LAW (1966)

Harris, Marvin. *Cultural Materialism, in* ENCYCLOPEDIA OF CULTURAL ANTHROPOLOGY 277 (David Levinson & Melvin Amber eds., 1996)

Harris, Ron. *The Private Origins of the Private Company: Britain 1862–1907* (2009), *available at* http://papers.ssrn.com/sol3/papers.cfm?abstract_id=1613206

HARRISON, LAWRENCE E. WHO PROSPERS: HOW CULTURAL VALUES SHAPE ECONOMIC AND POLITICAL SUCCESS (1992)

Hartwell, Robert M. *Demographic, Political, and Social Transformations of China*, 42 HARV. J. ASIATIC STUD. 365 (1982)

HARVEY, DAVID. THE NEW IMPERIALISM (2005)

HAYASHI MEGUMI, CHU SHI KONAN NOSON SHAKAI SEIFO KENKYU (1953)

He, Weifang. *The Judicial System and Governance in Traditional China, in* THE RULE OF LAW: PERSPECTIVES FROM THE PACIFIC RIM 91 (Mansfield Center for Pacific Affairs ed., 2000)

Heffetz, Ori & Matthew Rabin. *Conclusions Regarding Cross-Group Differences in Happiness Depend on Difficulty of Reaching Respondents*, 103 AM. ECON. REV. 3001 (2013)

HEGEL, G.W.F. THE PHILOSOPHY OF HISTORY (J. Sibree trans., 1956)

Heijdra, Martin. *The Socio-Economic Development of Rural China During the Ming, in* 8 THE CAMBRIDGE HISTORY OF CHINA 417 (Denis Twitchett and Frederick Mote eds., 1998)

Hisayuki, Miyakawa. *An Outline of the Naito Hypothesis and Its Effects on Japanese Studies of China*, 14 FAR EASTERN QUARTERLY 533 (1955)

HO, PING-TI. STUDIES ON THE POPULATION OF CHINA, 1368–1953 (1959)

HO, PING-TI. THE LADDER OF SUCCESS IN IMPERIAL CHINA; ASPECTS OF SOCIAL MOBILITY, 1368–1911 (1962)

Hoffman, Philip T. *Taxes and Agrarian Life in Early Modern France: Land Sales, 1550–1730*, 46 J. OF ECON. HIST. 37 (1986)

HOFFMAN, PHILIP. GROWTH IN A TRADITIONAL SOCIETY: THE FRENCH COUNTRYSIDE, 1450–1815 (1996)

HOLDSWORTH, WILLIAM. A HISTORY OF ENGLISH LAW (2d ed., 1937)

Houston, Rab. *Custom in Context: Medieval and Early Modern Scotland and England*, 211 PAST & PRESENT 35 (2011)

Hoyle, R.W. *An Ancient and Laudable Custom: The Definition and Development of Tenant Right in North-Western England in the Sixteenth Century*, 116 PAST & PRESENT 24 (1987)

Hoyle, R.W. *Tenure and the Land Market in Early Modern England: Or a Late Contribution to the Brenner Debate*, 43 ECON. HIST. REV. 1 (1990)

HSIAO, KUNG-CHUAN. RURAL CHINA: IMPERIAL CONTROL IN THE NINETEENTH CENTURY (1960)

HUANG, JINGBIN. MINSHENG YU JIAJI: QINGCHU ZHI MINGUO SHIQI JIANGNAN JUMIN DE XIAOFEI [CIVILIAN WELFARE AND HOUSEHOLD ECONOMICS: RESIDENT CONSUMPTION IN THE LOWER YANGTZE FROM THE EARLY QING TO THE REPUBLIC] (2009)

HUANG, PHILIP C.C. CIVIL JUSTICE IN CHINA: REPRESENTATION AND PRACTICE IN THE QING (1996)

HUANG, PHILIP C.C. CODE, CUSTOM, AND LEGAL PRACTICE IN CHINA: THE QING AND THE REPUBLIC COMPARED (2001)

Huang, Philip C.C. *Development or Involution in Eighteenth-Century Britain and China?*, 61 J. ASIAN STUD. 501 (2002)

HUANG, PHILIP C.C. THE PEASANT ECONOMY AND SOCIAL CHANGE IN NORTH CHINA (1985)

HUANG, PHILIP C.C. THE PEASANT FAMILY AND RURAL DEVELOPMENT IN THE LOWER YANGTZE REGION, 1350–1988 (1990)

Huber, J.D. *Religious Belief, Religious Participation, and Social Policy Attitudes across Countries* (Columbia University, Working Paper, 2005)

HYMES, ROBERT H. STATESMEN AND GENTLEMEN: THE ELITE OF FU-CHOU, CHIANG-HSI, IN NORTHERN AND SOUTHERN SUNG (1986)

Iannaccone, L. *Introduction to the Economics of Religion*, 36 J. ECON. LIT. 1465 (1998)

INOUE, TOHRU. ZHONGGUO DE ZONGZU YU GUOJIA LIZHI [CHINA'S LINEAGES AND RITUAL INSTITUTIONS OF THE STATE] (Qian Hang trans., 2008)

ISETT, CHRISTOPHER. STATE, PEASANT AND MERCHANT IN QING MANCHURIA: 1644–1862 (2007)

JACOB, MARGARET. SCIENTIFIC CULTURE AND THE MAKING OF THE MECHANICAL WEST (1997)

Jiaoyu, Shi. *"Yiduan" Li Zhi de Chuantong Sixiang [The Traditional Thought of the "Heretic" Li Zhi]*, 16(2) CHONGQING ZHIYE JISHU XUEYUAN XUEBAO [J. CHONGQING TECH. INST.] 78 (2007)

JING SU & LUO LUN, QINGDAI SHANDONG JINGYING DIZHU JINGJI YANJIU [ECONOMIC ANALYSIS OF QING MANAGERIAL LANDLORDS IN SHANDONG] (1984)

JONES, ERIC L. GROWTH RECURRING: ECONOMIC CHANGE IN WORLD HISTORY (1988)

Karasawa, Yasuhiko, Bradly W. Reed, & Matthew H. Sommer. *Qing County Archives in Sichuan: An Update from the Field*, 26 LATE IMPERIAL CHINA 114 (2005)

KE, CHANGJI. ZHONGGUO GUDAI NONGCUN GONGSHE SHI [RURAL COMMUNES IN CLASSICAL CHINESE HISTORY] (1988)

KELSEN, HANS. PURE THEORY OF LAW (1989)

KERRIDGE, ERIC. AGRARIAN PROBLEMS IN THE SIXTEENTH CENTURY AND AFTER (1969)

King, Peter. *Legal Change, Customary Right, and Social Conflict in Late Eighteenth-Century England: The Origins of the Great Gleaning Case of 1788*, 10 LAW & HIST. REV. 1 (1992)

Kiralfy, Albert. *Custom in Mediaeval English Law*, 9 J. LEGAL HIST. 26 (1988)

Kirby, William C. *China, Unincorporated: Company Law and Business Enterprise in Twentieth Century China*, 54 J. ASIAN STUD. 43 (1995)

Kishimoto, Mio. *Ming Qing Shidai de "Zhaojia Huishu" Wenti [The Issue of "Zhaojia" and "Dian" Redemption in the Ming and Qing]*, in III-4 ZHONGGUO FAZHISHI KAOZHENG [EMPIRICAL STUDIES ON CHINESE LEGAL HISTORY] 423 (Terada Hiroaki ed., Zheng Minqin trans., 2003)

Korobkin, Russell B. *What Comes after Victory for Behavioral Law and Economics?*, UCLA School of Law, Law-Econ Research Paper No. 11-10 (March 15, 2011), *available at* http://ssrn.com/abstract=1787070

KURAN, TIMUR. THE LONG DIVERGENCE: HOW ISLAMIC LAW HELD BACK THE
MIDDLE EAST (2010)

LANDES, DAVID S. THE UNBOUND PROMETHEUS: TECHNOLOGICAL CHANGE
AND INDUSTRIAL DEVELOPMENT IN WESTERN EUROPE FROM 1750 TO
THE PRESENT (1969)

LANDES, DAVID. THE WEALTH AND POVERTY OF NATIONS: WHY SOME ARE SO
RICH AND SOME SO POOR (1999)

Lavely, William & R. Bin Wong. *Family Division and Mobility in North China*, 34
COMP. STUD. IN SOC. & HIST. 439 (1992)

LEE, PAULINE C. LI ZHI, CONFUCIANISM, AND THE VIRTUE OF DESIRE (2012)

LEVENSON, JOSEPH R. CONFUCIAN CHINA AND ITS MODERN FATE: A TRILOGY
(1968)

Levy, Gilat & Ronny Razin. *Rituals or Good Works, Self and Social Signaling in
Religious Organizations* (London School of Economics, Working Paper, July
2011)

LI WENZHI & JIANG TAIXIN, ZHONGGUO DIZHU ZHI JINGJI LUN [ON CHINA'S
LANDLORD-BASED ECONOMY] (2005)

Li, Bozhong. *"Rengeng Shimu" yu Mingqing Jiangnan Nongmin de Jingying
Guimo ["Ten mu Per Person" and the Scale of Jiangnan Agriculture in the
Ming and Qing]*, 1996(1) ZHONGGUO NONGSHI [CHINESE AGRICULTURAL
HIST.] 1

LI, BOZHONG. AGRICULTURAL DEVELOPMENT IN JIANGNAN, 1620–1850 (1998)

LI, HUAIYIN. VILLAGE GOVERNANCE IN NORTH CHINA, 1875–1936 (2005)

LI, LILLIAN M. CHINA'S SILK TRADE: TRADITIONAL INDUSTRY IN THE MODERN
WORLD, 1842–1937 (1981)

LI, LILLIAN M. FIGHTING FAMINE IN NORTH CHINA (2007)

LI, LILLIAN. *Review of* State, Peasant and Merchant in Qing Manchuria: 1644–1862, 38
J. OF INTERDISCIPLINARY HIST. 644 (2008)

Li, Pingliang. *Jindai Zhongguo de Xinxue, Zongzu yu Difang Zhengzhi [New Learning, Lineages, and Local Politics in Early Modern China]*, 8(2) ZHONGGUO
SHEHUI LISHI PINGLUN [COMMENTARIES ON CHINESE SOCIAL HISTORY]
86 (2007)

LI, WENZHI & JIANG TAIXIN. ZHONGGUO ZONGFA ZONGZU ZHI HE ZUTIAN
YIZHUANG [LINEAGE INSTITUTIONS AND COMMON PROPERTY IN CHINA]
(2000)

LI, WENZHI ET AL. MING QING SHIDAI DE NONGYE ZIBEN ZHUYI MENGYA
WENTI [THE QUESTION OF "SHOOTS OF AGRICULTURAL CAPITALISTM" IN
THE MING AND QING] (1983)

LI, WENZHI. *Lun Yapian Zhanzheng qian Dijia he Goumai Nian [On Land Prices and
Purchase Years before the Opium War]*, 1988(2) ZHONGGUO SHEHUI JINGJI SHI
YANJIU [STUD. OF SOC. & ECON. HIST.] 1

LI, WENZHI. MINGQING SHIDAI FENGJIAN TUDI GUANXI DE SONGJIE
[THE LOOSENING OF FEUDAL LAND RELATIONS IN THE MING AND QING]
(2007)

LI, ZAN. WAN QING ZHOUXIAN SUSONG ZHONG DE SHENDUAN WENTI [THE
ISSUE OF ADJUDICATION IN LATE QING COUNTY-LEVEL LITIGATION]
(2010)

Li, Zehou. Zhongguo Xiandai Sixiang Shi Lun [On the Intellectual History of Modern China] (2008)

Liang, Zhiping. Qingdai Xiguan Fa: Shehui Yu Guojia [Qing Customary Law: Society and State] (1996)

Licht, Amir N. et al. *Culture Rules: The Foundations of the Rule of Law and Other Norms of Governance*, 35 J. Comp. Econ. 659 (2007)

Licht, Amir N. *Social Norms and the Law: Why Peoples Obey the Law*, 4 Rev. L & Econ. 715 (2008)

Lieberman, Victor. 2 Strange Parallels (2009).

Lin Ji. Changjiang Zhongyou Zongzu Shehui ji qi Bianqian: Ming Qing zhi 1949 Nian [The Lineage Society of the Middle Yangtze Region and Its Evolution: From the Ming and Qing to 1949] (1999)

Lin, Ji. *Guomin Zhengfu Shiqi de Lianghu Xin Zuxue yu Xiangcun Zongzu [New Lineage Schools and Rural Lineages in Hunan and Hubei during the Republican Era]*, 2004 (2) Jindai Shi Yanjiu [Studies on Early Modern History] 117

Lin, Qian & Zhang Jinfan. *Zailun* Chongde Huidian, Hubu Zeli *de Falü Shiyong [Restudying the Legal Application of the* Chongde Huidian *and* Hubu Zeli]*, 5 Faxue Qianyan [Frontiers of Legal Scholarship] 197 (2003)

Liu, Guoqiang. *Qingmo Minguo shiqi xingfadian jianshe zhong qinshu lunli guanxi de chuancheng yu biange [Continuity and Change in the Treatment of Kinship Ties in Late Qing and Republican Criminal Codes]*, 2012(4) Daode yu Wenming [Morality and Civilization] 67

Lowry, S. Todd. *The Agricultural Foundation of the Seventeenth-Century English Oeconomy*, 35 Hist. of Pol. Econ. 74 (2003)

Lu, Baoqian. Qingdai Sixiang Shi [Intellectual History of the Qing] (2009)

Ma, Debin. *Economic Growth in the Lower Yangzi Region of China in 1911–1937: A Quantitative and Historical Analysis*, 68 J. Econ. Hist. 355 (2008)

Ma, Jialu. *Sima Guang Shehui Sixiang Tanxi [An Exploration of Sima Guang's Social Thought]* (M.A. Thesis, Qingdao Univ., 2009)

Ma, Ye & Tianshu Chu. *Living Standards in China between 1840 and 1912: A New Estimation of Gross Domestic Product per capita*, Paper presented for the European Historical Economics Society Conference (2013)

MacAulay, Stewart. *Non-contractual Relations in Business*, 28 Am. Soc. Rev. 55 (1963)

Macauley, Melissa. Social Power and Legal Culture: Litigation Masters in Late Imperial China (1998)

MacCormack, Geoffrey. The Spirit of Traditional Chinese Law (1996)

Macfarlane, Alan. The Origins of English Individualism: Family, Property, and Social Transition (1978)

Mair, Victor V. *Language and Ideology in the Written Popularizations of the Sacred Edict, in* Popular Culture in Late Imperial China (David Johnson, Andrew J. Nathan, & Evelyn S. Rawski eds., 1985)

Mann, Susan. Local Merchants and the Chinese Bureaucracy, 1750–1950 (1987)

Marks, Robert B. *China's Population Size during the Ming and Qing* (on file with author)

MARKS, ROBERT B. TIGERS, RICE, SILK, AND SILT: ENVIRONMENT AND ECONOMY IN LATE IMPERIAL SOUTH CHINA 226 (2006)

Marsh, Robert M. *Weber's Misunderstanding of Chinese Law*, 106 AM. J. SOCIOL. 281 (2000)

MARX, KARL. CAPITAL (1867), *available at* www.marxists.org/archive/marx/works/1867-c1/ch31.htm

MATHIAS, PETER. THE FIRST INDUSTRIAL NATION (1969)

MATTEI, UGO. BASIC PRINCIPLES OF PROPERTY LAW (2000)

Mattei, Ugo. *Three Patterns of Law: Taxonomy and Change in the World's Legal Systems*, 45 AM. J. COMP. L. 5 (1997)

MAZUMDAR, SUCHETA. SUGAR AND SOCIETY IN CHINA: PEASANTS, TECHNOLOGY AND THE WORLD MARKET (1998)

McAdams, Richard H. *Comment: Accounting for Norms*, WISC. L. REV. 625 (1997a)

McAdams, Richard H. *Signaling Discount Rates: Law, Norms and Economic Methodology*, 110 YALE L.J. 625 (2000)

McAdams, Richard H. *The Origin, Development, and Regulation of Norms*, 96 MICH. L. REV. 338 (1997b)

McAleavy, Henry. *Dien in China and Vietnam*, 17 J. ASIAN STUD. 403 (1958)

McDermott, Joseph P. *Charting Blank Spaces and Disputed Regions: The Problem of Sung Land Tenure*, 44 J. ASIAN STUD. 13 (1984)

MILSOM, S.F.C. HISTORICAL FOUNDATIONS OF THE COMMON LAW (2d ed., 1981)

MILSOM, S.F.C. THE LEGAL FRAMEWORK OF ENGLISH FEUDALISM (1976)

MOKYR, JOEL. THE ENLIGHTENED ECONOMY: AN ECONOMIC HISTORY OF BRITAIN 1700–1850 (2010)

Moll-Murata, Christine. *Chinese Guilds from the Seventeenth to Twentieth Centuries*, 53 INT'L REV. OF SOC. HIST. 213 (2008)

MOTE, F.W. IMPERIAL CHINA 900–1600 (2003)

Muramatsu Yūji, *A Documentary Study of Chinese Landlordism in the Late Ch'ing and Early Republic Kiangnan*, 29 BULL. SCHL. ORI. AFR. STU. 566 (1966)

MURAMATSU YŪJI, KINDAI KŌNAN NO SOSAN – CHŪGOKU JINUSHI SEIDO NO KENKYŪ [TENANCY IN THE EARLY MODERN LOWER YANGTZE: RESEARCH ON CHINESE LANDLORD INSTITUTIONS] (1970)

MUSSON, A., ALBERT EDWARD, & ERIC ROBINSON. SCIENCE AND TECHNOLOGY IN THE INDUSTRIAL REVOLUTION (1969)

MYERS, RAMON H. THE CHINESE ECONOMY, PAST AND PRESENT (1980)

MYERS, RAMON H. THE CHINESE PEASANT ECONOMY; AGRICULTURAL DEVELOPMENT IN HOPEI AND SHANTUNG, 1890–1949 (1970)

Myers, Ramon. *Land Distribution in Revolutionary China*, 8(5) CHUNG CHI J. 62 (1969)

NAGANO, AKIRA. ZHONGGUO TUDI ZHIDU DE YANJIU [RESEARCH ON CHINA'S LAND INSTITUTIONS] (Qiang Wo trans., 2004)

NAQUIN, SUSAN & EVELYN RAWSKI. CHINESE SOCIETY IN THE EIGHTEENTH CENTURY (1987)

NATSUI, HARUKI. CHŪGOKU KINDAI KŌNAN NO JINUSHI SEI KENKYŪ [A STUDY OF LANDLORD INSTITUTIONS IN THE EARLY MODERN LOWER YANGTZE] (2001)

NEALE, R.S. CLASS IN ENGLISH HISTORY (1981)

NG, CHIN-KEONG. TRADE AND SOCIETY: THE AMOY NETWORK ON THE CHINA COAST, 1683–1735 (1983)

NORTH, DOUGLASS C. & ROBERT PAUL THOMAS. THE RISE OF THE WESTERN WORLD: A NEW ECONOMIC HISTORY (1976)

NORTH, DOUGLASS C. INSTITUTIONS, INSTITUTIONAL CHANGE AND ECONOMIC PERFORMANCE (1990)

O'Brien, Patrick. *State Formation and the Construction of Institutions for the First Industrial Nation*, *in* INSTITUTIONAL CHANGE AND ECONOMIC DEVELOPMENT (Ha Joon Chang ed., 2007)

Ocko, Jonathan. *I'll Take It All the Way to Beijing: Capital Appeals in the Qing*, 47 J. ASIAN STUD. 291 (1988)

OVERMYER, DANIEL L. FOLK BUDDHIST RELIGION: DISSENTING SECTS IN LATE TRADITIONAL CHINA (1976)

PALMER, ROBERT C. ENGLISH LAW IN THE AGE OF THE BLACK DEATH 1348–1381 (2001)

Peñalver, Eduardo Moisés & Sonia K. Katyal, *Property Outlaws*, 155 UNIV. PA. L. REV. 1095 (2007)

Perdue, Peter C. *China in the World Economy: Exports, Regions, and Theories*, 60 HARV. J. OF ASIATIC STUD. 259 (2000)

PERDUE, PETER C. CHINA MARCHES WEST: THE QING CONQUEST OF CENTRAL EURASIA (2005)

PERDUE, PETER C. *Property Rights on Imperial China's Frontiers*, *in* LAND, PROPERTY, AND THE ENVIRONMENT (John Richards, ed., 2001)

Perdue, Peter C. *The Qing State and the Gansu Grain Market, 1739-1864*, *in* CHINESE HISTORY IN ECONOMIC PERSPECTIVE 100 (Thomas G. Rawski & Lillian M. Li eds., 1992)

PERELMAN, MICHAEL. THE INVENTION OF CAPITALISM: CLASSICAL POLITICAL ECONOMY AND THE SECRET HISTORY OF PRIMITIVE ACCUMULATION (2000)

POLANYI, KARL. THE GREAT TRANSFORMATION: THE POLITICAL AND ECONOMIC ORIGINS OF OUR TIME (Rinehart ed., 1944)

POLLOCK, FREDERICK & FREDERIC WILLIAM MAITLAND. THE HISTORY OF ENGLISH LAW BEFORE THE TIME OF EDWARD I (1968)

Pomeranz, Kenneth. *Land Markets in Late Imperial and Republican China*, 23 CONTINUITY & CHANGE 101 (2008)

Pomeranz, Kenneth. *Ten Years After: Responses and Reconsiderations*, 12(4) HISTORICALLY SPEAKING 20 (2011)

POMERANZ, KENNETH. THE GREAT DIVERGENCE: CHINA, EUROPE, AND THE MAKING OF THE MODERN WORLD ECONOMY (2000)

POMERANZ, KENNETH. THE MAKING OF A HINTERLAND: STATE, SOCIETY, AND ECONOMY IN INLAND NORTH CHINA, 1853–1937 (1993)

POSNER, ERIC A. LAW AND SOCIAL NORMS (2000)

Posner, Eric A. *Law, Economics, and Inefficient Norms*, 144 U. PA. L. REV. 1697 (1996)

Posner, Richard A. *Social Norms and the Law: An Economic Approach*, 87 AM. ECON. REV. 365 (1997)

Postema, Gerald G. *Custom, Normative Practice and the Law*, 62 DUKE L.J. 707 (2012)

POWELL, RICHARD R.B. *Determinable Fees*, 23 COLUM. L. REV. 207 (1923)

QI PENGFEI, JIANG JIESHI JIASHI [THE FAMILY HISTORY OF CHIANG KAI-SHEK] (2007)

Qiu, Hansheng. *Songmin Lixue yu Zongfa Sixiang [Song-Ming Neo-Confucianism and Lineage Rituals and Thought]*, 1979(11) LISHI YANJIU [HIST. STUD.] 63

Radin, Margaret Jane. *Personhood and Property*, 34 STAN. L. REV. 957 (1982)

RAMSEYER, J. MARK & ERIC B. RASMUSEN, MEASURING JUDICIAL INDEPENDENCE: THE POLITICAL ECONOMY OF JUDGING IN JAPAN (2003)

RAWSKI, EVELYN S. AGRICULTURAL CHANGE AND THE PEASANT ECONOMY OF SOUTH CHINA (1972)

RAWSKI, EVELYN S. EDUCATION AND POPULAR LITERACY IN CH'ING CHINA (1979)

Rawski, Evelyn S. *The Ma Landlords of Yang-chia-kou in Late Ch'ing and Republican China*, in KINSHIP ORGANIZATION IN LATE IMPERIAL CHINA, 1000–1940 (Patricia Ebrey & James Watson eds., 1986)

RAWSKI, THOMAS G. ECONOMIC GROWTH IN PREWAR CHINA (1989)

REED, BRADLEY W. TALONS AND TEETH: COUNTY CLERKS AND RUNNERS IN THE QING DYNASTY (2000)

ROBERTSON, H.M. ASPECTS OF THE RISE OF ECONOMIC INDIVIDUALISM; A CRITICISM OF MAX WEBER AND HIS SCHOOL (1950)

ROSS, H. LAURENCE. SETTLED OUT OF COURT (rev. ed. 1980)

Ross, Richard. *Commoning of the Common Law: The Renaissance Debate over Printing English Law, 1520–1640*, 146 UNIV. PENN. L. REV. 323 (1998)

ROWE, WILLIAM T. CHINA'S LAST EMPIRE: THE GREAT QING (2009)

ROWE, WILLIAM. SAVING THE WORLD: CHEN HONGMOU AND ELITE CONSCIOUSNESS IN EIGHTEENTH-CENTURY CHINA (2003)

RUBIN, G. R. & DAVID SUGARMAN. LAW, ECONOMY, AND SOCIETY, 1750–1914: ESSAYS IN THE HISTORY OF ENGLISH LAW (1984)

Ruskola, Teemu. *Conceptualizing Corporations and Kinship: Comparative Law and Development Theory in a Chinese Perspective*, 52 STAN. L. REV. 1599 (2000)

Ruskola, Teemu. *Law, Sexual Morality, and Gender Equality in Qing and Communist China*, 103 YALE L.J. 2531 (1994)

Ruskola, Teemu. *The East Asian Legal Tradition*, in THE CAMBRIDGE COMPANION TO COMPARATIVE LAW 257 (Mauro Bussani & Ugo Mattei eds., Cambridge Univ. Press 2012)

Sabel, Charles & Jonathan Zeitlin. *Historical Alternatives to Mass Production: Politics, Markets and Technology in Nineteenth-Century Industrialization*, 108 PAST & PRESENT 133 (1985)

Saito, Osuma. *Land, Labour and Market Forces in Tokugawa Japan*, 24 CONTINUITY & CHANGE 169 (2009)

Schirokauer, Conrad & Robert P. Hymes. *Introduction*, in ORDERING THE WORLD: APPROACHES TO STATE AND SOCIETY IN SUNG DYNASTY CHINA 1 (Robert P. Hymes & Conrad Schirokauer eds., 1993)

SCHMUDDE, DAVID A. A PRACTICAL GUIDE TO MORTGAGES AND LIENS (2004)

Scott, Robert E. *The Limits of Behavioral Theories of Law and Social Norms*, 86 VA. L. REV. 1602 (2000)

Sen, Amartya. *Internal Consistency of Choice*, 61 ECONOMETRICA 495 (1993)

Shaw-Taylor, Leigh. *The Rise of Agrarian Capitalism and the Decline of Family Farming in England*, 65 ECON. HIST. REV. 26 (2012)

Shaw-Taylor, Leigh. *Working Paper on Agrarian Capitalism* (2008), *available at* www .geog.cam.ac.uk/research/projects/occupations/abstracts/paper7.pdf

Shi, Yingying. *Wang Anshi Jingxin yu Jingshi Sixiang Lunshu [On Wang Anshi's Ideology of "Heart-Cultivation" and "Social Cultivation"]* (Ph.D. Thesis, Pengjia Univ., 2011)

Shi, Zhihong. *20 Shiji San Sishi Niandai Huabei Pingyuan Nongcun de Tudi Fenpei ji Qi Bianhua [Land Distribution and Change on the North China Plain in the 1930s]*, 2002(3) ZHONGGUO JINGJISHI YANJIU [STUD. ON CHINESE ECON. HIST.] 3

Shiga, Shuzo. *Qingdai Susong Zhidu zhi Minshi Fayuan de Kaocha [Research on the Legal Origins of Civil Law and Adjudication in the Qing]*, in MING QING SHIQI DE MINSHI SHENPAN YU MINJIAN QIYUE [CIVIL ADJUDICATION AND CIVIL CONTRACTS IN THE MING AND QING] 54 (Wang Yaxin & Liang Zhiping eds., Wang Yaxin et al. trans., 1998)

SHIROYAMA, TOMOKO. CHINA DURING THE GREAT DEPRESSION: MARKET, STATE, AND THE WORLD ECONOMY, 1929–1937 (2008)

SIMPSON, A.W.B. A HISTORY OF THE COMMON LAW OF CONTRACT: THE RISE OF ASSUMPSIT (1975)

SIMPSON, A.W.B. A HISTORY OF THE LAND LAW (1986)

Singer, Joseph William. *How Property Norms Construct the Externalities of Ownership* (Working Paper 2008), *available at* http://ssrn.com/abstract=1093341

SMITH, ADAM. AN INQUIRY INTO THE NATURE AND CAUSES OF THE WEALTH OF NATIONS (Joseph Nicholson ed., 1895)

SMITH, THOMAS C. THE AGRARIAN ORIGINS OF MODERN JAPAN (1959)

SOMMER, MATTHEW H. SEX, LAW AND SOCIETY IN LATE IMPERIAL CHINA (2000)

STEPHENS, THOMAS B. ORDER AND DISCIPLINE IN CHINA: THE SHANGHAI MIXED COURT 1911–1927 (1992)

Stokes, Gale. *The Fates of Human Societies: A Review of Recent Macrohistories*, 106 AM. HIST. REV. 508 (2001)

Stone, Lawrence. *Social Mobility in England, 1500–1700*, 33 PAST & PRESENT 16 (1966)

Stross, Randy. *Numbers Games Rejected*, 10(3) REPUBLICAN CHINA 1 (1985)

Suchman, Mark C. & Lauren B. Edelman, *Book Review: Legal Rational Myths*, 21 LAW & SOC. INQUIRY 903 (1996)

Sugarman, David & Ronnie Warrington. *Land Law, Citizenship, and the Invention of "Englishness": The Strange World of the Equity of Redemption*, in EARLY MODERN CONCEPTIONS OF PROPERTY 111 (John Brewer & Susan Staves eds., 1996)

Sugihara, Kaoru. *Labour-intensive Industrialisation in Global History*, Kyoto Working Papers on Area Studies No. 1 (2007), *available at* www.cseas.kyoto-u.ac.jp/edit/ wp/Sugihara_WP_Web_081018.pdf

SUI, HONGMING. QINGMO MINCHU MINSHANGSHI XIGUAN DIAOCHA ZHI YANJIU (2005)

SUN, LIJUAN. QINGDAI SHANGYE SHEHUI DE GUIZE YU ZHIXU: CONG BEIKE ZILIAO JIEDU QINGDAI ZHONGGUO SHANGSHI XIGUAN FA [THE RULES

AND ORDER OF QING COMMERCIAL SOCIETY: INTERPRETING QING CHINA'S COMMERCIAL CUSTOMARY LAW FROM STELE INSCRIPTIONS] (2005)

SZONYI, MICHAEL. PRACTICING KINSHIP: LINEAGE AND DESCENT IN LATE IMPERIAL CHINA (2002)

Tang, Lixing. *20 Shiji Shangbanye Zhongguo Zongzu Zuzhi de Taishi – Yi Huizhou Zongzu wei Duixiang de Lishi Kaocha* [*The Trends in Chinese Lineage Organization in the First Half of the 20th Century – A Historical Study on the Lineages of Huizhou*], 34(1) J. SHANGHAI NORMAL UNIV. 103 (2005)

Tefft, Sheldon. The Myth of Strict Foreclosure, 4 U. CHI. L. REV. 575 (1937)

TER HAAR, BAREND. THE WHITE LOTUS TEACHINGS IN CHINESE RELIGIOUS HISTORY (1992)

Terada Hiroaki, *Shindai Chuuki no Ten Kisei ni Mieru Kigen no Imi ni, in* TOUYOU HOSHI NO TANKYUU 339 (1987)

Terada, Hiroaki. *Ming Qing Shiqi Fazhixu zhong de "Yue" de Xingzhi [The Nature of "Yue" in Ming and Qing Legal Order], in* MING QING SHIQI DE MINSHI SHENPAN YU MINJIAN QIYUE [CIVIL ADJUDICATION AND CIVIL CONTRACTS IN THE MING AND QING] 178 (Wang Yaxin & Liang Zhiping eds., Wang Yanxin et al. trans., 1998)

THE BRENNER DEBATE (T.H. Aston & C.H.E. Philpin eds., 1987)

THE CITY IN LATE IMPERIAL CHINA (G. William Skinner ed., 1977)

THE RENAISSANCE OF CONFUCIANISM IN CONTEMPORARY CHINA (Fan Ruiping ed., 2011)

Thomas Buoye, *Litigation, Legitimacy, and Lethal Violence, in* CONTRACT AND PROPERTY IN EARLY MODERN CHINA 94 (Madeleine Zelin, Jonathan K. Ocko, & Robert Gardella eds., 2004)

Thompson, E.P. *Eighteenth-Century English Society: Class Struggle without Class?*, 3 SOC. HIST. 133 (1978)

Trubek, David M. *Toward a Social Theory of Law: An Essay on the Study of Law and Development*, 82 YALE L.J. 1 (1972)

Tsoulouhas, Theofanis C. *A New Look at Demographic and Technological Changes: England, 1550 to 1839*, 29 EXPLORATIONS IN ECON. HIST. 169 (1992)

Turner, R.W. *The English Mortgage of Land as a Security*, 20 VA. L. REV. 729 (1934)

UNGER, ROBERTO. LAW IN MODERN SOCIETY: TOWARDS A CRITICISM OF SOCIAL THEORY (1976)

University of Nottingham, Copyhold Land, *available at* www.nottingham.ac.uk/mss/ learning/skills/deeds-depth/copyhold.phtml (last visited May 6, 2009)

University of Nottingham, Mortgage by Conveyance, *available at* www.nottingham .ac.uk/manuscriptsandspecialcollections/researchguidance/deedsindepth/mortgaged/ conveyance.aspx (last visited July 5, 2013)

University of Nottingham, Mortgage by Demise, *available at* www.nottingham.ac.uk/ manuscriptsandspecialcollections/researchguidance/deedsindepth/mortgaged/ demise.aspx (last visited July 5, 2013)

Upham, Frank. *From Demsetz to Deng: Speculations on the Implications of China's Growth for Law and Development Theory*, 41 N.Y.U. J. INT'L L. & POL. 551 (2009)

Upham, Frank. *Political Lackeys or Faithful Public Servants? Two Views of the Japanese Judiciary*, 30 L. SOC. INQUIRY 421 (2005)

Voigtländer, Nico & Hans-Joachim Voth. *Why England? Demographic Factors, Structural Change and Physical Capital Accumulation during the Industrial Revolution*, 11 J. ECON. GROWTH 319 (2006)

VON GLAHN, RICHARD. THE SINISTER WAY: THE DIVINE AND THE DEMONIC IN CHINESE RELIGIOUS CULTURE (2004)

Vries, Peer. *The California School and Beyond: How to Study the Great Divergence?*, 8 HISTORY COMPASS 730 (2010)

WANG, HUI. XIANDAI ZHONGGUO SIXIANG DE XINGQI [THE RISE OF MODERN CHINESE THOUGHT] (2008)

WANG, HUNING. DANGDAI ZHONGGUO CUNLUO JIAZU WENHUA [LINEAGE CULTURE IN CONTEMPORARY CHINESE VILLAGES] (1991)

Wang, Shanjun. *Fanshi Yizhuang yu Songdai Fanshi Jiazu de Fazhan [The Fan Philanthropic Estate and the Development of the Fan Lineage in the Song Dynasty]*, 2004 (2) ZHONGGUO NONGSHI [AGRICULTURAL HISTORY OF CHINA] 89

Wang, Shanjun. *Songdai Zongzu Zhidu de Shehui Zhineng ji Qi dui Jieji Guanxi de Yingxiang [The Social Functions of Song Lineages and Their Effects on Class Relations]*, 1996(3) HEBEI DAXUE XUEBAO [ACADEMIC J. OF HEBEI UNIV.] 15

Watson, Rubie S. *Corporate Property and Local Leadership in the Pearl River Delta, 1898–1941, in* CHINESE LOCAL ELITES AND PATTERNS OF DOMINANCE 239 (Joseph Esherick & Mary Rankin eds., 1990)

WATT, JOHN R. THE DISTRICT MAGISTRATE IN LATE IMPERIAL CHINA (1972)

WEBER, MAX. ECONOMY AND SOCIETY: AN OUTLINE OF INTERPRETATIVE SOCIOLOGY (Guenther Roth & Claus Wittich eds., Ephraim Fischoff et al. trans., Bedminster Press 1968)

WEBER, MAX. MAX WEBER ON LAW IN ECONOMY AND SOCIETY (Max Rheinstein ed., 1954)

WEBER, MAX. THE PROTESTANT WORK ETHIC AND THE SPIRIT OF CAPITALISM (Peter Baehr & Gordon C. Wells trans., Penguin 2002)

WEBER, MAX. THE RELIGION OF CHINA: CONFUCIANISM AND TAOISM (1920)

Weiss, Yoram & Chaim Fershtman. *Social Status and Economic Performance: A Survey*, 43 EUR. ECON. REV. 801 (1998)

White, C.M.N. *African Customary Law: The Problem of Concept and Definition*, 9(2) J. AFRICAN L. 86 (1965)

Whitman, James Q. *Enforcing Civility and Respect: Three Societies*, 109 YALE L.J. 1279, 1320 (2000)

Wiens, Mi-chu. *Lord and Peasant in China: The Sixteenth to Eighteenth Centuries*, 6 MODERN CHINA 29 (1980)

Williamson, Oliver E. *The New Institutional Economics: Taking Stock, Looking Ahead*, 38 J. ECON. LIT. 595 (2000)

WILSON, THOMAS A. GENEALOGY OF THE WAY: THE CONSTRUCTION AND USES OF THE CONFUCIAN TRADITION IN LATE IMPERIAL CHINA (1995)

WITTFOGEL, KARL A. ORIENTAL DESPOTISM: A COMPARATIVE STUDY OF TOTAL POWER (1957)

Wong, Bobby K.Y. *Dispute Resolution by Officials in Traditional Chinese Legal Culture*, 10 MURDOCH UNIV. ELECTRONIC J. OF LAW, *available at* www.murdoch.edu.au/elaw/issues/v10n2/wong102_text.html (2003)

WONG, R. BIN & JEAN-LAURENT ROSENTHAL. BEFORE AND BEYOND DIVERGENCE: THE POLITICS OF ECONOMIC CHANGE IN CHINA AND EUROPE (2011)

WONG, R. BIN. CHINA TRANSFORMED: HISTORICAL CHANGE AND THE LIMITS OF EUROPEAN EXPERIENCE (1997)

Wood, Andy. *The Place of Custom in Plebeian Political Culture: England, 1550–1800*, 22 SOC. HIST. 46 (1997)

WOOD, ELLEN MEIKSINS. THE ORIGIN OF CAPITALISM (1999)

WRIGHTSON, KEITH. ENGLISH SOCIETY, 1580–1680 (2003)

Wu Tao, *Qingdai Jiangnan de Yitian Liangzhu Zhi he Zhudian Guanxi de Xin Geju*, 2004(5) JINGDAI SHI YANJIU

Wu Zhihui. *Qingmo "Li Fa zhi Zheng" de Pingjia yu Qishi [Evaluating and Learning from the Late-Qing "Ritual and Law" Debates]*, 2013(26) RENMIN LUNTAN [PEOPLE'S FORUM], *available at* http://paper.people.com.cn/rmlt/html/2013-09/11/content_1311789.htm

Wu, Tianxia. *Chuantong Xiaodao de Chuancheng yu Yanbian [The Inheritance and Evolution of Traditional Filial Piety]* (M.A. Thesis, Shaanxi Normal Univ., 2008)

WU, XIANGHONG. DIAN ZHI FENGSU YU DIAN ZHI FALÜ [THE CUSTOMS AND LAWS REGULATING DIAN SALES] (2009)

Xing, Long. *Jindai Huabei Nongcun Renkou Liudong ji qi Xiaozhang [Demographic Mobility and Change in Early Modern Rural North China]*, 2000(4) LISHI YANJIU [HIST. STUD.], *available at* http://economy.guoxue.com/article.php/1480

XU MAOMING, Jiangnan Shishen yu Jiangnan Shehui, 1368–1911 [GENTRY AND SOCIETY IN THE LOWER YANGTZE, 1368–1911] (Shangwu Press 2004)

Xu, Huailin. *Chenshi Jiazu de Wajie ji "Yimen" de Yingxiang [The Disintegration of the Chen Lineage and the Influence of the "Yimen"]*, 1994(2) ZHONGGUO SHI YANJIU [STUD. CHINESE HIST.] 56

XU, MAOMING. JIANGNAN SHISHEN YU JIANGNAN SHEHUI [THE JIANGNAN GENTRY AND JIANGNAN SOCIETY] (2004)

XU, XIAOQUN. CHINESE PROFESSIONALS AND THE REPUBLICAN STATE: THE RISE OF PROFESSIONAL ASSOCIATIONS IN SHANGHAI, 1912–1937 (2001)

XU, XIAOQUN. TRIAL OF MODERNITY: JUDICIAL REFORM IN EARLY TWENTIETH-CENTURY CHINA, 1901–1937 (2008)

XU, YANGJIE. ZHONGGUO JIAZU ZHIDU SHI [A HISTORY OF LINEAGE INSTITUTIONS IN CHINA] (1992)

Yamana Hirofumi, *Shinmatsu Konan no Giso ni Tsuite [Late Qing charity estates in the Jiangnan area]*, 62 TAYO GAKUHO [EAST ASIAN STUDIES] 99 (1980).

YANG, GUOZHEN. MING QING TUDI QIYUE WENSHU YANJIU [RESEARCH ON LAND CONTRACTS IN THE MING AND QING] (1988)

Yang, Guozhen. *Shilun Qingdai Minbei Minjian de Tudi Maimai [Discussing Land Transactions in Qing Northern Fujian]*, 1 ZHONGGUOSHI YANJIU [STUDIES ON CHINESE HISTORY] 29 (1981)

Yang, Wanrong. *Shilun Minguo Shiqi Nongcun Zongzu de Bianqian [On the Evolution of Rural Lineages in the Republican Era]*, 2002(2) GUANGDONG SOC. SCI. 103

You Jianxia, *Suzhou de Dizhu yu Nongmin [Landlords and Peasants in Suzhou]*, in 3 SUZHOU WENSHI ZILIAO [LITERARY AND HISTORICAL DOCUMENTS FROM SUZHOU] 57 (1990)

YOUNG, LOUISE. JAPAN'S TOTAL EMPIRE: MANCHURIA AND THE CULTURE OF WARTIME IMPERIALISM

Yu, Tongyuan. *Ming Qing Jiangnan Zaoqi Gongyehua Shehui de Xingcheng yu Fazhan [The Creation and Development of Jiangnan Industrial Society in the Ming and Qing]*, 2007(11) SHIXUE YUEKAN [J. OF HIST. SCI.] 41

Yuan, Hongtao. *Zai "Guojia" yu "Geren" Zhijian – Lun 20 Shiji Chu de Zongzu Pipan [Between "Country" and "Individual" – On the Criticism of Lineages in the Early 20th Century]*, 119 TIANFU XINLUN [NEW OPINIONS FROM SICHUAN] 119 (2004)

Zelin, Madeleine. *A Critique of Rights of Property in Prewar China*, in CONTRACT AND PROPERTY IN EARLY MODERN CHINA 17 (Madeleine Zelin, Jonathan K. Ocko, & Robert Gardella eds., 2004a)

Zelin, Madeleine. *China's Economy in Comparative Perspective, 1500 Onward*, in ASIA IN WESTERN AND WORLD HISTORY 474 (Ainslie Embree & Carol Gluck eds., 1997), *available at* www.upf.edu/materials/huma/central/abast/zelin.htm

Zelin, Madeleine. *Managing Multiple Ownership at the Zigong Salt Yard*, in CONTRACT AND PROPERTY IN EARLY MODERN CHINA 230 (Madeleine Zelin, Jonathan K. Ocko, & Robert Gardella eds., 2004b)

ZELIN, MADELEINE. THE MAGISTRATE'S TAEL: RATIONALIZING FISCAL REFORM IN EIGHTEENTH CENTURY CH'ING CHINA (1992)

ZELIN, MADELEINE. THE MERCHANTS OF ZIGONG: INDUSTRIAL ENTREPRENEURSHIP IN EARLY MODERN CHINA (2005)

Zelin, Madeleine. *The Rights of Tenants in Mid-Qing Sichuan: A Study of Land-Related Lawsuits in the Baxian Archives*, 45 J. ASIAN STUD. 499 (1986)

Zhang Yan. *Qingdai Jiangnan Shouzu Jigou Jianlun [A Brief Discussion of the Rent-Collection Institutions in the Qing Lower Yangtze]*, 1990(4) HANGZHOU SHIFAN DAXUE XUEBAO [ACADEMIC JOURNAL OF THE HANGZHOU NORMAL UNIVERSITY]

ZHANG, JINFAN. ZHONGGUO FALÜ DE CHUANTONG YU JINDAI ZHUANXING [THE TRADITIONS AND EARLY MODERN TRANSFORMATION OF CHINESE LAW] (1997)

Zhang, Jinjun. *Qingdai Jiangnan Zongzu zai Xiangcun Shehui Kongzhi zhong de Zuoyong [The Role of Lineages in the Qing Lower Yangtze]*, 34(3) J. ANHUI NORMAL. UNIV. 353 (2006)

Zhang, Peigang. *Qingyuan de Nongjia Jingji [The Agricultural Economy of Qingyuan]*, 7 SHEHUI KEXUE ZAZHI [J. OF SOC. SCI.] 1 (1936)

ZHANG, PEIGUO. JINDAI JIANGNAN XIANGCUN DIQUAN DE LISHI RENLEIXUE YANJIU [A HISTORICAL ANTHROPOLOGICAL STUDY OF EARLY MODERN LAND RIGHTS IN THE LOWER YANGTZE] (2002)

Zhang, Xiaotian. *Status Inconsistency Revisited: An Improved Empirical Model*, 24 EURO. SOCIOL. REV. 155, 156 (2008)

Zhao Yancai. *Lue Lun Liu Shipei de Jiazu Zhidu Sixiang ji qi Lunli Jindai Hua Guan [A Brief Study of Liu Shipei's Thought on Lineage Institutions and the Early Modernisation of Ethics]*, 2004(11) XUESHU YANJIU [ACADEMIC RESEARCH] 89

ZHAO, GANG. ZHONGGUO TUDI ZHIDU SHI [HISTORY OF CHINESE LAND INSTITUTIONS] (2006)

ZHENG, ZHENMAN. FAMILY LINEAGE ORGANIZATION AND SOCIAL CHANGE IN MING AND QING FUJIAN (Michael Szonyi trans., Univ. of Hawaii Press 2000)

ZHONGGUO FAZHI TONGSHI [HISTORY OF CHINESE LAW] (Zhang Jinfan ed., 1999)

ZHONGGUO MINFA SHI [THE HISTORY OF CHINESE CIVIL LAW] (Kong Qingming, Hu Liuyuan, & Sun Jiping eds., 1996)

Zhou, Qirong. *Rujia Lijiao Sichao de Xingqi yu Qingdai Kaozheng Xue [The Rise of Confucian Ritualism and Evidential Scholarship of the Qing]*, 2011(3) NANJING SHIDA XUEBAO [ACADEMIC J. NANJING NORMAL UNIV.] 7

ZHOU, YUANLIAN & XIE ZHAOHUA. QINGDAI ZUDIANZHI YANJIU [RESEARCH ON QING TENANCY AND DIAN INSTITUTIONS] (1986)

ZHOU, ZHUWEI ET AL. ZHEJIANG ZONGZU CUNLUO SHEHUI YANJIU [A SOCIAL STUDY OF LINEAGE VILLAGES IN ZHEJIANG] (2001)

ZHU, YONG. QINGDAI ZONGFA YANJIU [STUDIES ON LINEAGE RITUALS IN THE QING] (1987)

Chinese Terms

COUNTY AND VILLAGE NAMES

Baxian	巴县
Baodi	宝坻
Danshui-Xinzhu	淡水-新竹
Houxiazhai	后夏寨
Houjiaying	侯家营
Lengshuigou	冷水沟
Longquan	龙泉
Ningbo	宁波
Shaxian	沙县
Shicang	石仓
Shunxi	顺溪
Sibeichai	寺北柴
Wudian	吴店
Wujiang	吴江
Wuxi	无锡
Zhaowen	昭文
Zhuji	诸暨

LEGAL OR ADMINISTRATIVE TERMS

Baojia	保甲
Dian	典
Diya	抵押
Fanshang	犯上
Huhun tiantu	户婚田土
Huishu	回赎

Juemai	绝买\绝卖
Sifabu	司法部
Tianmian	田面
Tiandi	田底
Xiangyue	乡约
Xiguan	习惯
Yamen	衙门
Yizhuang	义庄
Yongdian	永佃
Zeli	则例
Zhaojia	找价
Zuzheng	族正

Index

Printed in the United States
By Bookmasters